Praise for

THE THIRD RAINBOW GIRL

"*The Third Rainbow Girl* is a riveting excavation of the secrets time, history, and place keep. In a long-buried crime, Emma Copley Eisenberg has unearthed a story that reveals America."
—Alex Marzano-Lesnevich, author of *The Fact of a Body: A Murder and a Memoir*

"*The Third Rainbow Girl* succeeds on two levels: first, as a deep dive inquiry into the 1980 murders of two young women in Pocahontas County, West Virginia, and the ensuing, tangled investigation, and second, as an intimate and humane portrait of a close-knit Appalachian community, the kind of place that is often reduced by outsiders to little more than a cliché of itself…A remarkable book."
—Richard Price, *New York Times* bestselling author of *Lush Life*

"Emma Eisenberg has distinguished herself as a reporter of remarkable wisdom and conscience, and her powers are on full display in *The Third Rainbow Girl*. Eisenberg's meticulous, compassionate reporting does not promise any of the easy answers we might expect from true crime: neither about what happened to the 'Rainbow Girls,' nor about poverty, injustice, and the fate of outsiders—whether hippies, hitchhikers, carpet baggers, or journalists—who give and take in this country's poorest areas. Her insights are hard won, deep, and devastating, making this an unforgettable debut."
—Alice Bolin, author of *Dead Girls: Essays on Surviving an American Obsession*

"I blazed through this book, which is a true crime page-turner, a moving coming-of-age memoir, an ode to Appalachia, and a scintillating investigation into the human psyche's astounding and sometimes chilling instinct for narrative. A beautiful debut that will stay with me for a long time, whose story mesmerizes even as it convinces you to find all mesmerizing stories suspect."

—Melissa Febos, Lambda Literary Award winner and author of *Whip Smart* and *Abandon Me*

"Eisenberg has crafted a beautiful and complicated ode to West Virginia. Exquisitely written, this is a powerful commentary on society's notions of gender, violence, and rural America. Readers of literary nonfiction will devour this title in one sitting."

—*Booklist*, starred review

"*The Third Rainbow Girl* is a fascinating hybrid work of true crime and memoir…In following the twists and turns of the case, Eisenberg paints an affectionate portrait of Appalachia that complicates and contradicts stereotypes about the region."

—*Shelf Awareness*

"[Eisenberg] reconstructs the case with a brisk pace and a keen sensitivity… offers a nuanced portrait of a crime and its decades-long effects. A promising young author reappraises a notorious double murder-and her life."

—*Kirkus Reviews*

THE
THIRD
RAINBOW
GIRL

THE THIRD RAINBOW GIRL

THE LONG LIFE OF A DOUBLE MURDER IN APPALACHIA

EMMA COPLEY EISENBERG

NEW YORK   BOSTON

Hachette Books
Hachette Book Group
1290 Avenue of the Americas
New York, NY 10104
hachettebookgroup.com
twitter.com/hachettebooks
instagram.com/hachettebooks

First Edition: January 2020

Hachette Books is a division of Hachette Book Group, Inc.

The Hachette Books name and logo are trademarks of Hachette Book Group, Inc.

Lines from "Darkness Poem" by Irene McKinney used with permission.
Lines from "At 24" by Irene McKinney used with permission.
Lines from *Southern Migrants, Northern Exiles* by Chad Berry used with permission.
Maps of West Virginia and Pocahontas County by Liz Pavlovic.

Photo credits: Page 7, photo of Nancy Santomero: courtesy of Jeanne Hackett. Page 7, photo of Vicki Durian: courtesy of John Durian. Page 47: courtesy of the author. Page 79: courtesy of Jacob Beard. Page 127: courtesy of Jerry Kauffman. Page 177: courtesy of Jerry Kauffman. Page 217: courtesy of the author. Page 253: courtesy of Liz Johndrow. Page 312: courtesy of Jerry Kauffman.

The publisher is not responsible for websites (or their content) that are not owned by the publisher.

The Hachette Speakers Bureau provides a wide range of authors for speaking events. To find out more, go to www.hachettespeakersbureau.com or call (866) 376-6591.

Print book interior design by Abby Reilly.

Library of Congress Cataloging-in-Publication Data has been applied for.

ISBNs: 978-0-316-44923-6 (hardcover), 978-0-316-44920-5 (ebook)

Printed in the United States of America

LSC-C

10 9 8 7 6 5 4 3 2 1

For my parents

If I am missing in any sense, it is a missingness I created for myself in order to be free.

—Dawn Lundy Martin

CONTENTS

AUTHOR'S NOTE

What follows is the result of five years of reporting and research I conducted in seven states. To understand and conjure the historical sections, I drew on police records, court documents, newspaper reports, scholarly articles, social media posts, and the personal archives of those involved.

The voices of the living are here, with the exceptions of Bobby Lee Morrison, Winters Walton, Robert Allen, and Steve Hunter, who declined my requests for interviews. I included their point of view where it is available by other means, but no doubt this book would have profited from their insights. If interviewees' contemporary memories differed from their earlier statements in the public record, I have noted the discrepancy.

The sections chronicling my own time in Pocahontas County were aided by journals, letters, photographs, and emails. Quotation marks indicate verbatim speech, while passages without quotation marks convey speech reconstructed to the best of my abilities. I have changed some names and identifying details to protect individuals' privacy. For certain names and nicknames, where official documents and court records used different spellings, I chose the most commonly accepted spelling.

In one instance, where the privacy of minors was involved, I chose to make "the red-headed girl" a composite of several real people.

The perspective offered here is mine alone. I don't claim to speak for the people of Pocahontas County, though I hope that this book speaks to them as well as other audiences. I have tried to see the telling of truth in this book like the drawing of an asymptote, a line that continually reaches for the heart of the matter, even as it does not—cannot—meet it.

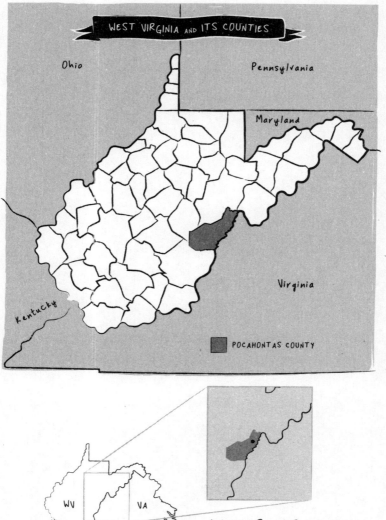

WEST VIRGINIA AND ITS COUNTIES

Ohio

Pennsylvania

Maryland

Virginia

Kentucky

POCAHONTAS COUNTY

WV

VA

National Radio Quiet Zone
● GREEN BANK TELESCOPE

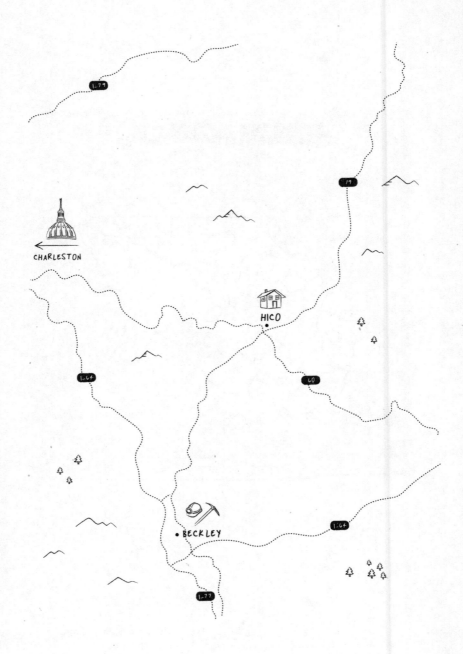

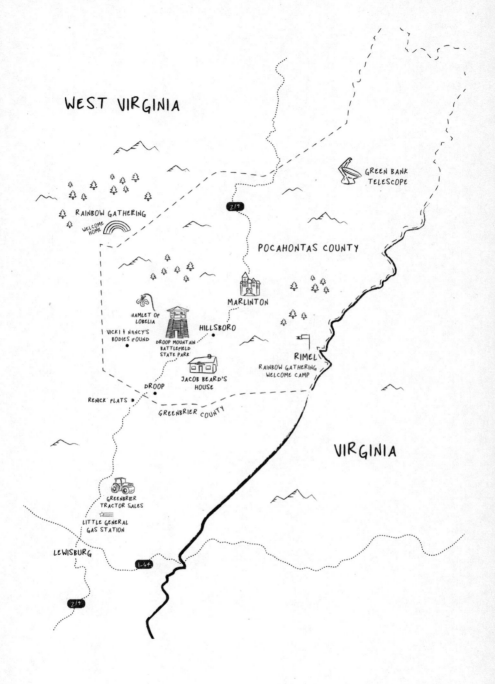

TRUE THINGS

Here are some true things:

1. In the afternoon or early evening of June 25, 1980, Vicki Durian and Nancy Santomero were killed in an isolated clearing in southeastern West Virginia. They were twenty-six and nineteen, hitchhiking to an outdoor peace festival known as the Rainbow Gathering, but as the result of two and three close-range gunshot wounds respectively, they never arrived. Vicki was from Iowa but was working as a home health aide in Arizona. Nancy had dropped out of college in New York and was working at a Tucson thrift store. They had not had sex on the day they died, nor were they raped. Their killings have been called the Rainbow Murders.

2. They died in Pocahontas County, a sparsely populated area that consists largely of protected national forest and sits along West Virginia's eastern border with Virginia. At the time of their murders, thousands of travelers from all over the country had come to this area to attend the Rainbow Gathering. Local reaction to the festival, organized by outsiders, varied widely. One faction of Pocahontas Countians was upset at the disruption of their lives and, assisted by prominent state politicians, filed an unsuccessful injunction to stop the event. Some speculated a causal link between the festival and the deaths. Because of this, as well as the remoteness of the clearing where the two women were found, citizens and law enforcement mostly believed that the killer was local.

3. The murders were a trauma experienced on a community scale. Wherever they went to eat or relax or pray, residents discussed these crimes and the fact that the killer was likely still living among them. Two young women had come to their home place for a peaceful celebration and instead ended up dead. Hillsboro, the closest town, held less than three hundred residents. Neighbor accused neighbor.

4. No one was prosecuted for Vicki and Nancy's murders for thirteen years. Eventually, nine local people were arrested and charged with crimes connected to the killings. Three more were named as suspects by law enforcement. Two confessed. Four accused another in sworn statements or testimony. All this and more was reported, in great detail, by the local paper, the *Pocahontas Times*, each Thursday morning. The accused were all men who made their living by working the land—farming, hauling timber, cutting locust posts, or baling hay.

5. In 1993, the state of West Virginia chose to pursue a trial against one man only, a local farmer named Jacob Beard, whom it deemed the "trigger man." Beard was convicted and sentenced to life imprisonment without the possibility of parole. The state's case rested on the word of two of the nine men, both offered immunity in exchange for their testimony. Three men, prosecution witnesses testified, had picked up Vicki and Nancy hitchhiking and then driven them to the woods, where the other men joined the party. The men drank and smoked weed, the prosecution's theory continued, and then they tried to rape Vicki and Nancy. When the women struggled too much and threatened to go to the police, Beard was said to have shot them. One of the witnesses had less than a third-grade education, and the other said he had repressed his memories of the murders for many years but later recovered them. Both witnesses were physically assaulted by West Virginia State Police officers.

6. In 1984, a man named Joseph Paul Franklin, already incarcerated in a federal prison in Illinois for a series of murders he had committed throughout the late 1970s and early 1980s, told an investigator that he

shot and killed two women in the woods of West Virginia. Franklin had a tendency to make claims that he would later disavow, and he had been diagnosed with schizophrenia. Law enforcement deemed his confession less than platinum, and the judge in Beard's case agreed. But in 1996, after learning that Beard was doing what Franklin felt to be his time, Franklin grew more insistent in claiming responsibility for Vicki and Nancy's deaths. With Franklin's cooperation, Beard was granted a new trial in 1999 and found not guilty in 2000.

7. I lived in Pocahontas County, West Virginia, from May 2009 to November 2010 and have spent approximately two hundred additional nights here, mostly in summer. I came as a Volunteer in Service to America (VISTA), a corps of domestic service volunteers created in 1965 to "alleviate poverty" in America's most distressed regions that sits under the broader program AmeriCorps. It was my job to empower the teenage girls of southeastern West Virginia by fostering their academic excellence, their knowledge of the ecology and history of their home state, and their healthy emotional development. I eventually moved away from Pocahontas County but have since been back many times as a friend and worker and later as a reporter—that troubled and troubling term—because once I heard the story of Vicki and Nancy and the nine men, it would not leave me.

8. Though it was my job to work with the girls of Pocahontas County, most of the people I was closest to here were men. They worked construction jobs to make the money they needed and shared with me their music and their land. I existed in a relationship with them essentially as a friend and neighbor and fellow researcher looking into the word "alive."

9. The idea of Appalachia is well understood; the real place, less so. It is a borderland, not truly of the South or the North, and West Virginia is the only state entirely within its bounds. Because of its enormous natural resources and their subsequent extraction, which has largely profited corporations based elsewhere, the relationship between the people of West

Virginia and the broader United States of America is often compared to that between a colonized people and their colonizers. The programs of Lyndon Johnson's War on Poverty that funneled national dollars and aid workers to central Appalachia, though founded on humanitarian ideas, also furthered this troubled interdependency.

10. Pocahontas County life demanded that women and girls be powerful in ways that the more urban places I've lived have not, or have even categorically denied. The masculinity I saw in Pocahontas County also encouraged emotional and physical closeness between men in ways I have rarely seen elsewhere.

11. If every woman is a nonconsensual researcher looking into the word "misogyny," then my most painful and powerful work was done in Pocahontas County. It could have been done in any other place, because misogyny is in the groundwater of every American city and every American town, but for me, it was done here. Looking into the Rainbow Murders became part of this work.

12. According to the most recent FBI data, 74 percent of women who are murdered are murdered by men. In 84 percent of cases, the act of murder was not related to the commission of any other felony such as rape or robbery.

13. In America, protecting or avenging white women from a violation of their safety or sexual autonomy has been used time and time again to justify the unlawful incarceration of men—particularly poor men and men of color. To be conceptualized or to conceptualize oneself as a victim, as my friend the writer Sarah Marshall often reminds me, is the thing more than any other that inhibits personal and moral growth.

14. White men accounted for nearly 80 percent of suicide deaths in 2017, and men in West Virginia are committing suicide at a rate of almost three times the national average, according to the most recent comprehen-

sive data by the US Centers for Disease Control and Prevention (CDC). These numbers do not take into account deaths by drug overdose, car accident, or workplace accident.

15. Friedrich Nietzsche famously wrote that in all desire to know, there is a drop of cruelty. The same may be true of the impulse to turn the messy stuff of many people's lived experience into a single story. At the same time, stories are responsible for nearly everything in this life that has made me more free. Which stories are which and to what extent this story is an example of the former idea or the latter or both is an essential question of this book.

16. Elizabeth Johndrow hitchhiked with Vicki and Nancy across the United States. In the mythology of these events, Liz is known as "the third girl," though she did not die. She's not a girl anymore, but a woman with a son and a rich network of love. When I think of all this as a story, I think of her.

PART I:
WELCOME HOME

To love a familiar patch of earth is to know something beyond death, "westward from death," as my father used to speak it.

—Louise McNeill

Nancy Santomero, 1979

Vicki Durian, 1977

1

IT STARTS WITH A ROAD, a two-lane blacktop called West Virginia Route 219 that spines its way through Pocahontas County and serves, depending on the stretch, as main street and back street, freeway and byway, sidewalk and catwalk.

It is June 25, 1980, just after the summer solstice, and a young man named Tim is driving home for the night. He had driven to Lewisburg, the big town almost an hour away, and is coming back now, with fresh laundry and groceries.

The road is made of black tar with a healthy gravel shoulder that gives way to ditch and then forest on both sides except when it climbs up or down a mountain, which is often. On those stretches, the ditches are replaced by tight metal guardrails with reflective yellow arrows that point drivers around the hairpin turns, some nearly one hundred and eighty degrees—a true switchback. To drive this road requires skill, to know when to tap the brake and when to press the gas. Tim is new in town and still learning. It is tempting to slam on the brake every time he sees a switchback, but the better move—for safety, gas efficiency, and natural enjoyment—is to do nothing, to let the speed ride and then, halfway through the turn, give it more gas. Beyond the guardrail is a steep drop-off into a valley where happy cows huddle together under ancient trees. The stakes of driving this road are high for Tim, as the many dents and welds in the guardrails remind him.

If a traveler were so inclined, she could drive this road in its entirety, all 524 miles of it, from Buffalo, New York, to Rich Creek, Virginia. Just south of the modern Mason-Dixon Line, this road roughly traces the original boundary between the land to the east called Virginia and the land to the west that has had so many names: West Augusta, Trans-Allegheny Virginia, Kanawha, and finally, when it declared itself a sovereign state, West Virginia.

In the beginning, the Seneca and the Cherokee used a route that would become this road to travel the wilderness from where the St. Lawrence River flows through New York state all the way to Georgia, long before there were any white people here.

Soon the white people came, first only to the coast at Jamestown but then crashing west across the forest floor. To stop the flow of blood, King George III issued the Proclamation of 1763, declaring what would become this road as the dividing line between what was "rightful" English settlement and what was not. Whites were forbidden to settle west of this boundary, and any who had already crossed were commanded to return; likewise Native Americans were forbidden to go east of it. But do the white people listen? They do not listen.

Choosing this road as the boundary wasn't arbitrary, nor was it empathy for the rights of Native Americans, just sheer capitalist pragmatism. West of this road was wild, and not in a good way: it was steep and craggy mountainsides unsuitable for farming—"trash land." But for those who had left England seeking opportunity in the New World—largely the poor, the criminal, and the disenfranchised—many found that such opportunities were not easily forthcoming in Virginia. A powerful class-stratification system had quickly been established, a scramble for power that left some on top but most out in the cold. Those who had come with slightly more resources and ties to the upper classes back in London rushed to expand their claims over those who had fewer. By 1770, less than 10 percent of the white colonists owned over half the land in Virginia. To everyone else, the land beyond this road, forbidden or not, looked good.

Before long, smoke from the fires of simple timber homes marked the presence of a different kind of settler than the Virginian gentleman farmer: the intrepid woodsman squatter. To choose this place meant choosing violent struggle and disobedience, meant choosing years of raiding and being raided by the Seneca, meant choosing to sign up to fight in the American Revolution against England in such great numbers and with such enthusiasm that George Washington said of the region, "Leave me but a banner to plant upon the mountains of West Augusta, and I will gather around me the men who will lift our bleeding country from the dust and set her free."

Tim's car clears the hamlet of Renick, and the road flattens and straightens into a stretch called the Renick flats. Route 219 winds up and to the left, and the world becomes darker as the sun falls away and the pavement narrows and begins to hug the side of Droop Mountain. "Pocahontas County," the sign says, and then Tim is on the mountain's summit, where the road flattens again and takes him past a church marquee and the two-story farmhouses and single-wide trailers of his neighbors, past the pens where they raise chickens and sheep and pigs.

Take your right hand, and give the world the middle finger. Extend your thumb. If this is West Virginia, Pocahontas County sits in the thumb's fleshy heel, a jagged raindrop of land nearly the size of Rhode Island. It was named after the Native American princess we know so well, but there all familiar stories end.

Half the county is Monongahela National Forest. Eight major rivers have their headwaters here, rivers that feed the Gauley, then the Kanawha, the Ohio, and eventually the Mississippi, so that water that begins in Pocahontas County flows as far south as Louisiana. This is not coal country. Instead, its main exports are timber and people.

Each of Pocahontas's nine thousand residents could have her own nine square miles of land, but all the kids go to a single high school. If the kid is athletically inclined, she can become a Pocahontas County Warrior—unremarkable in football and track and field, but excellent in agriculture and archery. Snowshoe Mountain ski resort is here, on land that was logged throughout the first half of the twentieth century, then left to burn. It's owned by out-of-state prospectors, though exactly who owns it and where they call home will change too often to keep track—a North Carolina dentist, a Tokyo development company.

The world's largest fully steerable radio telescope is here too, a mountain-sized white satellite dish atop a construction crane that is visible from most anywhere in the northern part of the county. In 1958, the federal government established the National Radio Quiet Zone, a thirteen-thousand-square-mile swath of land spanning the West Virginia–Virginia border inside which cell phone signals and Wi-Fi will be severely restricted to minimize interference with the telescope's work of detecting faint interstellar signals, and all of Pocahontas County sits inside it. Take this state of affairs, and layer on top the profit margins of private telecommunications corporations, and the result will be that even in the second decade of the twenty-first century, Pocahontas County will remain a white spot on AT&T's orange map.

This is a place where those who wish to be undisturbed by pings and rings can do so in peace. There is a deep awareness here of what the rest of America thinks a life should look like—the newest model, the fanciest vacation, the highest paying job with the best retirement plan—and, among many, a rejection of that life. Some people grow their own corn and make their own music and choose to give birth at home without beeping machines. Some are not just off the grid but off the record—no company knows their name. The Gesundheit! Institute, Patch Adams's movie-famous hospital for alternative healing, is here; ditto Zendik Farm, an intentional artist community originally formed in 1969 in California.

Some people teach school or fix cars or stack the plates of the tourists who come here to hike and fish and ski. Some people are nurses and doctors and home health aides and lawyers and Tudor's Biscuit World servers and Rite Aid employees. Many people cannot get work in their field of interest because the jobs do not exist here, and some cannot get jobs at all. Some are not able to work and subsist on disability. West Virginia ranks forty-fourth out of all the American states for overall physical health of its population and forty-eighth for quality of care. Despite having the second lowest average annual income in the country, West Virginians pay the eighth highest health insurance premiums under the Affordable Care Act. Though it has the worst mental health of any state according to the CDC, it is ranked forty-eighth for access to mental health services. A therapist or a specialist is often a drive of an hour or more; the state has a single abortion provider in the capital of Charleston, 140 miles from Pocahontas County.

Some vote in every election, picking up their elderly relatives, driving them into town to pull the lever, and putting signs for their candidates of choice, both local and national, in their yards. Others don't vote at all, because the government doesn't care about West Virginia, so why bother? Some call the sheriff's office with the slightest information; others don't trust its deputies—you could trace law enforcement corruption back more than a century, to when the railroad companies and logging companies used hired guns to force people off their land or to sell their mineral rights. This will happen all over again when fracking is invented and prospectors will draw the Atlantic Coast pipeline straight through Pocahontas County.

Tim puts on his turn signal and gets ready to pull the car off to the left at the small green sign for Lobelia Road. It is easy to miss, he is learning; if he sees the rectangular stone marker for Droop Mountain Battlefield State Park, he's gone too far. The park is a popular spot for picnics and family reunions and reenactments of what happened here more than a hundred years ago, a battle that sealed West Virginia's statehood forever. It is said that you can still find musket balls in the dirt there if you dig down deep enough.

The story of West Virginia's birth as a state and how that shaped Pocahontas County in particular is a tough and exciting one, full of pluck and verve and no taxation without representation, an American story of David against Goliath and freedom from bad rules.

Unlike eastern Virginia, where farms were massive agricultural operations powered by African-born people forced into slavery, western Virginia was still primarily small homesteads even into the nineteenth century. People fished, trapped animals for fur, or cut timber. Families raised small beds of crops and livestock to sell to the rich people in eastern Virginia. Few plantations here—not enough flat land, not enough money, but some families did keep small numbers of enslaved people in bondage. To bring lumber from the Great Lakes states to the booming cities of the East, the railroad companies laid track through western Virginia in the 1820s. Thousands of people could now hop a train from eastern Virginia to western Virginia, and thousands did, looking for cheap land. City land promoters sold immigrants arriving from Europe on the dream of western Virginia. In the 1840s and 1850s, the Irish fleeing the potato famine made these mountains their own. But most still did not legally own their land, and without legal claim, they had to continually guard against threats from other squatters and from powerful city people with money and laws on their side. All this made the people of western Virginia vigilant, scrappy, and resourceful, engaged in the constant task of survival.

Many in Richmond and Washington, DC, looked down on western Virginia, regarding it as a lawless place where poor families occupied land they didn't own and didn't farm, a lifestyle that was at odds with both the Puritan ideals of family and Southern aristocratic values. Something "had to be done" about this place. The Virginia government adopted a policy that anyone squatting on land in the western territories of the state could claim first rights to buy it, but if they couldn't come up with the cash fast, they would have to either start paying rent or move on. Most families in western Virginia made their livings from the natural world or bartered; they didn't keep money on hand. Great swaths of land were sold to rich investors in Baltimore, Philadelphia, and New York.

Further, new laws also made owning land a qualification to vote and participate in democracy. But even if they could scrounge up the money, the system was rigged against western Virginians. In a baffling rule, a farm animal was now taxed at a higher rate than an enslaved person, making it far more expensive to farm in western Virginia than in eastern. People here just couldn't compete with the big plantation operations that churned out crops at bargain prices.

Western Virginians did all their own work and without the evil of slavery, so they should pay less in taxes than the slave-owning farmers to the east, they figured, not more. Plus they always seemed to be getting the raw end of the deal when it came to public money to build courthouses, jails, and schools. They didn't have good numbers in the state legislature—partly there had always been fewer people here, partly enslaved persons counted toward population tallies in eastern Virginia (though, disgracefully, as only a portion of a human). As early as 1831, western Virginia farmers backed a movement to free all people enslaved in Virginia—though whether motivated by racial justice or financial self-interest no one can say for sure.

Western Virginians grew savvy and pissed off. They began to talk about separating and making their own state, and this in the midst of the larger conversation circulating in Richmond and throughout the American South about separating from Lincoln's Union. Western Virginians were squeezed in the middle once again—counties closer to Richmond with more flat land and financial prosperity were in favor of sticking around and following their mother wherever she might go, even if that meant following her away from the Union. But many of the westernmost counties didn't want war and weren't inclined to follow Richmond anywhere. Twenty-two delegates from the mountains met in secret and resolved that they would oppose secession and keep as much of Virginia as possible loyal to the Union, and that they would eventually, when the time was right, move for their own state.

Richmond did not approve. Western Virginia offered a plentiful supply of young men who could go off to the fight without the risk of leaving enslaved people "unsupervised." The mountains were also a necessary strategic and geographic link between the Confederacy's natural resources and the bulk of their troops. The two parts of Virginia were still united when the first shots were fired at Fort Sumter in 1861, and still together in May when a majority of Virginia's state delegates voted to secede, but after two years, a special convention, and a popular election to make official what had long been felt, West Virginia officially broke with Virginia to stay in the Union and become the thirty-fifth American state on June 20, 1863. Its motto was, is, *montani semper liberi*—"mountaineers are always free."

Yet in every county and town and household, the people of what was now West Virginia had to choose for themselves. West Virginia officially fought for the Union in the Civil War, sending approximately thirty-six thousand soldiers to the blue. But a hearty sixteen thousand soldiers took up for the gray. Neighbor against neighbor, et cetera, but in Pocahontas County, it really was.

We like to talk of turning points, of moments that swing the door open or shut forever, and if you believe in such things, the Battle of Droop Mountain was one. November 1863: a small brigade of five thousand Union soldiers was on its way to an area of southwest Virginia near Roanoke on a standard slash-and-burn mission when they ran smack into seven hundred fifty Confederates under the command of Mudwall Jackson, disgraced cousin to Stonewall, at a bend in Route 219 a few miles north of Droop Mountain. Vastly outnumbered, the Confederates scuttled up Droop Mountain, while the Union brigade stayed put. From their perch that night, Confederate soldiers could peer over the edge of the slope and look down into the valley, where thousands of Union campfires burned. They would fight, they knew, and they would die.

But that night, Jackson managed to send panicked word to another Confederate general who was camped in nearby Lewisburg with some 1,175 foot soldiers. In 1980, it would take Tim forty-five minutes to drive the thirty miles back from the grocery store, but in 1863 it took twenty-four hours of continuous walking. They marched all that day and all through the following night and reached the summit of Droop Mountain around nine the next morning. Within an hour, Union forces attacked. By the end of that day, blood was soaking the ground of Droop Mountain, and West Virginia would never be part of the Confederacy.

Wrecked men and women returned home to Pocahontas County after war's end. Virginia tried to sweet-talk West Virginia into getting back together, but West Virginia held strong. Those who had peeked over the mountain's edge and those who had lit fires in the valley, however, now found themselves once again sharing a town. Most had not wanted to be Confederate, but saying no to a thing is not the same thing as saying yes to its opposite. For years and maybe forever, the state would struggle to be fully and truly part of the Union.

* * *

At the green sign for Lobelia Road, Tim turns left off Route 219, follows the paved single lane steeply downward until it wrenches to the right, revealing a view of the giant maple at the valley's center, and then keeps going into the small hamlet of Lobelia. He slows a few miles from his home and turns off at a neighbor's driveway.

At twenty-one, Tim has just been discharged from the army and moved to Pocahontas County weeks earlier; it is supposed to be an interesting place to be, a haven of sorts. In the 1970s, this part of West Virginia, particularly along this road, became the chosen home of a critical mass of people who wanted to move away from cities like Philadelphia, New York, and San Francisco.

Throughout the late 1960s and into the early 1970s, many Americans felt dispossessed by where the country was heading and how it was heading there—the Vietnam War principally, but also the way the government had responded to the uprisings motivated by racial injustice in Los Angeles and Detroit. Fleeing cities, they went to "the land." Between seven hundred fifty thousand and a million Back to the Landers, as they were dubbed, lived in communes by the mid-seventies, and an additional million were homesteading, either as singles or as couples in some of the most rural parts of the United States. If Helen and Scott Nearing's *The Good Life* was the blueprint for this way of life, *Mother Earth News* was its instruction manual. In 1970, the magazine published an article on the country's most homestead-friendly land available for purchase. Its conclusion: "north-central Pennsylvania" and "almost the entire state of West Virginia."

In 1975, a gaggle of Back to the Landers from all over the United States set up a commune in Pocahontas County called Island of the Red Hood. They set up a small farm, though they struggled with the hard soil and narrow growing season. Other Back to the Landers came as couples and families, some having driven all over the country in Westfalia camper vans before finally settling in West Virginia. They bought land, built slipshod timber-frame houses, and tried to put gardens into rocky, frozen ground. They had come to live off this land, but they did not know how.

Some locals who had grown up here for generations enjoyed watching them fail and flail, some kept a polite distance, but most succumbed to empathy or pity or the thing that flows between neighbors. They showed the newcomers how to plant and how to can, how to insulate and how to dredge; they lent car parts and seeds; they brought wood and installed carburetors and fixed wells.

Friendships happened. One local woman whose husband worked for the state highway department and was gone for weeks at a time invited the commune women over for quilting and soup, and soon they were sharing child care, dog care, recipes, dreams, and fears. Many local Pocahontas County residents were surprised to find that these new people were a lot like them—neither group cared much for material things, and neither had many. They were surprised to find that the Back to the Landers shared many of their same values too—values like self-sufficiency and freedom.

But by 1979, the bonds of the Red Hood commune were fraying—people were having babies or getting divorced, or they were tired of the hard work and the meetings where so-and-so went on about whose turn it was to take the chainsaw to be sharpened. Some of the Back to the Landers returned to the cities from which they'd emigrated, but many stayed, remarrying and buying land as family units. Pocahontas County had been losing population at a steady clip since 1920, when the logging boom burst, but the 1980 census delivered a shot in the arm: numbers were up.

It is around a quarter to nine when Tim pulls out of his neighbor's driveway, but the sky still has some light to it. He turns off Lobelia onto Briery Knob, a narrow gravel road that pitches slightly uphill. He drives for two miles through the forest until the turnoff for his dirt lane appears. He turns in toward his lean-to cabin and drives a hundred fifty yards or so, as is his routine; the lane continues, but deep ruts up ahead will scrape the underside of anything but a pickup. When he leaves most mornings, he backs up into a patch of earth cleared of brush, where he can turn around and drive out again.

But as he drives into his lane on this night, Tim sees two people lying there in the cleared patch off to his left. The pair seems to be having a private moment, Tim thinks, having sex maybe, so he continues on through and parks. When he turns to look at them once more, something is not right, and it is in their bodies. Too still. Tim walks back to where they lie: two women, almost perfectly perpendicular to the lane, their feet to the road, their heads in the grass. They are on their backs, and their eyes are open. They have been shot. Fifteen minutes later, and the dark would have hidden them.

2

1980: OUT WITH JOAN BAEZ and Bob Dylan, all hail Iron Maiden and AC/DC. The first case of AIDS in the United States is reported to the CDC. Fifty-two Americans remain hostages in the US embassy in Tehran. Gas is dear, and national unemployment barrels toward a rate unmatched since the Great Depression. Ku Klux Klan membership is the highest it's been in fifteen years; in California, a Klan leader wins the Democratic nomination to Congress. Eight years after the Equal Rights Amendment passed both houses of Congress, the Republican Party withdraws its support, and the amendment will fail forever. The writer Alice Sebold is raped in a tunnel on the campus of Syracuse University and told by police that she is lucky—she lived.

In a televised address the year before, President Jimmy Carter diagnoses the feeling in the air as a "crisis of confidence": "Confidence in the future has supported everything else—public institutions and private enterprise, our own families, and the very Constitution of the United States." He wears a blue velour suit and a diagonally striped tie. "We've discovered that owning things and consuming things does not satisfy our longing for meaning." More than thirty years before Donald Trump will appropriate it for his own purposes, Ronald Reagan uses the slogan "Let's make America great again" in his bid for the Republican presidential nomination in the fall of 1980. "I need your commitment, your hope and your belief in this great nation's ability to begin again," he pronounces, in a dark brown suit and light brown tie. West Virginia will be one of only six states in the nation to vote to reelect Carter. When Reagan triumphs in November, everything will change.

But not yet. In the spring and summer of 1980, there is still the possibility that the future might turn out differently, that the striped tie might yet prevail over the brown one, that a doomsday diagnosis might, in its honesty, be more uplifting than magical thinking. Many in West Virginia do not want to begin again or are not buying the kind of new beginning Reagan is selling.

The paper of Pocahontas County is the *Pocahontas Times*, steered by the same family since 1892. Its main reporter and soon-to-be-editor is grandson Bill McNeel, who went away to Ohio and Oregon for school and then came back. The paper is still printed letter by letter with hand-set type and a phototypesetting machine like a journalistic x-ray. "Those days are gone!" a citizen of Pocahontas County writes in a campaign letter from this time. "Technology has brought us out of the 'hollers' and thrust us into the midst of a teeming, scheming, screaming society. Our people must be prepared to face the future."

Throughout the spring of 1980, the Survival Center at the University of Oregon in Eugene mailed thousands of flyers with gratis nonprofit postage to food co-ops and colleges and mailboxes all over America. "This is the Invitation and Information sheet to the 1980 Rainbow Family World Peace Gathering," the flyers read. "These Gatherings are Free and Everyone Everywhere is invited to Come and Share Together. Bring your Friends and all your Relations to Gather with us in the hopes of Spreading the True Truth that Humanity is Beautiful, that We can Live and Work Together in Cooperation and Joy." The flyer invited anyone who could get there to attend a peace festival that summer in the Monongahela National Forest in West Virginia.

Such was the habit of the Rainbow Family, a loose organization that aimed to revive the hippie spirit of the 1960s and had been converging on a different public land for a few weeks each July since 1972. A remote location was plucked off the map, word was mailed out, and several months later, people came—sometimes as many as twenty thousand. The group usually did not bother with permits because permits required the signature of a leader and the Rainbows do not believe in leaders.

The 1980 Gathering in West Virginia would be their first ever in the East.

"Our Relation with the Local People is Very Important," the flyer further advised. "Please be Perfectly Respectful of the Local People in whose area we gather. It is important that we be completely Sensitive, Clean and Polite in all our Dealings with These People. We have worked hard over the years to earn the Respect of the Forest Rangers and Local Citizens, but this is an area that can still use Improvement."

At other Gatherings, Rainbows turned the public bathrooms of several gas stations near their campsite into bathhouses, flooded a local diner for lunch and dinner for a week leaving only pennies for tips, and shoplifted prodigiously from the single general store. A Gathering meant thousands of people tromping, shitting, pissing, and parking their cars. Forest ranger presence had to be multiplied by five or ten, so staff had to be imported from other counties, and then everyone had to be paid overtime. Rainbow people had gotten sick, gotten hurt, inundated local hospitals. They were not malicious—some had gotten up to help waitresses at the diner serve meals, and a Rainbow leader wrote the wronged store owner a fat check as reparations—but they lived outside the rules and did what they wanted regardless of the consequences.

Common sense and good manners would dictate a generous period of advance warning, but it was the middle of May 1980—just a month before the Gathering was scheduled to begin—before Forest Service officials in West Virginia got word that the Rainbow people were on their way. Between five and fifteen thousand people were expected, the Rainbows advised. One hundred acres of woodland were needed, plus parking.

Fifteen thousand visitors! In 1980, all of Pocahontas totaled just below ten thousand. "It looks like we will have lots of company this summer in Pocahontas County," wrote McNeel, breaking the news to his readers. "We urge everyone to be sure of facts before stories are repeated—they have a habit of growing." Some were excited, eager to see with their own eyes the longhairs they had long been watching sit in and burn flags on the nightly news. But would they be naked, lurching around the woods? Would they be food stamp freeloaders?

The Rainbows wanted a spot in the Monongahela National Forest called the Three Forks of the Williams River, which sat smack above the headwaters for nearly every major waterway in Pocahontas County. Perhaps the Rainbows might like to camp at another spot instead? No, the Rainbows said—only that spot would do.

Movies like *Easy Rider* told a story that positioned "hippies" from the city and "hicks" from rural areas as irrevocably opposed to one another. Yet how much actual hostility citizens of Pocahontas County felt toward the Rainbows in the months leading up to the 1980 Gathering depends on whom you ask. Certainly different belief systems seemed to be colliding. There were incidents in nearby parts of West Virginia around that time involving locals confronting people they perceived as different, sometimes aggressively, and the more liberal newspapers in Charleston printed glowing stories celebrating Rainbow values at the expense of the more traditional local way of life.

Pocahontas County had already been intimately exposed to outsiders for years in the form of their Back to the Lander neighbors, and though it was difficult to avoid hearing about the Rainbows' impending arrival, there is little evidence to suggest that all or even most of the people of Pocahontas County harbored serious ill will toward the Rainbows.

Governor John "Jay" Rockefeller, a New Yorker who had come to West Virginia as an Appalachian Youth volunteer and stayed, called the Rainbows' impending arrival "disruptive." Other government officials called them "leeches" and "derelict misfits." 1980 was an election year, and in what was likely a bid for votes, Secretary of State James Manchin fanned the embers of hostility by declaring that Rainbow people were not welcome in the state because they did not practice West Virginia values. Encouraged by Manchin, several prominent Pocahontas County residents filed a request for an injunction in federal court to block the Rainbow Family from gathering in the Monongahela, but a judge threw it out. The Rainbows would come, and they would camp where they liked.

They came by car and by VW bus. They came on bike and on foot. "By not having a camera, we missed an opportunity Monday to take a picture of a young lady walking to the Rainbow Gathering with her mule; the mule was well-loaded with gear and supplies," wrote McNeel for the *Poca-hontas Times*. "She walked all the way from New Jersey, and had been on her way for a month."

Estimates vary, but between two and six thousand people arrived in Marlinton throughout the month of June 1980 and into early July and then made their way further into the forest for the festival. Some say they stole. There were reports of Rainbows going into Foodland and using the vegetable crispers to wash their mud-caked hands. Some scandalized citizens reported that Rainbows had run naked through a car wash near Main Street. Other citizens were excited and set up lawn chairs on the bridge that spans the Greenbrier River to watch the visitors roll in. In nearby Richwood, some Rainbow People showed a slide show of past Gatherings and then answered questions from more than a hundred locals. "While some were a little stunned by such Rainbow exotica as a young man who introduced himself as 'Water Singing on the Rocks,'" reported the *New York Times*, "the meeting ended with Rainbows and Richwood residents alike joining hands and singing the old hymn 'Will the Circle Be Unbroken?'"

More than five hundred local people from Marlinton and the surrounding hamlets drove the switchbacked roads into the national forest to check out the Rainbow scene, a far greater local presence than usually showed up at the Gatherings. The one-lane dirt road to the Gathering was littered with hitchhikers—some locals picked them up; some didn't. Rainbow volunteers directed traffic, inquiring of visitors if they were just staying for the day or planning to camp overnight, and parking was suggested accordingly, with cars arranged in neat rows.

A half mile farther down the road was a gate with a sign that said no alcohol, drugs, or weapons beyond that point. The camp was meticulously clean, as if the Gathering was instead a convention of Boy Scouts. Some visitors were greeted near the gate by a Rainbow bluegrass band, totally naked behind their strings.

Handwritten signs on tree trunks divided the camp into sections— drug-free, clothing, clothing optional, organic foods. A Rainbow man passed out copies of the unofficial newsletter, printed with each day's events on a press set up in the back of someone's VW bus. Food, carried in from across the country and supplemented from the grocery in nearby Cowen, was prepared by a team of designated volunteers at five canvas-topped kitchen tents. Inside each tent, men and women stirred enormous pots—soupy mixes of brown rice, tomato paste, potatoes, and carrots—and gave it away to anyone who was hungry; all you had to do was listen to the talk and maybe peel a potato or two.

"I was impressed by the Family members because I believe they are doing something that all of us, even conservatives like myself, have dreamed of doing sometime," wrote Bob Scott, a visiting journalist. "Saying the heck with material things and the mortgage, and running off to live wherever the spirit and the winds and an old Volkswagen bus will take us."

Inorganic matter was carted off in plastic or burlap sacks to another part of the camp; early arrivals had also dug out a pit for compost and another long trench that served as an open-air outhouse. Several plastic buckets of lime were available, and people were encouraged to sprinkle a little bit on their dump, whether pre- or post-digestion.

McNeel made the trip too, perhaps out of personal curiosity or merely professional obligation. There were workshops, he reported—Yoga, Grain and Organic Vegetable Farming, Knot Tying and Scissor and Tool Sharpening, Appalachian Folk Dancing, Poetry Reading. "This writer noted, however, that many people at the Gathering seemed not to be interested in the workshops but in visiting, talking, and being with each other."

On the edge of the festival grounds was a swimming hole backed by a hillside that led up to where visitors had parked. Many swam naked here, and the sight of so much flesh in such clear, clean water was special. A few local men took to standing on the far side of the hole and harassing the Rainbow women as they swam, hooting and guffawing their laughter and discomfort. Other local people dove right in. A writer for another local weekly wrote, "And what did your intrepid reporter do when faced with the spectacle of several hundred skinny-dippers? Why, the only sensible thing. I stripped down and joined them."

It rained every night, and every morning a fog filled the holler of the Three Forks of the Williams River that did not lift until noon. Then it lifted, and there was the sun, a sun that saturated the moss and the grass and hit the maple and oak leaves so richly they looked Technicolor. The clouds moved fast across the sky, the weather moved in fast from the west, and the Rainbow People learned, as any citizen of Pocahontas County could have testified, that here it could go from full sun to full-on pouring in ten seconds flat.

There were those who came for a music festival, those who came to soak up the strength that comes from fellowship, and those who lacked a sense of purpose in their lives and came seeking answers or a cosmic message. Some lived the Rainbow life year-round, hitchhiking or sleeping in the back of their vehicles. When you are at a Rainbow Gathering, everyone is connected, everyone is related, you are encouraged to call everyone you meet "sister" or "brother," and you are to hug them and welcome them "home." Their slogan was "May You Always Be All Ways Free." Every so often a shout of "We love you!" went up from one kitchen tent and was passed to the next, around and around, until it returned to its origin. This usually took place at dawn, as a kind of reveille, or in the evening, as a way of calling Gatherers from around the camp to converge for dinner. They held hands before eating, taking a moment of silence before the din.

3

BIG SKY, NO STARS, NO edge. The drama of a crossroads where two country routes meet at perfect right angles, and the quiet, a quiet that feels different than it does in the East—windblown, ringing through the telephone lines. The Dutch Country Inn, the Tequila Grill, the Hard Luck Cafe, and the Amish bakery. House, job, church, kids. Happy wife, happy life. This is Washington County, Iowa, a square thirty miles southwest of Iowa City.

No edge here, literally—the road is flat and flows right up against the parking lot of the gravel plant without any shoulder. Few people walk from one destination to another here, except kids in the middle of empty roads, two miles from where the bus drops them off.

Vicki Durian wanted to walk. She was born in 1953 to farmers—eighty acres of corn and beans and hogs for one hundred and twenty-five dollars a head; timber in the summer. Eight kids, Vicki the second and the oldest girl. The boys worked the fields and the hogs with dad; the girls worked the house with mom—cooking, cleaning, and doing dishes. When it was time for the boys to come in for lunch, it was Vicki who called them. "She could really whistle," says her younger brother, John Durian.

For a long time, Vicki was good—good girl, good citizen. Her parents were often in the *Kalona News* for hosting luncheons at the Catholic church, bearing palls, and chairing committees. Vicki curled her hair, kept "trim," joined Future Homemakers of America, had many friends at school and lots of cousins who slept over in tents in the Durian backyard on the weekends. Saved the sixteen candles from the cake the girls gave her at lunch, taping them into her scrapbook.

She had a horse for a while, had dogs and cats, loved animals. All the kids ran around the property. Camping, fishing, playing in the swimming hole behind the Durian farmhouse. "Right in the English River," says John, "which I wouldn't do now."

Vicki loved school, Mid Prairie Middle then Mid Prairie High— "Homecoming 1970, we love you hawks!" Football games, basketball games, the winter dance—"I am a Mid-Prairie Golden Hawk Booster." Made invitations for suppers—"Bring the latest gossip!" Made clothes— "Vicki, Thanks so much for making that dress for me! I just love it and I know I'll get a lot of good out of it!" Did she do well in school? "A lot better than you boys!" says dad Howard. Critical, it seems, but only of herself: "Not the greatest play—but I even had a part," she wrote in her scrapbook.

She knew how to have fun. She dressed brothers John, Mike, and Tom as little princesses and walked them around to meet the neighbors, which people still talk about. When Vicki and her cousins slept in those tents, she would sneak off on foot and walk down to the river and then cross it to the Wassonville Cemetery and the bridge, a wooded area far from the gravestones that was the party spot then and is still the party spot now. Her best guy friend was a boy from school who drove a noisy motorcycle. Howard didn't like it when the boy parked at the farmhouse and would tell him to get lost. "I heard it all the way to his home."

Vicki liked the dark, was fascinated with vampires and a show called *Dark Shadows*. She liked television in general, images beamed in from far away. At fifteen she watched the hippies gather for Woodstock, and the picture stuck—she wanted to go, but she was too young, born too late. She bought her first album: a greatest-hits record by the Grass Roots. She lay on her floor and listened.

In 1971, seventeen now, Vicki went to see the movie *Love Story*— catchphrase "Love means never having to say you're sorry"—escorted by a boy named Robert and pasted the ticket stub in her scrapbook. Soon Vicki was receiving Christmas cards addressed to her and Robert. Robert came over for Christmas dinner and gave her a blouse and a pair of electric scissors.

The world was beginning to change. The farming business was faltering.

Howard took a job working the third shift at a refrigeration factory near Cedar Rapids. Vicki's mother, Clarabelle, who had been working as a lunch lady at Mid Prairie, took a second job at the Pull'r Inn cleaning rooms. Robert saw other girls. "This is the last year I'll have an obligation to Mid-Prairie," Vicki wrote in her scrapbook under her senior year class schedule.

One day her cousin DeAnn, whose family visited often from Colorado, heard the back door slam and voices—Vicki and Robert—arguing down by the river. Vicki came back in and told her parents she was pregnant. Howard and Clarabelle said, it's your choice—go to Colorado and have the baby and come back when you're better, or stay here and marry him. Robert and Vicki went to prom together in June 1972, he in a light blue tux, she in a yellow dress with ruffles around the throat and wrists, but there is no joy in these photos.

Throughout the 1960s and into the early 1970s, nearly 80 percent of babies born to white women without legal spouses were relinquished for adoption. "The right thing to do to protect your parents was to get out of town, go into a home," wrote Joni Mitchell, who gave up a child to adoption at the exact start of this boom—1965. "The homes were full.…Movies were getting sexier. It was very confusing to be a young woman then."

By the mid-1970s, as sex outside marriage, contraception, abortion, and single parenting became more common and less socially shameful, this rate would plummet to 12 percent; by 1983 it would be just 4 percent. The Supreme Court decision that legalized abortion nationwide came down in 1973, a year after Vicki got pregnant, but in 1972 Iowa, no one felt it coming.

Vicki arrived at her cousins' house in suburban Colorado in the summer of 1972, freshly graduated from high school and five months pregnant. The Catholic adoption agency got her a job so she wouldn't be idle, and she watched movies and sewed with DeAnn and the rest of the family. She bore it all cheerfully. "That was Vicki," DeAnn says. She had the baby in November, on the same day as her own birthday, or very near. She held her son, and then a nurse came and took him.

One day afterward, DeAnn leaned against Vicki's bedroom door while

Vicki lay in bed and asked if Vicki ever regretted her choice, if she ever cried for her baby. "I cry for him every day," Vicki replied.

"She loved that baby," DeAnn says now. "I think some counseling would have been a good idea. She never got any."

Back in Iowa, Robert came over for Christmas again. He was enraged. He wanted the baby. He was still seeing other girls. The Durians could hear him shouting through every wall. Vicki told him to get out and not to come back. In Vicki's scrapbook from 1972 there is a page with an inscription in Vicki's blue swooping writing: "The last note this year from Robert." Only a discolored square exists where this note once sat.

Most days, Vicki picked up her sister Mary and their brothers from school, then went to work at Shenk's Nursing Home. There she would be, driving her dad's big stick-shift pickup truck with her tanned arm lolling out the window. "Get in," she would say, laughing and gesturing to the truck bed, then flooring the gas.

Vicki began to talk about going to San Francisco, about going to see the Grateful Dead. She cut her hair, stopped wearing makeup, started wearing flowing dresses and baggy pants. She had always gotten excited for Earth Day, but now she became "a real hippie." On a family trip to Lake Geode, when her brothers threw their soda cans out the window, she lectured them on how long it takes for aluminum to biodegrade—five hundred years. She became a vegetarian, started making her own granola, started using chopsticks instead of a knife and fork, stopped touching the mounds of meat Clarabelle asked her to prepare for dinner, placing big bountiful salads on the family table instead. "We eat meat around here," Howard said one night, and Vicki got up from the table and ran up the stairs. Her brother John heard her lifting the needle and playing her Grass Roots record over and over again, and he knew: Vicki would leave, and he would inherit that record.

She moved to Iowa City for a little while, living in a big communal house near what is today the Prairie Lights bookstore. She tried Davenport, near Moline, so she could go to the nursing school there. Her aunt and grandmother had been nurses, and she figured she might as well try for her degree.

But Vicki wanted to go farther, go faster—she just wanted to go. She wanted California, she wanted ocean, but she had no money for all that. She started hitchhiking.

Nancy Santomero had never hitchhiked outside of Long Island before. Her father, Joe, had traveled through the West when he was in his teens, but he came back. He met Nancy's mother, Jeanne, an "independent woman" with a good job as a bank secretary, playing tennis on a Brooklyn court. It was Joe's friend who asked Jeanne for her number, but Joe prevailed on the friend to sell it to him for thirty-five cents. Jeanne and Joe married at a small Catholic church in 1955 and set up their home in Levittown, that first gleaming and mass-produced suburb, designed to house soldiers returning from the Second World War and their families. Once just potato and onion fields, the town was built assembly-line style; at the peak of construction, a house was said to be completed every sixteen minutes. Jeanne had a good eye and was a snappy dresser whose garden was always the most elegant one on the street. She was the product of a happy marriage and a doting father. "I thought all fathers were like that," she says. "I expected my husband to be the same kind of man. But he was not."

Joe's job as a Wise potato chip salesman kept him mostly on the road, driving his truck all over Long Island, and Jeanne stayed home to raise the kids—five of them born in quick succession, one almost every year. Joe wanted a boy, but Jeanne gave birth to girl after girl after girl after girl. The last one was Nancy. Patricia was just a year older than Nancy, but because Patricia was a shy child with a speech impediment, their mother decided to hold her back, and the two ended up in the same grade. "That way she could be with Nancy," Jeanne says. "Nancy would protect her." Nancy and Patricia had all the same friends and were sometimes mistaken for twins.

Levittown remained a completely white suburb into the 1960s because of a policy that explicitly banned people of color, and Jeanne worried about her kids growing up in such a place. She went back to work at the hospital as a ward clerk, and many of the people who came in for treatment lived in nicer neighborhoods in the Long Island towns to the east—farther from the city, closer to the Long Island Sound. The houses in these towns had more space between them; the crowds who played in the parks were more diverse. Joe drove his potato chip truck through these towns too and smelled their cleaner air. The couple crunched the numbers and decided they could afford the leap.

In August 1969, when Nancy and Patricia were going into the fourth grade, the Santomero family moved into a two-story house on a quiet cul de sac in the new development of Huntington. The kids could walk to school and downtown to Main Street, where there were restaurants and a small bookstore. They walked to the Walt Whitman mall, to the big H shopping center where there was a Sears, to the Woolworth counter, and the movie theater.

The theme of Nancy's childhood was variety—shifting, trying on many different outfits to see if they fit. She wasn't very concerned with her clothing, though, favoring jeans and peasant shirts. She was friends with everyone—the potheads, the disco people, the lacrosse players, the hippies. She was into art—painting and sculpture mostly, though for a time she talked about becoming a professional photographer—and liked everything from Joni Mitchell to Ayn Rand.

But she was an athlete too—a top-notch basketball player who played center. "I would throw the ball to her right away, and she would take it to the hoop," remembers Patricia. Nancy liked being outside, a preference she got from her mother. "I had never been to the ocean until Nancy's mother took us," says Jo-Ann Orelli, Nancy's best friend from that time.

The sisters shared one room and one bed. "We'd face [one] way and scratch each other's backs," says Nancy's sister Jeanne, the second oldest, "and then we'd roll over and scratch [the sister on the other side]."

Nancy's father was "traditional Italian," he was "macho," he believed "the man was the head of the household," says Catherine Shea, who grew up on the same street as the Santomeros. Joe worked long hours and wanted dinner on the table when he came home. Nancy's sisters and her brother, Peter, the youngest of all the kids (Joe got his boy after all), mostly deferred to Joe's wishes.

"Nancy was stubborn," says Patricia. "She was just like my dad—they were so similar. And the rest of us had to live with them."

If there was a party too far away to walk to, the sisters and their friends sometimes hitchhiked along the local roads, a common practice at that time. "Everybody did it," Orelli says. "We used to hitchhike with eight people, get picked up and jam into a car. If there were seatbelts, nobody wore them."

Nancy wasn't the one riding shotgun, but she went, squished into the backseat. The parties sprawled like the towns; they spread from kitchen to living room, living room to yard, yard to woods, woods to the shore, and then right on out to the Sound.

She liked to drink, says Orelli, but not more than anyone else. "We'd get a beer and all share it, passing it around and getting buzzed off the bubbles." She had crushes, most notably on the brother of a friend of one of her sisters, and dated a boy for a while, but unlike Patricia, who met her husband in high school, Nancy's relationships never got serious. Patricia went to the prom, but Nancy didn't; going to the prom stag was not a thing at that time, Orelli says, nor was girls asking guys out. Neither was caring much about school or grades. Nancy was an "average student" at best.

"In high school, no one asked me if I was going to go to college," says Kathy. "It's nothing like now. I think we were just on the edge of change."

After high school, Nancy rolled upstate to SUNY Buffalo. But it was brutally cold there, and she didn't like her roommate. She got an apartment off campus right away, which she paid for herself—Joe and Jeanne couldn't afford to help.

It is tempting to call Nancy "tough," but Orelli says it wasn't so. She was loving; she wasn't hard. "She was a strong person.... What she did, I could never do—when she went to school in Buffalo…she was kind of on her own.... She was independent. She just had more guts [than the rest of us]."

Nancy did not hide it when she suffered. "My nerves are acting up," Nancy wrote to Orelli. "Can't eat, can't sleep. I always thought myself to be a calm person. Tricked again!"

After her freshman year, she dropped out of school. "I really feel that I will find a more suitable place elsewhere," Nancy wrote to her sister Jeanne in the fall of 1979. "Exactly where is unknown, but I am going to search for it."

She spent that summer going downtown with her high school friends to the bars around Huntington. No one had any money, so the friends would buy six-ounce cans of Miller High Life called "splits," which cost about ten cents.

The drinking age was eighteen then, and that wasn't the only difference. "It was easier back then to get ahead," says Orelli. "Now to live someplace like [where we grew up]…it costs a lot of money."

Nancy told her friends that she had dreams, things to do, but she didn't know what they were exactly or where. She thought she might like to become a forester or a park ranger, so she could work outside or close to animals. She had two cats named Thunder and Lightning.

Her moods seemed changeable that summer, recalls her sister Jeanne. "She would have very highs and lows. She would be really happy and then really sad."

"Primarily she was happy," Patricia says. "If she was sad, it was because she felt lost. When you don't know what you're doing, what your life is, it torments you."

A school friend of the Santomero sisters, who was studying at the University of Arizona in Tucson, was also back home in Huntington for the summer. It's warm there, she told Nancy over a split. By the fall, Nancy and her cats were there.

"I'm sure Iowa has been in its peak autumn colors by now. I miss that," Vicki wrote home to her sister Mary in October 1978. "There is a definite season change here also but only slight.… There will be five planets lining up in Scorpio in a few weeks and I feel the earth will go through some drastic changes. Me too!"

She was in California. She had found that when she smiled, people stopped their cars. Someone called her Bright Star because of that smile, and soon it was her name.

Where some searchers are essentially one—all movement, all desire, all muscle and hair—Vicki was two, both street cat and house cat. There was the dream, sure, there was the need to be free, but also, somewhere that was always with her, there was the farm in Iowa, the bills that were due, the father and the mother, and the seven siblings who stayed. Vicki knew she had busted the set, disturbed the order by leaving.

When Mary got married, Vicki caught a ride home and stood dutifully with the other bridesmaids in the ceremonial half moon. She had forgotten how to wear makeup so completely that one of Mary's friends had to do it for her. The dress—a floor-length gown of "tyrol red fashioned with empire waist, front opening with stand-up collar, long puffed sleeves with cuffs accented with white pearl buttons"—felt odd against her skin, but she wore it.

By 1980, Vicki had moved to Tucson and found work as a home health aide, a job she liked because it was flexible enough that she could be gone for weeks at a time. She scrimped, but she got by. She had a big vet bill to pay off for her dog, Jake, and a truck that wasn't running. "I don't feel boggled and down with any of it," she wrote home to Mary and Mary's new husband, "and feel light and happy that everything is working out just fine."

In Tucson, Nancy lived with her sister's friend for a while and worked at a thrift store. But when she was off, she explored downtown. Down Fourth Avenue, where the buildings are low and tall cacti poke over fences into alleyways like trees, sat Food Conspiracy, Tucson's organic food cooperative. The building was red brick with a front window, and Nancy liked to sit there. One day, a woman came out of the store and stopped. It was Vicki.

Soon they were walking together along the avenue and talking. They were both Scorpios. Vicki arranged for Nancy to move into a group house she knew. "I live in a nice large house with ten other humans," Nancy's letters from this time show. "Four men, three women, three children. Crazy crew."

Vicki and Nancy may have gone on other adventures during this time. "Traveling with a beautiful lady named Bright Star," Nancy wrote to her friend Orelli, "learning an awful lot from her." Nancy also had plans to travel with another friend and possibly to leave Tucson altogether for California, Oregon, or Washington.

"She has invited me to join her in her travels. So I'm off...to explore the unknown. In search of exactly what I don't know—when I find it I'll fill you in," Nancy wrote her sister Jeanne.

Ultimately, she changed her mind about moving West, but she remained restless. She wanted to leave her job, which she hated.

"I'm finding Tucson to be a bit of a drag. It's really a nice place, but not the place for me," Nancy wrote to Jeanne. Then to her whole family, "I plan on selling everything I own and traveling with a backpack and my cats of course. Thunder…is just growing up. He has a lot of battle marks on his body. He is learning the art of survival."

When another friend of Vicki's named Liz called from the outlaw commune and asked Vicki if she wanted to leave Arizona for a few weeks and go to the Rainbow Gathering in July 1980, Vicki was down. But she wanted to bring Nancy along—Nancy could use the experience. The trio made plans to meet up at Vicki's parents' farmhouse in Iowa and then hitchhike to West Virginia together from there. Vicki's sister had a new baby, and her brother was graduating from high school.

For several days, Vicki, Nancy, and Liz slept in Vicki's childhood bedroom. They went to Mary's baby shower. Vicki held her new nephew, and a camera flashed, capturing the moment. Was Vicki remembering her own baby then? She didn't say, and no one asked. "It wasn't a secret," says her brother John. "We just didn't talk about it." Her father, Howard, didn't think much of "all this Rainbow business" and told the three women so. Her mother, Clarabelle, wanted Vicki to stop all the wandering and come home and settle down. Vicki said it would probably be her last big trip. Of the coming-home part, she said she would think about it.

It was time to go. "The visit here with y'all has been delightfully wonderful. Thank you for sharing your space & food and love with us, it is gratefully appreciated indeed," reads a note signed just from Vicki and Nancy. "As we travel the east coast of the country we will remember all of you Durians with prayerful thought. May you be blessed abundantly with all you need."

Vicki's brother Tom was working at Amishland Sausage in Kalona, so they left him a note. "I hope all in your life is terrific, please be careful,"

Nancy wrote to him. "I hope you are feeling good now," Vicki wrote, with a happy-face sign. "Love and take care of yourself. See ya."

Vicki's mother didn't want to drive them the half hour to the closest interstate ramp, but she did. After Clarabelle had cried and cried and then driven away, Vicki remarked to Liz and Nancy that this was the first leave-taking that had made her mother cry.

4

Trooper Gary Hott drove through the widely gridded streets of downtown Marlinton, another trooper sitting shotgun. As ever, Eighth Street—the main drag—was empty except for the occasional peckish teenager walking the bridge, which spanned the rushing Greenbrier River and connected Main Street to route 219 and the gas station with its mini-mart. The lunch counter, the hardware store, and the auto dealership were all dark. The only lights were the hospital's illuminated emergency sign and the bank marquee. It was 9:15 pm—Wednesday, June 25, 1980.

A call came in over the radio then, the words cutting through the sounds of katydids and frogs: one of the Pocahontas County sheriff's deputies had responded to a call about a couple of bodies up on Briery Knob and was requesting assistance. Bodies—a thing that almost never happened there. Hott acknowledged receipt of the message, pulled the car onto the smooth blacktop of Main Street, then hung a fast left at the traffic light to head south on 219. When he pulled off Lobelia Road toward Briery Knob, he drove slowly and took directions from his passenger. Hott had been through this area once or twice, but the back roads this deep still confused him.

By the time Hott arrived on Briery Knob Road at 9:55 pm, there were already two other vehicles there—Tim's car and a cruiser belonging to a sheriff's deputy. Hott approached where the two men were conferring, and they led him over to the bodies. Hott saw one woman lying on her back with her left arm out to the side and her right arm up over her head. She wore a University of Iowa sweatshirt and the back of her pants seemed like they'd been pulled up. The other woman wore a white cotton blouse with blue flowers that had also hiked up a bit and exposed some of the flesh of her stomach. She was lying on her side, so it was difficult for Hott to see her face.

He set to work walking the scene and marking its essential features. He walked farther down Tim's dirt lane with a high-powered flashlight and found that it ended in deep ruts and was closed off by a log placed across it. On a rock lining one of the ruts, Hott discovered some metal flakes and a scrape of orange paint, as well as a set of tire tracks. The right front tire of the car looked to be a summer tire, while the left rear tire mark looked to be made by a winter tire.

It was Hott who took the eight photographs of the bodies that night that would be the only record of how they were found, but to take some of them, Hott decided it was necessary to roll one of the bodies onto her back.

Judy Cutlip wasn't especially surprised when her kitchen phone rang and it was the fire station saying she was needed right away. It was her night on call. She worked in the business office in the hospital, so being a volunteer EMT allowed her a more physical kind of work, plus she liked helping people if she could. It hadn't been a walk-on situation, though; she'd gone through a rigorous eight-week training process in everything from first aid to dodging bullets. So far she'd mostly been called to respond to car accidents and elderly people who'd slipped and fallen.

Pocahontas County had only been offering ambulance service to the citizens in the southern parts of the county like Hillsboro and Droop Mountain for three years. In the 1950s, hospital workers rode to emergency calls throughout the county in a hearse, and if the hearse could not make it up a particularly rough or snowy road, the family would be obliged to carry the injured or sick person the rest of the way. In the 1960s, the Marlinton Fire Department had a single ambulance to service the whole county, but if two calls happened to come in on the same night, the hearse method might still be employed. This was no way to live, people had been telling the county commission for years, but Pocahontas County officials pled funding shortages. Then in the late seventies, the state subsidized the purchase of two ambulances, and good ones too—four-wheel drive and equipped with a winch and cave rescue equipment, which would come in handy for fool-hardy cave enthusiasts—and the commission jumped on it. The Hillsboro Volunteer Fire Department got one of these ambulances, and that was the one Judy Cutlip rode to Briery Knob.

On a clear night and moving at average speed, it might take a pickup truck twenty or twenty-five minutes to cover the eleven country miles be-tween the Hillsboro Fire Department and the clearing on Briery Knob Road, but it took the ambulance forty-five minutes at least to navigate the steeply sloping and switchbacked curves, four-wheel drive or no. One of Cutlip's neighbors did the driving, a great guy who could load and unload a human being, though he wasn't an EMT. Cutlip and another man were the trained personnel responsible for whatever might happen when they got there. They exchanged few words if any the whole trip, except near the end, when the driver called out to hold on and the ambulance bounced from asphalt onto potholed dirt.

Flashlights shone this way and that in the dark. One of the law's cars had its flashing lights on but without the sound. There was some maneu-vering of the ambulance to be done in order to park it as close as possible without disturbing the scene. Tim was concerned the ambulance would obscure the tire tracks Hott had found—plaster casts hadn't been taken yet. The ambulance driver assured him that he would not drive over them. It was dark, Judy Cutlip remembers, and surprisingly quiet, no bustle, just the voices of four men talking together and the tick-tick of the ambulance engine cooling.

She was the one who leaned over to feel the carotid arteries of the two women and say that they were dead. They were still warm, very warm—rigor mortis had not set in at all—and she remembers thinking that they must have been killed very recently. Their eyes were open, and Cutlip looked in them. She had picked up corpses before and touched them, but this was the first time she had ever touched a body that had not died on its own terms.

Cutlip, the other EMT, and the ambulance driver loaded the corpses onto two gurneys. As the driver backed up the vehicle, Hott looked on and helped with directions. The ambulance proceeded back down the dirt road toward the hospital in Marlinton, but it bounced and jiggled more loudly now with the added weight of its cargo.

Trooper Robert Alkire of the West Virginia State Police was halfway asleep in his home two hours north when the phone clanged and the voice on the Pocahontas County end of the line told him that two women had been shot on Droop Mountain and that he should get in his car and drive.

Alkire passed through Marlinton and then into the hamlet of Buckeye when headquarters radioed again, telling him to turn around and go to the Marlinton hospital instead. He walked into the small, cold morgue. One of the women had been shot twice in the chest, the other three times—in the head, neck, and chest. One wore a red University of Iowa sweatshirt and was missing one of her foam sport sandals. The other was carrying a pocket knife and a folded flyer that offered handwritten directions to the Rainbow Gathering.

Above the typed text of the flyer was a hand-drawn map of southeastern West Virginia that suggested that the best route to the Gathering was to approach from Virginia, taking newly minted Interstate 64 to Lexington, then following a quiet two-lane into Marlinton, county seat of Pocahontas, where the Rainbows would have a welcome station to help guide travelers on into the wilderness. "Dotted roads are uptight," read the handwriting. All local roads in West Virginia were drawn dotted. Because their eyes were still open, no matter where Alkire walked around the table, it seemed as though the women were quietly watching him.

Alkire stayed with the bodies until they were airlifted to Charleston to be autopsied. Day broke. It was Thursday. Alkire followed several squad cars of Pocahontas County sheriff's troopers down Route 219 and then onto the dirt roads to the clearing where the women had been found. Alkire noted the browning blood in the grass and the tire tracks, but little else. Back into the car caravan and on into the Monongahela National Forest to the Rainbow Gathering, which was now nearly in full swing. The officers showed around the photos Trooper Hott had taken of the women's dead faces, but no one seemed to know them. A

Rainbow leader promised to get the photos into the festival newsletter the next day.

"No belt, no brassiere or underpanties. No socks…" medical examiner Irvin Sopher in Charleston wrote Alkire. "No evidence of sperm, no evidence of sexual assault." One of the women had a blood alcohol level of 0.01, less than a can of beer or a shot of whiskey consumed within an hour of dying, while the other's was 0.08—about three or four drinks. They had most likely been shot within three hours of being discovered, making their time of death around six or seven in the evening. They had not been shot as they had been found but had either fallen or been moved after impact. The weapon was either a rifle or a pistol; the bullets had passed cleanly through the bodies and left only small particulate fragments. But the trajectory was very unusual—markedly downward at about a forty-five-degree angle, as if they had been kneeling, crouching, or sitting while someone had shot them from above. And the "level of destruction" was very high—the bullets were of a large caliber and been shot at such close range that the back of one woman's right hand and the left side of the other's face had been charred by the blasts.

The Rainbow leader was good to his word. He went to the back of his VW bus and printed and mimeographed the faces of the unidentified corpses into the daily festival newsletter with the question "Does anybody know who these women are?"

George Castelle was a lawyer who had traveled from nearby Charleston to attend the Gathering. He watched as people passed around copies of the Rainbow newsletter with the faces of two dead women on it. His friends spoke of the two "sisters" who hadn't made it. People were afraid—is there a killer traveling around picking up Rainbows and killing them? Is this going to be a problem on the way out?

"I had hoped the Gathering would be successful and that the Rainbows would come back often," says Castelle. "It was really demoralizing. After so many years of peaceful gatherings in Western states, they come to West Virginia, and people start getting slaughtered."

No one came forward to claim the women in the photos. A week later, the Gathering ended, and the members began their steady exit out of Pocahontas County by the feet and cars and buses and mules by which they'd come, and the Forest Service came in to survey the damage, of which there was remarkably little in the end. The Rainbows had broken down their camp with shocking precision and cleanliness; no arrests or hospitalizations had occurred at all.

Of the Santomero children, Kathy Santomero was the most like Nancy; the two shared a love of organic foods and travel and, unlike their other sisters on Long Island, never wore much makeup or polish on their nails. Kathy, too, had heard about the Rainbow Gathering, and several of her and Nancy's friends from home were also going. Kathy and Nancy made a plan to meet at the Gathering at a white van belonging to friends and then travel together back to New York. When Kathy arrived, she found the white van and Nancy's friends, then waited for Nancy herself. As the days passed, she didn't worry, she says; she just assumed Nancy had found something better to do. Kathy ate brown rice and watched the sun rise and fall and the rain roll in and swam in the rivers, and then someone passed her friend the small Rainbow newsletter with the black-and-white photos of the dead women, and the friend passed it to Kathy. One of the women was wearing her hair in braids.

"I was like, 'I wonder if that's my sister,'" Kathy says. "But when I said that to my friend, he said, 'They're Indian girls. It's not your sister.' So I dismissed it."

Kathy returned to New York, but days after she got back to her university in Geneseo, Nancy had still not called. A friend of Kathy's who had gone with her to the Gathering did instead. He kept looking at the two small pictures of the dead women in the *Pocahontas Times* he'd grabbed in town on the way out, he told Kathy. "I think one of them is Nancy."

"He was awesome," Kathy says. "He said, 'Kathy, whatever you want to do, if you want to be by yourself, if you want to go get drunk, there's no rule book.'" Still unsure if the dead woman was really Nancy, Kathy wanted to handle it herself, and without telling her parents. She and a friend got into a borrowed car and drove to Charleston, where the newspaper reported the bodies were being kept pending identification. The whole drive there, all five hundred miles past Buffalo and Cleveland and Parkersburg, West Virginia, Kathy was able to stay positive. It wasn't going to be her. There was no need to worry, no need to fear. Once in Charleston, they drove around and around looking for the morgue, and Kathy grew frustrated, then incensed.

When they finally found the right place and the right room and the right official and were shown the two women's bodies, Kathy looked at them and still didn't think either of them was Nancy. But one of the bodies was wearing a woven bracelet just like one Kathy had made for her.

"She had my bracelet on," Kathy says, "and then I knew." The morgue staff were brusque and insensitive to Kathy and her friend as they stood in the viewing room. "I was fighting mad as we left. I was probably venting on them. What do you call that? Misplaced, displaced anger." Kathy called her mother in Long Island and told her she was coming home, and nothing else—she wanted to tell her mother in person—and then the friend drove her there.

Nancy's sister Patricia, who everyone thought was Nancy's twin, was twenty at the time, working as a fitness instructor in Huntington and living at home with their mother. On the night of the murders, June 25, 1980, she says, she had been teaching an exercise class when she began to feel a terrible pain in her chest and head. She came home from work and went straight to the bathroom without eating dinner. She ran the water, then got into the tub.

"I had the strange sensation, a very strong knowledge that I was going to die," Patricia says. "I lay there in bed, and I wrote out my will. I wrote out what everyone would get and how I wanted to be buried. My head was hammering—I felt awful. I was able to get out of the bath, and I got into bed, and I said, 'Okay, if this is what is happening, I accept it.' I was ready to die. And then I woke up the next morning, and I had not died. And then I wondered where Nancy was."

It was a week later, a morning in early July, when Patricia heard Kathy pull into the driveway. She figured Nancy was in the car too, that the two of them had come home from West Virginia together. Nancy had a habit of greeting Patricia by jumping on her and tackling her in bed. Patricia waited five minutes, ten, then twenty minutes for Nancy to come busting into her bedroom. She heard Kathy talking to her mother in the next room and then the sound of their mother crying. Patricia got up from bed, opened the door, and stood in the jamb between the two rooms. Kathy was holding her mother's hand, and her mother was still crying.

"And I said, 'Where is Nancy? What is wrong with her? Did she do something wrong? Is she in jail?' And they told me she was dead."

Kathy Santomero was able to tell the West Virginia State Police Vicki's full name, and word was sent to the police in Wellman, Iowa, who told the Durians. Kathy knew that Nancy and Vicki had not been traveling as a duo, but rather as a trio, but she only knew the third woman's first name—Liz.

It stood to reason that if three women had traveled together and two had ended up dead, the third should be dead, too, or in mortal danger.

PART II:

A DIVIDED HEART

Dear Mr. President, I said, Dear Dean,
Dear Husband, Dear Our Father, Dear Tax Collector,
you don't know me. I don't know what I am,
but whatever it is, you can't have me.

—Irene McKinney

Valley off Lobelia Road, 2009

1

THE SPRING I WAS TO graduate college, there rose up in me the desire to drop so hard out of my life that I could hear my life trying to get in touch. Call it the loss of faith that coincides with economic crisis, call it American nostalgia for the pastoral, call it what you do when you still believe that there must be someplace left to go where anything is all the way true. At my liberal arts college outside of Philadelphia, I destroyed every God—religion, literature, politics, feminism, art—with my self-important words, dismissing each as problematic and essentially worthless. I dismantled every system to make a new world, but then I had to live in it. My friends and I burned a Christmas tree on a patch of concrete behind our cinder-block apartment complex. I'll never forget how fast it went—whoosh, gone.

Several years earlier, word of a nonprofit organization for teenage girls in West Virginia called Mountain Views had begun to circulate among my crowd—women's center employees, residents of the environmental and Quaker houses, players of ultimate Frisbee. I applied and, instead of returning home to New York City, spent the months after my sophomore year in Pocahontas County working as an intern for the residential camp that Mountain Views became each summer.

A dense and crackling ten weeks. I slept in a house that looked out onto a pen of horses, made copies and phone calls in a log cabin office, and did everything else in the campground—half a football field of cleared clover grass circumscribed by an oval of dirt road. On the narrow ends sat the wooden picnic shelter for meals and the shower house, built by girls past, where the water was heated by a wood fire. The fat ends were dotted with small screened-in and tin-roofed cabins, big trees for hammocks, and a campfire ring with six benches arranged in a hexagon.

Everywhere I went in that campground was the loud counsel or good-natured yelling of the Founder. The hair on the Founder's head was brown, thick, and arranged in a pattern of crisscrossing layers so the effect was a kind of fabulous mullet. She had small round glasses and wore indigo denim jeans and button-up flannel shirts ordered from hunting and out-door catalogs or purchased at Cabela's. She was tall and tan, her muscles visible under her rippled sixty-something skin.

She was from California and had wanted to be a professional fiddler but found her way to being a teacher for the gifted and talented program in the West Virginia public school system instead. Over the course of many years, she saw eighth-grade girls—hand-raising, answer-knowing, laughing girls—turn quiet in high school. She convinced a friend to sell her the Mountain Views land for a dollar, and a West Virginia judge arranged for a state prison crew to come and clear it.

In the summer of 1996, the Founder asked her two daughters and their friends to come and be the counselors. The first campers were girls from the local middle schools who slept in green army tents. It rained the whole two weeks, and their sleeping bags became heavy with the moisture. Many of the girls wanted to quit. The Founder gathered them together and pointed down the embankment toward the town of Hillsboro. Everyone down there thinks we're going to come down, she told them. Do we want to prove them right, or do we want to tough it out? They stayed.

The Founder's vision was simple: girls going into ninth grade would live together for about two weeks in the woods. No computer, no cell phones, no boys. Meals were healthy and contained foods outside a fourteen-year-old's comfort zone. The campground was perched on a hill, and equestrian class (there was something special that happened between teenage girls and horses) was held on the plateau below; girls might climb the steep trail between them three or four times a day. Math and science classes were held daily, along with a creative arts class. Campfire every night, when the girls would read poems they'd written and sing songs—Janis Joplin, "Swingin' on a Star," old cowboy songs.

As the years passed and girls went through the program and wanted to come back and see each other again, a second camp session was established, and year-round programs too—academic tutoring, college advising, ACT preparation, and trips to visit college campuses. The thought was: What if there was a place you could go where no one would judge you, where you would be taken in for exactly who you are?

This was not a camp for "needy" girls. It was a camp for girls who wanted to do hard math problems, create wild art, learn the names of medicinal plants, and make friends with other girls who also wanted to do those things. No savior complexes or outsider bullshit would be tolerated, the other interns and I, who mostly came from schools throughout Appalachia and the East Coast, were told during training. But facts were facts, and the director of Mountain Views, one of the Founder's daughters whose blond bangs shook when she spoke, needed us to know them just the same.

Some of the girls Mountain Views served rode the bus an hour and a half each way to the county's single high school; going to the doctor could be a similar time commitment. Women in West Virginia are less likely to work outside their homes than women in any other state in the nation. For every dollar made by a man working full-time in West Virginia, a woman in West Virginia earns seventy-four cents (the national figure is eighty cents). Thirty-two percent of West Virginia women and girls smoke (the highest rate in the nation), and they report much more stress, anxiety, and depression in their lives than women nationally.

The Director gave us poems and novels and academic articles to read that showed poverty was a false god imposed on Appalachia by outsiders and spun into a story that had been used for harm. As Helen Lewis writes, the region's history "demonstrates the concerted efforts of the exploiters to label their work 'progress' and to blame any of the obvious problems it causes on the ignorance or deficiencies of the Appalachian people." I learned that by the late 1920s, the state of West Virginia had been completely deforested: after it was logged, nearly all the old growth forest that remained had burned in forest fires. When it rained then, it flooded—valleys where towns sat filled up with water; topsoil got washed away into streams and silted up waterways that West Virginians were still trying to use for transportation and industry. The streams became so polluted with sawmill and coal waste that many of the fish and plants died. Conservationists established the Monongahela National Forest in 1920 to protect more than half of the total 1.7 million acres—much of it in modern-day Pocahontas County—and ensure the regeneration of some forest land, but could not reverse the damage that had already been done.

The Director gave me Denise Giardina, the great chronicler of the years when West Virginia's miners fought back against exploitative mine owners, and local poets Louise McNeill and Irene McKinney. She gave me Nikki Giovanni, and bell hooks, and taught me about the rich Affrilachian community that had been thriving in the region for centuries. I read Chad Berry, who directs the Loyal Jones Appalachian Center at Berea College in Kentucky, and learned about his idea of "the divided heart," a condition of divided allegiances and longings that some believe most centrally defines the experience of being Appalachian in America. After the timber and coal industries came to Appalachia, Berry writes, "People were suddenly faced with a number of decisions: stay on the homeplace or move to a new coal camp or mill town; try to continue the traditional life or venture into the more modern; migrate temporarily, perhaps to Atlanta, Nashville, or any of a number of growing southern towns or even to Cincinnati, Detroit, or Akron, and then return home; be hungry, poor, but happy in the South or be comfortable but perhaps unfulfilled in the North; stay near family and kin or light out on one's own; be content or curious."

One in nine American girls will experience sexual abuse or assault by an adult before she turns eighteen, and one in six women will be the victim of a rape or attempted rape in her lifetime. From that summer, I learned that Pocahontas County is not immune to this epidemic and that its workings here felt even more difficult to understand or prevent. Rural towns are farther from educational programs, crisis centers, and laws designed to protect children. Communities where everyone knows and needs each other pose unique problems for reporting sexual violence, as well as for healing.

Leaving was gendered, I began to suspect—the girls, if they had good grades, by and large left; if they didn't, they mostly got married and had kids and lived in houses that sat far from 219, their lives already lived in private. The boys stayed.

I stood at the highest point in West Virginia that summer. I learned what stinging nettle feels like on the skin of my calves (a ferocious itch), that the antidote to stinging nettle was jewelweed, and that Mother Nature, in her kindness, usually made sure the two grew side by side. I learned how to make my hands into the shape of animal paws and how to ask teenage girls questions that could not possibly lead to one-word answers (how, why, describe). As a New York City kid, I'd taken driver's education classes at eighteen but had little impetus to actually get my license until applying for the internship at Mountain Views, which required one. I was a brand-new driver, and it was painfully obvious to all the other interns and staff—in the way I couldn't reverse a Mountain Views van full of coolers of water even a few paces without ending up in a ditch; in the way I full-body startled and pulled over when a gunshot rang out in the song coming through the van's speakers.

I learned how to pump gas into a car that summer, how to pump gas into a plastic container, how to change a tire in the rain, how to take the batteries out of a smoke detector, and that most problems in the physical world could be solved if you simply got down on your knees to look and believed in your own ability to find a solution.

The intern house sat in a small grassy clearing; above us was the mountain and the campground where the girls slept, below us the steep dirt driveway one had to climb up to the Mountain Views property, which was occasionally blocked by a big brown horse called Delilah. Next door to me slept a girl from Kentucky who had short hair and wore a baseball cap with a heart on it.

I learned how to use a weedwacker. You've got to prime it. The girl from Kentucky showed me how, pushing her thumb over and over against the plastic circle button as it filled with dark oil. We weedwacked the whole campground in preparation for the campers' arrival, and I discovered that in the hum of that machine and afterward, my body coated with bits of grass and oil, I felt good—working felt good.

My cell phone got no signal—not even when we descended the mountain in minivans and bought snacks at the gas station in Hillsboro. In this absence, some space loosened up. On nights off, the girl from Kentucky taught me to like the taste of beer and then excused herself to go to the Mountain Views office so she could talk to her man in Massachusetts. A trans man, I learned, with a small name like a girl's cut in half.

I don't want to be one of those girls who doesn't shave her legs and then shaves them when her boyfriend comes to visit, I said at some point that summer, standing in the pantry of the office building where we stored our cans of beans. I had a gentle floppy-haired boyfriend from college, who would be arriving any minute.

You don't want to be, the girl from Kentucky said, tapping her foot against an interesting rock she'd dragged inside. But you are.

I came back from that summer in despair. I sat in my childhood bedroom in New York City, which had recently been repainted purple. Outside my door, my mother's sadness sat just beneath our stippled ceilings like a layer of warm air. I could feel my father standing at the closest window looking down at the street. *Pick up your feet, pick up your feet*, he had been directing me since childhood (I scuffed them when I walked), and I had learned to comply.

The people I'd met that summer at Mountain Views sat heavy on my mind. I felt blocked, squeezed, a tightness in my chest that kept tightening. Ideas had been introduced, ideas about the lived experience of sexism and rape culture as it intersected with rural life and Appalachian history, but I still didn't know what they had to do with me.

I went to study in France. In Paris, as we rode a crowded metro train to the outskirts of town for a day of flea market shopping, a man stuck his hand up my friend's skirt and inserted his knuckles inside her. I watched how suddenly her face changed—one moment she was just living her life; the next she wasn't. On a different dry afternoon, we were followed by two men who, when we ceased replying, called us *slut*, *bitch*, *whore*. They followed us for a long time, touched the backs of my hands, my palms, kicked my feet, threw a plum that splattered against a nearby rock. I couldn't comprehend it—so blatant, so unequivocally there, in the light of day. As my friend and I stood with our backs against a low brick wall covered with wisteria and waited for the full minute of silence that meant these men had left us for good, something sparked alive in me, then caught. It was a bubbling in my throat like hiccups you couldn't hear, a vibration in my thighs you couldn't see. My heart began to beat faster, and the energy spread through the fat of my upper arms and down into my elbows, knees, and hands.

"Reflect on a personal violence you want undone," directs the poet CAConrad. "Some terrible THING that removed the beauty you once lived with."

That night, I listened to my roommate whistle through her nose as she slept. She was a German and a good girl who never left our sterile apartment complex after ten at night. I wanted to burn my body, or both our bodies, to throw a bomb down one of Paris's metro passageways, just pull the pin and let this whole old and graceful motherfucking city burn. *Hmm,* I thought. *What's this?*

Back in America, I read Paulo Freire. I read Nancy Scheper-Hughes. In a class for people who had done summer internships similar to the one I had done at Mountain Views both in America and abroad, we had debates on "cultural relativism," the idea that people steeped in one culture, particularly a Westernized or dominant culture with wealth, should not judge the ideas or practices of people living in another culture, particularly those of people living in developing nations.

We learned about meddling white people who imported giant fish into a lake in East Africa to help "save" their food supply, but then the imported fish fed on all the indigenous fish, destroying the lake's naturally diverse ecosystem. We learned about the ways in which mostly white, middle-class American or European feminists passed judgment on traditional practices important to other cultures, dictating which behaviors could be considered liberatory and which oppressive. Trying to help was an inherently privileged and colonialist position, and besides, it only made whatever it was that was wrong worse.

We also read about moments when people or organizations chose not to intervene in the face of violence or suffering in favor of what they felt was the more important act of witnessing it or recording it for all the world to see. A documentary filmmaker continued filming while young girls in Kenya were genitally circumcised and filmed still as they cried out, "I don't want it," and "You're hurting me." Photojournalist James Nachtwey photographed the atrocities of wars in Kosovo and Rwanda and, among many other subjects, a family who lived hungry and exposed to the elements along a Jakarta railway track. On the one hand, some of his photographs sparked meaningful humanitarian action and financial resources. On the other, as critic Susie Linfield writes of the people in Nachtwey's work, "I do not think their spirits are intact. In showing us the many ways that the human body can be destroyed, Nachtwey's pictures can inspire revulsion more easily than empathy." Nachtwey himself was plagued by this ethical imbroglio. "Do I make a living from other people's suffering? Has their suffering and misery been my ladder to success? Do I exploit people? [Am I] the vampire with the camera?"

There was nothing an empathetic and politically involved person could do, it seemed, from text after text we read, that wasn't in some way catastrophic; there was no direction to move in that wasn't flawed or corrupt. Cultural relativism, in its sense of compromise and lack of active harm, seemed like a good place to stop thinking.

But some nights, alone or beside my sleeping boyfriend, my mind could not find rest and wandered further down the path. What was that kind of judgy Feminism with a capital *F* anyway? If it was saying that we should strive to make women living in minority cultures "like us," to be free in the ways that we were free, wasn't that also fundamentally flawed because even I, a middle-class American white woman, was profoundly aware of the effects of sexism, profoundly not free? But, further, if we as engaged people striving for liberation dismissed our own gut reactions and moral convictions on the grounds that it was fucked up to have those feelings in the first place, wasn't that just further patronizing and ghettoizing minority and historically dispossessed cultures by making a line between our own supposedly neutral culture we could judge and an "other" we couldn't?

I started to have the suspicion that there might still be room for saying,

"I think that is a problem," and, under very specific circumstances, "I want to do something about it." At the end of that class, I wrote a paper arguing for the views of an anthropologist named Sally Merry, who wrote that cultural relativism is "primarily about tolerance for differences and is incompatible with making any moral judgments about other societies." But, she continued, "this incompatibility depends on how one theorizes culture. Thinking about culture as a homogenous, integrated, and consensual system means that it must be excepted or criticized as a whole." Cultures could be taken apart and considered piecemeal, with nuance. It was possible to keep some parts without keeping all, and to lose something without losing all.

But did I learn? I did not learn. Another professor gave me Adrienne Rich, who said that all heterosexual sex with men was inherently oppressive and that the only way to find freedom was to live a life in which you did not depend on men for love, pleasure, or money. I broke up with my boyfriend for a tall woman I'd been watching in my poetry class. This alleviated the pandemonium in my mind for a season, but still the air was wrong.

What was wrong in the world was metastasizing inside me. I became metastasized. On the outside I was alive and cared about people and school, but on the inside I was hollow and didn't. People of color, poor people, indigenous peoples, women and queer people were being diminished and killed every day I was alive. Cement mix sloshed rocky through my veins. I became a concrete girl. Walking around campus, I recognized other concrete people—in particular, a young black man who often stood apart at parties tapping his wing tips. Once, by the pretzels, I tried to speak to him, but his face said one word: *don't*. I didn't.

It was 2009. National unemployment reached 10 percent, the highest since 1983; the unemployment rate for twenty- to twenty-four-year-olds peaked at 16 percent. May was coming. I watched other people make interesting or sensible or desperate decisions—a job at a nonprofit in Philadelphia, law school, Teach for America. All these things were part of the problem, I had decided. They trained you to know things or teach people things or make things, none of which were real.

I knew the very position of dissenting and dismay was a privileged one and that my rejection of these choices made, to rational people and people with less class and race privilege, very little sense. Yet there is a particular cognitive dissonance that sets in when you have many of the advantages this life can bestow but have seen, up close and in slow motion, what they mean for those to whom they are denied. You start to think maybe you can abdicate your privilege like a crown, if only you try hard enough, and that maybe that will settle the score.

I felt broken and running from the system in my mind in which the only choices were to dominate or be dominated, stay completely still or get annihilated by my feelings and the terror of history. It was a system of impossible twos and endless double binds, and I was afraid to move within it or choose anything. I felt that no one I knew had a clue about America, its true texture and shape and flavor, and that the ways I had been taught to live in it were no longer working.

Mountain Views called me on a bright April afternoon. Did I want to come back to Pocahontas County again for a year or maybe two? They said I had done a good job as an intern, that I had worked hard, that a few of the girls had been asking about me. If I said yes, they said, I would technically have to apply and be accepted into the federal aid program AmeriCorps VISTA and then be placed with them. They said they had new ideas, new projects in the works, that it was an exciting time to live there. A little light went on—I cared.

I spent a week thinking about it. During nights eating cereal in my college library and supposedly working on my thesis, I looked at road atlases of the United States instead. I had a collection of ideas about West Virginia, but I had a hunch that they were all gross misinformation, plus none of them agreed: coal and the end of coal. Poverty and a mansion on a stripped mountain. Pickup trucks and VW buses. OxyContin and Jesus. Mother Jones and Don Blankenship. Knobby elbows and the fattest city in America.

None of it made any sense, and I knew that it would not, likely, for a very long time. I would tell my family and friends that my reasons were service, sacrifice, and to see a new part of the world, and they would seem to accept this. But in truth, I did not understand my own feelings or the instinct, below language, that was driving me back toward Pocahontas County. I felt mixed-up, with the sense of foreboding guilt that always accompanies our most important lies. I called Mountain Views back and said yes.

2

GIRLS GOT DROPPED OFF AT Mountain Views by every conceivable family member, from grandma to oldest sister's boyfriend. Some girls hopped out of shiny pickups with extended cabs and diamond-patterned metal boxes in the back, trailed only by a sturdy dad in a reflective state roads vest. There were Subaru Outbacks driven by feminist moms who worked in tourism in Greenbrier County and lowrider sedans owned by grandfathers who wore black buttons telling the world they had served proudly in Korea. Asked to reflect on what they hoped for their girl campers during these weeks, many said they simply wished for their kids to get to be kids, to have fun and make friends. It was always the toughest-looking dad with the highest-lifted truck and the most beautiful girlfriend who got choked up and said that he wanted his daughter to learn to love herself.

Name games in the field. The buzzing of katydids as the parents drove away. Running, the losing of shoes, the messing-up of makeup. All the girls carried camp-issued rectangular canvas satchels with their names written in duct tape, and plastic reusable water bottles. They screamed through the campfire ring. They were looking for their tribe, moving in packs, swinging in hammocks in groups of three and four and five, a cluster of heads bent over a single drawing in a spiral-bound notebook.

I taught drama to the older girls. I dredged up my childhood piano lessons and will forever know the introductory piano moves to "Take Me or Leave Me" from *Rent*, chosen by a student who had a facial scar as shiny and lovely as Harry Potter's. I taught writing: *Does the story have more than one point/idea/theme?* my notebook reflects that I instructed.

Could it be read in more than one way? Does the character have flaws and contradictions? Are all the words carefully chosen? Is every word necessary? Is it physical? Include at least three images/sentences/lines that contain the senses—touch, taste, smell, hear, see. Avoid abstractions—love, hate, shy, scary, nature, friendship, beautiful.

Before dinner each night, as per Mountain Views tradition, the girls would raise their hands to tell each other and the staff what they were grateful for. The student with the shiny scar often sat up against the wall of the picnic shelter writing poetry. A redheaded girl took the seat beside me; I would braid her hair and decorate it with daisies. She liked me, I think, in the way that some like weak people in power they can get to do their bidding. She was always asking me to bend the rules for her, and I was always doing it—I wanted that much to be liked.

I'm grateful for knowledge, to know things, said one of the older girls.

I'm grateful for this place, said the red-haired girl. She gestured at the shape of the mountain that was just visible still, in the gloaming, across the field, and the other girls stomped their feet and clapped in agreement.

There was the sense that an experience was happening here, and it was the experience of feeling big and possible and being shoved forward, and it was for the girl campers and not for me or the other adults. There was something in that—not for you—that felt good. After putting my cabin of campers to bed each night, I crossed the open field, the air minty and cold in the mouth, the stars whiter and sharper than they had been in any other place. There was the sound of girls walking to the outhouse in twos, the occasional shriek, then quiet. The moon glowed so completely I could turn off my flashlight and follow the path through the ferns to the staff bunk without it.

Nights I stayed in the campground, I slept on a green army cot that snapped together and sometimes apart. Our cots and bunk beds were arranged around the perimeter of a screened-in shack where the staff women slept. Others were usually there by the time I got back; I was slow and read too much. *Reee-ah-reeee-ah-reee-ah*—the sound of Betsy's wind-up flashlight. She would enter, eyes wide, and perch on her cot; then she might get out her guitar and play something low and sexy and fantastic.

Talia, who had once been a Mountain Views camper, would stretch out on the floor to listen, and then the Director would come in, lugging a big backpack.

What'd I miss?

The Director had taken over running Mountain Views just a few years earlier. She had grown up in Pocahontas County and gone to the public schools here, then to Harvard. But after a year of her accent being mocked, she came home to help her mother start Mountain Views and fell in love with the man who would become her husband. She went back and graduated from Harvard soon after, then moved home again, marrying on the Mountain Views land.

At night, she sat in the doorway by the old-fashioned red gas lantern and listened as we gave the nightly report. I looked to the Director for cues as to how I should respond to each bit of news. Then the clicking-off of flashlights, then silence. The enraged sound of sleeping bag zippers. Sometimes the sound of grown women crying in the night and trying to be quiet about it. When it rained, that tin roof was a steel drum, filling the cabin with sound. In the morning the trees dripped, and the girls were in rain boots, and the Director was draining the coffeepot again, and the fog didn't lift off the mountain until lunch.

3

By day, I served teenage girls. But by night, starting in the fall after the camps ended, I hung out, learned to play bluegrass music, and drank beer with a group of grown men.

I lived first in an upstairs bedroom in a square two-story brick house that I rented from Sam, a supporter of Mountain Views who was also a teacher at the local middle school. The house was in Hillsboro, a town of around three hundred in the southern part of Pocahontas County, and sat on one of the few side streets that ran perpendicular to Route 219. As you drove into Hillsboro, there was the town's only restaurant on your right and the road that led down to the prison; on your left, a car shop and the Presbyterian church. The elementary school—go Red Devils—and its fields and the public library came up fast on the right, and across from them was the Marathon gas station. Beyond this, a beauty parlor, a Laundromat full of gleaming rows of rarely used machines, and then done—219, more two-lane road, heading north. The writer Pearl S. Buck was born here while her parents were on furlough from their missionary work in China and visiting Buck's maternal grandparents; she returned often.

You could sit on Sam's porch and know what transpired in all of Hillsboro—at the Marathon station or at the elementary school soccer field just beyond view. Sam's porch had an ironic light-up palm tree and a sign that showed a parrot drinking a martini and the words "It's Five O'Clock Somewhere." When I sat on the porch couch on my days off from Mountain Views, zombified and chugging something cheap, Sam would come out and refill my glass with Maker's Mark, then take a seat on her barstool. She might talk to me or talk to her beau on the phone or pay bills or work on her lesson plans for September, while I stared at the plants growing through her trellis.

If she talked to me, it was about child development and group psychology, how to make a girl who hated herself feel loved in the eyes of a strange adult. She didn't insist or lecture; she mused, floating these ideas on the breeze for me to pluck off if I wished. She had taught young people for years and would go on to become one of the most influential educational organizers in the state. I listened.

Sometimes—I in the red chair, she stretched on the green couch under a chenille blanket—we watched *The Bachelor*, though we agreed we preferred *The Bachelorette*. We always liked the same men—the quiet ones who wore the least hair product. I did not mention that I'd been dating women, though she would not have been fazed.

Sometimes she'd call a pizza in to the Marathon gas station, and I'd walk over to pick it up. Across from the Marathon in a little gravel turnout, a gaggle of trucks sometimes idled in the dark, their frames lifted high enough to insert two Frisbees end-to-end. They were boys and men, pulled up side by side, passenger talking to driver. The Marathon's sign illuminated its small gas plaza, and the boys and I watched each other as I stepped into the light.

As summer became fall and the work migrated down from the campground and into the log cabin office building, I drove Route 219 every morning on my way to Mountain Views. I drove it first in a green Volvo station wagon with New York plates borrowed from my parents that lost a fog light when I mangled a baby deer in its undercarriage, and I drove it later in a white Toyota pickup with West Virginia wildlife plates that I bought with money orders from the Hillsboro post office. I still didn't really know how to drive a car, let alone drive one on a road like 219. I had no trust—if I couldn't see that the road continued beyond a modest crest, I assumed it did not and slowed to a crawl. I sat hunched forward over the wheel and drove so slow the pickups roared past me, swerving into the other lane. Or I rode the brakes, slamming them as I fishtailed down every switchback.

But there was a straight stretch I liked just after leaving Hillsboro. On one side, hay fields and a pond where cows sat and drank. On the other, a two-story white board-and-batten house with lace woodwork trim and then the wide valley floor, the Alleghenies rising, layer by layer, mountain on mountain, then sky. In the morning, the valley was dunked in fog, and I could see the houses that lined the road but not much else. At night, the hills were black against the Prussian blue sky. In the fall, a patchwork of oranges. In the summer, a green so blaring it looked fake.

When the work was done, around nine or ten o'clock, I drove this stretch of road in the dead dark. I used it to exhale the day and inhale the night, and then I pointed my nose toward wherever the party was—in a pool shed in the woods or in the living room of a clapboard house near the Greenbrier River.

One day near the end of that summer while sitting on Sam's porch, I sensed a commotion over at the elementary school field. It was a community soccer game, and Sam was there, talking to a group of young men. One of them leaned against a yellow Chevy station wagon that sported an "I ♥ MOUNTAINS" bumper sticker.

They're fracking lines, the man, whose name was Trey, was saying. Up on Briery.

He was handsome and solid with a shock of red hair that stuck up in the front. Didn't look at me, but looked at me.

I didn't see Trey again until a few weeks later at Sam's house. Walking home from the Marathon station, I spotted the yellow wagon parked in the grass near Sam's tomatoes. While people chatted in the yard, Trey sat with Sam on her porch under the parrot sign and talked to her about Buddhist philosophy. His words came through the porch window screen perfectly, to where I sat in Sam's dark living room. Then he suddenly got up and opened the door.

You can come outside and join us, he said, if you want.

Trey made delicate pencil drawings of trees and rolled his own Bali shag cigarettes and listened to NPR all day on the job site where he hung drywall, and he always had things to tell me about apple pickers in Texas or butterflies in Peru. He was usually unreachable by phone, and was a fan of the show-up and the stop-by and the I'll-see-you-around-sometime. His favorite book was *Siddhartha*. "Truly, nothing in the world has taken up so much of my thinking as this I of mine," writes Herman Hesse, "and about nothing in the world do I know less about than me."

Trey's best friend at that time was a large boy named Peter who wore his black hair up in a topknot and drove a blue Toyota pickup I coveted—it had a swooping silver racing stripe. Trey and Peter were working together on the same job site in Hillsboro just a few hundred meters from Sam's house, and that whole month of August I was on vacation from Mountain Views, I would keep one eye on the book I was reading and the other on 219 for Trey's wagon or Peter's truck. I'd "run into them" at the Marathon station, where they would be guzzling gallon jugs of water or shooting the shit with the old men who liked to take in the sun on the iron bench outside the store, and they'd sometimes invite me to go swimming. Usually we took Peter's truck, and Trey gave me the front seat. Between turns to look at Trey's hair blowing in the hard wind, I learned that Peter had gone to college in Morgantown, then come back, and that his father was the town doctor. His sister had gone to Asheville, where she worked as an artist, painting murals under bridges and on the sides of buildings.

The swimming hole was where the road dead-ended at the Greenbrier River. Peter would park his truck off to the side, half in the road and half in the dirt. A bottle of Dr. Bronner's soap would magically appear from behind the truck's bench seat, and a towel, and Peter would bounce off toward the river, over the old railroad tracks, which had been turned into an asphalt biking trail, while Trey walked behind with me. I took off my shirt and swam in my sports bra and athletic shorts, nervous about whether Trey would think I was too fat and whether these were the right clothes to swim in a river anyway, but neither Trey nor Peter was looking or seemed to care. They were already swimming easy circles, splashing each other and throwing the Dr. Bronner's back and forth like otters.

Toward late summer Trey took me to his house. He showed me the stone wall he was building and the hoop house where he grew vegetables for sale, then led me into the woods. He taught me to play a word game as we hiked uphill for several miles, occasionally stopping to point out a tasty mushroom or put his whole body inside the dying husk of a tree. "Look," he said, when we had finally crested the ridge and reached a sunny rock from which the whole valley was visible, open as an ocean. I like to come here, he said. He pointed to a mountain on the far side that he thought looked like a pregnant woman. I agreed. Back in his room, a lofted space with new windows and many blankets, he explored the inside of my thighs with his hand. He smelled acrid and good.

Let's just sleep, he said, leaving his hand there all night.

"Where are you, again?," people I had known in the northeast—my parents, friends from high school or college—asked through the crackling line. "How's the weather in Kentucky?" "What's it like in the South?" "What's it like in Maryland?" "Are you near the ocean?" "Can you see horses?" "I hear it's nice over there in South Carolina." "Where are you?" "Where are you again?"

"West Virginia," I said. "Pocahontas County."

Hmm, they said.

These questions were dumb, but on some level I understood. I lived now in a real place that existed, but I struggled to express to them where that was. The words "West Virginia," it seemed, were insufficient to convey a satisfactory reality. Even expanding the purview or adding modifiers—south central, near the border of Virginia—did not seem to help things.

I began to notice that a certain twoness or a bothness lived here. It was in the symbols displayed on the houses—here a white one with a small Confederate flag flying over its porch, there a yellow one with a sprawling garden in the back and a truck with a "No Farms, No Food" sticker parked smartly in the drive. In the Walmart parking lot in Lewisburg, I sometimes sat and looked at cars. The Walmart was open twenty-four hours, which made it a popular choice not only for me to pee and buy ice cream but also for people to leave their cars overnight while they carpooled to work or to a party, so the sample size was larger. There were lifted Ford 150 trucks with signs that said "Rebel Pride," and "You can pry my gun out of my cold dead hands," and "Real women drive trucks." But in equal or greater numbers there were Subarus and Toyota Tacomas that said "Birthplace of Rivers" or bore stickers for the Human Rights Commission or that said FRACKING in an oval with a line drawn through it.

On the one hand, inside the boundaries of Pocahontas County was a traditional music institute, an antique bookstore, and an artisan cooperative. Just about everyone I knew, local or transplant, had a garden—tomatoes, kale, cucumbers. A coworker of mine at Mountain Views lived in a highly functional home made partly from hardened layers of mud and outfitted with solar panels.

On the other hand, there was the fact that when driving up the steep rocky road to the Mountain Views' campground, if you turned off at an earlier driveway you would end up at a property registered to a neo-Nazi group.

Oh, I think they got tired and moved on, the Founder said, waving away the idea with her hand, and, at last check with the Southern Poverty Law Center, she was right.

The only restaurant in Hillsboro, which had been closed for years but reopened my first year there to much community rejoicing, was owned by Sam's neighbor and her husband. Their kids were the only kids of color in Hillsboro Elementary School; years later, she would wake up to the words "NIGGER LOVER" sprayed across the side of her café. Scores of neighbors, the Director included, came out in the snow to help her scrub them off.

Was I in the South? Some people, both in Pocahontas County and not, seemed to think I was. True, I could call up an image of passing a billboard for "Mason-Dixon Auto Auction" off of I-81 on the way there, memorable because above the billboard had twirled a real commercial eighteen-wheeler truck lifted on a metal pole. West Virginia is a Southern state according to the US Census. But so are Maryland and Delaware. Some sources now say a better geographical border are rivers—the Potomac on the East and the Ohio on the West. If this is so, West Virginia is split vertically by the Potomac River watershed, with Pocahontas County almost exactly on the dividing line.

In a piece the *Atlantic* published called "Where Does the South Begin?" the author suggests that religion is as good a way as any to draw the boundary. On these grounds, "The divide roughly follows the Ohio River, but it cuts across West Virginia, where the southern tier is Baptist and speaks [with] a drawl and the northern tier is ethnic and cheers for the Steelers." On this map, Pocahontas and its neighboring county to the north are colored a forest green for Methodist, but the counties to its south and west are red for Baptist.

My friend from college felt sure that politics were at the heart of all things. In the American imagination of recent years, "the South" means Republican and conservative states, "the North" liberal Democrats. But here still, a snafu: from 1932 to 1996, West Virginia voted Democratic in every presidential election except three—1956, 1972, and 1984.

In 1988, when Michael Dukakis got slammed by father Bush and Dan Quayle, West Virginia did not help in delivering the blow. While Virginia, Pennsylvania, Ohio, and even New Jersey and Connecticut jumped aboard and voted red, West Virginia joined New York, Massachusetts, and Oregon as one of ten states nationwide to opt for the Greek-Orthodox pro-choice candidate who used Neil Diamond's immigrant anthem "America" as his theme song. It wasn't until 2000, when George W. Bush narrowly pulled out the state's five electoral college votes—and won the election by that exact number—that West Virginia's red era began, a color that's been darkening ever since.

Another possibility that people kept suggesting was that I was simply in Virginia. People could grasp "Virginia." Though she had driven there with her own hands and watched the state welcome signs appear with her own eyes, a friend of mine could not grasp that West Virginia was a sovereign state distinct from the western portion of Virginia. I once lived in Richmond, a woman at a conference told me. I hear it's lovely over there, especially in Roanoke, a man said to me later on a plane.

I took a drive to Harrisonburg, Virginia, one day, where there was an Indonesian restaurant I liked. This necessitated crossing the West Virginia–Virginia border on two-lane back roads so I could see if there was a discernible difference.

There was. The surface of the road changed on the Virginia side—it was smoother there, fewer cracks, more shoulder. There was more brick, less clapboard; more sky, fewer trees. The houses were set farther back from the road. There were swaths of lawn and horses and other cars with foreign plates—North Carolina, Texas—and flags. All kinds of flags.

To look into what distinguishes West Virginia from its neighbor and parent Virginia is to see a state that prefers fewer laws circumscribing the behavior of its citizens—regardless of the content of those behaviors. In contrast, Virginia's history is one of being highly involved in governing the intimate lives of its citizens and legislating the protection of the social status quo.

No law is the best law seems to be the unspoken slogan of West Virginia. It has been legal to have gay sex in West Virginia since 1976; the comparable figure for Virginia is 2003. In 2006, the state of Virginia ratified a constitutional amendment defining marriage as between a man and a woman and prohibiting the Commonwealth from creating or recognizing any legal status for relationships between people who weren't married. A similar constitutional amendment was proposed in West Virginia in 2009 but was overwhelmingly voted down by the House of Delegates.

In 2018, a nonprofit called the Population Institute released a nationwide "report card" that evaluated each American state on its reproductive health services. West Virginia's grade was a C, Virginia's an F-. For years, Virginia law has required women to have a vaginal ultrasound before an abortion in which the provider "must offer the woman the opportunity to view the image." Though 90 percent of women in West Virginia live in a county without an abortion provider, the state never passed any such law.

West Virginia's state motto, *montani semper liberi* or "Mountaineers are always free"—which I had now seen tattooed in classic black ink on no less than eight hot young West Virginians—comes with a simple image. Two men in rounded brown cowboy hats carry an axe and a pickaxe and chill against a large boulder inscribed with 1863, the date of the state's founding. There is also some corn and a swath of green lawn upon which sit two crossed rifles and a red cap that seems plucked from the head of a Smurf.

Contrast this with Virginia's *sic semper tyrannis* or "thus always to tyrants," which makes Virginia fundamentally a place of opposition—to the supposedly sinister force of tyranny. "Mountaineers are always free" takes another tack: this is who we are; this is the state we're in—free.

That fall of 2009, I worked in a wooden lodge cut into the side of a mountain at a desk that had been decorated with my name. I attended meetings and wrote grants and wore out the words "social change" and "empowerment." But mostly I was in charge of girls who came to our programs who lived in nearby Nicholas County. I was assigned a list of about fifteen girls I would call every Sunday night so they maintained a connection to our programs throughout the year and also so we could know if they would come to the dinner and tutoring sessions we held at the Mountain Views office every Tuesday night. I was also in charge of planning college trips; many of the Mountain Views girls wanted to go to college, and their parents wanted this for them too. Still, some would be the first in their families to go, and the idea of a trip to visit campuses, particularly campuses as far away as North Carolina or Pennsylvania, was unfamiliar or out of reach for some families.

I liked making these calls, which I would do from the landline at Sam's house. Because Pocahontas County and its environs are in the federal Quiet Zone, practically all the numbers of the students I called were landlines, and most times I had to ask a parent or sibling if I could speak to the girl in question. More than a few times, these family members had to ask me to repeat myself—I spoke fast, and I spoke New York; my pacing was brusque and wrong. But I got better. I learned to say, Good evening and how are you? I learned to breathe more between words and to wait longer without getting impatient when a brother went rogue and forgot to tell his sister I was waiting on the other end of the line.

The conversations I had with the girls were sometimes short but always instructive. What are you doing? Writing a paper about turtles. About to go for a walk down to Fas-Chek. Can you come to tutoring on Tuesday? No, I have to help dad out with digging a ditch. No, I have to watch my sisters, statewide testing, my boyfriend's soccer game, detention. What'd you do? Spoke up when I was being bullied, asked why the dress code wasn't being enforced on the boys too, skipped ahead three chapters in the textbook because class was too easy.

Every Tuesday night, all the girls who wanted our programs left their schools, separated by miles and mountains, and took school buses to the bottom of the dirt road that led to Mountain Views. Before big pots of spaghetti and sauce, we asked the girls to tell us again what they were grateful for. I'm grateful for my body because it helps me run and play soccer; I'm grateful for my family and for the fence posts they won't buy because they're sending me on the college trip to Virginia instead.

I studied the ACT so I could teach it those nights and lead small classes for three or four girls on the parts of a sentence, the American electoral college, how to write a poem. The student who'd sung "Rent" usually came, bringing love poems. Also the redheaded girl who had often sat with me at camp. Her mood was different by that fall. When I worked with her on math, she cracked jokes, then cracked pencils, then refused to answer my questions at all, preferring to sit on the seventies-patterned cushioned chair and stare at her hands in silence.

Word reached me that a horse trainer who worked with Mountain Views and lived on Lobelia Road was looking for a roommate for her farmhouse, and I leapt at the idea, remembering that hike with Trey and the mountain that looked like a pregnant woman. She had split with Trey's friend Bill and was looking for someone to help with her mortgage. By October, I hauled my clear bins of books from Sam's place in Hillsboro and moved into Anya's two-story farmhouse, which looked out on a round pen where she trained horses. She and I took long hikes through the rambling woods and neighborhood, a close-knit hamlet of people who lent sugar, lent trucks and trailers. They threw me a welcome party of homemade elderberry wine and bread on a stick and venison canned the previous year, and, as ever, people took out instruments—a mash-up of the fiddles of the native West Virginians with the harmonicas and cellos of the aging hippies. On one of her trail rides, Anya was adopted by a fluffy, troublemaking orange kitten and, knowing my obsession with such creatures, brought him home for me.

Soon Trey was often at the farmhouse with me, frying an egg or cleaning a pan, petting the dog or brushing the cat, helping me feed the fire in the wood stove or the three very free-range pigs. The pigs had belonged to Bill, but Anya didn't have the heart to make him get rid of them.

One Saturday the pigs escaped their pen; I came down the stairs and fumbled in the kitchen for the kettle, and my hand hit a pig. Later, I got a phone call from the woman in the closest house over the hill. Normally a bastion of calming energy, her voice was urgent: all three pigs were over at her house, digging underneath the foundation. Bill appeared a half hour later on the road in his red Subaru wagon. He banged his hand on the driver's-side door and called, "Here piggy piggy piggies," and in a matter of minutes all three pigs perked up their ears, ceased their digging, and trotted obediently after his wagon like a mother ship.

In high school, Trey and Bill and some ten other men I would come to know had called themselves the Droop Mountain Holler Boys, in homage to this valley where they had all, more or less, grown up. For short and in jest, they sometimes still called themselves the DMHB. The DMHB were in some ways an unlikely bunch, both the sons of Back to the Landers who'd stayed after the commune disbanded and the sons of Pocahontas County locals for generations. They tended to like different kinds of music from the other boys at school and preferred being outside and making up games together to partying every weekend. They were in their twenties and thirties now, working construction jobs around the county to pay for the little they needed. Pool night on Fridays was their tradition, and it was Bill who first brought me there.

I'd often walked this way down the road, past the small cemetery and the house where the dog barked at me, but I'd never kept going. Bill kept going, then eventually turned off and parked in a grassy field near a gray-blue weathered shed from which a station wagon stuck out. As we got closer, I saw that the engine of the wagon was hooked up to a generator, which was powering the light in the small shed.

As we entered, two men were in the middle of shooting a game on a grand, oversized pool table. One of them was boisterous and dark-haired; the other, his brother I gathered, was quieter. One more man, in shorts and thick wool socks, sat in an old iron barber's chair with his feet up drinking an Old Milwaukee beer. The shed smelled like the night and the wood smoke coming from a nearby house. A small boom box played Nine Inch Nails. Peter and Trey took turns swinging a length of string with a ring on the end of it toward a hook by the door.

Yes! Trey called out, having hooked the ring.

No way, no way, Peter said, you were over the line, you were cheating.

The boisterous brother turned to face me and wiggled his eyebrows like *watch this*, held the pool cue behind his back, and shot. He missed the ball so badly and so hard that he knocked the eight ball off the table. It rolled beneath the station wagon, and his brother and the man in the chair heckled and booed while he retrieved it. I was the only woman there that night, and many other nights after.

Bill rolled his eyes and tossed me a beer, which I was sure I'd drop, but didn't.

Good catch, Trey said, hugging me. A small compliment but enough to relax me and push me out of my own mind and into the action.

Wanna play? Peter asked me, gesturing toward Trey and the ring game. But from some need for distance, or hard pride maybe, I didn't want to spend time with Trey only, or let him know I'd come for him.

I think I want to play pool, I said, turning toward the table.

Uh oh, careful, Bill said. It's not a standard table, so it plays weird.

He was right. The table's size made the balls roll faster and farther, and every shot felt smoother and more languid than on tables I'd encountered before.

At a certain point that first night, after we'd had a few, not drunk but heading there, the song "Brown Eyed Girl" came on the boom box.

Oh oh oh oh, said the louder brother, and the man in shorts leapt up from the barber's chair. It was a group joke of theirs—whenever this song came on, they'd replace the subject of the title with "squirrel." Peter put his arm around me from one side, and Trey from the other. "Laughing and

a-running," they began to sing, and I was just there, not a woman necessarily, but a friend who could stay as long as I wished.

There were instincts I found I had about what makes a good life that
were more applicable to life in Pocahontas County than they had ever
been to life in New York City. How people sometimes slept on a stuffed
cotton mattress in their cars overnight if they'd had too much to drink
or just felt like it and then kept the party going in the morning, not with
drink but with sleepy faces and coffee and eggs and bacon. People stayed
and waited and carpooled and dropped off and dropped in. There weren't
many people at the parties, but there were old people and young people
together, and there was a kind of determination in these parties, a drive
that matched mine.

No one was in a hurry; no one was climbing the ladder; no one's first
question was "What do you *do*?" The DMHB worked only as much as was
absolutely necessary and then spent their leisure time playing music, hiking, or relaxing with their families; people were more than the calculus of
their profession or their ambition. If I wanted to hang out, there was only
one place to go, and everyone I wanted to see would probably be there. I
could relax. There was no question of where the night would take me. I'd
keep drinking, or I'd go home.

Anya and Bill split again, and Anya moved out, and left Bill and me
and the animals alone together in the farmhouse. I probably should have
moved out, too, when she did, but I didn't—stubbornness I guess, plus
sheer dumb love for that house. Its back field was a plateau that covered
the space between the house and the nearest mountain, and it attracted
deer in the gloaming.

Even on Saturdays, Bill got up at four or five o'clock in the morning
and played NPR at top volume while he made breakfast and fed the pigs.
Then he'd go off to see about a fence or visit a friend, and he'd say something true and cutting to me on his way out, and I'd be diminished and
scuttle away.

I didn't know how to live right in a house like that. I was always building the fire wrong; or doing the dishes wrong, letting the water run or
draining the sink too soon; keeping the heat in too long or letting it out

too soon and killing the plants. Often I worked late at Mountain Views, and if Bill was gone on a job or hunting or delivering a horse in North Carolina, I'd come home to a cold house, and the chickens and the pigs had not been fed, and there was a woodshed full of wood but no kindling. I'd take the headlamp that hung from a nail by the front door and go out to the dark woodshed and do my best to cut kindling with the axe the way Trey and Bill had shown me.

It was at a meeting of a writers' group I joined that fall, hosted by Peter's aunt, who wore her hair in pigtails and poured homemade elderberry wine into thick crystal goblets, that I learned about the two women who had died up on Briery Knob almost thirty years earlier. I had been to his aunt's house many times before: she also hostessed a Sunday night music night that was full of tambourine and "I Shall Be Released."

The other four members of the writers' group took their seats on a red sofa, a leather wingback chair, and a knitted pouf. They were all in their fifties, all transplants to West Virginia who had come in the 1970s. We sat around a low table sipping our wine. We had all brought a piece of writing, which we cradled in journals or legal pads on our laps. One by one we read. A tan man with a white ponytail read a short story. Affirmations were murmured. Then it was Tim's turn to share. He was Peter's father and the doctor at the local jail ever since it had switched over from being a hospital.

My journal entry tells me that the light was thin that day and wind blew around the leaves that had already fallen on the grass outside. Tim wore a cloth baseball cap and tapped the toes of his boots against the carpet. He retrieved a square of folded-up paper from the back pocket of his jeans and began to read it in a quiet, steady voice. It was a poem, and it was a dream: he is walking through the woods, and then he finds two women's bodies. After he finished reading the poem, he refolded the piece of paper and then began to cry, pressing his thumb and fingers to his eyes like a duck's bill and shaking out the tears.

Asked about this day, Peter's aunt said she believes that it was finding the bodies that led Tim to become a doctor but that Tim was a stoic man who she doesn't believe would have shared his feelings about the murders so openly in a group setting.

In my memory, Tim's wife brought his head to her shoulder. She looked down at the carpet, then back up at our hostess and the rest of us. She smiled and sighed in a kind way, and then her smile faded to a sadness that seemed to say, "Still?"

PART III:
THE RELEVANT NECESSARY PEOPLE

I have heard it said that Georgians are unable to drive in snow, and that Arizonans go bonkers behind the wheel in the rain, but no true-blooded West Virginia boy would ever do less than 120 mph on a straight stretch, because those runs are hard won in a land where road maps resemble a barrel of worms with Saint Vitus' dance.

—Breece D'J Pancake

Jacob and Linda Beard, year unknown

1

BY THE MORNING AFTER THE murders, Thursday, June 26, 1980, the news covered the southern part of Pocahontas County like a fog and then moved north toward Marlinton. Wives called their husbands at work. Children turned to face their classmates on the school bus and then told their parents over dinner what they'd learned. In the restaurant of the Marlinton Motor Inn, at Miss Kitty's beer joint, at Dorie's lunch counter, in the front yard of Oak Grove Presbyterian Church in Hillsboro, the story spread: two girls had been found on Briery Knob shot to death. Nineteen and twenty-six, so young, so young. A fear that gripped the throat and stomach—some parents wanted to keep their children home from school.

Outside the Marathon station in Hillsboro was an ice machine and a bench for shooting the shit, usually occupied by retirees and older men drinking coffee from Styrofoam cups. By the gas pumps, a volunteer ambulance driver for the Hillsboro Fire Department was holding forth for a small crowd.

I had a hell of an ambulance call last night, he said. He had been the one to drive the dead women's bodies from Briery Knob to the hospital in Marlinton. Someone asked if the women were local, and the ambulance driver said no, but the rumor was the people who did the killings were. Those gathered agreed—no one not from Pocahontas County would know how to get to Briery.

June 25 was a Wednesday and the *Pocahontas Times* went to press Wednesday nights, so the news of the young man's discovery in the woods didn't hit kitchen tables until a full week later. "Tragedy struck the

County with the finding last Wednesday night of the bodies of two young women on the Briery Knob road," the *Times* reported. In an effort to identify them, the paper ran two thumb-sized photos of the corpses.

For days after Nancy's sister identified the bodies, sheriff's deputies in West Virginia and Iowa searched for the elusive "Liz." Authorities in every American state were sent her description. "It seems now that a third girl may be involved," reported McNeel. "She is believed to be a tall, slender, blond named Elizabeth." The area around Briery Knob was checked and rechecked for this "third Rainbow girl."

A week later, Alkire's phone rang at the state police headquarters.

My name is Elizabeth Johndrow, the voice said. And I'm alive.

Liz met Vicki Durian at the co-op grocery store in Tucson, just as Nancy had. Liz was hanging outside the store with her backpack when Vicki tore off a hunk of the crusty bread she'd bought and handed it to her. Liz had hopped out of a van headed west earlier that day and didn't know anyone in town; Vicki had put down some roots and had a mentor's warm energy. They walked the three blocks to Vicki's apartment, which she shared with two other women. She'd been in Tucson about six months and worked as a nurse in the homes of elderly people in the area to pay the bills. There were already a few people camping in tents in her backyard, and another couple living out of a truck that was parked in the front. All Vicki had left for Liz was a closet. Would that work? It was a big closet.

When Vicki wasn't working, she and Liz walked all over Tucson. Vicki knew the restaurants, supermarkets, bakeries, and produce suppliers that threw away perfectly good food, so they dumpster-dived and prepared what they found in big dinners for whoever happened to be staying at Vicki's that night. They sat on the steps of Vicki's house with the other travelers and talked. Someone knew beadwork, and from then on that's what they did with their hands. Vicki took Liz to parties at the sprawling communal house where Nancy had stayed, but Liz and Nancy didn't meet each other. The house was a real hippie household; they juiced everything in sight, drank wheatgrass, and kept a kombucha mother in the fridge, which did not surprise Liz.

Almost nothing surprised Liz then. She was eighteen, but she felt much older, felt that she had seen it all, done it all, drugged it all. So when, a few months after arriving in Tucson, Liz heard about a hippie outlaw commune in the desert, she figured it was as good a time as any to head there. Its residents were several families from Arkansas who had been caught growing pot by the kilo and others who were hiding out from the law. Some of them had been to last year's Rainbow Gathering. Go, they told Liz. She had saved some money, but it was stolen at the commune. She went.

Liz was in a school bus on her way to Washington State—another adventure—but then Mount St. Helens erupted, covering the entire Pacific Northwest from Idaho to Alberta in ash. She caught a ride out of Portland, and arrived in Iowa a few days after Vicki and Nancy.

Liz could calculate the miles they needed to cover and about how long it should take them to get there, but it was Vicki who would lean over and make people stop, and Vicki who would talk to them about who they were and where they were headed, while Nancy hung back on the road's shoulder. There was the woman who drove past them because she was too scared to pick up three hitchhikers and then turned around and came back because they were women and she felt she should. They got a ride in an RV from another woman who told them, Send me a postcard when you get where you're going. A truck driver let them off at a truck stop in Illinois and told them about a baseball field nearby where they could get a safe night's sleep. There was a Christian guy who took them home to his family for dinner. They had a gun pulled on them. The guy told them he just wanted them to know he had it. Then he put the gun away and drove on. In Louisville, they were riding in a semi truck with a bench seat, and the driver started grabbing at Vicki, who was sitting next to him. When they stopped at a traffic light, Vicki grabbed his deodorant can and sprayed him in the face with it, and the trio hopped out and ran. Vicki taught Liz how to juggle. They had a tent but never used it; that's how clear the sky was. Vicki had brought a small drum in a velvet case, and she played it if she couldn't sleep.

The three friends reached Charleston, West Virginia, ahead of schedule.

Vicki wanted to go to the beach, said they had time, and Liz and Nancy agreed. A guy picked them up and drove them to a big old mansion on Sullivan's Island, South Carolina. He had home brew, he made his own furniture, and the women talked with him awhile, swam with him off the coast, and spent the night in his rambling home. They'd intended to spend another night camping on the beach, but it rained. They left the next day, catching a ride in an empty Trailways bus up into North Carolina, and planned to make it to the Gathering the following day.

That night, Liz had a feeling she should call home and acted on it. Her father was getting remarried in Vermont that week, she learned, so she decided to part ways with Vicki and Nancy. At a truck stop in Richmond, Virginia, the three women said their good-byes; Liz stood on a road headed north; Vicki and Nancy stood across from her so they could catch a ride west toward the Gathering. A truck stopped and picked her up, Liz told Alkire, and she didn't know what happened to her friends after that.

Most every business owner along all the routes Vicki and Nancy might have taken from Richmond to Droop Mountain had something to tell Alkire. A woman in a county to the east swore she had seen Vicki and Nancy sitting in her diner. Another woman in Hillsboro was equally sure they had walked by her house and shown her a Swiss army knife. Feeling swamped, Alkire took the ones he could, then gave a stack of tips to other officers, both state police and Pocahontas County Sheriff's Department.

Feeling was not Alkire's first language. His father was military and moved the family to Wisconsin, Oklahoma, Alabama, Germany, then back to West Virginia to Buckhannon, a small city that contained a rigorous liberal arts college and that looked more like Pittsburgh than like Pocahontas County. The family stayed in town just long enough for Alkire to finish high school, and then they were gone again. But so was Alkire—without them. His great-uncle had been a state police officer, and Alkire wanted to be too, but the timing was wrong. Nine days after graduation, he signed up for the navy. At seventeen, he stood on the deck of the

USS *Quillback* headed for Spain. Later Guantanamo Bay and Key West. It would be years before Alkire would see the United States again, or anyone he had known.

The *Quillback* crew was close. "Truly one of the great experiences of my life," writes one of Alkire's contemporaries on a website that promises reunion with old navy buddies. Another writes, "Looking for shipmate Hinkley, first name not known. [While] on board Quillback, had operation on lower jaw?" But Alkire didn't haul or scrub like the rest; he collected information, he watched and recorded, and shaped it all into plans and coordinates. "Best boat I was ever on," writes a third. "Was on 5 boats all out of Key West, FL. Anyone remember me?"

No one remembers Alkire. He kept quiet, did his work, and came back to West Virginia. In rapid succession throughout the 1970s, as if checking off boxes on a to-do list, he got his degree from West Virginia University, got married, had his first son, entered the state police academy, had a second son, and graduated. He had a thick head of brown feathered hair and had developed a low, loping gait. He didn't want to write tickets; he wanted to solve murders and, once given the opportunity, set himself fully to the task. The state police divided West Virginia into four quadrants, and Alkire had C company—some six thousand square miles, including Pocahontas and nearby Greenbrier counties, as well as more populous counties to the north and west. Throughout the late 1970s, he solved a lot of murders, and rose from trooper to trooper first-class and then eventually to corporal. Whenever a case needed help or a fresh look, they'd call Alkire, and he'd go.

The Rainbow Gathering map Vicki had been carrying suggested that travelers exit Interstate 64 in Virginia just east of Pocahontas County and then use a two-lane road to cross into West Virginia, eventually ending up in Marlinton. But based on the fact that Vicki and Nancy's bodies had been discovered on the southern side of Pocahontas County, off Route 219, Alkire began to work with the theory that they might have overshot their target and taken the interstate farther than recommended, getting off at the exit for Lewisburg.

In our time, Interstate 64 runs a comfortable 189 miles, crossing the state of West Virginia horizontally, but in 1980 its line was fresh and broken—a few sections west of Pocahontas County remained yet unfinished. If a traveler wished to continue past that point, she'd reach Beckley and then have to exit and take a steep two-lane road into Charleston. This state of affairs remained unchanged until 1987, when the gap was finally closed, making it one of the last and, because of its steep grade, most expensive stretches of interstate to be constructed in the United States.

In 1980, the Lewisburg I-64 exit sign advertised access to Route 219, which may have been why Vicki and Nancy took it—219 was marked on their hand-drawn map as an alternate, though not recommended, route. If a traveler were to pull off I-64 and head north toward Pocahontas County, the first place to get gas was the Little General store.

A woman who worked as a cashier at the store gave a statement saying that on June 25 between 5:30 and 6 o'clock in the evening, two women came in and bought something, though the woman could not remember what, and paid for it with some coins from a green velvet change purse. They told her they were from Arizona, which she remembered because it was so odd—the desert. Then they left and got into a black Chevy Nova driven by a young man who had purchased six dollars' worth of gas. He was "tall and thin, wasn't a hippie, blond hair. No glasses, no beard, or mustache." The Nova turned right, the woman said, continuing north on 219 toward the Rainbow Gathering.

Alkire began looking for dark Chevy Novas, starting with several in the county that met the store owner's description. Alkire also looked for people with a history of run-ins with the law; there was a local "flasher" with a history of nonconsensually masturbating in front of women, who didn't have a firm alibi. Just two houses were within earshot of the spot where Vicki and Nancy died: one belonged to a deaf octogenarian, and the other to a man named Arnold Cutlip and his partner, Virginia Schoolcraft, who said that she had heard several gunshots on June 25 between 4:00 and 4:15 pm. When Alkire asked around about Cutlip, he was told that Cutlip was a heavy drinker who sometimes abused Virginia.

Alkire and his associate, a Sergeant FW Dickinson, clacked out a list of three possible suspects: (1) The flasher, (2) Arnold Cutlip, who "was in the area at the time of murders and is capable of drinking or committing acts of murder....Appears to know more than he is telling," and (3) Paulmer Adkison, a local young man who had been spotted in the area around Droop Mountain Battlefield State Park on the day of the murders and was already being investigated for another local death—a murder for hire.

In a pleasing parallel, the neat report also offered three possible motives: (1) "For sexual satisfaction, as one of the suspects has a known history of being a 'flasher,' and after exposing himself may have become hostile and upset if he was laughed at or ignored." (2) Robbery, since Vicki and Nancy were known to have backpacks and a tent when they parted ways with Liz, but those had never been found. (3) "That of personal satisfaction in the killing of two individuals connected to the Rainbow family."

But two of these three suspects had alibis—Arnold Cutlip had a friend, a man named Johnnie Washington Lewis, who, to the great chagrin of Cutlip's partner, Virginia, essentially lived on Cutlip's couch. Cutlip and Lewis were inseparable, everyone said; wherever Cutlip went, so went Lewis. Lewis said that he and Cutlip had been together all day, cutting downed locust trunks into posts to sell, then drinking at a beer joint in Hillsboro.

The summer of 1980 ended. At the end of deer season, hunters found Vicki and Nancy's backpacks under a laurel bush near Hico, West Virginia, about sixty miles west of Briery Knob. All their belongings were there—their sleeping bags, their tent, even the small velvet case that had held Vicki's travel-sized drum. So much for the robbery motive. Alkire was left with Rainbow hate. He and his fellow investigators crisscrossed the county from Snowshoe ski resort all the way to Interstate 64 again, following stories of "hippie killers" and dark Chevy Novas. Nothing held.

For two months, Alkire drove the sixty-five miles of switchbacking 219 between the West Virginia State Police office in Marlinton and his home in Elkins before he finally admitted the commute was untenable. The

Motor Inn in Marlinton let him rent a room by the week and take his meals there, too, and he worked out of the trunk of his car, storing a growing trove of case notes.

When the full ballistics report came back from the Charleston lab, Alkire took it into his motel room and spread the pages out over the thin bedspread. Next to the official case number, the firearms examiner had written "Rainbow Family Murders"—the title, later shortened to "Rainbow Murders," that would become the case's moniker. In some official documents, Vicki and Nancy are simply called "Rainbows," marked forever by a group they never joined, a destination they never reached.

The bullet fragments lodged in Vicki and Nancy's bodies were, taken as a group, too small to yield any useful leads, the report concluded. But one revealed that the bullets used in their killings were a Sierra brand, .41-.44 caliber—thick ammunition, big in diameter, and very powerful. The examiner could still not be sure whether the gun that had fired them was a revolver or the short rifle known as a carbine. Nine types of revolvers could have fired the bullet as well as two carbines, including the .44 Magnum made popular by Clint Eastwood in *Dirty Harry*.

Alkire paged forward and back through this report and also reviewed the full autopsies of "Red Sweat Shirt" and "Blue Sweat Shirt" as the medical examiner had called them before their identities were known. It was Nancy who wore the red University of Iowa sweatshirt, though it was Vicki who came from that state—Nancy must have borrowed it. Every part of Nancy's body was examined, and while the coroner noted that she was "slightly obese" and had dirty feet and fingernails that were "crudely manicured," he found her corpse otherwise "without note." Vicki had two rings on her little and ring fingers, white metal rings with a turquoise heart and star, but her body was no more revealing. It was Nancy who had the higher blood alcohol content—.08, the current legal limit to drive—while Vicki had had maybe one drink.

"There has been no new development in the murder case concerning the two girls but the investigation is continuing," McNeel had reported on July 31, 1980. "Every bit of information or evidence is being checked carefully."

Vicki and Nancy's case, it seemed, would not solve. The scene had yielded little, ditto the lab results. Everyone in the county with any relevance had been examined or eliminated. Yet the clearing was just too remote for a stranger to find, Alkire felt. Over and over again, in briefing meetings with other state police officials and sheriff's deputies, Alkire told the room that whoever had killed the women had to be local.

Alkire's sons were eight and two by then, and it might be a month before he got home to them. Enough, his wife, Elaine, eventually declared after two years. Land was cheaper in Pocahontas anyway, she pointed out, so why didn't they just buy a lot there and build their own place? Alkire was promoted to corporal and officially transferred to Pocahontas County full-time in November 1982. Elaine Alkire enrolled their two sons in Marlinton Middle School. They were Pocahontas Countians now.

The funeral service for Vicki Durian took place on July 15, 1980, at St. Joseph's Catholic Church, the same place where her sister Mary's wedding had taken place. She was buried in the cemetery where she and her brothers used to hang out and drink and watch the weather roll in. Newspaper reporters from as far away as Cedar Rapids kept showing up at the farmhouse, knocking on the front door, and lifting the shades. Neighbors and family members kept showing up too, leaving casseroles and condolences. Clarabelle took to her bed. It was winter before the doorbell and phone stopped ringing incessantly. But by 1982, two years had passed, and even Alkire had ceased calling. Now they were wishing for its ring again.

One Friday in late July 1982 around 9 o'clock, it did. Odd to get a call so late, as most people knew the Durians kept farming hours and wouldn't call after supper, so Howard answered it with a tightness in his chest. It was a man's voice. He said he was calling from Pocahontas County, West Virginia, and that he was real sorry that Howard's daughter had been killed where he lived. The caller said that he had gone to high school with some of the investigators who were working Vicki's case and that the guys were small-town, not the brightest bulbs in the box. Mr. Durian might want to try to get the FBI in there or something.

Howard said nothing until the caller was finished and then asked the man's name. The caller wouldn't give it. I am not the murderer, he said. Then he hung up.

Howard put the phone's receiver down, then immediately picked it up again and called Alkire. A tap was placed on the Durian line, in case the guy was dumb enough to call back. He was.

"That," says Alkire, "is the first I ever heard of Jacob Beard."

2

JACOB WILSON BEARD LIKED THE idea of having the power to join one piece of metal to another and make someone forget that they had ever been separate. His dad had been raised in Pocahontas County, in a big white house where one county road met another, and Beard was raised there too. It still stands today, on a road named after the Beards, in a hamlet called Beard. During Beard's childhood, the family ran a prosperous cattle farm that grew corn and hay and had the new-looking pickup trucks to show for it. For extra money, Beard's father had also worked as a State Farm insurance salesman. Before she married, his mother had taught school; afterward, she worked occasionally as a substitute teacher and then "finally" became a housewife.

Jacob Beard grew up a busy farm kid—pigs for Future Farmers of America, calves for 4H. When he turned sixteen, there was a new car waiting for him. School was easy; he dated girls, chiefly Linda, a majorette—all that twirling. It was 1964 when Beard graduated from Hillsboro High School, placing twelfth in a class of twenty-three. Most people who could afford some other kind of education left the county after high school. A lot of the guys went into the service. A lot of the girls looked for husbands. Some guys would go to West Virginia University in Morgantown to study farming or how to teach school, but if they were lucky, they found jobs back home.

Beard moved to Nashville and enrolled in a technical school specializing in automotive mechanics and welding, then got a job an hour north of Philadelphia at a factory where they made box trailers. But the chemical fumes hurt his eyes, even with the goggles, and a doctor told him he'd soon go blind if he kept it up. In the first of what would be a long string of returns, Beard drove home to West Virginia and started working construction. In 1965, he and Linda married.

The marriage was rocky and short-lived. Beard wanted to be gone again; he started taking trips to the Washington, DC, area, one of which ended in an arrest for drunk and disorderly conduct, and soon moved there. In 1967, he and Linda divorced. Beard took a job as a mechanic at a Chevrolet dealership in Arlington, Virginia, until 1969. His parents, as the *Pocahontas Times* was fond of chronicling, wintered in Florida near Daytona Beach. During the winter of 1969, Beard went down to visit them. It was 70 degrees in December, and he found work as a mechanic, again at a Chevy dealership, and soon became its service manager too. On a visit back to West Virginia, Beard called Linda up, and they were soon back together; in 1971 they remarried, and in 1974 Linda became pregnant with their first daughter, Teresa.

While Beard had been traveling, Linda had gone back to school to become a nursing assistant and easily found work in Florida. But in 1976, just as they were feeling rooted, Beard's dad called to say he and Beard's mother were getting older and they needed Beard to come back to Pocahontas County to take over the farm. Back he and Linda and their daughter went.

Now Beard was feeding and tending the cattle, putting up hay, chopping grass for silos, and also tending the big garden abundant enough to feed both his young family and his aging parents. In 1978, he took a second job at Greenbrier Tractor Sales in Lewisburg. Sometimes this hustle was too much to handle alone, and Beard was forced to hire help, local guys who could make hay or cut posts.

Beard wanted to quit working in town and open his own shop on the family land, but he hurt his ankle badly and could barely hobble. He hired members of the nearby commune to rebuild a sagging barn and paint the kitchen. Another Back to the Land couple had a horse farm just above the Beard land, and Beard liked them just fine.

Beard drank—too much by his own standards and the law's, catching another charge for drunk and disorderly during Pioneer Days, Marlinton's summer version of Mardi Gras. But these are not uncommon crimes in the mountains, where police have little else to do but park outside the bars and wait.

When the Rainbow people came to town the following year, they came into Marlinton, the other side of the county from Beard's home. He may have seen a few hitchhiking on the road, but he doesn't think he picked any up. Linda worked at the hospital down the road from their farm and occasionally worked Saturday night into Sunday morning. If Linda was working, Beard would take his two daughters to church and then take them out for a Happy Meal. Any empty moments were swallowed up by the farm—there was always a cow that was sick or a field that needed to be cut for hay.

But wherever he went that summer, talk followed of the two "Rainbow" girls who had been shot up on Briery Knob and who might have done it. Not just at the Marathon gas station, but at the grocery store, the river, the beer joint, at church. Who had seen whom out driving that day. Who beat his wife. Who was frustrated because he had lost his job. Like Alkire, many citizens of Pocahontas County talked about how the killer had to be local.

Beard spent most of his working hours out on service calls to fix farm equipment in nearby Virginia counties, but he'd often run into people from Pocahontas or Greenbrier County on the job, and they'd want to talk about it too. Still Beard didn't think too much about the killings. As with most rural areas in the early 1980s, sudden death was not completely foreign to Pocahontas County—usually there were one or two deaths each year by accidental gunshot or suicide or bar dispute. But one day in 1982, after the murders had largely fallen out of the pages of the *Pocahontas Times*, Beard was sitting outside the office where he worked eating a sandwich when a neighbor from Droop Mountain stopped by to wait on a piece of machinery that was being fixed. Beard listened to the man discuss the case—what they knew about the dead women and what they didn't, what the investigation had revealed and what it hadn't. For the first time, Beard really let his mind linger over the killings, and they started to work on him. It just didn't fit, that two girls would be dead on isolated Briery

Knob. He started thinking about it every day; it would pop into his mind while he was working and driving and at odd moments. It was a mystery.

The years rolled by. He and Linda had another daughter, Tammy.

"Jacob, when he was sober, was a fine guy," a county official told a Long Island weekly paper. "When he was sniffing gas or smoking pot, he was meaner than hell."

"If you look into his background," former Pocahontas County Sheriff Jerry Dale told me, "he's a real Dr. Jekyll and Mr. Hyde."

The story goes that the idea for the *Strange Case of Dr. Jekyll and Mr. Hyde* came to Robert Louis Stevenson in a fever dream while he was swarming with tuberculosis. His lungs were hemorrhaging blood and drowning in mucus. He would create a character, he saw—a man—who would struggle aboveground with the things he and so many other men suffered with below it. "With every day, and from both sides of my intelligence," Stevenson writes, "the moral and the intellectual, I thus drew steadily nearer to that truth…that man is not truly one, but truly two."

The idea to call Vicki's dad came to Jacob Beard with a similar kind of urgency. July 2, 1982, was a Friday night. Beard had worked all day and was hot, tired, thirsty, numb. He says he had had a few drinks that night but wasn't drunk. There on the coffee table, he says, was a copy of the *Pocahontas Times* with an "anniversary" article about the Rainbow Murders. Two years. It was just really bothering him, and no matter the television program he watched or the beer he drank, thoughts of the murders wouldn't leave him.

Beard says he called the Durians in Iowa instead of the Santomeros in Long Island because it was an hour earlier in Iowa. Plus he didn't know how to pronounce "Santomero." He made the call from his home, which he says he wouldn't have done if he had been trying to hide his identity. He also says he called only once.

Whether once or twice, Beard put calling the Durians out of his mind so much so that when, a few weeks later, he stopped to talk to a friend at the Marathon gas station and a sheriff's deputy squad car pulled up alongside his red truck, he says he was completely surprised. Even when the deputy told him that the state police wanted to speak to him and could Beard please follow his car, he still did not connect the dots.

In the examination room sat a small officer with a square head, hook nose, and chlorine-blue eyes who introduced himself as Corporal Robert Alkire. Come on in, the officer said to Beard. You must know what this is about.

Beard was bigger than Alkire had expected—tall and wide with a head like a potato and seventies-style aviator glasses without the tint.

No sir, Beard replied. I've no idea what this is about.

At first Beard denied making the phone calls to the Durians, but then he admitted it. Sure, okay, he told Alkire. It was just that I felt so bad for those girls and their families.

Why didn't you give your name, then? Alkire asked. Can you see how that seems odd, even suspicious?

I don't know anything, Beard said. So I didn't want to make it seem like I did, or get too involved.

Alkire was interested in Beard's whereabouts on the late afternoon and night of June 25, 1980, since the medical examiner put Vicki and Nancy's time of death around 6 or 7 o'clock in the evening. So where was Beard?

Beard told Alkire that he left work at Greenbrier Tractor Sales in Lewisburg, made a house call to work on a piece of farm machinery until about 5:15 pm, stopped off at his home near Droop Mountain for a sandwich and a change of clothes, and then headed to a school board meeting with Linda, arriving by 7:00 or 7:30 pm. He wasn't in the habit of attending all the school board meetings, but this had been an important one: the board was voting on whether to close the Hillsboro school where Beard's two daughters would go. The proposal was to consolidate a few grade schools into a single school, which would mean busing kids from the southern part of the county, where the Beards lived, farther north each morning. Beard was dead against it, as were many of the other parents, and he had said so at the meeting. But they lost—the school was closed anyway. After the meeting, Beard continued, he went home with Linda's cousin, the cousin's wife, and another friend; Linda had to work the night shift at the hospital and left separately.

Had he seen any Rainbow girls on June 25? Alkire asked.

No.

Did he know anything or had he heard anything at all about the Rainbow Murders?

Local people did the killings, Beard said. That's what everyone is saying.

Without anything concrete to hold him, Alkire let Beard go, but told him to stay in touch. In case you remember anything, he said.

Beard's alibi seemed to hold after 7:30 pm; witnesses told Alkire they had seen him at the school board meeting, though one, Sis Hively, said he seemed drunk—red in the face, alcohol on his breath—and agitated, that as he addressed the school superintendent, he had yelled. Beard's cousin by marriage, Roger Pritt, confirmed that Beard had left the meeting with him and his wife.

Before 7:30 pm was squishier. Beard couldn't remember where he had gone on the service call, and by 1982 he wasn't working at Greenbrier Tractor Sales anymore. Alkire went and got Beard's old time card, which did indeed say that Beard had finished a house call at 5:15 pm, but it didn't say to whom and the time was handwritten in pencil. Common practice, Beard's old boss said, as many of the guys would go out on calls not knowing how long they would take, then fill in the time the next morning when they got back.

But Beard had lied to Alkire at least once in that first interview, Alkire discovered. Beard had a mistress, a teacher who lived in Greenbrier County named Patricia—a "fling," Beard says, that his wife knew about. He didn't leave the school board meeting in 1980 in a car of four people, but rather five—the extra passenger was Patricia, though Beard says they didn't go home together.

Alkire discovered the lie on December 26, 1982, when he got a call from the Pocahontas County magistrate's office. A Patricia had just filed a complaint against a Jacob Beard for animal cruelty. Did Alkire want her number?

On Christmas Eve, Patricia said, she was getting her four daughters ready for church when Beard called and said he was coming over. They had been seeing each other off and on since 1979, but things had started to go downhill, particularly since Alkire had summoned Beard for questioning about the Rainbow Murders.

Beard sounded drunk, Patricia said, and she told him not to come. He insisted—he really wanted to see her, needed to see her. No, Patricia said again. She told Beard that it was over and hung up the phone. Before she left, she checked on her English sheepdog and tabby cat, then buckled her kids into the car. When she returned from services, she found her dog, bleeding from a stab wound to its back. Her cat lay in her bed, still alive but snuffling in its own blood; it had been sliced from chin to tail. Her dog lived, but her cat did not.

A Pocahontas County sheriff's deputy arrested Jacob Beard for animal cruelty on December 27, 1982, knocking on his door that night. Beard denied the charge, but the magistrate found sufficient cause to hold him and set bail at $1,100, which Beard paid. He says he went home without spending the night, though official records reflect that he wasn't released from jail until December 28.

Several days into the new year in 1983, Beard drove back to Marlinton to meet with the county prosecutor at the time, a man named Steve Hunter, to see what might be done about the charges. Instead of Hunter, Beard found his assistant, a pale, round-faced man in his thirties who introduced himself as Walt Weiford and whom Beard vaguely recognized from growing up together around Pocahontas County.

The matter would go to trial, and Beard should get a lawyer, Weiford told Beard. A good one.

3

IF YOU WERE LOOKING FOR Walt Weiford, you might find him on the Blue Bridge that spanned a place in the Greenbrier River near Buckeye, just south of Marlinton. "I have crossed that bridge many, many times with various intentions…:)," he once wrote on Facebook, including but not limited to meditating, fishing, drinking, and rereading the Constitution of the United States.

Weiford was a "great man," a "good man," "one of the good guys," a "true man," say his friends and neighbors; he was "there for you," he "had your back," he "always knew how to say things"; he "offered words of wisdom" and "always pointed you in the right direction." He was "refreshing," a "straight shooter," "not political," "saw things from all sides," and "told it like it is." He had red-blond hair that he wore shaggy but a full beard and mustache that he kept groomed and even as a lawn. He was open, even effusive with his feelings of love and gratitude to be alive and to be a West Virginian and to have married his wife and have created his only child, a daughter, who was his favorite person. He wore dark blue denim overalls when he played three-finger banjo with his bluegrass band and tailored suits when he lawyered. He adopted rescue animals, liked lost causes and underdog stories. A self-identified liberal, he also read conservative news websites and didn't like when people "went too far" or "got out of hand." He believed that most conflict could be solved if people in this world could decide to "just be *human*." He liked to be outside, to sit on the hood of a car listening to the crickets buzzing in summer, to build a bonfire in the fall and stay out with it alone until it died.

Weiford was born in Marlinton and graduated from the high school there in 1969. Before he wanted to be a prosecutor, he wanted to be a spiritual warrior, to minister somehow to the sick and suffering. He left Pocahontas County for Marshall University in Huntington, where he copied down psychological diagnoses on yellow legal pads and memorized their symptoms. Becoming a case worker for Child Protective Services let him see the things that every CPS worker across America sees and some things unique to the Mountain State: the couple feeding their twin toddlers only dilly beans they'd meticulously canned over many summers, the second-grade teacher at the local school who had begun taking her students home with her so their parents could work overnight shifts as coal mine security guards.

Weiford got tired, got fed up. What good was it to minister to the suffering if you could not protect them, if their suffering would just keep repeating and repeating, ad nauseam and forever?

Weiford had an energy, a bounce, and struggling against what he perceived as injustice was its greatest fuel. Law school in Morgantown plugged him in and charged him up. He was two years a married man in June 1980, and it was the summer between his second and third years, when he came home to intern for then-prosecutor Steve Hunter for nothing but experience. He came into work one day, and Hunter told him there had been a double homicide up on Briery Knob and that was all they were going to do that day. Weiford was twenty-eight.

Weiford got into the car with his boss, and they drove 219; the summer fog had lifted by midday, and the sun shone hot and dry. Hunter turned sharply right onto Droop Mountain Battlefield State Park road and then kept on through. The lush trees blocked out the sun, and the rhododendron bushes dripped onto Weiford's arm, slung out his window, when Hunter steered the car too close.

It was easy to spot the place where the women had been found—perhaps ten officers were walking the scene, combing the grass. Weiford walked with them and listened. He trailed behind Prosecutor Hunter and wrote down what Hunter said and how he said it. The bodies were gone by then, but their blood was still there in the grass.

When the summer ended, Weiford went back to school in Morgantown.

He should have been studying—torts, civil procedure—but instead he was calling home, calling Hunter. What was happening on the case with the two Rainbow girls? Had their backpacks been found yet? He came back to Pocahontas County every break.

When Weiford graduated, he came home for good, this time as assistant prosecuting attorney, a volunteer part-time position he accepted with pride, though it paid zero dollars. To live, he went into private practice handling the divorces, wills, and deeds of Pocahontas County and even picked up a third job as counsel for a local bank.

When Alkire called the prosecutor's office with updates on the Rainbow case, it was often Weiford who answered. They'd talk for twenty, thirty minutes. Alkire was new to town and a little awkward; people around the county still considered him a city slicker. Weiford felt sorry for the guy and sometimes invited him out to eat by the river or to bring his sons to the drive-in movie theater.

1982 became 1983. Pocahontas County has the highest average elevation of any US county east of the Mississippi, and the snow was especially relentless that year. Alkire and Weiford shoveled their cars out every morning, again if they had a meeting after lunch, and again before the black drive home. Some kids—like Alkire's and Beard's—lived down one-lane back roads that school buses struggled to navigate dry much less in snow, so Pocahontas County kids missed weeks of school days, days they would have to pay back, sooner or later.

There may be no stronger bond than the one between two people who fundamentally do not agree about what happened in their story. Who was wrong and who was right, who was evil and who was innocent, who did what to whom and what it all meant. Alkire and Beard are bound to each other in this way.

After Alkire interviewed Beard about his calls to the Durian family and then learned about the animal cruelty charges against him, Alkire kept close tabs on Beard. He summoned Beard for an interview three more times in January and February 1983, though Beard said each time that he knew nothing more about the Rainbow Murders and that he was sorry he had ever made those calls. Alkire asked Beard if he knew Arnold Cutlip, suspect number two from Sergeant Dickinson's first report who lived in the house closest to the clearing where Vicki and Nancy had been found. Beard said he knew Cutlip by face and to say hello because he had hired Cutlip a few times to cut some timber on the Beard farm, but that was all. Alkire showed Beard pictures of Vicki and Nancy's dead faces, taken when they were found on Briery Knob and asked Beard to show the pictures around the county to see if they triggered any recognition. Alkire still thought Beard knew something more. He might make a suitable ambassador or informant of sorts, rattle the people truly involved out into the open.

Beard began to look more and more disheveled each time he came in to meet with Alkire—burst blood vessels in his cheeks, heavy circles under his eyes. When Alkire asked why, Beard said his father had just died and that money was tight on the farm, so he had taken a second job as an overnight security guard at a dam more than an hour away. Alkire asked around and found that Beard had become friendly with another Pocahontas County man who worked at this same dam and that they would sometimes carpool to their shifts together. The new friend also had a teenage girl staying with his family, and the rumor going around was that Beard was sleeping with her.

Alkire called the prosecutor's office. As usual, Weiford answered. The two men discussed applying this rumor as pressure to see if Beard might finally give up whatever information he knew. Plus there was still the animal cruelty charge to resolve.

On a Thursday in early February 1983, Alkire called Beard to arrange a meeting. Just a few more questions, he said. But this time, Alkire asked Beard to come to the courthouse in Marlinton, to Prosecutor Hunter's office.

Beard looked even worse than the last time Alkire had seen him, and he reeked of alcohol. Alkire dropped the rumors of an affair between Beard and his friend's teenage houseguest and watched Beard for how it landed. Beard got agitated and denied it. Weiford reminded Beard of the cat murder charge. Finally, Prosecutor Hunter spoke very slowly: Is there anything you may have forgotten to tell us about the Rainbow Murders? Beard's lawyer told him that the state would grant him immunity for whatever he might say.

Yes, Beard said. On his way home from his service call on June 25, 1980, around 5:30 pm, he drove by the entrance to Droop Mountain Battlefield State Park and saw several cars parked at the mouth of the entrance road, known locally as "Lovers' Lane." He recognized one of them as belonging to a female friend of his from high school and another was a little red Buick that belonged to a woman named Christine Cook. Beard saw Cook sitting inside the car. He also saw two men standing on either side—Paulmer Adkison, Cook's boyfriend, who had been suspect number three on Alkire's original list, and a friend of Adkison's named Bill McCoy. There were also two people inside Cook's car, he said, and they might have been women—they seemed to have long hair—though Beard couldn't say for sure. He hadn't told this to Alkire before, he said, because he hadn't seen the high school friend herself and came to believe her car was only there because it had happened to run out of gas nearby and he didn't want to get her in trouble.

Beard then asked if he could have his $1,100 back for "the cat thing." Prosecutor Steve Hunter said he could, and that in exchange for Beard's continued cooperation he would make sure that a continuance was granted for the animal cruelty charge—vague wording that Alkire and Weiford interpreted to mean the charges would go away (Beard was never tried or convicted of animal cruelty, and his criminal record does not reflect this charge at all). Beard was then presented with an immunity agreement that protected him from prosecution as an accessory to murder before the fact but provided no immunity if it turned out Beard had been the one to shoot the Rainbow girls. Beard's lawyer motioned for him to sign it, and Beard did.

Alkire was sweating as he watched Beard sign the document; he didn't like the idea of anyone getting immunity until he could clearly grasp the whole case in his hands. But Beard had given information where there was none, so Alkire ran with Beard's facts, setting off straightaway to interview Christine Cook. Since Paulmer Adkison had always been on Alkire's list, and Cook was his girlfriend and the mother of his child, Alkire had already talked to her several times over the years; Adkison had been arrested for that unrelated crime shortly after the Rainbow Murders. Around the county, Cook was known as a nice, polite girl; no one including Alkire could figure out why the two kept gravitating back together. When Alkire had interviewed her in July 1980, she had said that yes, she had been in Droop Mountain Battlefield State Park with Adkison earlier in the day to sell a truck to Arnold Cutlip, but they had left the park in the early afternoon. She had not been in the park in the evening, and she had certainly not seen any Rainbow girls or hosted them in her car.

Interviewed again, she told Alkire that she might have been on Droop Mountain that evening after all, with Adkison and his friend Bill McCoy, just as Beard had said. Also, two more of her boyfriend's friends had been there—Richard Fowler and Gerald Brown. But there had been no women besides her there, she said, she was sure of it. And she had not seen Jacob Beard at all that day.

When Alkire checked, he found that Richard Fowler was indeed a friend of Bill McCoy's, that they were often a duo, local guys in their late twenties who worked as day laborers in a slow 1980s West Virginia economy when they could get the work. Gerald Brown was older and better off, a logging contractor with a wife and a trailer on Droop Mountain. He sometimes hired McCoy and Fowler to cut posts when he had the work to give them.

Then, three days after Beard signed the immunity agreement, Alkire's office phone rang. It was a Sunday, early, and Alkire wasn't in.

"It's pretty important," Beard allegedly said to the trooper who answered. "I want to tell [Alkire] about the third Rainbow girl."

To hear Beard tell it, that winter after the phone call to the Durians, Alkire would not leave him alone. It was constant. Alkire kept calling him, wanting him to come down to the station to talk about the Rainbow Murders, and Beard kept going in. He had been raised to believe in the law, he says, and felt that if an officer of the law needed help, you helped.

Beard says that he was the one who ended the affair with Patricia, and that he ended it long before Christmas Eve because he decided he loved his wife and wanted to stay with her. On Christmas Eve, he and Linda had been invited to a friend's house to play cards, but Linda didn't go, instead staying at home with their daughter. Beard went for a couple hours, he says; he loves dogs and would not hurt one.

Beard's father died in January 1983, and after that, Beard says, he began to lose it with grief. Despite getting into the car and driving straight to Florida at his mother's call, his father had still died before Beard could say good-bye in person.

"And for a month or six weeks, the only time in my life I ever drank much was then, when I lost my dad because I loved him and I think about him every day yet," says Beard.

Before, Beard says, he only drank on weekends, but now he was drinking every day. Also, he had indeed made a friend at his new job, and they'd carpool to the dam, which was more than forty miles away in Virginia. His friend was no help on the drinking front, even encouraged it. Beard got into the habit of going over to his friend's place early, and they would play a couple of rounds of cards and drink together before they had to leave for their shift, which started at five in the evening and meant Beard didn't get home till nearly 4 o'clock in the morning. Then he'd get up in the late morning and put up hay.

When Alkire called Beard in February 1983 and asked if they could meet, Beard says he was exhausted, strung out, bone tired of Alkire and his harassing calls. But still feeling obligated to the law, he went. They met in Steve Hunter's office, with Hunter and Weiford, as well as Beard's lawyer, though Beard can't remember asking him to be there.

The prosecutors had drawn up an immunity agreement for him, Beard says, though he couldn't understand what he might need immunity for. But his lawyer seemed unconcerned—tell them something, anything, sign it and you can go home—all this will be over. Beard really wanted to go home, he says. So when Hunter asked if there was anything he had forgotten to say, Beard told them something he knew wasn't related to the Rainbow Murders—the tip about the cars on Droop Mountain Battlefield State Park.

Can I go now? Beard says he remembers asking. He signed and left.

That Sunday, he had started drinking early. He was still distraught about his father's death just a month before, after all. Alkire called yet again, and left a message, Beard says. Again Alkire asked if Beard could come down to the station for a chat. Beard was dreading returning the call. He wanted to tell Alkire he was finished with all that. But, he says, he called Alkire back and, after a few minutes on the phone, gave in yet again.

The trooper who answered the phone at the West Virginia State Police office when Beard called hung up and then picked the phone back up again to call Alkire at home. Alkire returned Beard's call, then called the trooper back at the office. "Called this officer and advised that Mr. Beard had told him that Arnie Cutlip and Paulmer Adkison had run a girl through a corn chopper at his farm back in September 1980," read the trooper's notes from that day.

Alkire had arranged to meet Beard at the state police office in Marlinton that evening. They met. Beard spoke in more detail. Alkire typed up his words in a written statement, which Beard then read and signed:

> It was in the first part of September, 1980. I was at my shop in Beard, WVa. I was working on my chopper, that is what is used to chop up silage. Arnie Cutlip and Palmer Adkison drove up in Arnie's green Chevrolet pickup truck. Arnie was driving. They got out of the truck. Arnie had been drinking. I couldn't smell anything on Palmer. I had oiled the chopper and it was sitting there idling. Arnie was looking for Gerald Brown. I told him Gerald was not here. Palmer started to walk around the wagon and tripped over the tongue. When he got up he looked into the chopper that was running. He said, "Arnie, I think there is the answer to our problem."

According to this statement, Paulmer Adkison then went to the back of Cutlip's truck and took out the pale undernourished body of a young woman wrapped in a dark gray smock. The two men put her through

Beard's corn chopper, directed Beard not to tell anyone they had done so, got back into Cutlip's truck, and drove away.

No, Beard says, that's not how it happened at all.

At the station, Beard was buzzed, fatigued, overcome with grief, he says, vulnerable and weak. His resolve to resist Alkire had left him. Alkire again accused him of having a sexual relationship with his work friend's young female houseguest. According to Beard, Alkire then said that he would see to it that Beard went to jail for statutory rape if he didn't make a statement incriminating Adkison and Cutlip for the Rainbow Murders. That's when Beard began to feel truly afraid. Could Alkire really do that? And if he could, what else might he be capable of?

Beard refused to make the statement. Alkire persisted. After several hours, Beard says, Alkire then said, Come on. If you were going to get rid of a body on your farm, how would you do it? And Beard allegedly responded, Through my corn chopper.

He claims those words—"the third Rainbow girl"—weren't his and never were. He says that Alkire wrote up the statement himself, that Alkire would suggest a few lines, then Beard would throw out some ideas, and they made it up together as they went along. Beard says he only signed it.

Alkire had become obsessed with the idea of Beard's guilt, Beard alleges, for what reason he can't say. In his phone calls to Vicki's dad, Beard had stated that police investigators were not doing their jobs; maybe Alkire had taken it personally. Or perhaps because of the animal cruelty charge, Alkire had gotten it in his mind that Beard was violent and cruel to women.

Whatever the truth, the statement was written. It was signed and presented to a magistrate. Arnold Cutlip sputtered a denial and called Beard a liar, but Cutlip was arrested anyway. Paulmer Adkison remained incarcerated for another crime. It is unclear who investigators thought this allegedly murdered woman was, for Alkire had already spoken to Liz Johndrow at length.

Alkire sent officers to interview Cutlip's partner, Virginia Schoolcraft, again. "When [Cutlip] gets drunk he slaps her around a lot," read the WVSP trooper's notes from the interview, "and the next day after he sobers up he doesn't remember anything that happened when he was drunk." A magistrate declared there was probable cause to hold Cutlip for murder and set a high bail, forcing him to remain in the Pocahontas County jail.

Beard helped Alkire disassemble his corn chopper so that it could be shipped to the West Virginia state crime lab to be tested for human remains. At Cutlip's preliminary hearing, Beard repeated the corn chopper story under oath, and it made the papers. By spring's end, every citizen of Pocahontas County knew what the words "the third Rainbow girl" meant.

A few months later, the results of the tests performed on the corn chopper came back negative for any blood or tissue. After being incarcerated for more than 180 days, Cutlip was released. For years afterward, whenever Cutlip showed his face at a town festival or a family reunion, people tilted their heads toward their companions and whispered, "There goes the corn chopper man."

4

IN 1912, AN OREGON SUPREME Court judge presiding over an arson case wrote, "It is not an easy task to unring a bell, nor to remove from the mind an impression once firmly imprinted there." In so writing, he coined the legal phrase "You can't unring the bell." A ruling in 1962 from the Fifth Circuit Court of appeals offered similar sentiments: "After the thrust of the saber it is difficult to forget the wound"; and, memorably, "If you throw a skunk into the jury box, you can't instruct the jury not to smell it." A story, even one debunked as false, lingers.

This is also the truth undergirding our defamation and libel laws; as a society we have decided that false stories are so permanently damaging as to constitute a crime. Defamation suits require the plaintiff to show that their life—or that more amorphous idea, their reputation—has been injured by the false story beyond repair. *There goes the corn chopper man.*

Yet it may not be as easy as we might think to distinguish telling a true story from telling a false one. Lies and fictions do not come from nowhere; they come from our experiences, the newspaper obituaries column, and perhaps our deepest wishes, curiosities, and instinctual drives. Psychoanalysis would label these "phantasies," the *ph* connoting that they reside in a mental reality rather than an objective reality. Freud believed that phantasies were primarily about bodies—the desires to possess one's own body or that of another and to destroy it.

He also believed that criminals were not those who lacked a moral conscience but rather people with overactive consciences. "Paradoxical as it may sound," he wrote, "I must maintain that the sense of guilt was present before the misdeed, that it did not arise from it, but conversely—the misdeed arose from the sense of guilt." Once the crime was committed, Freud posited, the phantasy was relieved. At least now they knew why.

The mind then, has its own facts, connected to objective facts, but not always in agreement with them. Before a story can be told to someone else, we must first tell it to our self.

That image of a young pale girl in a loose smock and of a man looking into the maw of a corn chopper and deciding it would be a good place to "solve the problem" of a dead woman's body—where had that come from? Alkire says Beard. Beard says Alkire. Someone had told himself that one before.

Bobby Lee Morrison may have been the last person in all of Pocahontas County to learn about the Rainbow Murders. He was seventeen in 1980 and had just dropped out of Pocahontas County High School to support his girlfriend and their infant daughter by cutting locust posts. He showed up even in bad weather. He cut down trees, then cut them into six-foot segments with a chainsaw, then used a splitter until the pieces were thin enough to sell to farmers. Gerald Brown paid the best, so Bobby mostly worked for him.

According to his girlfriend, Bobby Lee Morrison was on a fishing trip with two other men on June 25, 1980. When his girlfriend came to pick him up the next day, she told the men about the murders. "Well," Morrison said, "I am glad I know where I was."

Years passed, and Morrison began working for Jacob Beard by a kind of accident. "[Beard] had some two calves or something that went wild," Morrison would testify in court. "They had been chasing them. Couldn't get them. They needed more help. I think [my friend] told [Beard] I would probably help him if he would come and get me."

Morrison started doing odd jobs for Beard. Many boys had already lost their licenses to DUIs by the time they were seventeen, but not Morrison. When Beard opened a small auto body shop on his land, he hired Morrison as a mechanic, and there Morrison worked every day without event for about a year, until the night of April 3, 1983, when a local man walked into the Greenbrier County Jail and said that he had heard secondhand that Bobby Lee Morrison, now twenty years old, had watched Gerald Brown kill the Rainbow girls.

Morrison was picked up at Beard's shop on April 6, driven to a West Virginia State Police interrogation room and questioned for approximately six hours. He signed a rights waiver in high school perfect cursive and then a statement saying that he had been riding in Gerald Brown's pickup truck when they picked up two women walking just outside Hillsboro. The women said they were "with the Rainbows," so he and Brown drove them into Droop Mountain Battlefield State Park—a shortcut to the Gathering—where they stopped to drink a little moonshine, then drove up to Briery Knob road. There, Morrison alleged, they stopped again, drank some more moonshine, and talked "about partying and how much we used to drink." Brown then propositioned the women for sex, but they refused.

> They said no they were sorry but they weren't going to do it.
>
> Gerald took off then and started driving towards Briery Knob again. I went to sleep. I heard something and when I woke up I heard a gun shot and saw a flash. Then I heard another gunshot and saw another flash. The gun shots were three or four seconds apart....I asked him why he did it. He said he wanted to get some pussy off of them and they wouldn't give it to him and it made him mad.

According to Morrison, Brown shot the women as they stood along the passenger side of the pickup. Asked how many times, Morrison said, "I only heard two shots; there might have been more than that." He and Brown dumped their bodies in the clearing where they had been found. Later, Brown chucked the women's backpacks under some brush along a two-lane county road heading west toward Beckley.

Morrison was held in the county jail, and Alkire set about getting a warrant for Brown. When picked up, Brown said he didn't know anything about what happened to the Rainbow girls and that on that day in June he had gone to a beer joint in Hillsboro and drank six beers. He said he did not remember whom he talked to or who was in the beer joint with him, but he certainly had not seen Morrison at all that day, though he did remember seeing an ambulance go through Hillsboro headed north on 219 around nine or ten o'clock at night. The investigator's report goes on to state, "[Brown] did remember that he did tell someone that he had killed the Rainbow girls but he didn't remember who he told it to."

Brown was quickly arraigned, and bail was set at $100,000; off he, too, went to the county jail. As for motive, his 1983 investigation report reads "anger due to being refused sexual gratification." While in the back of a police car en route to the magistrate's office for arraignment, Brown told the trooper driving that it didn't matter what happened to him and that if he was brought to trial for the Rainbow Murders, he would plead insanity. "'It's possible I was there with Bobby and the girls,'" the trooper's notes reflect, "'and it's possible I did do it, but if I did, I was drunk and I don't remember doing it.'"

In the weeks that followed, Alkire and his troopers looked for evidence that further incriminated Brown. He had apparently been confessing to murder all over the place. "I am a hippie killer," he told the owner of a nearby inn.

Like Beard, Brown also had a wife and a girlfriend. Brown's girlfriend lived in Maryland but had started coming down to Pocahontas County in the late 1970s to visit her mother. "On different occasions we would go to the Droop Mountain Park and he would drive over the mountain on a steep road," notes the statement she gave on April 12, 1983, days after Brown was arrested.

> Sometimes he would stop at a wide place and he would be really upset, he would be crying. Then he would tell me that he had done some awful things….One day he and I were riding around together and I made the comment that one of these days I was going to kill my husband. Me and my husband were separated and weren't getting along. Gerald said, "No, you wouldn't want to kill anyone, believe me, I know how it feels."

One day, the girlfriend also found a small turquoise cross necklace in Brown's truck. He gave it to her, saying that it had belonged to one of his "Rainbow friends" but that they wouldn't be back for it.

Later that spring, Morrison recanted his accusations against Brown and his statement in its entirety. He said that in fact he and Brown had nothing to do with the murders, that he had made the whole statement up because his boss, Jacob Beard, had told him to do so and threatened to hurt his girlfriend and child if he refused. Beard had given Morrison a few details, Morrison claimed—the location of the bodies and how they had lain, that one girl had drunk a little and the other a lot—but he knew nothing else. All charges against Morrison were dropped, and he was released from the county jail in early May 1983.

Beard says he never threatened Bobby Morrison into making a statement against Brown and can't understand why he would say that. Beard has a different theory for the chain of events with Morrison and Brown based on rumors he's heard: Morrison had a family member who was in some trouble with the law, and his family was putting pressure on Morrison to try to exchange information in the Rainbow case—which everyone in the county knew law enforcement desperately wanted—for his family member's freedom.

Walt Weiford, for his part, was not surprised by Morrison's recantation—law enforcement themselves had come to doubt what Morrison had said. After offering his confession, Morrison consented to do a ride-along to the scene of the crime. Weiford and Alkire sat in the back, a sheriff's deputy drove, and Morrison sat in the passenger seat, his head leaning out into the open air. Alkire asked Morrison to retrace the path he said he and Brown had taken that day. Without hesitation, Morrison led them to the wide spot on Briery Knob where Vicki and Nancy had been found, showed how the bodies had lain perpendicular to the road, and said that their clothing had been disheveled—all true facts. He said that he and Brown continued straight after dumping the bodies but had to turn around shortly afterward because the road dead-ended, also consistent with the tire tracks and paint scrape found at the scene.

But then Alkire asked Morrison to take them to the site where he and

Gerald dumped the women's backpacks. Morrison said he didn't remember. He had the trooper turn down the nearest paved road and fifteen minutes later halfway gestured at a spot off to the right. There, he said, without conviction.

"He wasn't within fifty miles of the place," Weiford says. "It wasn't like he was even close."

Meanwhile, even after Morrison was released, Brown remained in jail, unable to pay his bail. He was a "pauper"—so read the affidavit he had to submit to prove he was too broke to hire a lawyer—so the court appointed him two for free. He listed his income per month as zero dollars, likewise his cash savings and assets; he was unemployed and was receiving twenty-five dollars a month in food stamps. After Brown was kept in jail over a month, his lawyer filed a motion to reduce his bail, arguing that Brown was a native and lifelong resident of Pocahontas and Greenbrier Counties with no felony record and that $50,000 per count of murder was "excessive in relation to his financial ability." The motion was refused.

The wheels of bureaucracy turn so slowly. In late October, the case having unraveled, the prosecutor's office requested that the indictment be dropped against Brown, but Brown's case was not officially dismissed by a judge until the middle of January 1984. By the time the jail doors slid open for him, Brown had been in prison seven months.

5

PERHAPS IF THE PICTURES OF Vicki and Nancy with their eyes open and the smell of their blood on the grass of Briery Knob had not worked their way down into Walt Weiford's sternum and sat there like a stone, the investigation into the Rainbow Murders might have ended in 1984—with two stories he couldn't do much with: the evidence against Bobby Lee Morrison and Gerald Brown was circumstantial at best, and Jacob Beard seemed to be either deeply confused or a teller of monumental lies.

Weiford was still volunteering his time as the assistant to the county prosecutor—taking care of traffic stops and drug charges and juveniles who went AWOL. When Hunter's term was up in 1984, he gave Weiford his blessing. Weiford ran for county prosecutor that year but lost by twenty votes. Deflated, Weiford continued building his private practice, but he kept calling the new prosecutor and asking questions—What about Vicki and Nancy? His victor was no friend of Weiford's former boss and did not share Weiford's devotion to the Rainbow killings.

It's cold, he told Weiford. Leave it alone.

Alkire was no more encouraging—he was being transferred to Parkersburg, nearly Ohio, to work on a different murder case. Keep in touch, he told Weiford before leaving, and the two men promised they would.

Weiford's daughter grew up, tumbling over logs and swimming in the Greenbrier River. He taught her how to play music, what notes were, what a scale was, to strum a guitar but pick a banjo.

Soon it was 1988; Vicki and Nancy had been dead eight years. That fall, Weiford ran for prosecutor again at the age of thirty-six, and this time he won. In an act of God or complete coincidence, Alkire had been promoted to the rank of sergeant and then first sergeant in the West Virginia State Police just a few months before and reassigned to Pocahontas County.

In January 1989, just days after he took office, Weiford called a meeting between Alkire's West Virginia State Police officers and the Pocahontas County Sheriff's Department headed by Sheriff Jerry Dale to discuss the status of the Rainbow Murders investigation. Alkire had at times, he was the first to admit, pushed aside the help of Dale's deputies, and they in turn had at times resented this and been hesitant to turn over information to Alkire.

Can't you just try to work together, please? Weiford pleaded with those gathered that day, and both Alkire and Dale agreed they would try. Just go through everything again, Weiford said. Share all your information, go over every note again, every interview—together. See if one of you has something that the other doesn't know about. Maybe something will turn up.

Nothing did. Two more years passed. Then one day in the winter of 1991, a sheriff's deputy found a small handwritten note made in 1986 on a scrap of loose-leaf paper. "Alice Roberts seen Ricky Fowler pick the girls up at Renick Valley," the note read, referencing a spot in the unincorporated hamlet of Renick, just south of Droop Mountain. The note further added, "Jake Beard—blue car."

Had anyone, either sheriff's deputy or state police detective, ever followed up with this Alice Roberts? Nobody had. When found, Mrs. Roberts said, Oh yes, I think so. But if you really want to know the story, you should go talk to my daughter, Pamela. She was living in another county by then, but Alkire found her and drove the miles. And she said, Oh yeah. I saw the whole thing.

Pamela Wilson was a bored teenage girl on June 25, 1980, with nothing to do but stare out the window of her house, which sat along a rare straight stretch of Route 219 known locally as the Renick Flats. It was afternoon, she said, somewhere between 2 and 6 o'clock. "I saw two hippie-type girls standing at the road," Wilson told Alkire in a sworn statement. "The girls were not obese, but they were bigger and heavier than average. Ritchie Fowler pulled up in his van. He was there about a minute and the girls got in the van and drove it off towards Droop Mountain." Fowler was a familiar name to Alkire by then, since he was one of the friends of Christine Cook's boyfriend whom Cook had alleged was hanging out in Droop Mountain Battlefield State Park that day.

That wasn't all. Wilson told Alkire that she thought she also saw two more men in the van, Bill McCoy—the same man Beard supposedly saw outside a car with two women in it at Droop Mountain Battlefield State Park on the evening of the murders—and Winters Walton, a friend of McCoy's. But, she cautioned, she wasn't sure.

"I told my mother at the time that those girls shouldn't have got in with them," she continued. She said that she knew Fowler from growing up around the county and felt that he was a drinker with "a bad reputation." She knew his van, which she described as being light blue, either a Ford or a Chevrolet with "a bubble window" on the back. Wilson further said that a week or two after she'd seen the two women getting into the blue van, Bill McCoy had threatened her in the supermarket, cautioning her not to tell anyone what she'd seen.

Alkire thanked Wilson and drove home to Pocahontas County. "Things just started happening then," he says.

Throughout the winter of 1991 and into 1992, Alkire and the sheriff's deputies interviewed and reinterviewed dozens of Pocahontas County residents who lived on Droop Mountain or nearby. By that winter Alkire and Weiford had a story: three men—Fowler, McCoy, and Walton—had picked up Vicki and Nancy on the Renick Flats. They then assembled a bigger group of men to party at the mouth of Droop Mountain Battlefield State Park. Then one of the men—they were not yet clear on which one—shot Vicki and Nancy.

At trial, Weiford would refer to this group of men as the "relevant necessary people." Alkire, too, used this term. "It seemed like no matter who we talked to," Alkire says, "it kept coming back to those guys and the blue van."

* * *

Five of the men had already fallen under suspicion—Jacob Beard, now forty-six; Gerald Brown, fifty; Arnold Cutlip, fifty-four; Bill McCoy and Ritchie Fowler, thirty-six and forty respectively. By 1992, Bill McCoy was locked up for a DUI in Nevada, and Fowler too had left the state, having moved his family to Virginia. Some were new—Johnnie Lewis, fifty-nine, the man Cutlip let sleep on his couch, and Winters Walton, forty-two, a gentle man who'd taken a job at a lumberyard. They had all grown up in southern Pocahontas County, and in 1980 if not in 1992, most of them still lived there.

The relationships between these men were diffuse and various; by 1992 they were not a group anymore and perhaps had not truly been one even in 1980. Some of the men were certainly friends—Fowler and McCoy, McCoy and Walton, Cutlip and Lewis. McCoy, Fowler, Cutlip, and Lewis had been day laborers for hire in 1980, and all had worked for either Brown or Beard. Brown and Beard knew each other to say hello, as business owners and competitors. Brown drank and hung out with these men when he hired them; Beard says he did not.

Though it was twelve years later, a handful of Pocahontas County residents, on being reinterviewed claimed to remember relevant facts from June 25, 1980—facts that either were new or had never made it into the investigative record. They said the day and the days after were etched into their memories, like the day Kennedy was shot.

A resident of Droop named Steven Goode told Alkire that he had seen Ritchie Fowler's blue van at Gerald Brown's trailer on Droop Mountain at around 6 o'clock on the evening of the murders. The van had been "backed in" toward Brown's trailer, and he had seen Ritchie Fowler, Bill McCoy, and Jacob Beard there. His first thought, Mr. Goode reported, was that they had "gotten an illegal deer."

Another Droop resident, Mike Hively, who is in fact Gerald Brown's half brother, also swore that he saw Fowler's van at Gerald Brown's trailer that night. His wife, Sis, Gerald Brown's sister-in-law, claimed that she saw Jacob Beard's red truck at the entrance to Droop Mountain Battlefield

State Park between 5:30 and 6:00 pm on the day of the murders and reiterated that she felt Beard was aggressive at the school board meeting that night and seemed drunk.

Yet another, William Scott, said that he saw Jacob Beard driving out of Droop Mountain Battlefield State Park at around 3:30 or 3:45 on the day of the murders. And Virginia Schoolcraft, Arnold Cutlip's partner, repeated what she had said in 1980—that she heard two rapidly fired gunshots on June 25, 1980, between 4:00 and 4:15 in the afternoon. An older woman named Betty Bennett, who had been Ritchie Fowler's "friend" in the early 1980s, now swore that Fowler had confessed to her that he had been there when the Rainbow girls were killed. She was also a friend of Bobby Morrison's mother and said that she had witnessed Jacob Beard threatening Morrison's family.

Why have you waited so long to tell us this information? Alkire and the sheriff's deputies inquired. Most of these witnesses had by then been interviewed several times—in 1980 and perhaps again in 1985 or 1986. They cited fear, specifically of Jacob Beard.

The tangible material needed to prove this story—the blue van for example—proved elusive. In central Virginia, where Fowler now lived with his wife and son managing a recreational horse farm, Fowler had heard that his name was often in law enforcement's mouths. He called Alkire up and demanded to know what in the actual fuck this was all about. Alkire told him. Fowler said that he didn't know anything about the Rainbow Murders and that he had wrecked his blue van on a tree in 1986 and then had it crushed for scrap. But it didn't matter anyway, Fowler said, because he had already been living in Virginia by June 1980 and only came home on the weekends, so he couldn't have killed any Rainbow girls on a Wednesday.

Nevertheless, Alkire said, could Fowler come back to town to answer some questions? Fine, Fowler said, agreeing to travel to the Pocahontas West Virginia State Police office, now located in the hamlet of Buckeye just south of the county seat. The station was moved after the flood of 1985, which devastated Marlinton, washing houses and bridges down the river.

Fowler had picked up some Rainbow hitchhikers once, he recalled to

Alkire, but there were six or seven of them, and they had a dog. In the end, Fowler said that he might have been on Droop Mountain on June 25, as it was possible that he had taken the day off, and it was also possible that someone had borrowed his blue van without his permission—he had been a heavy drinker at that time.

Did he have any proof of that? Alkire asked. Fowler then cut the interview short and stormed out. Later, he agreed to take a polygraph exam near where he lived in Virginia, but after that he got a lawyer and never answered any more questions.

Alkire collected guns from all the relevant necessary people he could and had them tested against the bullet fragments pulled from Vicki and Nancy, but nothing matched. The medical examiner had also managed to extract a few paint chip fragments and some automobile glass from Vicki and Nancy's skin and clothes, but with Fowler's blue van destroyed, there was nothing to compare them to. Alkire called and wrote letters to Bill McCoy in Nevada, but no reply came. Without any evidence of McCoy's involvement beyond Pam Wilson's statement, Alkire could not force him to answer questions or bring him home to West Virginia.

Gerald Brown still lived in Pocahontas County in a trailer on top of Droop Mountain and still worked as a logging contractor. When he was arrested and then charged with the murders in 1983, he had refused to answer any of Alkire's questions or give any formal statement. There were those statements about the times Brown told others that he was a killer and the statement from his girlfriend about the necklace he had given her, but they were all hearsay and could not be corroborated. Brown's attitude was the same in 1991: he never offered an official alibi and summarily refused to discuss the matter. A man who worked for himself when he worked and did all his business in cash, he was not inclined to trust any system of power, law enforcement included, who had already incarcerated him for seven months.

Arnold Cutlip agreed to answer additional questions in the winter of 1992 but gave the same story he had been giving all along: he and his friend Johnnie Lewis had spent the day cutting locust posts on his property on Briery Knob, then driven their haul to a farm near Marlinton to sell them, and then gone back to Hillsboro to hang out at the beer joint for the afternoon. Later he and Lewis followed Adkison, in his girlfriend Christine Cook's car, to the mouth of Droop Mountain Battlefield State Park, where they hung out for a while, and then went home. He never saw any Rainbow girls.

If one of the "relevant necessary people" was going to open up further to Alkire then, it was going to have to be Johnnie Washington Lewis, Jacob Beard, or Winters Walton. At age fifty-nine, Lewis was the oldest, and he was also the only one with no permanent address. He bounced around between the homes of friends and relatives; Cutlip's couch was just one in a long string of generosities. Lewis had dropped out of school in the third grade and had a reputation around town for being "simple."

"Mr. Lewis is—I don't know that 'shy' covers it," state police detective Michael Jordan later added. "Mr. Lewis is—and not being derogatory towards him…a recluse." When interviewed, Lewis confirmed Cutlip's story—they had been together all day cutting posts and then drinking beer and had not seen any Rainbow girls.

Alkire and Weiford say that Beard was not an active suspect between 1985 and 1991, though they had not forgotten that he had made those calls to Vicki's father, nor that he had given that statement about the corn chopper and the "third Rainbow girl."

In those years, Beard had taken a job with a farming contractor that put him on the road planting corn in North Carolina and all up the East Coast. He and Linda had moved to neighboring Greenbrier County for the better schools and proximity to Interstate 64. He says he didn't have time to even think about the Rainbow Murders and never went back to Pocahontas County—there was no one there he cared about or who cared for him. On a trip back down to Florida in 1991, when Beard was just "rambling around" on a short solo trip to see friends in Daytona Beach, he visited his old Chevrolet dealership in Crescent City. His old boss had just fired his service manager the day before and asked Beard if he would come back. Beard jumped at the idea and convinced Linda and his daughters, now seventeen and nine, to move once again to Florida. Within weeks, they had sold their house in West Virginia and were gone.

6

THE NAME ON HIS BIRTH certificate is Winters Walton, but everyone called him Pee Wee. He was solid and thick-limbed with light brown hair and pale skin that, when he became embarrassed or scared or shamed, flushed a deep red that started in his forehead and spread. He liked to work and be among friends and ride his motorcycle across the flat, wide scenic highway in the sun.

When Morrison and Brown were in jail on Morrison's incriminating statement from 1983, Pee Wee Walton was hanging out at Denmar State Hospital in the hamlet of Denmar near Hillsboro one day when he heard some people talking—rumors of a girl who had seen the two Rainbow women get into a blue van. That hit something in his brain, which hit something else. Had he been there? He felt that he had, he would later tell investigators. But at first he told no one.

Pee Wee Walton and Alkire spoke for the first time in 1991 at Walton's house in Hillsboro, where he lived with his mother—they took care of each other. Alkire parked his car in Walton's yard, and Walton came out into the chilly September sun. Alkire wanted to know if Walton knew Fowler, and if Fowler had indeed owned a blue van in the summer of 1980. "Yes I do, yes he did," said Walton. "And where were you on June 25, 1980?" Walton said that as best he could remember, he and Ritchie Fowler and Bill McCoy had been riding around that day, shooting groundhogs and drinking beer in Fowler's blue van. For a while they had sat on top of Droop Mountain in the parking lot of a store called CJ's. But they hadn't seen any Rainbow girls and certainly hadn't killed any.

Several months later, Alkire called Walton again and asked him to come into the state police office and take a polygraph. Alkire also called the state police office in Charleston and asked them to send over someone who could administer the polygraph test; they sent a Sergeant R. D. Estep.

Walton took the test, repeating the story he'd given to Alkire in his yard. Estep, a tall, large man, accused Walton of being deceptive. Walton denied it. Alkire stood and left Estep and Walton alone in the room together for the better part of an hour. A week later, Walton called the state police office and said he had remembered more details and wanted to talk.

April 15, 1992—tax day. In the spring in Pocahontas County it's cold as winter until noon, and everything is wet, and then the sun comes out and dries up the mountainside, and the roads are bathed in light. That afternoon, Estep was back in Marlinton, helping Alkire again. At Alkire's request, Estep drove north out of Marlinton on 219 to the hamlet of Edray, where Walton worked at a lumberyard. Estep told Walton that he needed to get into the squad car and come down to the state police office again—Alkire had a few more questions for him. But the car did not turn around and take the direct route to the station. Instead, Estep directed his partner to pull the car onto a back road. Estep got out of the passenger seat and got into the back of the car with Walton.

"And you were scared," a defense lawyer would later ask Walton.

> A: Yes I was.
> Q: And when he got in the back seat with you, he told you, hell I'd a just beat you up, didn't he?
> A: Yes he did.
> Q: Told you he'd just as soon throw you in a ditch and shoot you. Right?
> A: Yes he did.

> Q: He told you he could do that and get away
> with it, didn't he?
> A: Yes he did.

Then, according to Walton, "[Estep] reached around and slapped me up-side of the head with his hand," a blow that bent his glasses but did not break them.

Back at the station in Buckeye, in the room alone with Estep, Walton says, the abuse continued.

"He jerked me off the chair onto the floor. And then he said, 'you lay there in the floor, don't you get up.' And then he stuck his foot up toward my head and was leaning back on the desk. 'I will kick your head through the door if you don't tell me what I want to know' and stuff like that. He was wanting me to say who done it. I said I think maybe Jacob done it, I don't know."

Then Estep opened the door and left. "Ready to talk," he told Alkire.

Alkire came into the room. Walton had a stunned look about him, his face was red, his clothes were disheveled, and his glasses were wonky. Walton then told Alkire that he thought he had had a dream about these women, about how he was there when they were killed. He told Alkire about the day in 1983 that he first heard the rumors about the Rainbow women getting into a blue van.

"They said they had somebody down at Renick's valley that seen them getting in a vehicle down there, and that kind of struck something right then," said Walton in his testimony to the grand jury. "I said, 'Wow, we was down there. We picked up two girls down there.'"

But he couldn't be sure if he'd truly been there or if he'd dreamed it.

"I had—I thought it was a dream. I dreamed about the field and coming down off Briery Knob, and waking up in the dream, and it was real to me, and then back into a dream, and then waking up at home in bed."

"But you didn't tell [Alkire] about this, did you?" Weiford would ask Walton.

A: No, I didn't.

Q: Why not Pee Wee?

A: One thing, I couldn't remember it.

Q: Okay. Are you saying that you feel you blocked it out?

A: Yes.

The door to the interview room kept opening and closing. Alkire and several other law enforcement officers interviewed Walton for several more hours. "And I told them I thought Jacob [Beard] might have done it, I don't know for sure," Walton would testify. "And they just kept up, 'We got to know for sure,' they said. I told them—I finally broke down and said, 'Yeah, Jacob done it.'"

Johnnie Lewis was also picked up on tax day 1992 and interrogated by Estep for fifteen or twenty minutes. "Ready to talk," Estep told Alkire again, and again Alkire went in. But still Lewis backed up Cutlip's story—the two men had been together the whole day cutting locust posts and drinking beer. There had been no Rainbow girls, and he had no information about their deaths.

Lewis also was not spared Estep's methods. When Estep was again alone in the room with Lewis, he told Lewis that there were many witnesses against him and that if he went to jail he would suffer and suffer. "He shook his handcuffs at me," Lewis would testify later. "About to hit me in the face with them. I ducked back."

Then Walton gave his statement about his dream and everything else he had remembered and signed it. And the next day, according to Alkire, Lewis came back, put his head down on the investigation room table, and said that he'd seen Jacob Beard shoot the two girls.

Lewis's statement also said that he was with Gerald Brown, Arnold Cutlip, Bill McCoy, and Ritchie Fowler, but it does not say that Walton was there—nor did Walton's statement say that Lewis was there. Could there have been other people present when the girls were killed that Lewis didn't see? "Could have been."

After Lewis gave his statement, Weiford charged Walton and Lewis with two counts of first-degree murder each. Ditto Gerald Brown and Arnold Cutlip, who were promptly picked up and taken to the county jail. Warrants were prepared and sent to police in Virginia, Nevada, and Florida for the arrests of Fowler, McCoy, and Beard.

"A renewed investigation of the case led this week to the arrest of seven men in four states," reported the *New York Times* on April 19, 1992.

"This case had not been out of anyone's mind or thoughts in 12 years," reads Weiford's quote.

A Hillsboro resident named Eugene Walker told the *Charleston Daily Mail*, "No one wanted to be a rat, I guess. One of them took one of those wild fits and did it just in a rage."

"It's all you hear about," Hillsboro postmaster Priscilla Sheets told the same publication. "Everyone who comes in here has got their own version of what happened."

Alkire, Weiford, Pocahontas County sheriff Jerry Dale, and all the officers who had helped with the renewed investigation met at the Buckeye West Virginia State Police office on the night of April 19 for a little party.

Alkire faxed the arrest report for Jacob Beard to the chief of police in Crescent City, Florida, cautioning him that Beard was "extremely dangerous, use extreme caution," and advising the use of a SWAT team for his capture. But Beard had young children in his home; as a compromise, the police chief called Beard's boss at the Chevy dealership and had him call Beard late at night with a ruse—the alarm was going off over at the dealership again; could Beard drive over and check it out?

When Beard pulled up in his pickup, he was thrown to the ground, and automatic weapons were pointed at his head. He stayed in the local Florida county jail for a week until West Virginia could send a plane down to get him. When Beard stepped onto the tarmac in West Virginia, there was Alkire.

PART IV:

A PERFECT STORY

What one does not remember dictates who one loves or
fails to love.... What one does not remember is the serpent in the garden of one's dreams.

—James Baldwin

Jerry Dale (left) and Walt Weiford (right), 1993

1

WE DON'T KNOW HIM, BUT we know his story: the man who lives in the woods and goes a little bit crazy. He lives too far from the civilizing forces of law, commerce, and family, so he goes too far with his own body, his own impulses, and his own power. He lives off the land but is too close to it—he gets dirty, wet, unpredictable; he drives a monster truck, or he walks. He doesn't trust outsiders and will do anything to them in order to maintain his freedom. He is Frankenstein and Wolf Man and Grendel and Rumpelstiltskin and the Cyclops; he is the rough honky-tonker who tries to rape Thelma in *Thelma and Louise*, the trucker who rapes Aileen Wuornos in *Monster*, the rural kids full of hatred who murdered Brandon Teena, and the rural kids full of hatred who murdered Matthew Shepard. He is the psycho killer of *Deliverance*, and of *I Spit on Your Grave*, *The Last House on the Left*, *Rest Stop*, *Vacancy*, *Wrong Turn*, *Eden Lake*, *Joy Ride*, and many others. He is chaos, anarchy, and wretchedness. He must be punished or killed if we are to live any kind of life.

"Monsters do not emerge out of a cultural void," writes scholar Tina Marie Boyer. "They have a literary and cultural heritage." In other words: he does not come from nowhere.

The hick monster story has deep roots in the history of West Virginia and is wound around the story of American industrialization and capitalism. Before you can dispossess a people from their own land, you must first make them not people.

The end of the Civil War and West Virginia on the winning side should have meant fat times aplenty, but it didn't. West Virginia found itself in an odd in-between space: not yet quite the North and too recently un-tethered from the South. It was uniquely poised, and thus uniquely poised for suffering. Unlike many Northern territories, it was not fostered for growth during Reconstruction, and like many Southern territories, it was punished.

West Virginia hadn't been a state long enough to have its own lead-ership and public infrastructure, so to rebuild, it ceded control of its railroad systems to Northern companies, which would operate them as subsidiaries—forever, it would turn out. Ditto with industries that had been nascent before the war—the oil fields near Parkersburg, for example—which would eventually flourish only when a Northern firm ac-quired and operated them. Gone were the wealthy plantation owners in Virginia who would buy agricultural products from West Virginia and pa-tronize its resorts and taverns. Gone were the livestock, plucked by roving Union and Confederate soldiers alike. Congress gave away free land to those who wanted to homestead west of the Mississippi, thus subsidizing the competition in the agricultural markets that had been mainstays of West Virginia's prosperity before the war.

But a new force did arrive in West Virginia: writers. In the 1880s and 1890s, their sharp eyes flicked over the forested landscape and created a new genre, "local color" novels that capitalized on the nostalgia and curiosity people in the South and North alike felt for fast-disappearing regional differences. Stories of "simple people" in country villages and hollers called back the free life many white people had lived in the South before the war came. Pieces in *Harper's* and the *Atlantic Monthly* sold at a healthy clip, as well as later books like John Fox Jr.'s *The Trail of the Lone-some Pine* and Horace Kephart's *Our Southern Highlanders*, marking West Virginia and other mountainous regions as the home of "backwards," "strange," and "childlike" people.

"This was the period when Appalachia was discovered and named by observers for whom the differences that separated Appalachia from the rest of the nation were more compelling than the factors that united them," writes John Alexander Williams in *Appalachia: A History*. This pe-riod gave us two portrayals of Appalachia and two alone, Williams writes:

"the Appalachian mountaineer, noble and stalwart, rugged and independent, master or mistress of the highlands environment; and the profligate hillbilly, amusing but often also threatening, defined by deviance and aberration."

Scholars, educational reformers, and lawmakers hardened the ideas espoused by these novels into the idea of Appalachia as a place with a singular and strange culture. This was not a coincidence, for it is far easier to dominate a people that many regard as "other." These simplistic stories played a key role in allowing absentee corporations to gain control of the region's natural resources.

Near the end of the nineteenth century, two-thirds of West Virginia was still covered in forest, mostly ancient-growth hardwood. Soon the lumbering companies that had been in the region multiplied, establishing larger milling operations. Then came the railroads, rendering the method of floating logs down the river obsolete and allowing production to explode. Railroads needed huge amounts of cash—a commodity that was still scarce in the mountains. Enter absentee owners who lived in cities. As a girl, the poet Louise McNeill watched the trains stream over Gauley Bridge just outside Charleston. Her people toasted, she writes, "To the biggity bugs of the N&W/Who sent regrets they can't be here."

Most West Virginia officials and judges welcomed these out-of-town investors and promoted the growth of industry as progress that would create jobs. They bent laws, wrote new ones, and interpreted the constitution in favor of industrialists at every turn. With this influx of capital, lumbering exploded in the 1890s. Now equipment could be transported into, and lumber out of, territory that was previously considered too remote and craggy. More track was laid down. Jobs were abundant, and people were arriving every day to fill them, including African Americans, who flocked west from Virginia in search of greater equality and better pay.

If change had been slow to come to West Virginia directly after the Civil War, by 1900 the lumber industry was cooking with gas. To turn a profit, companies needed to harvest the timber from enormous tracts of land—and fast. For this kind of productivity, they needed lots of capital and took on heavy debt. To remain solvent in the face of all this debt, they had to be constantly producing; it was often cheaper for them to continue cutting even at a loss than to stop production for a single day.

As the machine of big lumber churned, reaching its peak in the first decade of the twentieth century, the result for West Virginians was the slashing and burning of their forests without the benefit of any lasting economic infrastructure. The land of West Virginia was skinned at a staggering pace. This was not a lumber industry, in which trees were cultivated as a crop and cut as more were planted; this was mining. A company stayed a few months, extracted the trees, and moved on.

Jobs followed the decimation—once a forest had been cut, those holding the axes and operating the mills were out of work. Some West Virginians became migratory, following the work; others would spend their lives trying to match the wages they'd made for a few months. Some tried to turn back to the farms they'd worked before, but they were gone—the forests where farmers had let their livestock roam and from which they'd drawn wood, water, and food were wastelands now. From 1880 to 1920, many West Virginia families who had previously made a good living from their farms were forced off their land and into wage labor. Or they left.

Enter coal. Of the 24,230 square miles that make up West Virginia, a total of 9,500 square miles, or 39.2 percent, is underlaid with coal—forty-three of the fifty-five counties, in whole or in part. Small-scale coal mining had been happening sustainably in pockets of the state since before the Civil War, but as the logging industry died, perfectly good railroad track was left behind, and coal rose up to take its place. Out-of-state industrialists began approaching local mining companies and offering to expand their operations, or they stole their methods and drove them out of business. Soon the great coal fields of southern West Virginia were accessible by rail, and coal towns sprang up, consisting of a mine, whatever housing the coal company decided to provide for its workers, and a store where they were obligated to buy all their goods. From 1880 to 1917, the number of miners in West Virginia grew from about four thousand to ninety thousand; the state had swapped one extractive economy for another.

"Today," say the writers of the 1941 *West Virginia: A Guide to the Mountain State*, "the State has no self-sufficient communities."

The lumber and mining booms would not be the last times Appalachia was "rediscovered" by outsiders; there were several more such occasions. When the Mine Wars raged in West Virginia from 1912 to 1922, the sophisticated organizational tactics of the coal miners and the violence of the Battle of Blair Mountain, called "the largest insurrection in US history outside the Civil War," attracted national attention. In the mid-1960s, President Kennedy's trip to the region and Lyndon Johnson's War on Poverty meant photographs of real or perceived Appalachian destitution blanketed kitchen tables across America. Finally, in the second decade of the twenty-first century, as reporters and pundits sought to explain the surging enthusiasm for Donald J. Trump, writers and cultural critics, me included, considered Appalachia with renewed interest. Again, reporters zoomed in and out and had days to construct a totalizing story. If Appalachia was "the heart of Trump country," as it was called in a flurry of articles and think pieces in 2016, it was suddenly urgent for us to understand its beating. Yet, as has been true all along, whatever blood pumps through Appalachia pumps through all of us. "The nation awoke on November 9," writes Elizabeth Catte, author of *What You Are Getting Wrong About Appalachia*, "to the news that we were all now residents of Trump Country."

2

WITH THE ARRESTS OF SEVEN local men in the spring of 1992, the
Rainbow Murders drew their first in-depth media coverage from outlets
outside West Virginia. Reporters visited Pocahontas County for a week at
a time, and citizens could spot their New York plates driving too slow on
219 or parked outside Dorie's lunch counter in Marlinton, which only fueled the community buzz over the crimes. The articles wove a narrative of
drunken backwoods hicks and sexy hippie women, of two profoundly separate value systems that had touched because of the Rainbow Gathering,
then wished they hadn't.

"The culture clash was thought to carry the potential for violence," a
September 1992 article in the *St. Petersburg Times* declared.

"The women were outsiders," wrote a *Newsday* reporter in 1992, and
"the suspects were locals....A lot of people in Pocahontas County didn't
want the hippies there, and many thought the women should know better
than to hitchhike unescorted."

These outlets also told the story that Pocahontas County was home
to "both rugged physical beauty and a few rugged people," characters
that were capable of "backwoods intrigue." The place was rural, and it
was scary, they made clear. "The bodies turned up near the driveway to
Arnold Cutlip's home, an address so remote the television was powered
by batteries."

Further, went the logic, the twelve-year lag between the murders and
the arrests was because Pocahontas County's central motivation was the
protection of its own "clan" rather than rooting out the truth.

"Local sentiment was that hillbillies killed a pair of hippies as an expression of anger over the Rainbow Gathering.... It has been suggested by several residents that the investigation dragged because the victims were from somewhere else."

"Weiford and the police deny that there was any xenophobia against the victims and point to their persistence in eventually bringing charges as proof of their lack of bias," the *Newsday* article continued.

"Jake Beard goes to a party with axes," a Hillsboro resident was quoted as saying. Other neighbors told stories that he had chainsawed animals, that he had waved a pistol at a man who had damaged his fence. A Pocahontas County resident who had moved to the area as part of the Back to the Land movement offered this view to the *St. Petersburg Times:* "Everyone knew who did those murders. I'd say a big reason nobody talked is they were all afraid of Jake Beard."

Weiford brought charges against Beard first, since he was "the trigger man," and the grand jury had found there was sufficient evidence to try him for two counts of first degree murder. In the state of West Virginia in 1992, premeditated intent could legally be formed in a tiny gap between the idea of killing someone and its execution—even a few minutes is sufficient.

Weiford's term had technically run out—he had campaigned for reelection in 1992 and lost again. But he'd spent his career steeped in the Rainbow case, so his successor deferred to Weiford, allowing him to remain on the case as a "special prosecutor."

During the winter of 1993, Pocahontas County got pounded by more than twenty inches of snow. The stream of cars that drove past Walt Weiford's house and honked hello slowed to a glide, then a skid; soon it stopped altogether. Not even the guys who had plows strapped to the front of their trucks wanted to brave it. No school for Weiford's daughter. Silent days, and Weiford spent them at home hunched over his desk, preparing his case against Beard.

A persuasive story in a court of law turns out to mean pretty much the same thing as it does in literature. Echoing Aristotle's rules for compelling drama, expert trial lawyers say that a good trial story is one in which people have reasons for the way they act, accounts for all the known facts, is supported by details, makes common sense, and is organized in a logical way, so that each piece of information naturally follows the one before it based on cause and effect.

"Your case must have both a theory and a theme," advises Steven Lubet, author of *Modern Trial Advocacy: Analysis and Practice*. A winning theory "has logical internal force," and it should be simple and easy to believe. "Even 'true' theories may be difficult to believe because they contradict everyday experiences," writes Lubet. "You must strive to eliminate all implausible elements from your theory."

The theme is the emotional center of the story that ensures that your theory will stick and persuade a jury. "Just as your theory must appeal to logic, your theme must appeal to moral force…. The most compelling themes appeal to shared values, civic virtues, or common motivations."

The hick monster story was certainly "simple" and "easy to believe" and offered more than a hint of moral force, but Weiford had his doubts about it, possibly because he himself did not believe it. "To me it wasn't a hicks versus hippies sort of thing," Weiford told the *St. Petersburg Times*. "It's not that simple."

Vicki and Nancy had not been raped; there was no evidence of sexual assault or that they had had sex of any kind before they died. Yet the story that gender and thus sexuality had played an essential role in their deaths—a flavor in the groundwater we assume we taste whenever a woman is killed—had already solidified. Alkire had been telling it to himself since the first day their bodies were found; his earliest hypotheses included "the flasher: for sexual satisfaction." Bobby Morrison told it—"Gerald Brown said something about going somewhere and getting some nookie or something like that." Gerald Brown's arrest report told it—"anger at being denied sexual satisfaction." Pee Wee Walton told it, too—the men wanted to get Vicki and Nancy somewhere alone "to see if [they] would put out."

"[The men] decided they were hippies and you know they figured, 'Hippie girls, free sex,' so they picked them up," a senior law enforcement official who asked not to be identified had also told *Newsday*. "There is no indication that these girls were interested in any kind of sexual activity, there is no indication that they were in any way 'loose.' Our impression is that [Vicki and Nancy] thought these were *nice* guys who were going to give them a ride to the Rainbow Gathering," the source continued.

Further, a great deal was made in the 1992 media coverage of the fact that Vicki and Nancy were not especially pretty. "The girls were not obese but they were bigger and heavier than average," Pam Wilson, the witness who said she had seen the women getting into the blue van, told police. Vicki was frequently described in the press as "bucktoothed" and Nancy as a "tomboy."

"Her sisters were beautiful girls," Jo-Ann Orelli, Nancy's childhood friend says. "Not that Nancy wasn't pretty, but she was stockier. Nancy was more regular [looking]."

Nancy's sister Patricia protests: "She was fine looking, she didn't look any different than us, and she certainly wouldn't have noticed or felt jealous." But Patricia's husband pipes up from the background: "Out of all of you she was definitely the least attractive."

"They were all very naturally beautiful girls," Catherine Shea, who grew up next door to the Santomeros in Huntington, told me. "Great skin, blond hair. But they weren't aware of it somehow. Their mother was the same way, able to look just wonderful without a lot of makeup. Nancy looked more like her dad."

Why do we care if a murdered or missing woman is pretty? I don't know, but we care. In 2004, Gwen Ifill of *PBS* coined the term "missing white woman syndrome" to describe what happens when, as a nation, we become obsessed with following the case of a missing or murdered white girl. Eugene Robinson of the *Washington Post* instructs that to qualify for the full treatment, the missing or murdered girl must be middle-class or higher and she must be white. "The disappearance of a man, or of a woman of color, can generate a brief flurry, but never the full damsel treatment," Robinson writes. "She must be attractive—also non-negotiable."

"It's the meta-narrative of something seen as precious and delicate being snatched away, defiled, destroyed by evil forces that lurk in the shadows, just outside the bedroom window," Robinson writes. "It's innocence and optimism crushed by cruel reality. It's a flower smashed by a rock."

When asked by the *St. Petersburg Times* in 1992 if he committed the Rainbow Murders, Jacob Beard responded by looking at photos of Vicki and Nancy and then, in a move that reveals the strange yet pervasive logic that a woman's likelihood of being raped is equal to her supposed sexual appeal, replied, "They were definitely not the type of women I'd want to have sex with. They weren't the slimmest, trimmest little things."

Vicki and Nancy were not ideal damsels then—a narrative problem, likely why the story of their deaths never became a consuming national media sensation. Weiford would have to find some other way to make them flowers and some other way to make their killer a rock.

"Lawyers must therefore pay careful attention to the fact finder's frame of reference, which in turn will be determined, at least in part, by his or her education, training, background, experiences, preferences, and biases," Lubet, the trial expert, further advises.

Weiford needed a story that would appeal specifically to a West Virginia jury—a jury that would be made up of ten West Virginia men and just two women. A bunch of guys drinking, a blue van, that straight stretch of road, went the story taking shape in Weiford's mind. Two girls (they must be girls, not women, if they are to be innocents) murdered by a group of men (they must be men, not boys, if they are to be rocks).

The theme would be how female naïveté inevitably gets smashed by male lechery and violence, and the consequences of dangerous masculinity. But not just any masculinity—specifically, local masculinity. The killer was local. The badness had come from within, and it was still within, Weiford felt. As long as Vicki and Nancy's case went unprosecuted, that bad feeling would remain. The most appealing story was not only about men crushing women, but it was also about the redemption of Pocahontas County maleness: convict this one bad apple, and our community can be made whole again. Convicting Jacob Beard would be a cleansing, a return to moral correctness and safety, the way of the gentleman and the family. This was the story Weiford chose.

3

JACOB BEARD USED HIS PHONE call when he arrived at the Florida jail in April 1992 to call not his wife but his former boss—a powerful West Virginia farmer named Charlie Long.

Long had heard rumors that Beard could be aggressive, but he never saw that behavior. Beard, he says, was sweet to his wife and young children. "If he needed a hammer, he would ask to use it before he used it. When he partied, he partied hard, when he worked, he worked hard....I don't know what his previous life was, but he was always good to me."

We'll get you the best, Long promised Beard, the absolute best. And a couple days later, two men in suits from Charleston showed up to shake Beard's hand. Robert Allen, who had once been an assistant in the US attorney's office, was in his early fifties and had a large square face. He was the senior lawyer, and it was his name on the door. This is a witch hunt, he told Beard. Pure and simple.

Stephen Farmer was a newly christened partner in Allen's firm in his early thirties. He sat with his arms crossed at that first meeting and said little, but he would be the one to give up nights and weekends preparing for Beard's case.

Allen and Farmer promptly set about trying to secure a change of venue, arguing that because of the media coverage that had saturated Pocahontas County since 1980 and the surge of articles since Beard's arrest, in which he was said to "go to parties with axes and chainsaws," he could not possibly receive a fair trial at home.

"I asked [a friend] what he thought [about the Rainbow Murders]," testified a defense witness at the hearing held to determine whether this change was necessary, "and he said, 'Well, everybody knows Jake Beard did it.' And generally speaking, I think that's the consensus of opinion."

Weiford then asked the witness where specifically he had heard the case discussed.

"Gosh, everywhere you go, Walt....K.C.'s Bar. Miss Kitty's. The Diner. Frontier Restaurant. Everywhere you go, it's discussed."

"The community appears to harbor such a fear of Beard, bordering on hysteria, deserved or not, that Mr. Beard's culpability in their eyes has already been established," Farmer wrote in his successful brief. "A change of venue must be granted, moving the trial to a location where Mr. Beard's reputation is not an issue. Only then can it be reasonably guaranteed that fact will be separated from fantasy."

Weiford had bigger problems. In June 1992, Johnnie Lewis had been reinterviewed in preparation for trial, but instead of incriminating Beard, he recanted his April 16 statement, returning once more to the original story he had told investigators in 1980 and on April 15: he had been with Arnold Cutlip all day and seen no Rainbow girls.

Then Walton told a West Virginia State Police officer that his statement had been coerced by Estep. By the middle of July, Weiford's case was screwed. The state police superintendent called all the law enforcement officers involved to an emergency meeting in Charleston. Well, he asked Weiford, can you make the case or not? Weiford told the group he had no choice but to drop the charges. "Improper investigative procedures" used by the state police had "seriously compromised the case and were going directly to the credibility and sustainability of the evidence on which they were obtained," Weiford told the Associated Press.

Back home in Pocahontas County, Weiford called Alkire. The two of them talked a long time. What about hypnosis treatment? Alkire hadn't heard of it, plus who knew if Walton or Lewis would consent to the procedure. One more time, Weiford asked, just pick them up one more time. Alkire agreed to do it.

Once again that October, Alkire drove to the Walton home in Hillsboro. Once again they stood in the yard. Would Walton be willing to be hypnotized to help him remember things? He would. He remembered. Summoned one final time for questioning without his lawyer present, Lewis again said that he'd seen Jacob Beard shoot Vicki and Nancy. Weiford recharged Beard for the murders, as well as Fowler, Brown, McCoy, and Cutlip, and filed a "conspiracy to abduct with the intent to defile"—a sex crimes charge—against Beard. Walton and Lewis were both granted immunity for their testimony but remained incarcerated "for their own protection."

Yet even in the midst of this legal cloud, the men, released on bail, went about living their lives. Brown went out drinking with McCoy's brother one night in the winter of 1993, then went back to the McCoy house afterward. Brown was in the kitchen by himself a long time, so McCoy's mother went to check on him and found him sitting in a chair, silently choking on a bite of the ham sandwich he'd made. She called for help, but no one came.

"It's called a café coronary," the medical examiner in Charleston said when they got his body. "People trying to eat, get choked on something, have a heart attack, and die. Happens all the time."

4

SUSAN STRONG ALWAYS WANTED TO be Lois Lane. A junior high teacher told her she could write, and after reading about how Woodward and Bernstein uncovered Watergate, reporting was all she wanted to do.

As Vicki and Nancy's lives as adult women were ending, Strong's was just beginning. She was two years out of high school and had been working all through the month of June 1980 fixing up the house that she and her fiancé, a man she had known since she was a freshman and he a senior, would move into. She would be leaving her parents' farm and moving up onto Droop Mountain, where she knew no one except her husband's cousins, Gerald and Drema Brown. When the Rainbow people started coming, she was excited; she went down to Marlinton to watch them arrive and wave. Then the bodies of two girls from somewhere else turned up on Briery Knob. Three weeks later, she and her husband were married.

Like most others in the county, Strong kept up with the Rainbow Murders in the paper and heard talk of the case when she went out to eat or shop for groceries or pump gas. For a time, she didn't believe the killer could be local. She preferred not to put stock in rumors. But over time, she began to believe.

By the time Strong turned thirty-three, she had two daughters and had gone back to school to get her bachelor's degree in English. She and her husband volunteered at their Lutheran church and for the Democratic Party and the Family Refuge Center. She had interned at the *Pocahontas Times* under the elderly Bill McNeel, learned fast, and gotten hired afterward.

The defense's motion for a change of venue was granted in the spring of 1993, after Beard was rearrested, and McNeel's health was failing. The trial was expected to last three weeks. Would Strong be up for making the long drive and covering it freelance? She would.

Beard's trial was assigned to Judge Charles Lobban, a balding man in his sixties with a patrician diction and a military record. His courtroom was in Lewisburg, county seat of neighboring Greenbrier County, where Beard had lived and worked for many years—not quite the distance Beard's lawyers had hoped for.

The Greenbrier County Courthouse room was neither grand nor shabby, but simply utilitarian: cream-white walls, linoleum floor tiles, windows with slatted blinds. The only things that distinguished the room from a modest Presbyterian church were the dark wood judge's podium, which matched the wood tone of the spectator benches.

Each day, Strong left her home on Droop Mountain and drove the forty minutes to the courthouse in Lewisburg. She wasn't alone, as media went; the same television firm that had covered the first Rodney King and Jeffrey Dahmer trials wanted to film the Rainbow Murder trial and air the footage on Court TV.

The defense team objected—the Lewisburg courtroom was not well-suited to being televised. There were no podiums for the lawyers upon which microphones could rest. Wires would have to be run up and behind the bench, which didn't thrill the honorable Judge Lobban, who was a few years out from retirement and prone to tripping. "Don't you want to be on national television?" the representative from Court TV asked Beard's attorney, Robert Allen. "No," responded Allen, "I would rather be on the farm."

But Court TV prevailed. The accommodations were made, and people around the United States could now watch a West Virginia murder trial on their television for the first time. "As you leave the courtroom you might smile," the affable Judge Lobban would later tell a group of children visiting the proceedings for a school trip. "You may find you're on camera."

The potential jurors were exceedingly polite to Beard's lawyers and to Weiford during jury selection. Though they had large farms to run, gardens to weed, children to watch, and sick parents to care for, they were not eager to evade jury service—*No, it's fine; my farm is rented. It's no problem; I'll get a babysitter.*

Two male potential jurors had mothers who were retired correctional officers at the women's prison in Alderson, twenty miles away, where Martha Stewart would one day do her time. One juror had a father who had been murdered. One potential juror had himself been a correctional officer.

"Do you think that that has had any impact or influence on your thinking as to people that have been accused of a crime?" asked Mr. Allen.

"No," the juror responded. "If anything, in my opinion, it would probably be for me more reassuring that I did have an open mind, from seeing, you know, both sides of the tracks. I deal with the facts. I mean, if I don't see it, it didn't happen."

Lobban addressed the potential jurors. How many of the jurors had already read something about the case? All but three jurors responded that they had. Read something about it in the last two or three days? Nine hands. Talked to someone about it? Ten.

Mr. Farmer then asked a question. "Have any of you ever been involved in a situation where you felt that something happened in a certain way, and therefore tried to reconcile or conform facts to support that view of what happened?"

Judge Lobban interrupted: "That's probably human. Everybody does that some."

5

THERE WAS ONLY ONE MOTEL in Lewisburg—the Brier Inn—and everyone ended up there. Nancy's mother, Jeanne, and her sister Kathy, coming from Long Island, took a room, as did Vicki's sister Mary and her cousin DeAnn. Nancy's father, though traveling separately, got a room there too.

Defense attorneys Allen and Farmer also took rooms at the inn, and Allen's room ended up being next door to Mary and DeAnn's. Allowed to go free on bond during the trial, Beard stayed there, too, in his own room. He and Linda had separated in December 1992 after his arrest in Florida. "Mr. Beard reports that they were having problems for 'a couple of years,' and then charges pertaining to the current matter were filed," reads a court form. "That ended it."

Allen told Beard it was important to look rested, but Beard had trouble sleeping. No family or children or friends came to support him, though from time to time there would be someone in the courtroom he knew. After the proceedings each day, he'd go out to eat alone at one of Lewisburg's restaurants and then meet with Allen and Farmer in Allen's room to go over the next day's testimony. At night and through the wall, Vicki's sister and cousin could almost hear Beard and his attorneys' voices asking questions, cracking sodas, cracking jokes.

The *State of West Virginia* v. *Jacob Wilson Beard* lasted twelve days, during which time reporters and camera people from news outlets both West Virginian and national sat in the press benches and bumped into each other on the stairwell landing on the way to the courtroom. Strong soaked up as much advice as she could from the other reporters. She took a liking to the seasoned vet representing the *Roanoke Times;* anytime he took a break for a cigarette or a cup of coffee, Strong asked him the questions for which she hadn't been able to get answers. What's it like to get hate mail? How do you get an interview with someone who won't return your calls?

Walt Weiford, commuting from his home an hour away, sat alone at the desk reserved for the prosecution, though Robert Alkire and Sheriff Jerry Dale, also making the long daily drive, were never far away. Nancy and Vicki's female relatives sat together in the first row, four across. Twenty-five citizens of Pocahontas County were called as witnesses, and over the course of the twelve days, they, too, were there.

May 19, 1993, was a Wednesday. Bill Clinton had been president for five months. The most listened-to song on the radio was Janet Jackson's "That's the Way Love Goes." Judge Lobban smiled for the camera, then told special prosecuting attorney Walt Weiford to proceed. The back of Weiford's head was the only part of his body that was visible to a courtroom observer when he rose from his wooden chair and stood, angling his body toward the jury. He spoke slowly and without great passion.

"Yesterday, several times we had the opportunity for some levity and a laugh or two," he said. "We were able to break the ice and sort of get familiar with each other. But today I am sure you understand by looking—with the looks on your face, we are about serious business."

Weiford then addressed what he felt had been two widespread misconceptions: first, Vicki and Nancy were not interchangeable members of an ideological group, but rather individuals—real women with real families and friends. Second, the Rainbow people were much less strange and organized than they had been made to seem. "It's not a sect. It's not a cult. It's a group of people with a common view of life that get together, spend time with each other."

Weiford tugged on his tie, then on each of the cuffs of his starched white shirt in a series of movements he repeated as he spoke—tie, cuff, cuff; tie, cuff, cuff; a gesture of nerves perhaps, or only a way to mark his internal rhythm.

"There was some partying going on there. The testimony will even suggest that there were efforts to engage the girls in sexual activity. An eyewitness will even say that there was some struggle. Some man-handling of the girls. That they began to be concerned again about their circumstances, and even suggested if they weren't allowed to leave or weren't taken somewhere, they were going to go to the law.

"Now, the testimony will tend to show that shortly after these comments were made by these young women, and really for reasons that may never be clear, absolutely clear to anybody, perhaps out of anger, perhaps out of ridicule, frustration, for whatever purpose—and it would have been a senseless purpose—this defendant, Jake Beard"—a long pause here, a turning toward Jacob Beard and an arm gesturing at him with fingers splayed—"obtained a gun and shot both girls dead."

Weiford explained to the jury that there would be little in the way of physical evidence. No murder weapon was ever found. There would be no fingerprints and no DNA evidence, which was not widely used in the United States until the mid-1990s. Instead the prosecution's case would be made by two witnesses, Pee Wee Walton and Johnnie Washington Lewis. Their testimony would not be spotless, Weiford conceded— Lewis was "not [a] very sophisticated" person, and Walton had been highly intoxicated—but they were determined to tell the truth as best they knew it.

Weiford spoke a long time before he realized he'd gone on too long, then rushed to wrap up. He asked the jury to keep their minds open and their eyes "on the ball."

"Now, if you will do that, and if you will do what I am asking you right now, then the defendant will receive a fair trial. And that's what he asks for, and that's what he has a right to.... And if you will do those things, the verdict that you reach will be a correct one, according to the law and the evidence and the instructions of the court, and justice will be done."

Stephen Farmer rose and buttoned his suit jacket. His head stood significantly higher than Weiford's had, a great tuft of dark bushy hair, the top of which bobbled slightly as he spoke. He stood at a small music stand the Court TV man had procured as a podium, and the camera caught him in exact side profile. His air was more urbane than Weiford's but less polished.

"Bob Allen over here, and I, are proud to stand before you on behalf of Jacob Beard, a fellow who grew up over in Pocahontas County, and who is charged with killing these two girls," Farmer said, at a louder volume than Weiford had been using. "Mr. Beard is a man who is not guilty. And it is my job to give you the facts and to show you that he is not guilty."

Farmer reminded the jury that it is not the defense's job to prove Beard innocent but rather to prove that the state had not succeeded in making its case beyond a reasonable doubt. With that, he turned to poking holes in the state's version of events. But where Weiford's statement flowed and centered around a single theory and theme, Farmer's jumped from idea to idea in a seemingly arbitrary manner.

He framed his case as a reaction to that of Weiford, saying that the state's problem was not what they would say, but what they would leave out. "The state did not tell you that their witness, for instance, Winters Walton…witnessed two girls being shot to their death at point-blank, and forgot it for thirteen years. Not that he didn't tell anybody. Not that he was trying to hide anything. Just that he didn't remember it."

Farmer recapped Beard's phone call to the Durians and Morrison's confession against Gerald Brown and argued that from 1983 forward, Alkire and Weiford were focused on Beard as a suspect to such a degree that they consciously disregarded evidence of other theories.

"Now, ladies and gentlemen," Farmer concluded. "I concur with the one thing the prosecutor said, that this is a very serious situation. Mr. Beard wants you to pay attention to this case. Wants you to listen to the evidence. Wants you to determine whether or not he is guilty or not guilty. Ladies and gentlemen, from the evidence in this case, we believe that you will have only one conclusion, and that is that Mr. Beard is not guilty. Thank you."

By the second day, the trial was drawing forty spectators. Barry Adams, a Rainbow member who had attended the 1980 Gathering and helped Alkire pass the photos of the dead bodies around the camp, sat in the last row with a small group of other Rainbows. "We're here to see what kind of a show trial this is," he told the *Charleston Gazette*. Adams tended to believe that Vicki and Nancy were murdered as an attack on the Rainbow people and their way of life; he was suspicious of those in power in Pocahontas County and of law enforcement. "Police, government folks, they tend to be on our case. They tend to think we're outlaws. And in reality, we're pretty strong about the principles of the Constitution."

Barbara Thymius, a retired nurse and volunteer with a Greenbrier County organization that offered services to abused women, came every day of the trial and watched the proceedings from the second row, sitting just behind Nancy's mother. She was propelled by a desire to witness and to keep watch, she said, as women often did not get a fair shake at trial, whether as victim or defendant.

"I think it's a liars' contest if you want to know the truth," Thymius said.

Tim, who had found Vicki and Nancy's bodies late that summer night thirteen years earlier, took the stand for the prosecution as the very first witness after opening statements. He wasn't a young man anymore, but an accomplished local doctor who had built a life for himself and his family in these mountains. He laid out all the back roads in tenths of a mile and yards and all the possible ways the clearing could be accessed from each direction. He described to the court how the bodies looked—rumpled, as if they'd fallen or been moved. He told the courtroom how isolated and little-traveled Briery Knob was. He lived still, he told the jury, only a few minutes' drive from that spot.

Dr. Irvin Sopher, sporting a head of gray hair more robust than would be expected of a man in his sixties and a face so pink it looked slapped, testified next. Now the chief medical examiner for the state of West Virginia, Sopher had once participated in the exhumation of Lee Harvey Oswald. Sopher spoke in elegant jargon like the television doctor Quincy. He cocked his hands into guns and leaned far back in the witness chair. To better gesture at enlarged line drawings of two human bodies punctured by bullets, he wanted to use an easel.

"If that would be helpful, you may do that," Judge Lobban told him. "If there is room to set it up there. Maybe it will lean."

The two bullets that killed Vicki, Sopher testified, were discharged from a distance of about a foot, entered through the top of her left breast, punctured her heart and lungs, and exited her back near her right kidney. The shot paths were roughly parallel to each other, Sopher explained, indicating that they had been fired in quick succession.

"This is a markedly downward path," Sopher emphasized, about a forty-five-degree angle, which would be very unusual if the person was shot while standing upright. He suggested that Vicki must have been seated or bent over. "Unless someone were standing on a ladder or a chair, but that doesn't make much sense, you see."

Nancy was also shot at a close range of about a foot, once in the head at an angle more or less parallel to the ground and twice at a downward angle—one shot entered her chest near her collarbone and exited through her back near her right lung. The other had "a very peculiar angle," Sopher testified, entering and exiting her right breast from top to bottom, suggesting she may have been bent forward at the time of impact. Unlike the other two, either one of which would have been enough to kill, this shot would not have been fatal and the lack of hemorrhage suggests it might have been fired after Nancy's heart stopped beating.

Cross-examining Sopher, Allen then asked, "Are any of those wounds consistent with anybody running away and running up a hill?"

"If they were flexed at the waist. But they would have to be running toward the weapon."

The time of death, essential in establishing the prosecution's theory of the crime, was hotly disputed. Sopher had originally said that the women most likely died around 7 pm, which would make it hard for Beard to have been the killer, since he was at the school board meeting in Marlinton, about forty minutes away, by 7:30 pm. On the stand, Sopher now said that he could not be certain. He was not Quincy after all. By his best estimate, the murders probably occurred between 6 and 9 pm but could have happened as early as 2 pm.

Christine Cook took the stand next. Pee Wee Walton had said in police statements that he saw Cook on Droop Mountain that day talking to the Rainbow girls, so she was an important element of propping up one of the main eyewitnesses to the crime. By now she lived in Morgantown, working as a unit clerk for the army and even had a new name, having separated from Paulmer Adkison. She now said that she "could not swear to it," but she thought that Johnnie Lewis was there, riding with Arnold Cutlip. Later, she said, a "bunch of people" ended up on Droop Mountain. "I think Bill McCoy was there. And Richie [misspelling in transcript] Fowler. I think Gerald Brown may have stopped by." Cook said that everybody was talking about the Rainbow family and wondering why they had come to Pocahontas County. Some of the men had been out to the Rainbow camp to check out the scene. When asked if she knew Beard or had ever met him before, she said she didn't think so and didn't think he had been there that day on Droop.

Cook was equally vague on the sequence of events. She said she thought the latest she was on Droop was 5 pm, but again she was not certain.

"Did you see any girls there that day there at the park?" asked Walt Weiford.

A: I don't believe so. Again, I couldn't swear to it, because it's a long time ago. And I don't believe there was any girls in the van . . .

Q: Was there drinking going on there at the park?

A: Yes, there was.

Q: A great deal?

A: Yes. They always drank a great deal.

Q: What was being consumed?

A: Seven and seven—and I forgot what all they drank. A lot of liquor and a lot of beer.

Q: Do you recall advising Sergeant Alkire that this was a time of your life that you wanted to forget?

A: Yes, because it's a lot of bad memories. I am sure people like to put their pasts behind them.

On the morning of the third day, locals William Scott, Sis Hively, and Steven Goode testified to seeing Beard racing his truck up the road at the entrance to Droop Mountain State Park, Beard's intoxication at the school board meeting, and his presence at Gerald Brown's trailer that night on Droop Mountain, respectively. Pamela Wilson, narrow, with power bangs, read into evidence her 1992 statement that she'd seen two "hippie-type girls" get into a blue van driven by Richard Fowler.

Bobby Lee Morrison was thirty by now, work-strong and handsome in a flannel shirt, with a thick mustache and hair that hung down past his collar. When the Court TV footage aired, the anchor asked the guest commentator if Morrison was dressed appropriately for court. She would have thought not, the anchor said, "but hey, you're in West Virginia."

Weiford needed Morrison to testify that Jacob Beard had bullied and threatened him into making false statements; Farmer wanted to offer Morrison as a possible alternative suspect—after all, he had once given a detailed murder confession that lined up with some of the facts.

During cross-examination after the lunch break, Farmer took Morrison through every element of his later recanted 1983 confession against Gerald Brown, demanding to know where Morrison "got" various details—how much each of the women had to drink, the mud puddle he had described, the brush under which their backpacks were found. Morrison again claimed that Beard had told him key pieces of evidence about the events so that his statement incriminating Brown would be more believable. But Morrison gave conflicting information about the source of his facts—he had told the grand jury that the police gave him the information that one of the women had drunk more alcohol than the other, but at trial, he said that Beard had told him that. As Farmer cross-examined him, Morrison's jaw, set in anger, clicked back and forth. His knee, where his baseball cap rested, jiggled up and down.

> Q: You also told them that you just made that information up out of the whole cloth, didn't you?
> A: I don't think so.
> Q: "Answer: I was—that was made up."

"Question: Who made it up? Answer: I did." Nobody told you that information, did they?

A: Mr. Beard told me that one of them was supposed to have drunk and the other one wasn't supposed to have drunk.

Q: Then why did you tell the grand jury in 1983 that you just made it up?

A: I think that was recanted wasn't it?

Q: That's what you're saying here. . . . That's what you said isn't it?

A: I don't remember . . .

Q: If Sergeant Alkire and Trooper Lanham would say that you were threatened in jail by Gerald Brown to change your story would that be a lie?

A: I don't think so, because I don't think I was threatened in jail by Gerald Brown.

Q: Did you tell these law enforcement people that the reason you were changing your story to implicate Jake Beard after being in jail with Gerald Brown . . . was because Gerald Brown had threatened you, would that be a lie?

A: I don't know, cause I don't think I was ever threatened in jail by Gerald Brown.

Q: Did you tell these gentleman, these law enforcement people, that you were threatened by Gerald Brown to change your story to implicate Mr. Beard?

A: I don't think so.

Q: You don't remember?

A: No, I don't.

Q: How many murders have you witnessed?

A: I have never witnessed any murders.

Q: How many murders have you given statements on and confessed to?

A: None, that I know of.

Q: This is the only one?

A: Yes.

Q: And you don't remember?

A: No I don't.

To observers, including the Court TV commentators, it was hard not to wonder about the truthfulness of Morrison's testimony. After a commercial break, the anchor turned to her commentator. "Let me ask you, Matthew, about what we just saw with the cross-examination of this witness who at one point snapped at the defense attorney there."

"Well, I'm upset, and let me tell you why," responded her guest. "[Morrison] remembers something from thirteen years ago, doesn't remember something from yesterday. He says he's been threatened by Mr. Beard.... What's he holding back?"

In his closing argument, Farmer, too, would harp on Morrison's hostility and strange demeanor.

"How many times did [Bobby Morrison] say 'I don't know' to a difficult question? Did you notice that the entire time he was in the courtroom he did not look at you, he did not look at me, and most of all he never once laid eyes on Jake Beard? The entire time he testified he looked directly at that back wall and thought to himself, when is this hell gonna be over?"

Alkire's testimony and cross-examination, with the aid of a big black binder of his notes, took up the better part of the trial's second week, interspersed with other witnesses for scheduling reasons. Though only in his early forties, the hair on both sides of Alkire's head was a distinctly lighter shade of gray than the top and front, which flopped, Bieber style, onto his forehead. His green, short-sleeved West Virginia State Police uniform was adorned with black and gold patches on both shoulders and the metal badges that marked him as a first sergeant. He looked attentive, eager, and exhausted—the dark areas underneath his small eyes were the size of quarters. He answered many of Weiford's questions with a quick, courteous "yes, sir" or "no, sir."

Alkire testified that Beard fell under suspicion because of the telephone calls he placed to the Durian house in 1982, but after that, Beard was an informant of sorts, providing investigators with ideas, none of which led to any evidence in the case.

"Local people did the killing," Alkire quoted Beard as saying.

Stephen Farmer conducted a long cross-examination that pushed hard on Alkire. Farmer stood on Alkire's left and very close, such that Alkire was obliged to turn his head to look at Farmer and answer his questions, and the cameras took Alkire mostly in right profile. Farmer was combative, aggressive even, while Alkire seemed calm, folksy, wrongly attacked. Farmer read Bobby Morrison's confession back to Alkire.

Q: Did you provide him with that information or did he provide it to you?

A: He provided it to me.

Q: You did not lead him or provide him with any of that information?

A: No sir.

Q: To the extent that he says that you provided him with any information, is he not telling the truth?

A: That I provided him with this information? I did not provide him with this information.

Q: Were you careful not to ask him questions in a manner that would give him the answer?

A: Well, absolutely, yes sir.

Q: So if he says that you intentionally or inadvertently asked him questions in a manner which would clue him into the answer, would that be a lie?

A: It would be an accident on my part, if I did. I can't say that I don't make mistakes. I could have asked a leading question, but I try to stay away from that, yes sir.

Farmer continued reading Bobby Lee Morrison's statement and underscored that in 1983, Alkire had felt that Morrison had so much information about the case—including information not released to the public—that he had to have been there. Alkire agreed that he had felt that way in 1983 and had testified as such to a grand jury, but had since changed his mind and lost confidence in Morrison's statement. Over and over, Farmer tried to show that Morrison's story was specific and accurate, while Alkire tried to politely push back, asserting that it was more or less in line with the facts, if a little vague.

"If you're going to vent your anger at a witness and you're gonna try to prove that some sort of conspiracy had taken place, pick on Bobby Lee," the Court TV commentator said later. "The jury would much prefer that than picking on nice old Officer Alkire."

He also criticized Farmer's overall strategy: "Why not start right out and say, 'There are other people who had motives; there are statements that were made....' This is thirteen years later. They can't go after the dead man [Gerald Brown], so why not go after Mr. Beard? Nobody likes him anyway!" He felt Farmer was not presenting a strong story, wholly separate from the story Weiford was telling, to the jury.

Liz Johndrow, now thirty-one and living in Vermont, traveled with her boyfriend for the trial. Walking through the hallway, she came face-to-face with Nancy's dad. He took Liz in his arms. A lot of weeping.

Liz was sorry, she told Nancy's dad, but she couldn't give him what he was looking for.

Liz's hair was cut short and held back by a thick black headband. She wore a beige suit jacket that was too big for her, even with its prominent shoulder pads. Her face and lips were pale too; the only color on her person came from her nose, which was red, and her eyebrows, which were dark and thin and perfectly horizontal. On the witness stand, she looked focused yet far away, determined to remember the truth, but with little access to it. She took long pauses after each question and a few times counted things out on her fingers.

After she had been sworn in, Weiford asked Liz where she lived now, and she answered him—but very quietly.

"If you would speak up so that everyone can hear you. You say you live in Brattleboro, Vermont?"

Weiford continued to struggle to hear Liz. Later in the testimony, Stephen Farmer also interrupted Liz, saying he could not hear her.

Judge Lobban turned to Liz then. "Miss Johndrow, I think the jury is straining also to have to hear you.... Your testimony is going for naught."

Weiford led Liz through each step in her journey with Vicki and Nancy. After leaving the beach in South Carolina, the trio boarded an empty Trailways bus that took them to Fayetteville, North Carolina, where Liz called home and decided not to go to the Gathering. After informing Vicki and Nancy of her change of heart, Liz testified, "they would head to the Gathering, and I would head to Vermont." Liz looked down at the courtroom floor a long time as she said the word "Vermont" and did not lift her eyes even when Weiford started his next question.

The next morning, Liz testified, they got a ride north on I-95 with a commuter headed into work who dropped them at a truck stop outside Richmond, Virginia. There was a diner there, and the women went in, even though they had no money—loose change, maybe.

"It was like morning," Liz testified. "People were in there having breakfast. This person bought us coffee. And we were just kind of saying our good-byes and making plans for Vicki and Nancy to come up to Vermont after the Gathering."

As she spoke, Liz put a question mark at the end of each of her sentences. "And then we walked out to the road, and I don't remember exactly what road? And I just remember, I—when we parted, I was on one side, they were on the other? We were headed"—Liz held her hands out wide to her sides then brought them together—"in different directions?"

"Still hitchhiking?"

"Yeah, and they waited until I got a ride because they were concerned. You know, about me taking off by myself."

"So they were still there when you got a ride?"

"They were still there."

In some newspaper articles from 1980, Liz is quoted as saying that she left Vicki and Nancy around noon or one o'clock on June 25, the day they died, and in others the same time on June 24; Alkire's notes from that time indicate that she told police June 25. In court, however, Liz testified that she left them on June 24. The date matters—it would help prove or disprove the prosecution's theory that Vicki and Nancy had been killed in the afternoon of June 25 in time for Jacob Beard to make it to the school board meeting at 7 o'clock that night. Richmond sits about 235 miles from where Vicki and Nancy were found, a drive of about six hours at 1980 speed limits, so if Liz parted from the women at noon at the earliest on June 25, the state's timeline of the women getting killed in the afternoon would not work.

As Stephen Farmer cross-examined Liz, pointing out the different date she had given in 1980, she listened to his questions but again stared at that spot on the courtroom floor, not meeting his eyes. She scrunched her eyebrows and moved her lips while Farmer spoke, repeating the names of the places he mentioned. She touched her fingers to her eyes and leaned back heavily in the wooden chair.

"Is Charleston, South Carolina, near Sullivan's Island?" she asked Farmer at one point instead of answering his question. "I don't even know where Charleston, South Carolina, is."

Farmer reminded Liz that when she first spoke with him in preparation for this trial, she was still convinced that she left Vicki and Nancy on Wednesday, June 25, not least because she remembered she arrived home in Vermont later that day and her mother and brother were out at their Al-Anon meeting, a thing they usually did on Wednesday nights. Liz made the switch to Tuesday, June 24, she testified, after talking with Alkire and other members of the state police, who helped her to count the days the trio were on the road and map their route. "It kept coming out to being the 24th," she testified.

"Both attorneys on Beard's defense team reacted visibly," Strong reported, when Liz said this.

Criminal trials are long, tedious affairs, more paperwork and logistics than dramatic utterances, and by the time Pee Wee Walton took the stand, it was the trial's seventh day, Thursday, May 27, 1993. When Walton was sworn in that morning, his face was already red, and his eyes, behind clear aviator-style glasses, looked wet. His hair was parted to the side, and he wore a brown blazer over a navy blue, vertically striped, button-up shirt; the top button was undone, so his white undershirt was exposed. He interlaced his hands in front of him.

"Do you have a clear recollection of the events of that day?" Weiford asked, consulting his notes, which were handwritten on a yellow legal pad and sat on the music stand he was using as a lectern.

"Yes, I do," Walton said in a jaunty, eager voice that was a bit at odds with the somberness of the occasion.

The beginning of Walton's testimony was unchanged from the story he'd first told Alkire on his lawn, but the ending was different. Yes, he and Ritchie Fowler and Bill McCoy had been sitting at the top of Droop Mountain off Route 219 at CJ's store on June 25, 1980. Yes, they had spent the morning going to town for liquor and beer, then driving around shooting groundhogs and drinking. Yes, they had a .22 caliber pistol they had been using on the groundhogs. But then, Walton's story now continued, someone drove by and told him and the other men that there were two girls hitchhiking down on the Renick Flats. Walton didn't want to go and asked Fowler and McCoy to take him home if they were going to pick up the women. But Fowler, who was driving, lobbied for it and said they could just go and look at the girls—they didn't have to pick them up.

"Okay. What did you all do?" Weiford asked Walton. Walton responded:

```
    A:  We drove down there in Renicks Valley, and
where the girls was at. We slowed down a little
bit. And drove by. . . . We seen two girls standing
along the road. . . . They was standing there just
with their knapsacks on the side of the road,
waiting for a ride, I think. We drove on down to
the next road that turned—secondary road, right
below there, and turned. We sat there
```

```
awhile. . . . Rich and Bill was discussing picking
them up. I thought they was just going to go on by
and not pick them up.
```

But they did turn back and pick the women up, according to Walton. It was McCoy who got out, talked with Vicki and Nancy, and helped them get their belongings inside. Fowler's van was a '70s captain's style with big seats and a plush bed in the back. According to Walton, Fowler told Vicki and Nancy he was headed the way they were going but first needed to stop at his boss's—Gerald Brown's—trailer on Droop Mountain to pick up a paycheck. They went there and stayed about an hour. Walton claimed that when they got to Brown's trailer, McCoy called around to more friends, "Let's have a party. We picked up a couple of girl hitchhikers." They then drove on to the entrance of Droop Mountain Battlefield State Park, where they drank more and met up with Arnold Cutlip, Johnnie Lewis, Gerald Brown, Paulmer Adkison, Christine Cook, another man named Larry Dean, and Jacob Beard.

```
A:  I heard something, said that they was won-
dering where they could take them to.
Q:  . . . What do you mean?
A:  They was wanting to take them somewhere, to
get them off the road by theirself or something.
```

According to Walton, Cutlip then came over to the van to look at the women, then returned to where his vehicle was parked to discuss potential secluded spots where they could take the women. After that, he said, Cook left with Adkison.

```
Q:  What's the next thing you can remember?
A:  . . . Rich and Bill had—said something about
they was going to see if the girls would put out
for them or something. And they got in the van
with them.
```

Q: When you say "put out," Pee Wee, what do
you mean?
A: Have sex with them.

This many men meant several vehicles, and the caravan then proceeded deeper into the state park and then through the park to a popular party spot. Two of the men then assaulted Vicki and Nancy, Walton claimed, pulling their hands behind their backs and feeling them up. McCoy asked Walton for his pistol so he could threaten the women into having sex. When asked what Vicki and Nancy were doing at this point, Walton described "the shorter one"—Nancy—as not putting up much of a struggle.

"The other one"—Vicki with "the teeth that stuck out"—"was fighting with Bill quite a bit.... She was hollering that she was gonna go to the law."

"Then," Walton paused, stumbled on his words, reddened, and touched his mustache with the index finger of his left hand.

A: I believe, Bill said something like, uh,
"we kill people, we'll kill y'all," or
something. . . . The girl that had the teeth that
stuck out, she come over, got away from Bill some.
Bill was with Ritchie towards the other girl. She
came to me and she asked me. I was on the [van]
bed at that time sitting back in the corner. And
she asked me why was we doing this to them. And I
told her, I ain't doing nothing to you. And Bill
came back over and got her.

The women continued to refuse sex, according to Walton, and the men eventually gave up on the idea of raping them, which they seemed to regard as no great failure, according to Walton. "Rich said they ain't gonna put out for us...just party."

Soon more men showed up, apparently just cruising around the woods, or perhaps called to the party, and the tension was diffused. According to Walton, Vicki and Nancy were then left unattended while the men talked, drank, and went to check out guns, a homebrew operation, and a camper. Fowler had brought the weed and rolled a joint, which everybody smoked; some people, including Walton, were also drinking liquor and beer. Vicki and Nancy were now standing outside the van.

Sitting among the other journalists in the Greenbrier courtroom, Susan Strong watched Walton lose his composure as he spoke of what happened next. Walton stayed in the van while Fowler got out of it.

"What's the next thing you can remember?" Weiford asked, with great gentleness.

A: Everybody jumping up there in the van, I guess when the first shot was fired.

Q: Did you hear a shot?

A: At this time, I can't, I can't say if I did or not.

Q: Do you remember people jumping in the van?

A: Yes. Everybody stood up and was standing around . . .

Q: What's the next thing you can remember, Pee Wee?

A: The girl running up into the doorway and backing out.

Q: What doorway?

A: The sliding door on the side.

Q: Can you remember which girl that was?

A: I think it was the one with the buck teeth.

Q: Do you remember it clearly or could you be mistaken?

A: No it seemed pretty clear.

Q: OK. What do you remember next?

A: A person coming up into the doorway with a rifle. Like this.

Q: Do you remember who that was?

A: I'm not really sure. It had to have been
Jacob since he's the only one who had the rifle.

Q: You said it would have to have been Jacob?

A: Well I guess it couldn't have to have been,
I'm not for sure if there was anyone behind the
van or not.

Q: Did you ever see anybody else holding the
gun?

A: Just Arnie, they was up in front of the
van.

Q: Was it Arnie with the gun?

A: No.

Q: Was it Gerald?

A: No.

Q: Was it Bill?

A: I don't know.

Q: Was it Rich?

A: He was in the van.

Q: Was it Jacob?

A: All I can remember is just seeing the person right there with the rifle in his hand.

Q: What kind of condition were you in at this
point?

A: Pretty well just about ready to black out I
think.

Q: Because of what?

A: The whole mixture of things I guess. Drinking and smoking that pot and beer and whiskey.

Q: Were you afraid?

A: Um, I think it was a little too much
drinking to even be afraid. It I guess scared me,
had to.

Q: Do you remember what you did?

A: Just sat there, I think.

Q: You remember what you were looking at, what
you were seeing?

A: Just the girl and the guy and the gun.

During Walton's cross-examination, which would take the rest of the morning until lunch and then the rest of the afternoon after it, Stephen Farmer paced between his notes on the music stand and the dark wooden chair that served as the witness stand. Farmer pressed hard, asking when Walton first asserted that he remembered being there when the Rainbow girls were killed, and digging deeply into Walton's mental state.

Q: And you were convinced that over the years
on occasion you had dreamed it?

A: I thought I did, yeah.

Q: And during those years you drank daily, did
you not?

A: No not daily.

Q: Regularly.

A: Pretty often yeah.

Q: And when you drank you didn't drink socially did you?

A: No.

Q: You drank to get drunk. Correct?

A: Sometimes, yeah.

Q: Week in and week out, from 1980 to 1992. Is
it so?

A: Pretty well, yeah.

Q: You spent a significant portion of your
life between 1980 and 1992 drinking whiskey.
Right?

A: (Silence)

Q: Correct?

A: Pretty well, yeah.

Nearing the end of the morning session, Farmer pulled out a white piece of standard printer paper and held it in both hands with his finger tips. It was a list of names and facts that the West Virginia State Police officers had shown to Walton on April 15, 1992, Farmer said, the day Walton was interviewed and assaulted by Estep, and the day he made his statement against Beard. Walton stated that one of the officers—he believed it was Estep though he couldn't be sure—had shown him that piece of paper, which contained the phrase "blue van," and that it was the officers who had given Walton that detail and told him they knew he had been in a blue van that day.

Q: Now was this before Sergeant Estep beat you up or after?

A: I'm not sure.

Q: It was before you gave any statement wasn't it?

A: Yes.

Q: And they told you that they knew you were with Ritchie Fowler. It was not you telling them you were with Ritchie Fowler, it was them telling you that you were with Ritchie Fowler, correct?

A: Yes . . .

Q: And they also said, Jake Beard, Buddy [Adkison], Gerald Brown, Pee Wee Walton, Arnie Cutlip and Bobby Morrison, right?

A: Yeah.

Q: Those are the names on that piece of paper that the state police showed you before they took your statement that day, isn't it?

A: Yeah.

When Johnnie Lewis settled his beautiful body in the witness chair the following morning, the apprehension in the courtroom was palpable. Lewis was remarkably tall and thin; his cheekbones ran hard from his

long, slender nose straight back to his ears, which were so distinctly separated from his jawline that he looked as if he'd lost a part of it shaving. His
voice was low; he blinked often and looked down at his hands. He wore
a long-sleeved, thick, brown work shirt with a buttoned pocket on each
breast. He seemed unable to read or write and could barely sign his name.

Judge Lobban asked Johnnie Lewis if he understood he was under oath.
Lewis responded that he did. Lobban then told him, "Mr. Arbuckle is
your attorney, and he is seated at the bench and will be available if you
need to make any inquiry of him during your testimony."

Lewis acknowledged that he'd heard this, so Weiford proceeded, even
more gently than he had with Walton, speaking lower and slower. He
asked Lewis his name, and Lewis answered shyly.

"Johnnie, I just want you to relax," Weiford said. "You don't need to be
nervous, okay? All of these people just want to hear the truth, okay?"

"Okay."

Lewis was living then with another friend, helping him out on his
farm. Before that, he had lived with yet another friend, three or four
miles down the road from where he currently lived. When Weiford asked
where Lewis had lived during the summer of 1980, he said he could not
remember for sure.

Weiford led Lewis toward the moment when Vicki and Nancy were allegedly standing up against the van.

> Q: OK. Now, let me ask you Johnny [misspelling
> in transcript], were you paying a lot of attention
> to what was going on?
> A: Yeah. Not much. Not much attention.
> Q: Did you hear anything?
> A: No.
> Q: What's the next thing you saw?
> A: The girls fall. The gun cracked. The girls
> fall.
> Q: You heard a gun crack?
> A: Yeah.

Q: Where did the crack of the gun seem to be coming from?

A: Jacob.

Q: From Jacob?

A: His hand raised.

Q: Now which direction was he facing?

A: He was facing, his back to me.

Q: His back was to you?

A: Yeah.

Q: Was there anybody else standing around there?

A: Bill, Ritchie.

Q: Where were the girls at?

A: At the van.

Q: How close to the van was Jacob?

A: That table there . . .

Q: Now, did you hear the gun crack more than one time?

A: Three. Two times actually. Two times. Three times all together. I just hear it three times, all I can remember.

Q: What happened when you heard the gun crack the first time?

A: (Silence)

Q: What did you see?

A: The girls fall. A girl fell.

Q: A girl fell? Where did she fall at?

A: Behind the van.

Q: And when the gun cracked what did you see?

A: The girl fall.

Q: OK, anything else?

A: No. The other one started to run.

Q: The other one started to run? Did you see anybody move other than the girls?

```
A:  No.
Q:  Did Ritchie move?
A:  No.
Q:  Did Bill move?
A:  Uh uh.
Q:  Did Jacob move?
A:  No, he stood.
Q:  What's the next thing you saw?
A:  The other girl fall.
Q:  Did you hear anything?
A:  Two shots.
Q:  Where were the shots coming from?
A:  Jacob, I reckon. As far as I can tell.
Q:  How could you tell that?
A:  His arm raised.
Q:  And after the gun cracked again what did
you see?
A:  The girl fall.
```

Weiford paused, perhaps sensing he was reaching the end, and asked if Lewis knew Walton. "Yeah, I seen him," Lewis responded, but when asked if he had seen Walton that day, Lewis answered clearly that no, he had not, though he admitted it was possible that Walton had been in the van and Lewis had not seen him there.

```
Q:  Did you drink a good bit at that time
Johnny [sic]?
A:  Quite a bit.
Q:  Do you drink now?
A:  No.
Q:  Why did you quit drinking?
A:  Just quit.
Q:  Huh?
A:  Just quit.
```

Mr. Allen cross-examined Lewis, establishing that Lewis had talked to the state police right after the murders, on July 3, 1980, and told them that he had been with Arnold Cutlip all day cutting locust posts. The defense wanted the jury to see how long the road had been for Lewis, from July 1980 to the spring of 1992 to this moment, over a year later, and how many times he had changed his story during this period of thirteen years.

Q: If you decided to tell the truth, Johnnie, on April 15 and 16, then why after that did you start saying you weren't there, time and time and time again?

A: I just scared—reckon.

Q: You got scared?

A: Yeah.

Q: From who?

A: I thought I was—maybe I wasn't there or something.

Q: You thought maybe you weren't there?

A: Yeah.

Q: There was a doubt in your mind that you weren't there?

A: Got to thinking I was there.

Q: So sometimes you think you are there, and sometimes you think you weren't there. Is that correct?

A: Yeah.

Q: So you really are not sure, are you?

A: Yeah, I am sure now.

Q: Now, you are sure. Okay. What's happened between last summer when you were saying you weren't there, and right now, to make you sure, Johnnie?

A: Just studying over it. I know I was there.

On Friday, May 28, the eighth day of the trial, the prosecution rested its case. Farmer then rose and asked for a directed verdict of acquittal on all charges—it never happens, but you've got to try. But it did happen—partially. Judge Lobban dismissed the abduction-with-intent-to-defile charge, saying that no witness had placed Beard speaking to the victims or conspiring with the other defendants to "defile" Vicki and Nancy.

With one charge down, Farmer and Allen's defense strategy was to cast doubt on the integrity of the prosecution's whole enterprise: they argued that every step of law enforcement conduct, from investigation to evidence collection to prosecution, was tainted by impropriety and dubious conduct, and suggested other suspects with more motive and opportunity than Beard, chiefly Bobby Lee Morrison and, though dead, Gerald Brown.

The defense called Corporal Michael Jordan and Trooper First Class Dallas Wolfe with the West Virginia State Police, both officers who had come aboard the case starting in the spring of 1992 after the first round of arrests. Alkire needed help with all the interviews, particularly in taking the statements of Walton and Lewis.

Jordan told about how upset Walton had become when shown pictures of Vicki and Nancy alive, then Vicki and Nancy dead. He cried and cried. Jordan also took Walton on a drive to jog his memory. They drove along 219, south from Hillsboro, up to Droop Mountain, past the parking lot that had once been CJ's store, and down into Renick's Valley, where the road flattened and straightened and where Pam Wilson had allegedly seen the blue van pick up the Rainbow girls. Jordan asked Walton to point out the spot where he and the other men had picked up the two girls. There, Walton said, pointing to a spot in the road. It was Wilson's house.

Both Jordan and Wolfe voiced concerns about the truthfulness of the testimony Walton and Lewis had given in court. Jordan testified that he felt Lewis had been intimidated by Sergeant Estep and that he doubted the theory that Lewis was present when the Rainbow girls were killed. He also testified about another possible theory of the crime: that a man locked up in a state penitentiary in Illinois named Joseph Paul Franklin had done it. Wolfe said that Lewis had "told investigators what he felt they wanted to hear."

Marilyn Thompson, the lawyer appointed to defend Lewis in June 1992, testified next. A young lawyer, having only passed the bar in 1990, she showed an old-timer's expertise in advocating for her client. She pointed out that on April 15, 1992, Lewis had told police that he had not seen any Rainbow girls and had played no part in the murders, but the next day under duress from Sergeant Estep, and without a lawyer, his story changed drastically. From the point at which she became his lawyer going forward, she said, Lewis denied having seen any Rainbow girls, through five additional police interviews that summer. Only in October 1992, when she was not present, did Lewis again say he had seen Vicki and Nancy get killed.

That night, Strong drove home to Droop Mountain and put her daughters, then five and nine, to bed. The weekend was Memorial Day, so Monday was a holiday, and one she usually spent with her husband's family. They were a big clan, the Strongs, an old name in Pocahontas County and specifically on Droop Mountain, and many of their neighbors were in fact their relatives. But on this particular holiday, no one much felt like celebrating.

The trial was playing out like a mini civil war: two family members testifying for the prosecution and three, not counting Beard, testifying for the defense. Gerald Brown's ex-wife, Drema, was also Strong's husband's first cousin. Drema would testify the following week in defense of Jacob Beard and by proxy her late ex-husband. Roger Pritt, another first cousin by blood to Strong's husband, would take the stand for the defense.

Gerald Brown's own half brother had already testified for the prosecution—saying he saw Fowler's van at Gerald Brown's trailer on the night of the murders, and his wife, Brown's sister-in-law, had been the one to say that she saw Beard parked at Droop Mountain Battlefield State Park and then again at the school board meeting, where he was drunk and aggressive. Technically these prosecution witnesses were also related to Beard as well.

Strong, given the responsibility of chronicling the facts for the larger community, was stuck in the middle.

* * *

The following Tuesday, everyone reassembled in the courtroom, refreshed from their vacation or not. But they had an urgent matter to deal with: some of the Rainbow people who had been sitting in the back of the courtroom, in particular "the gentleman with the pigtails," had written and printed up many copies of a tract called "The Haunting of Pocahontas" and, on Friday before the end of the trial proceedings, placed them downstairs in the lobby of the courtroom as well as on many of the windshields of cars parked near the courthouse—including one that belonged to a juror.

"When I picked it up and turned it over, I seen Bobby Lee Morrison—whatever the guy's name is—up at the top. I just—I just turned it over and brought it in here to Mr. Miller. I didn't even look at it," the juror in question told Judge Lobban.

Each juror then had to be individually questioned to see if they had read it and if their ability to be impartial had been tainted in any way. "We're sorry to bother you," Judge Lobban told each member as he spoke with them. "Unfortunately, it's a commentary about the trial and the witnesses and the parties and our system of justice in West Virginia."

"Now," Lobban asked one juror, "if the…document is critical of our trial and our witnesses, our lawyers, our system, our state, does that cause you any problem continuing to be a member of this jury panel?"

"As much as I have criticized all those things myself," responded the juror, who then quickly added, "No."

Later that morning, Gerald Brown's ex-wife, Drema, was finally permitted to take the stand. She testified that she had been home the whole day on June 25, 1980, except for an hour in the early afternoon, because she was waiting for her mother and sister to arrive from Ohio. She claimed that no men in a blue van had come to their trailer that night, contradicting Pee Wee Walton's testimony.

Beard's wife's brother, Larry Dean, testified next. Pee Wee Walton had claimed that Dean had also been in the woods the night the Rainbow girls had been killed—he had come in his jeep to "party." Dean said that he had not been on Briery Knob that night at all and that he rarely if ever drove the jeep Walton had referenced. On cross-examination, however, Dean admitted that when he had first been questioned by police, he said that he believed Beard might have committed the murders.

Roger Pritt also offered testimony rebutting that of his cousin's husband's brother's wife, Sis Hively. He claimed that Beard had not been drunk or aggressive at the school board meeting but had seemed his normal self and that they left together.

"It's up to you; it's your life," Robert Allen told Beard when they'd discussed if Beard would testify on his own behalf. On the one hand, an appealing defendant who can offer a coherent story of their whereabouts elsewhere on the day of a crime or a humanizing insight into how their character would not allow for such acts can be a lifesaver. On the other, a defendant who seems nervous, hostile, distant, or otherwise unappealing can make a jury convict faster than any damning evidence.

In a bright white polo shirt, dark suit jacket, and gold watch, Beard settled himself into the witness stand on the morning of the tenth day of the trial, a Wednesday. Except for an occasional shake of his head, he didn't move his body at all as he spoke. Once, during his long testimony, he adjusted his glasses, also aviator-style, to sit more solidly below his large, shiny forehead. He didn't smile or cry. Instead, he frowned and looked straight ahead, answering Allen's questions with a "yes, sir" or "no, sir."

As Allen led Beard through his movements on the day of the murders, Allen drew an elaborate and confusing diagram on the green chalkboard.

"And where is the valley in relation to this intersection?" Allen asked.

"About where you have them squiggles," Beard said, trying to be helpful.

Beard reiterated his alibi—that he had been at work at Greenbrier Tractor Sales in Lewisburg, then out on a service call in the afternoon, after which he got some groceries, went home, and ate a sandwich with his wife. They arrived together at the school board meeting by 7:30 pm.

Beard told the jury how defending himself in this case had tanked his health. Allen and his firm now held a second mortgage on Beard's house, and he had been on a leave of absence from work since February 1993.

"My nerves got pretty bad," Beard said, without emotion. "I suffered a couple blackouts. My daughter found me on the floor one Sunday morning, and I was taken to the hospital. They determined that I had had a small stroke."

He again said he didn't know any of the "relevant necessary people" more than to stop and chat with, and some not even that much; he had never even seen Pee Wee Walton until the preliminary motion hearings in mid-April. The only interaction he'd had with Rainbow people, he said, was in late 1980, when he met two of them who needed help hauling a burned van. They told him that "the Rainbows as a whole felt that local people had done [the killings]."

"Did you kill these girls?" asked Allen.

"No, sir. Absolutely not," replied Beard.

The defense spent the afternoon session calling an expert they'd commissioned to do computer graphics of the bullet paths through Vicki and Nancy's bodies based on the findings of Dr. Sopher, but it was so convoluted that even Farmer and Allen seemed to have trouble following the expert's train of thought and its implications, if any, on Beard's guilt or innocence.

Closing arguments took place on Thursday, June 3, the eleventh day of the trial. The gallery was clear of most spectators by then—they'd run out of sick days, or money, or interest. Kathy Santomero and her mother had returned home to Long Island; Kathy was getting married the following week and had errands to run.

"The style of Special Prosecutor Walt Weiford, whose relaxed matter-of-fact statements were delivered in increasingly hushed tones, was compared to defense attorney Stephen Farmer, who delivered his arguments in seeming frustration and increasing fervor," reported Strong.

In his closing, Weiford said that the witnesses he presented were imperfect, which made them in fact more credible. "Johnnie Lewis was in a place he didn't want to be," Weiford told the court. "He saw things he wishes he hadn't seen. Now if the state wanted to invent a witness for you, the state might have invented somebody that might have had an easier time testifying than Johnnie Lewis had."

He also emphasized the sheer number of Pocahontas County citizens who participated in the prosecution to testify against Jacob Beard. "You will believe Mr. Beard and his relatives," Weiford told the jury, or believe innocent citizens with no reason to lie. The other theories of the crime— Bobby Lee Morrison, Brown, and the inmate in Illinois were "hardly even worth mentioning."

Farmer's closing was indeed feverish, and frustrated. He delivered it from his music stand, looking at the jury. On Court TV, his face was again caught in profile.

"Pee Wee lives in Hillsboro with his mother. Sometimes he is employed; sometimes he is not. In Hillsboro, the law is the law. He told the law that he didn't know what happened. He told the law that…what he was telling them could be a dream. What did the law do? The law made him captive. The people that were supposed to help him and the people who were supposed to be in search of the truth took him captive.

"They may not be able to do that to me. And they may not be able to do that to you all. But you saw Pee Wee. It's real. And Pee Wee knows, when this is over, you all get to go home. I get to go home. Everybody in this court room gets to go home. Pee Wee goes back to Hillsboro. And it's him and the law…"

"Johnnie Lewis may be the most tragic aspect of this case short of the tragic deaths of these girls." Lewis, Farmer continued, was "an unfortunate man.…Knowing his capabilities, and the fact that he is not as fortunate as most of us, knowing that he lives out in the woods with a caretaker, is unable to care for himself.…The law…came to see him again. Now, if Sergeant Alkire was in search of the truth…why did he go get Estep to come and see Johnnie?…So they ditched the lawyer, and in October, they bring Estep back in, and it had the desired effect.

"You see because Johnnie Lewis has to go home too. Johnnie Lewis has to go home where the power is vested in the very people that he told the truth to, and look what they did to him. Johnnie Lewis knows what he has to do to survive. Pee Wee Walton knows, within both of their lives, what they must do to survive. And that was to come here and tell what the state wanted to hear."

Farmer ended by appealing to the West Virginia jury's understanding of how essential it can be for ordinary citizens to resist those with power. "The people that formed this county and this country came here in large part because the country that they were leaving permitted the government to randomly walk on people the way Mr. Beard has been walked upon in this case," Farmer said. "This country is founded on the premise that it's people like you that can look at the government and say, 'No, it won't happen. It won't happen.' Mr. Beard is not guilty. Send Mr. Beard home to try to put his life back together."

After just over three hours of deliberation, the jury reentered the courtroom. Judge Lobban had them line up at the front of the gallery facing the judge's bench so that Beard, Farmer, and Allen as well as Weiford were looking directly at the jury's backs and butts. Judge Lobban read the verdict: Beard was guilty of the murder in the first degree of Vicki Durian and guilty of the murder in the first degree of Nancy Santomero. Beard did not move his head or his eyes or his face while these sentences were read aloud.

Strong did not linger at the courthouse. "The thirteen-year-old mystery," she typed, "of who killed 'The Rainbow Girls' has now been solved."

PART V:
THE COGS DON'T MEET

A great truth is a truth whose opposite is also a great truth.

—Niels Bohr

Robert Alkire, 1993

PART 4

THE GODS DON'T MEET

1

ONCE UPON A TIME IN 1950s Mobile, Alabama, there lived a boy
named James Clayton Vaughn. His father left when he was eight, but he
had a mother and two sisters and a brother and a house near a woods of
loblolly pine.

Vaughn lived in the Birdville neighborhood, close to the air force base
and the water of Mobile Bay and a stone's throw from the new interstate
they were building through town. Most of the homes in Birdville had gone
up fast during the Second World War to give temporary shelter to military personnel, and when the officers and their families left, you could
rent them for cheap. Later they would become a public housing complex,
which still stands today.

Nearly half of Mobile was black then, but only 275 black residents were
registered to vote out of a total of 19,000 voters. Alabama had passed
onerous provisions in 1901 requiring voters to own property, be able to
read and write an article of the US Constitution, have been employed for
at least one year, and have not been convicted of any crime, including va-
grancy and public intoxication. This eliminated nearly all black residents
of Mobile and many whites too, including Vaughn's family.

Because poor communities have their own kind of logic outside
middle-class rules, Vaughn's Birdville was more or less integrated; poor
black and poor white kids tossed balls back and forth and hit each other
with friendly sticks. Yet if Vaughn left his neighborhood even for a moment, the reality of white supremacy and black dispossession was everywhere. It was in the whites-only restaurants and stores and schools of
course, but it was also in the crosses that burned on Highway 90 and 42

and 45 and 43—the only roads into or out of Mobile. A Klansman ran for city commission in 1957 on the slogan "the Negro will be kept in his place" and promoted his candidacy with buttons depicting two black men hanging from a tree.

Vaughn's father was mostly gone. His mother starved and beat him and sent him to sleep under the loblolly pines. For reasons that were never clear, Vaughn took the brunt of his mother's rage. By his teenage years, he was blind in his right eye, and his skull was cracked many times over.

When he was seventeen, Vaughn stole a copy of *Mein Kampf* from the Mobile public library and took to carrying it around his house and to the loblolly pines when he was forced to go there. Now instead of waiting for the sky to turn light, he had something to read. He read of Hitler's poverty and hunger and gobbled the words into his mind. "Our own painful struggle for existence," Hitler wrote, "destroys our feeling for the misery of those who have remained behind." To be a poor white boy with the same amount of power as a poor black boy—none—it seemed, was to have the lowest kind of human life.

Vaughn started looking at Birdville with new eyes. He stopped playing with his black friends. One of his neighbors, a black woman, had always been kind to him, sometimes giving him food while he sat under the loblolly pine; now he pretended he didn't know her. Vaughn kept reading Hitler and joined the American Nazi Party and the Ku Klux Klan.

As soon as he was old enough to drive, Vaughn dropped out of high school and took off for points north and east, where, under various fake names, he worked in construction, at a real estate firm, and in a shoe store. At twenty years old, he started hurling insults at interracial couples on the street, then at interracial couples idling in cars. He became transfixed by the philosophy Charles Manson called "helter skelter"—a vague collection of ideas involving anger at being rejected by the world of the rich and powerful, as well as promoting violence designed to create an apocalyptic war between blacks and whites that would end the world as we know it.

When he visited his sister in Mobile in 1973, he could not stop shaking and yelling when he saw that she had a black woman working in her house as a maid. "He got so upset that it was almost necessary for her to call the police in order to get him to leave," his FBI case notes read. In Maryland, he worked as a maintenance man at a building complex. It seemed as if he had calmed down emotionally during this time, his other sister told the FBI. But she was wrong. That year, in Atlanta, Vaughn followed a black man with a white woman date, then sprayed them with mace. Then he changed his name, reinventing himself forever. The name he took was Joseph Paul Franklin—Joseph for Goebbels's efficiency; Franklin for Ben's ingenuity.

Bombs came next. In July 1977, and within days of each other, Franklin used a sophisticated electrical detonator to blow a hole through the front of the home of Morris Amitay, the face of pro-Israel politics in Washington, and then pushed fifty pounds of water gel explosives and five sticks of dynamite into a crawl space in a small Orthodox synagogue in Chattanooga. The synagogue was flattened to the ground, but its Torah survived.

In the month following his bombings, Franklin got it in mind to drive to Wisconsin to kill a judge who had released two black men accused of raping a white woman. But on his way there, in a shopping mall in Madison, he was driving through a parking lot when a car driven by a black man with a white woman passenger, both twenty-three years old, backed out in front of him. Franklin honked and honked his horn until the man opened his door to see what the hell. Franklin shot the man as he approached, then pulled up alongside the car, got out, and shot the woman. He never forgot this first couple, Franklin said. The look the man got in his eyes when he knew he would die and the way the woman turned away and covered her face with her hands. He remembered the bad smell of gunpowder, too, and the way their blood had gotten on his clothes.

From 1977 to 1980, thanks to the expansion of the interstate highway system that offered travelers much greater speed and anonymity, Franklin roamed American cities large and small and murdered black men, black men and their white girlfriends or white women who might become their girlfriends, and Jews. He kept handguns around but mostly used a sniper rifle to kill, robbing banks to cover his constant need for fresh cars, guns, and bullets.

He shot and killed a Jewish worshipper exiting a temple in a suburb of St. Louis. He shot a black man and his pregnant white girlfriend as they walked down the sidewalk near their home in northeast Atlanta, killing the man and paralyzing the woman from the waist down. Outside the Georgia courtroom where Hustler publisher Larry Flynt's famous obscenity trial took place, Franklin tried to kill Flynt because his photographs depicted interracial sex, but he failed, leaving Flynt partially paralyzed and using a wheelchair. In Chattanooga, Franklin waited in the grass outside a Pizza Hut, where a white woman who dated a black man worked, then shot them both in the parking lot. The man, a junior varsity basketball player at the University of Tennessee, was shot first, but he managed before he died to shout a warning to his girlfriend. She lived.

Franklin grew more associative. He shot and killed the manager of a Taco Bell in Doraville, Georgia, because the manager was black and waited on white women. He shot and killed a twenty-eight-year-old black man for no reason at all, through a plate-glass window of a restaurant in Falls Church, Virginia. He shot another interracial couple outside a grocery store in Oklahoma City, leaving the woman's ten-year-old son alive. Franklin had sex with a fifteen-year-old white sex worker and then killed her when she said she had had sex with a black man. He killed a twenty-two-year-old black man who was standing at the counter of a fried chicken carryout restaurant in north Indianapolis in early January 1980 and a nineteen-year-old black man who was buying extermination spray at a convenience store on January 14 in the same city. He killed a white college student hitchhiking her way home from college in an isolated state park in Wisconsin who said she had, or would consider having, sex with a black man. He shot but failed to kill civil rights leader Vernon Jordan outside a Marriott Inn in Fort Wayne, Indiana.

In Cincinnati, he camped out on a railroad trestle with his sniper rifle waiting for an interracial couple to come out of a motel. When they didn't, he got bored and shot two black children at random instead—cousins, age thirteen and fourteen, on their way to split a dollar at the candy store. They both died. In June 1980, he killed a twenty-two-year-old black man and his white girlfriend as they walked over the Washington Street Bridge in downtown Johnstown, Pennsylvania. That August, Franklin drove around Salt Lake City's Liberty Park, a bustling public park where teenagers of all races came to roller-skate and flirt and listen to music. When he spotted two black boys, age eighteen and twenty, jogging with two white girls, both fifteen, Franklin opened fire, dropping the two boys to the pavement, where they bled to death. The two girls came away with shrapnel in their skin but alive. Then, as ever, Franklin packed up his rifle, put it back in the trunk, and drove on.

2

IN THE FALL OF 1978, thirty-four state police cadets graduated from the West Virginia State Police academy. Their class was called "the Pioneers," for it contained, for the first time, five black cadets and three women, including Deborah DiFalco. She had grown up in Maryland but crossed over into Mountaineer territory for college in Wheeling, where she studied political science and made it into the school's basketball hall of fame. She just liked the idea of being a police officer; she thought it would be exciting. She took the police academy exam while she was still a college student and began training just days after graduation. The six months at the police academy were like boot camp. Military style. You would be in formation; you would be in PT; back in formation, you would march into meals. Classes all day. She loved it.

DiFalco started out as a field trooper in uniform, stationed in Charles Town, in the Mountain State's eastern panhandle, famous for its horse racing. She wasn't the first woman to be a state trooper in West Virginia, but she was the second. The first, a woman named Sharen Deitz, would later successfully sue the West Virginia State Police for gender-based discrimination; a trainer in the police academy called Deitz "it," she alleged, because she was butch, and the promotion she applied for was given to a much less qualified man.

Perhaps because DiFalco was femme and pretty, or perhaps for other reasons, this wasn't her experience. "I was confident," she says. "I was kind of oblivious to being a woman. I worked with a really great group of guys. They never made me feel like I couldn't do something—quite the opposite. Love the people of West Virginia. You couldn't be offended. They defended me. I was small. I was lucky."

DiFalco became the first woman to do undercover police work in West Virginia. Drugs, gambling, a lot of narcotics. A lot of work in Martinsburg, Charles Town's big-city neighbor, where she was assigned to a task force to work an open-air drug market. It was thrilling and scary. She was often alone out there.

She went into plainclothes, then into investigations as a detective, and was stationed in Randolph County, just up from Pocahontas. Each day DiFalco left the house that she shared with her husband in Buckhannon and drove the half hour to the state police headquarters in Elkins, a three-story building with a cafeteria and barracks upstairs, where officers fresh out of the academy could live for a while until they got on their feet. Detectives might catch an hour nap or so if they were working through the night.

The office in Elkins was full of jokes. You had to know how to have fun; otherwise you'd die of a heart attack or boredom. Alkire liked to have fun, and that's what he was doing in March of 1984—after Morrison had confessed, then recanted. The Rainbow Murders case was quiet.

The phone rang. It was Ernest Smith, special agent of criminal investigation for the state of Wisconsin. We've got someone here, he said to Alkire, by the name of Joseph Paul Franklin, and he says he did the murders where you are.

Franklin's flesh was peppered with tattoos, but it was the one of the Grim Reaper on his right forearm, done in delicate line work, that got him caught. In October 1980, a Florida blood bank employee recognized it as he waited, sleeves rolled up, to sell his blood at a plasma center. It was Utah that tried him first, for murdering the two young black joggers in Salt Lake City. Franklin was given two life sentences and transferred to a federal penitentiary in Illinois, where he became the recipient of visits from law enforcement agents from multiple states. He spoke to most of them and confessed to his crimes on his terms and on his timeline, except Missouri, which had the death penalty—at that time, he did not want to die. He would spend the next thirty-three years in prison, awaiting trial, being tried for crimes he'd committed in five states, and then awaiting death. He was convicted of eight murders in the courts, though if you include crimes to which he confessed but for which he was not prosecuted—why spend the resources on a man already on death row—you'll arrive at a count of at least twenty deaths.

Every state with an unsolved murder of a black man or a white woman had come calling on Franklin at the federal penitentiary in Illinois. Special agents from Wisconsin arranged to visit Franklin to ask about the young white woman who was killed in a Wisconsin state park while hitchhiking home from college. Franklin quickly confessed to that killing, then turned the subject to other crimes. Also, he said, he had killed two women hitchhikers in West Virginia, in "Beckley County."

Wisconsin Special Agent Smith said that wasn't enough; they would need more details. Franklin said he had just come from robbing a bank in North Carolina a day or two earlier and was traveling on an interstate highway in West Virginia en route to Lexington, Kentucky, in the late morning or early afternoon of June 25, 1980, when he picked up two female hitchhikers whom he described as of average build, one with medium brown hair and one with light brown hair, "looking kind of sleazy, hippie type, kind of scruffy looking."

He picked the women up, he said, and then took "a road that went off to the side past a gas station," where he stopped for gas while the women were with him. It took "a couple hours'" driving time from there to the place where he murdered them. He believed the women were into communism and had been friends with, or possibly dated, black men in the past, so he simply decided to "waste both of them." He said he got the two women out of his car and that neither screamed. He shot the first girl in the chest from the front and the other once "in the face or the head." Special Agent Smith then asked Franklin to draw a simple map of the area where he supposedly picked these women up, which Franklin did.

Agent Smith was troubled enough by this confession to call law enforcement in West Virginia straightaway. Alkire thanked Smith and put the phone down, but his mood was not elation. Though charges had formally been dropped against Gerald Brown two months after young Bobby Morrison recanted his confession, Alkire felt that it was likely Morrison had just lost his nerve. All of Alkire's waking hours were still being channeled toward investigating Brown and Morrison. But Agent Smith would not quit; he faxed a follow-up letter to Alkire four days later, which included the map Franklin had drawn.

Alkire called Weiford. They turned the map this way and that but still could not make it match the topography they knew so well. Both men felt that Franklin's map was inaccurate on the whole, putting the gas station where he allegedly stopped on the wrong side of the road, as well as the "winding dirt road." The Xs Franklin had drawn to indicate Vicki and Nancy's bodies were only a short distance from 219, when in reality they were a solid fifteen or twenty minutes' driving time at a minimum. Alkire thought maybe Franklin had read about the case in a crime magazine or watched it on a crime show. Weiford agreed.

When agents from Tennessee visited Franklin a month later about the bombing in Chattanooga, Franklin again told them he'd killed two women in West Virginia. The Tennessee officer was taken aback. "Have you given that to anyone else?"

"Yeah, yeah, I told that already to Madison," responded Franklin.

"Has Pocahontas County, West Virginia, been in touch with you about it?"

"No."

In August 1984, DiFalco had just made trooper first-class for working some drug cases and a few murders in the eastern part of the state when her captain called her into his office. There was a case down in Pocahontas County, he said, a couple of girl hitchhikers that won't solve. Yeah, she said, I've heard of it. Well, the captain said, something's come up. We got a call. Alkire is under water. Can you help him out?

DiFalco was pleased—it meant something that they would give this to her; it meant they trusted her. Alkire called her on her desk phone. Listen, he said, this guy Franklin has been confessing to every crime this way and that, crimes all over the nation. It's probably nothing when it comes to him and West Virginia. But go check it out.

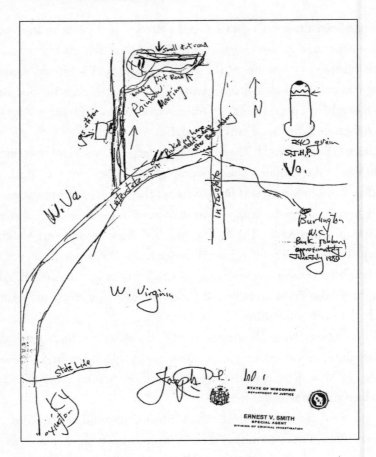

Hand-drawn map by Joseph Paul Franklin, 1984

Courtesy of Deborah DiFalco

On Monday, September 10, 1984, DiFalco drove the ninety minutes south along winding 219 to Marlinton. Aside from skiing at Snowshoe, DiFalco had never been in Pocahontas County before. She observed that the land was much steeper here than where she lived and that everyone seemed to know each other. Walt Weiford was waiting for her when she arrived at the state police office: an eager man with a round face who had a tendency to follow her around and rock back and forth on his feet from heel to toe.

Weiford gave her Franklin's map. On the map, DiFalco saw, Franklin had marked the West Virginia state line, the interstate he had been traveling, the exit road he had taken, the gas station, the winding dirt road he said he had turned down, and the "small dirt road" where he had supposedly left the bodies. Franklin had also written "Rainbow Meeting" along one of the roads, which according to what he had told Agent Smith, "the girls talked about either having just participated in or were hitchhiking to." Franklin had also told Smith that he used a .44-caliber revolver for the crimes and had drawn a picture of the 240-grain bullet he said he used.

DiFalco began by tracking down Corporal Gary Hott, the first officer on the death scene after young Tim had found the bodies, and showing him the map that Franklin had drawn. Does it work? she asked. Hott studied the map. Pretty well, yeah, he said, if you take Franklin's "interstate" to be I-64, the exit road he took to be Route 219 north, the "winding dirt road" to be Briery Knob Road through Droop Mountain Battlefield State Park, and the "small dirt road" to be the lane where they were found. Further, the "gas station" near the interstate could be the Little General store in the hamlet of Maxwelton near Lewisburg, where the initial investigators in 1980 had turned up the cashier that put two hippie women from Arizona in her store on June 25 with a tall, slim, clean-shaven man with light hair who drove a black Nova.

"Cpl. Hott advised that he felt the map adequately depicts the route to the murder scene and the position of the bodies," reads DiFalco's official "Report of Criminal Investigation."

DiFalco called the ballistics lab in South Charleston to check if Franklin's memory matched their findings. The fragments recovered from Vicki and Nancy's bodies were super small, they told her, but they could check the bullet jacket. They did, and indeed, the jacket appeared to belong to a 240-grain bullet, as Franklin stated. Franklin said that he had used the same gun and bullets in the Wisconsin hitchhiker murder as in the West Virginia ones, but the West Virginia fragments were too small for any conclusive comparison.

DiFalco kept calling different jurisdictions trying to check Franklin's facts. Pennsylvania told her that they had a murder of an interracial couple ten days earlier on June 15, 1980, that they thought was Franklin's, and according to their investigation, Franklin had short, light hair at that time and had been driving a dark metallic Nova. Florida sent her pictures of Franklin in the summer of 1980—short, sandy-blond hair, no facial hair.

North Carolina police said that there was indeed a bank robbery on June 24, 1980—North Carolina National Bank—and a little boy had seen the suspect getting into a black car. A special agent with the Chattanooga, Tennessee, office of Alcohol, Firearms and Tobacco said he had interviewed Franklin about the Chattanooga synagogue bombing, and, come to think of it, during that interview he had said something about West Virginia. Hold on, the agent told DiFalco. I'll send you the transcript.

> Q: "6/25/80, Pocahontas County, West Virginia, some killings there," asked the ATF agent.
> A: "Yeah, I did that," answered Franklin.
> Q: "What did they involve?"
> A: "Couple of race mixers."
> Q: "Women?"
> A: "Yeah."
> Q: "What happened on those?"
> A: "I just blew them away with a .44 magnum, said they went out with niggers."

DiFalco called the federal penitentiary where Franklin was being held in Marion, Illinois. She wanted to meet with Franklin herself, go over everything with him in person, and see if it added up. She wrote to the warden. She called. Finally, in early October, they called her back. Franklin had agreed to talk to her. Could she come next week?

That Monday, DiFalco and a trooper, Terry Snodgrass, set out on the nine-hour road trip in an unmarked police cruiser, sharing the driving as first signs for Huntington, then Lexington, then Louisville appeared and receded. Snodgrass was quiet, and there was little to talk about. Neither of them had interviewed a serial killer before. The last three hours beyond Louisville were dark, and they got dinner, then separate motel rooms. DiFalco read and reread her notes until she just shut the light off.

When DiFalco and Snodgrass reached the federal prison in Illinois just before ten in the morning, they were led down through one layer of the facility, then the next. "Just door after door. Seems like we just kept going down and down. Doors clanking behind us," DiFalco says. "I still tell people about it."

Finally they reached the very bottom of the prison and were led into a small square room. Franklin was brought in shackled. His eyes looked strange, off, possibly from the blindness in the right one. Right away he started looking at DiFalco, would only talk to DiFalco, and ignored Snodgrass altogether. Snodgrass put a tape recorder on the table. DiFalco said, Okay, tell us about the girls in West Virginia. But Franklin was "playing around," she says. He told them that he'd never shot anyone, never killed in his life. He told them that he was being held in prison for his political beliefs and that he had lied to the agents from Wisconsin and Tennessee about having killed girls in West Virginia. Everything I have ever said before is a lie, he said. This is the truth.

DiFalco and Snodgrass talked to Franklin for more than an hour, but there was no change. Finally, DiFalco showed Franklin pictures of himself in a wig and sideburns as he was robbing the North Carolina bank. He claimed he'd never robbed any bank but seemed interested in the pictures, even fond of them, and rubbed them with his fingers. Then DiFalco pulled out pictures of Vicki and Nancy after they'd been shot. Franklin would not look at them. No, no, don't show me that, Franklin said, turning away in his chair.

Finally, DiFalco called for the guard. This was a waste of time; they might as well put Franklin back in his cell, she said. But just after they had left the room and were outside in the corridor looking at Franklin behind bars again, Franklin motioned DiFalco over. He pressed his face through the bars and then lifted his mouth to her ear.

Let me put your mind at ease, DiFalco says Franklin said. I did it.

That's not enough, DiFalco says she told him. They needed details. She asked him what he did with the women's belongings. Franklin told her that he had hidden them in the woods far away from the murder scene on his way back toward Interstate 64. He told her that one of the backpacks was green. (Both Vicki and Nancy's sleeping bags were dark blue; Vicki had a bongo drum in a green case.) Franklin said he did not want to see anyone else go to prison for what he had done.

Back home in West Virginia, DiFalco found Nancy's missing sandal. It had been in the evidence locker of the Marlinton State Police all that time; she sent it to the South Charleston lab to be checked for prints, but there were none. She combed the original reports of investigation from 1980 and found a composite sketch of the driver of the black Nova given by the convenience store cashier who said she had seen the two women from Arizona get into his car. It looked a lot like the photographs that Florida had sent of Franklin.

She reinterviewed the cashier, who again said that she had seen women matching Vicki and Nancy's descriptions getting into a black or dark green Chevy Nova on June 25, 1980, with a tall, clean-cut man who didn't look to be from around there, adding that she remembered one of the girls made a purchase and paid for it with coins from a green change purse. She bought something from an aisle of the store that held snacks and cans of beans. This was consistent with the fact that a tan, pasty bean fluid was found in Vicki's stomach after her death, DiFalco noted. But the cashier couldn't identify Franklin's photo from a photo lineup. She was an elderly woman, and it had been years.

On a March day in 1985, DiFalco rose extra early. Her captain at the West Virginia State Police wanted her to present her report on Franklin to him, Alkire, Weiford, and Weiford's boss, and she wanted to be able to be comfortable enough with the material that she could look them in the eyes as she spoke.

Before this group, DiFalco presented the results of her labor. "I feel that Mr. Franklin had the motive, opportunity and capability to be the perpetrator of the crimes against the victims, Nancy Santomero and Vicki Durian," her report concluded.

The men in the room shifted in their chairs. Then Alkire spoke. He was not convinced, he told the room. He felt the facts of Franklin's confession were wrong—particularly the errors Franklin made when describing the road where he picked the girls up, the topography of the area, and the distances between where he picked the girls up, the road where he turned off, and the spot where he eventually killed them. Plus he had placed them in "Beckley County," which did not exist. He still suspected Franklin had heard about the case secondhand. Weiford agreed with him, suggesting that Franklin was talked to by so many investigators from so many different states, who was to say they hadn't perhaps filled in some of the details?

"Alkire felt that nothing was right about what Franklin said," DiFalco says. "He kept saying, 'It doesn't fit with what we know to be true.' He kept saying, 'The killer has to be local.'"

Why? DiFalco doesn't know, and it puzzles, especially considering that many citizens of Pocahontas County didn't believe Franklin's confession either, once they heard about it in the *Pocahontas Times*.

In the end, most of that 1985 meeting was spent discussing how Gerald Brown might still be the one and, if he was, how to prove it. They couldn't prove he'd fired the gun, but Weiford and Alkire strongly suspected that Brown had been there when Vicki and Nancy died. They were disturbed specifically by Brown's cavalier attitude toward the charges when arrested and his cavalier attitude toward death generally.

Worse, his wife, Drema Brown, had divorced him in 1983 on the basis of "extreme mental cruelty," and there was also the troubling fact that Brown had given his girlfriend a necklace that belonged to "one of my Rainbow friends" and several times driven her up to Briery Knob to cry.

At the end of the meeting it was decided that Alkire, DiFalco, and the other officers would continue investigating both Franklin and Brown as suspects. Then Alkire was transferred to Parkersburg, and DiFalco was also reassigned to another county; eventually she moved to northern Virginia to work with US Customs.

The first time Franklin called DiFalco was on February 14, 1985— Valentine's Day. He wanted to chat, to tell her about a newspaper article that someone was writing about him.

"He just took a liking to me," DiFalco says. "He was a little creepy, a little strange. He would call me, a lot, over the years." Sometimes during these calls, Franklin would drop into conversation the name of the small city in Maryland where DiFalco's parents still lived as a way, DiFalco felt, of saying, I know you. But she was not frightened of him, she says. "He mellowed over the years."

Okay, so I lied, Franklin said during that first Valentine's Day call. I did rob that bank in North Carolina. But that's it, I didn't kill anyone. Franklin asked DiFalco if she could send him the pictures of himself from the bank robbery. She told him no.

3

THE PRECISE PROCESS WE ARE talking about when we say, "believe," and where we think it happens—the brain? the heart? the stomach?—are poorly understood. DiFalco believed Franklin when he said he had done the killings, while Walt Weiford and Sergeant Alkire did not. We tend to treat believability as if it were synonymous with truthfulness or akin to solving a mathematical equation, but the relationship between what is believable and what is true and, further, what makes a story believable to one listener but not to another turn out to be some of the murkiest parts of human cognition.

The twelve jurors who voted to convict Jacob Beard were given the following instructions: "After making your assessment concerning the credibility of a witness, you may decide to believe all of that witness's testimony, only a portion of it, or none of it....In making your assessment, you should carefully scrutinize all of the testimony given, the circumstances under which each witness has testified, and every matter in evidence which tends to show whether a witness, in your opinion, is or is not worthy of belief."

The instructions also asked them to consider, when determining believability, "each witness's intelligence, motive to falsify, state of mind, and appearance and manner while on the witness stand." Yet much of this— "every matter in evidence," a witness's "appearance and manner"—leave great room for subjectivity. Judge Lobban several times directed the jury to use "common sense" and to view the evidence "in the light of your own observations and experience in the ordinary affairs of life," as if this would manifest twelve identical metal compasses.

For centuries we believed that humans are generally rational beings, applying rational thought and usually achieving sound judgment, except under circumstances where our feelings get in the way. But in the 1980s, just after Vicki and Nancy were killed, a sea change began to sweep through the scholarly community. What if it wasn't that our feelings were the source of our errors in logic, experts began to ask, but rather that our "machinery of cognition" contained errors in its very design?

Scholars who studied the processes of mind relevant to civil and criminal trial proceedings took up this idea with gusto. Researchers Nancy Pennington and Reid Hastie at the University of Colorado applied it to studying the workings of the minds of judges and juries and published a series of studies in the late 1980s and early 1990s that advanced a theory called the Story Model. Their theory holds that cognitively, instead of taking in each piece of information one at a time and judging it on its logical merits, humans judge legal evidence en masse, forming a story out of it. We then match the story we have built to the relevant legal term—guilty or not, murder in the first or second degree, and so forth.

Researchers found that the stories that judges and jury members construct influence their assessments of how credible a given witness is or the importance of a given piece of evidence. They also found that we tend to fill in any gaps in evidence with inferred causes and associations, consistent with the story we've built, and omit pieces of information that are unrelated or contradictory to our story. That is, if you've already started to tell yourself that the defendant is a good man wrongly accused of murdering his daughter, you will be more likely to disbelieve the ex-wife who takes the stand to testify to his violent temper and find reasons to discount the bloody footprint that matches his shoe.

The justice process is a war between competing stories and a quest to win the imaginations of the people who matter at every stage— investigators, prosecutors, judges, and juries. But what factors determine why these people choose one story over another?

Most experts in the field have come to the consensus that it is the "ease of story construction"—that is, the easier it is for the parties that matter to form a story out of the events in the first place, the more likely they are to believe that story.

According to the Story Model, two characteristics determine how "believable" an average person will find a particular story: coverage, or the extent to which the story accounts for evidence presented at trial, and coherence, or the story's wholeness, lack of contradictions, and "plausibility"—"the extent to which the story is consistent with knowledge of real or imagined events in the real world."

The more familiar the story is, then, the easier the narrative connection forged between teller and listener. At its most basic, many experts say, our brains work by slotting our experiences into molds of classic stories. Each time we hear a new story, we figure out what it means by trying to match it to one of our stored narratives. "We are always looking for the closest possible matches," write Roger Schank and Robert Abelson, professors at Northwestern and Yale, in their essay "Knowledge and Memory: The Real Story." "We are looking to say, in effect, 'Well, something like that happened to me, too,' or, 'I had an idea about something like that myself.'"

In terms of plausibility, it's not hard to see things from Alkire or Weiford's perspective. A mentally ill white supremacist serial killer roaming the nation is unfamiliar enough, let alone one who happens to be passing through one of the most rural counties in the United States, miles from any interstate, at the exact same time that thousands of other outsiders also happen to be passing through it. In America, where misogyny and violence against women are rampant, in a county where alcohol use is high, a story of local men fueled by alcohol killing women for no reason may feel strangely and deeply familiar.

It is also widely known that judges and jury members' perceptions of witness credibility are seriously influenced by seemingly irrelevant factors and that prepackaged stories from the world affect these judgments too. Jurors tend to see experts offering scientific testimony as more credible if they are attractive and confident. Rape victims who speak loudly or with anger or who do not break down in tears or who once went on a date with their rapist are less likely to be believed, studies show, because these actions deviate from the preconceived stories of rape we know. "When

creating their stories jurors rely on their mental scripts that include stereotypes and regular arrangements of events," writes scholar Katharina Kluwe
of Loyola University Chicago. "Accordingly, they use their existing knowledge and beliefs to fill in missing information, to sort out contradictory
evidence, and to determine the believability of a story." Our courtrooms
then, are where some of our most toxic stereotypes and flattest truths are
made and reinforced.

This view seems deathly dark unless you think of our brains less as
maliciously negligent and more as simply inclined toward rest and relax-
ation. This is essentially what Daniel Kahneman argues in his acclaimed
work *Thinking Fast and Slow,* in which he writes that we all have two "systems" working in tandem to conserve our mental resources and function
efficiently: System 1 is fast, instinctive, automatic, subconscious, and constantly busy generating impressions, intuitions, intentions, and feelings;
System 2 is logical, effortful, comprehensive, and slow. System 1 requires
little of us and is sufficient for most of our everyday functioning, but it's
not equipped to handle complex processes like long division, deciding
which house to buy, or holding two conflicting ideas in the mind at once.
Most of our mental questions are ones we do not even know we are asking, and they are answered by System 1, but when there is a question for
which System 1 has no reply, System 2 is pushed into action.

We don't like this idea that System 1—a force outside our conscious
control—exerts such enormous influence over our mental life, but according to Kahneman, it is so. "You believe you know what goes on in your
mind, which often consists of one conscious thought leading in an or-
derly way to another," he writes, "but that is not the only way the mind
works, nor indeed is that the typical way. Most impressions and thoughts
arise in your conscious experience without your knowing how they got
there.... You know far less about yourself than you feel you do."

System 1 is continuously taking in information from the world and
spinning a story from it. Your most intimate friend says a single word into
the telephone, and you know she is angry with you; a tall man on the sub-
way platform is shouting curses, and you sense a threat and move away.
System 1 also identifies incongruity and reacts with surprise; Kahneman

offers the example of an upper-class British man's voice saying, "I have a large tattoo on my back." Studies measured that the brains of participants had a response to this in just two hundred milliseconds: something is off; something does not make sense; people with moneyed British accents cannot also have large tattoos down their backs.

"If endorsed by System 2, impressions and intuitions [generated by System 1] turn into beliefs, and impulses turn into voluntary actions," writes Kahneman. "When all goes smoothly, which is most of the time, System 2 adopts the suggestions of System 1 with little or no modification. You generally believe your impressions and act on your desires, and that is fine—usually."

There is just one problem: System 1 is a blunt tool—it has so much work to do that it cannot afford to wade into the fine print every time—so it operates from the perspective of categories—the most typical case, the most plausible meaning—and thus produces the best story possible out of the information available. It tends to minimize ambiguity, suppress doubt, and exaggerate coherence—the degree to which the elements of the story go together, cause each other, and add up to a meaning or message—in order to tell stories that reinforce our existing judgments and beliefs. We are evolutionarily programmed to make links between our perceptions and their most likely meanings. "Coherence means that you're going to adopt one interpretation in general. Ambiguity tends to be suppressed. Other things that don't fit fall by the wayside, Kahneman instructs: "We see a world that is vastly more coherent than the world actually is."

Can such errors in thinking and judgment be overcome? Kahneman says, essentially, no.

4

AT THE FEDERAL PRISON IN Marion, Illinois, where DiFalco visited him, Joseph Paul Franklin lived in a special semi-isolated section called K Unit, which housed, in solitary confinement, celebrity prisoners and those who had committed the kinds of socially condemned crimes that made them vulnerable to attack. Franklin was both. He was sure the government wanted to kill him, that the guards were poisoning his food and mail. He threw away his letters and refused to eat. Then the K Unit was dissolved, and Franklin was moved into a prison unit that offered less protection. His delusions turned to hallucinations.

On a dark winter night in October 1994—he'd been locked up fourteen years—a "Spirit Guide" appeared to Franklin. It helped him, he said, and told him how to feel about what had become of his life. "Most of the time my Spirit Guide comes to me in dreams," Franklin told a reporter. "Sometimes I see my Guide in a dark corner of my cell, sometimes in the day, sometimes at night." His Guide told him that even though Missouri had the death penalty, in the case of the Jewish man exiting the St. Louis synagogue, it was time to confess, for it was fundamentally immoral to kill a person exiting a place of worship. Franklin spoke to an FBI agent and was soon whisked off to a Missouri jail. Other death penalty states came knocking once more about cold cases.

Melissa Powers was two years out of high school when cousins Dante Evans Brown, thirteen, and Darrell Lane Brown, fourteen, were murdered in that Cincinnati street under a railroad trestle. "This is one of the most horrible crimes that has ever happened in our community," Cincinnati prosecutor Joseph Deters said in a 1998 TV interview. "The nature of it was so cold-blooded and senseless."

Growing up in Cincinnati, Powers had wanted to be a fashion designer and had the genes and the blond hair for modeling, so she posed for fashion snaps and competed in runway competitions to pay for design school. She graduated, met a guy, had a son, separated from the guy, and went to law school while still modeling during her off hours, ending up in the Cincinnati district attorney's office. Her job was to do research for Deters, write briefs, and occasionally to argue a case—mainly traffic tickets and drunk and disorderlies.

Franklin had been a suspect in the Cincinnati murders of the two young boys after his capture in 1980; Cincinnati police could put him in the city at the time of the crime but had nothing more. To convict Franklin of the cousins' murders, a confession to a certified law enforcement official would be necessary. But Deters had had no luck—his requests for interviews with Franklin had all been rejected. Word had spread among law enforcement agencies who needed confessions from Franklin that he preferred women investigators and reporters, particularly if they were "attractive." Powers had heard this, too, and her ambition to solve the Brown murders had only grown as she researched and studied Franklin's crimes.

In the winter of 1997, Deters called Powers into his office, said he had something to show her, and popped a VHS tape into the player. In the taped interview, given a year earlier, Franklin's hair was lank and shoulder length, and the camera stayed tight on his face. "I am a natural born killer," Franklin said in the video. "You know what I'm saying?"

Deters asked Powers if she would be willing to journey to Potosi Correctional Center near Mineral Point, Missouri, where Franklin was then being held on death row.

"We told [Powers] flat out, I'm only asking you to do this because of the way you look," Deters said.

Powers agreed to try. When she contacted Franklin, she sent a picture of her prosecutor's photo ID card.

That April, Powers drove to Mineral Point for the meeting. Franklin freely admitted to killing the two young cousins. Why? Powers asked, recording the interview. "I was trying to get rid of all the ugly people in the world," he said. "I considered the blacks the ugliest people of all."

In an MSNBC documentary about these events, Powers says she felt that she had spoken to "somebody extremely evil, someone that is very much the devil walking on this earth." She also told the *Cincinnati Enquirer,* "He's evil and he's a weak person. Killing was his way of feeling powerful and important. This is a person who is alive when he is killing."

Three days after meeting with Powers and thirteen years after meeting DiFalco, Franklin called the Cincinnati prosecutor's office, asked to be connected to Powers, and told her that he'd killed two women in West Virginia and wanted to confess to that too. He'd heard that some guy in West Virginia was locked up for it. "The only thing I can say is he was convicted just due to the sheer number of people lying about it," Franklin told Powers.

He described the women and their clothing, said that he had stopped at a convenience store with them, that he had placed their bodies in a field after he shot them, and that he dumped their belongings—which he remembered as army military duffels—off the highway he took toward Lexington, Kentucky. He now said he'd shot the women inside his car while one sat in the passenger seat and the other in the backseat. He said he thought he had fired three shots—the actual number is five—but was sure he had been driving a Chevy Nova then. He said that his bullets went through their bodies and that the shots had maybe shattered the passenger-side window, which he had rolled down. He said he had killed the "dirty-hippie-type broads" because they admitted that they were "into race mixing." He asked Powers to contact the authorities in West Virginia and also to return and see him again, if she wanted another sworn confession.

Powers drove back to Potosi the following week.

"Did you get any emotional satisfaction out of killing either one of those girls or both of the girls?" she asked him.

"What do you mean?"

"Was there any—emotional, did you get, I guess, what was your feeling afterwards? Or during?"

"I'm not really sure, you know. It's not that you get emotional satisfaction. It's just that you, you know, it's someone you think should be wasted, you know. So I just went ahead and wasted them. You know?" Franklin said. "To me it was just, you know, something I had to do. It's a nasty job, but somebody had to do it."

"Can you see their faces in your mind? Can you see them?" Powers asked.

"Basically yeah, I can see them."

Newspaper reports exploded the next day with headlines like "Prosecutor Face to Face with Monster," "Former Model in Peril," and "High Fashion Prosecutor Gets Her Man." The MSNBC documentary produced later was dubbed *Beauty and the Beast*.

This title may speak to a truth about how many understood Franklin at the time, as well as his crimes, and the events that drew Powers into his orbit. Though we in the United States have adopted an eighteenth-century French version of *Beauty and the Beast* as our own, variations on the story of a young girl forced to marry a hideous animal because of her father's crimes exist in language traditions and countries all over the world, including Italy, Spain, Germany, Denmark, Switzerland, Romania, Ireland, Scotland, Norway, Russia, India, China, and Greece. A 2016 comprehensive that used two thousand "types" of stories from more than two hundred societies found that only fourteen stories could be traced all the way back to a time before languages split into their current branches, somewhere between twenty-five hundred and six thousand years ago. This story is one of them.

There was no animal and no father and no marriage in the real world of course, but the media comparison of Powers and Franklin to this tale tells us something in the language of story truth: people don't kill other people for no clear reason, we say; only animals do. Fathers rack up the balance. Daughters pay it.

5

THE WEST VIRGINIA STATE PENITENTIARY at Moundsville was under a state order to close when Jacob Beard stepped off the bus there in 1993. During a riot several years earlier, prisoners took control of the facility—guards were handcuffed with their own handcuffs, and three inmates were killed—earning the place a spot on the list of "The 10 Most Violent Prisons in America." Prisoners picked some of their cell locks easily; other locks hadn't worked in years. The cells didn't have solid walls or doors but were only bars facing the catwalk. It was common for inmates to smuggle flammable liquid out of one of the job shops, reach through the open bars of their target's cell, and throw it on the sleeping inmate, followed by a lit tissue. There were roaches in the food, and fat rats ran through the cells.

Beard had been given two life terms without the possibility for parole.

"I maintain my innocence," Beard said at his sentencing a month after his trial's conclusion, on July 16, 1993. "I was wrongly accused, and I was wrongly convicted. This past year has been a tragedy for myself and my family." His daughters were in the courtroom and intertwined their hands as he spoke, then hugged him and each other before he was taken away.

In prison, Beard's health plummeted. At the time of his sentencing, he was experiencing high blood pressure at near stroke-causing levels. "His blood pressure is so high I would consider it critical," his doctor wrote. "To my knowledge he had none of this medical problem until the present legal problems arose." Decades of heavy alcohol abuse had tanked his liver and his stomach. "Mr. Beard reports that he has not consumed alcoholic beverages since September 1990, but readily admits an alcohol problem," wrote his counselor.

He was also taking Tofranil, a drug indicated for major depression and suicidality. Prison medical records reveal Beard was struggling with severe anxiety episodes at first believed to be heart attacks. "This patient has a major stress syndrome and needs, very likely, hospitalization," a report noted. Beard had exhausted his finances. "He is so distraught over the legal matters he is unable to sleep or function."

Moundsville sits in the thin northern panhandle of West Virginia, which extends into Pennsylvania, and it was hard for Beard's family, split between Florida and Greenbrier County, West Virginia, to get there even if they had wanted to. He spoke to his daughters on the phone sometimes, but things were still strained with Linda.

Then in February 1995, Beard was on the bus that took the first forty prisoners to the new and more modern Mount Olive Correctional Complex in southwest West Virginia, which at least had solid cell walls. These early arrivers were to get the prison ready to open—clean, move tables and chairs—and got better cell assignments as thanks. Slightly improved, Beard could now participate in his appeal.

At the jump of Beard's trial, Weiford had made a motion to bar the defense from presenting testimony that suggested Franklin killed Vicki and Nancy, arguing that any such testimony would be unreliable hearsay. Beard's lawyers had wanted to bring Franklin in person to testify at the trial, but by 1993, nine years after Franklin whispered to DiFalco that he had done it, something had shifted in him again, and he was unwilling to cooperate, ignoring letters and calls from Beard's lawyers and refusing even to give a deposition that could be read as a sworn statement in court. Undeterred, Beard's lawyers planned to introduce into evidence Franklin's March 1, 1984, confession to Wisconsin agent Smith and to call DiFalco to the stand to testify about the hand-drawn map and her investigation.

"These statements have sufficient guarantees of trustworthiness and should be admitted by the Court," Farmer had written, adding that "the admission of these statements is in the best interests of justice."

Weiford argued that they were not. He reiterated the reasons why he felt Franklin's confession was not believable—the lack of route numbers on the map, the faulty distance estimations, the wrong name of the county where he had supposedly killed them.

Farmer cited Federal Rule of Evidence 804(b)(3), which states that a confession from someone other than the defendant "offered to exculpate the accused is not admissible unless corroborating circumstances clearly indicate the trustworthiness of the statement"; the map that Franklin drew was clearly corroboration, Farmer argued.

But Franklin had since gone back on the confession he gave to Wisconsin agents, Weiford countered, when he refused to talk on tape to Debbie DiFalco. Perhaps he was simply trying to snatch credit—build his murder portfolio?

Judge Lobban agreed and granted the prosecution's motion—mostly. "I propose to let our officers say what they did in the course of the investigation, but not say what he said specifically," Lobban stated, "other than he made statements that 'I did it,' and he made statements 'that I didn't.'" Invoking the four life sentences Franklin was already serving for crimes in other states, the judge called Franklin "a four-time loser" with nowhere further down to go.

In 1994, Beard's lawyers submitted his case to the West Virginia State Supreme Court of Appeals, raising as grounds the use of hypnosis techniques, the lack of competency hearings for Walton and Lewis, the state's use of witnesses who gave knowingly false testimony, and Judge Lobban's refusal to allow the defense to present evidence that would support a Franklin theory of the crime. Farmer, now a more established attorney in the firm, was the one to talk to Beard on the phone, visit him in prison, and prepare the briefs.

The court denied the appeal on most grounds, except for a legal technicality that acknowledged the police might have erred by using information Beard gave them at the meeting when he had been given immunity for "the cat thing"; it threw the decision on that back to Lobban. After reviewing all the evidence, Lobban ruled against Beard on this matter as well—he felt Alkire and Weiford had not erred and that the outcome in the case would have been unchanged.

Stephen Farmer stayed on Beard's case long after the money was gone. He felt the appeal process had given Beard only one option: to appeal Lobban's ruling on the technicality back up to the state supreme court. But Farmer also felt strongly that this was a fruitless path. Instead, in 1997, he filed a motion for a new trial based on the sworn confession Franklin had made to Cincinnati prosecutor Melissa Powers.

In Pocahontas County, Walt Weiford was no longer any kind of prosecutor but rather a regular lawyer in his own practice. Alkire had retired from the West Virginia State Police in 1994 and was now pursuing a political career running for county sheriff. Yet they both appeared for the hearing on Farmer's motion for a new trial, reprising their old roles. Weiford argued that Franklin had already confessed to the killings before Jacob Beard's 1993 trial and his statement was not newly discovered evidence; if the defense had wanted to use Franklin's testimony, they should have done so then. But Farmer reminded the court that Franklin had been unwilling to cooperate at the time, refusing all of Farmer's requests for an interview.

Well, Lobban said to Farmer, call your witnesses. Let's see what they've got to say that we haven't already heard.

Farmer called Powers first, then Deborah DiFalco.

"He was really disturbed after he found out someone had been convicted of these murders and was in jail. That seemed to bother him a lot," DiFalco testified. Franklin had kept calling her after Beard's conviction. "He would be talking about some idea, some philosophy he was reading, and then he would say, you know, I just don't understand why [the people in West Virginia] don't believe me."

"Do you believe him?" asked Farmer.

"I don't believe that he is lying. I don't know where he would get his facts from if he didn't have some knowledge about it."

Weiford called Alkire as a rebuttal witness to show that Franklin's facts—that he had fired three shots total, for example—were fundamentally flawed.

Farmer then cross-examined Alkire. "That's happened to you in other cases. When the guy says I shot x amount of times, and the physical evidence is different from that, right?"

Alkire agreed that this sometimes happened. "They usually shoot until the gun is empty."

Judge Lobban reminded those assembled that five conditions had to be met for a new trial to be granted on the basis of new evidence. First, he said, the evidence had to have been discovered after the trial, based on the affidavit of a new witness. Second, Beard and his legal team had to have been diligent in "ascertaining and securing" the evidence, and it had to be proven that such diligence "would not have secured it before the verdict." Third, the evidence "must be new and material," not "cumulative," that is, "evidence of the same kind to the same point." Fourth, the evidence would have to be sufficient to produce a different verdict at the second trial than at the first. Fifth, the "sole object of the new evidence" could not be to "discredit or impeach a witness on the opposite side." In order for all of these conditions to be met, Lobban needed to hear from Franklin himself. He ordered that Franklin be deposed and charged Farmer with doing it.

Farmer would not have to travel to see Franklin alone—members of the media wanted to go too. Thanks to Powers and a local Cincinnati journalist, Charlie Rose had heard about the case of Jacob Beard and the strange serial killer named Joseph Paul Franklin. In November 1998, a crew from *60 Minutes II* traveled to Potosi. Franklin wasted no time in front of the expensive camera setup. "I did it," he said.

Next stop: Pocahontas County. CBS's Charlie Rose spoke to Arnold Cutlip, who again reiterated the same version of events he'd been telling since 1980—he and Johnnie Lewis were together all day, cutting locust posts. Farmer took a statement from Cutlip to use in court: "At no time on that day did Mr. Lewis or I see the Rainbow Girls, Ritchie Fowler, Gerald Brown, Billy McCoy or Jacob Beard. At all times on June 25, 1980, Johnnie Lewis was with me, and at no time were we with the Rainbow Girls, Ritchie Fowler, Gerald Brown, Billy McCoy or Jacob Beard." Farmer filed Cutlip's affidavit as support for his motion for a new trial—if what Cutlip said was true, Lewis could not have witnessed Beard commit the killings.

On Friday, January 22, 1999, Judge Lobban came into the courtroom, called the parties to order, and without much fanfare announced that he was granting Beard a new trial.

Weiford took off his glasses and sat down. He didn't look well. Would Pocahontas County really seek to retry Beard a second time? Lobban asked. Without hesitation, Weiford stated that it would, though it would cost the county an estimated $100,000.

In a strange and nearly unprecedented move, Judge Lobban then set a bond amount for Beard. If he could pay it, he could walk free and stay free until his new trial began. Beard posted his bond with help from a bonding company, and two hours later, after being incarcerated for nearly six years, he boarded a plane to Florida.

The *Putnam County Courier Journal,* published in Crescent City, Florida, ran a front-page photograph of Beard being greeted at the Jacksonville airport by his two daughters. A bold one-inch headline proclaimed "FREE!" In Pocahontas County, there was mourning. The *Pocahontas Times* simply proclaimed, "Beard Out on Bond."

"The Case Against Jake Beard" aired on CBS on February 3, 1999. Franklin had gotten a haircut for television, his chin shone, and light reflected off his small round glasses. Cutlip appeared in front of a vaguely golden nineties background to tell his story, emphasizing that they were just regular Joes who cut posts and sold them for a dollar each, not murderers. Beard appeared in an orange jumpsuit to assert his innocence once again. Prison had not been kind to his body—he was pale, bloated. His heart was failing; also his kidneys and lungs.

While Beard was driving a tractor in Florida and attorneys were filing motions and going to court in West Virginia, Alkire, West Virginia State Police investigators, and the Pocahontas County Sheriff's Office launched yet another investigation. Weiford had been a hero in Pocahontas County after he'd convicted Beard the first time; now people touched him on the arm in Foodland and asked him how he was holding up. Both Weiford and Alkire came out of retirement to completely reconstruct their case against Beard—everyone who had been interviewed the first time around and was still alive was reinterviewed.

In May 2000, in a trial held an hour outside Charleston that took two weeks, all the original parties reconvened. All the prosecution witnesses from the first trial were present and told the same stories, even Johnnie Lewis, despite Cutlip's affidavit. Bill McCoy, the third alleged passenger of the blue van, was transported from Las Vegas, where he was incarcerated, to give testimony. But this time, to cast additional doubt on the testimony of Walton and Lewis, the defense hired a professor of psychology named Elizabeth Loftus as an expert witness.

In the late 1980s and early 1990s, a phenomenon called "repressed memory" rose to the public consciousness when a series of therapeutic patients, mostly women, experienced old memories of physical or sexual abuse surfacing with the help of their therapists, then sought to prosecute their attackers. One such case was that of Eileen Franklin-Lipsker, a young woman in suburban California who, in 1989, came forward to say that she had recently become aware of memories of her father molesting and murdering her best friend twenty years earlier. Her childhood friend's case was reopened by the prosecutor for San Mateo County, and Franklin-Lipsker testified in detail about riding in the car with her father when he committed the crime, and even recalled the ring her friend had been wearing when she died. The father was convicted of murder and sentenced to life in prison without the possibility of parole.

Similar cases followed, and approximately half the states passed laws allowing for repressed memory witness testimony. Franklin-Lipsker's father's sentence was later overturned, however, when it came to light that she learned the details of her testimony from a TV special that showed her friend's crime scene; many of the other cases also turned out to be flawed, and costly civil lawsuits accusing therapists of planting memories and prosecutors of using shady statements multiplied.

Elizabeth Loftus was something of the reigning queen in the field of repressed memory and its legal implications for eyewitness testimony, particularly when it came to disbelieving it. She had consulted or testified as an expert witness on hundreds of cases—the trial of the officers accused in the Rodney King beating, the Michael Jackson case, and the Oklahoma City bombing case among them—and advocated that the wording of the swearing-in of a witness be changed to: "Do you swear to tell the truth, the whole truth, or whatever it is you think you remember?"

"There is virtually no credible scientific evidence that memory of traumatic events can be massively repressed for prolonged periods of time and then reliably recovered," Loftus writes. She argued that memory does not work like a tape recorder, passively storing true observations that can be retrieved later. Rather, she believed, human memory is very fallible, susceptible to making mistakes in its recording and regurgitation as a result of many environmental factors—leading questions, the perceptions of others present at an event, "expectations of the self or others," and even small differences in language.

In one 1979 study, Loftus asked participants to view footage of two cars colliding and then prompted them to estimate the speeds at which the two cars were moving. She found that they gave much higher estimates if asked how fast they were moving when they "smashed into" each other than if the word "hit" was used, and that if prompted to discuss a broken headlight that didn't exist, participants were more likely to say it did if asked, "Did you see the broken headlight?" versus "Did you see a broken headlight?"

Another study by Loftus's colleagues found that 36 percent of participants claimed to have seen footage of a fictional news event called "the explosion in the Bali nightclub," and of these, all but one (97.2 percent) were "willing to provide details of where they were and who they were with at the time" when they watched the footage. Loftus coined the phrase "the imagination inflation effect" to explain the phenomenon of why people claim to have seen actual footage of highly traumatic public events that were never captured on film—the death of Princess Diana in 1997, for example. "The widespread news coverage of such events is bound to lead people to imagine the scene in their mind's eye which in itself may lead to the formation of false memories," the researchers concluded.

Loftus also set about to show that false memories can be implanted into the minds of subjects. Her studies successfully created false memories for impossible things—meeting Bugs Bunny (a Warner Brothers character) at Disneyland, for example, or experiencing fictitious medical procedures. Loftus found that many people could not differentiate between having memories of things they had actually done versus things they had imagined doing.

"If a person remembers that a trip on a ski lift badly scared him, he may choose to go cross-country skiing rather than downhill skiing next time," writes Loftus. "If a child remembers that she got horribly sick after eating chili last summer, she may find chili inedible in the future. However, do false memories have these same sorts of consequences for people's lives?" The answer is yes.

Studies further showed that social or interpersonal factors can have profound results on the production of false memories, like an interviewer with "high status" and a participant with "low status," or an extroverted interviewer and an introverted participant. Individual factors also matter. One study found that more aggressive people were more likely to form false memories for having perpetrated acts of violence or aggression.

In a 2013 study, Loftus and her team had college students undergo routine medical checkups performed by research assistants whose practices were videotaped and found to be free of any impropriety. The students were then called up and told that several other students had accused the research assistant (RA) who had examined them of inappropriate behavior, and then (1) asked about their experiences with the RA and (2) asked to sign a formal complaint against the RA; the interviewer, participants were told, "just needed a few more students to sign on" so they could fire her.

The study found that 17 percent were suggestible and suggestible participants were more likely to make a false accusation, but an additional 27 percent of participants agreed to sign the complaint even "after repeatedly denying that the accused research assistant had behaved inappropriately during their own encounter." Like a Venn diagram, then, two groups emerge with an overlapping portion in the middle: those who are genuinely "suggestible" and believe the false information to be true, and those who don't but are willing to tell a false story anyway because of social pressure. The result, of course, is the same.

* * *

Beard's defense team sent Loftus copies of Lewis and Walton's testimony, which she read and annotated.

"In the testimony of both of these persons, they claim to have lost and then subsequently recovered memories of the events of June 25, 1980, involving the death of the victims in this case," she writes. "The claims of both Mr. Walton and Mr. Lewis with regard to their lost and recovered memories are contradicted by generally accepted scientific studies regarding the working of memory. Consequently, the validity of their memories is highly questionable."

As citizens of Pocahontas County who had read numerous newspaper accounts of the crimes, including from the Bobby Morrison and Gerald Brown era, Walton and Lewis were steeped in case details and speculation. There was also Walton's dream and the hypnosis treatment he had been subjected to.

"Numerous scientific studies of memory demonstrate that such suggestive techniques can create the illusion of memory—that even the act of imagining an event can create a 'memory' of an event that never occurred."

Yet at the first trial, both Walton and Lewis seemed very sure that what they remembered was fact. "Did these events that you've told the grand jury, did they happen, Pee Wee?" Weiford had asked in 1992. "Yes," Walton responded. "Are you sure?" "Yes."

Yet, Loftus says, the degree to which a witness is convinced of the truth of their memories is not always an accurate predictor of their actual basis in fact.

"I have little doubt that Eileen Franklin believes with every cell of her being that her father murdered [her friend]," Loftus writes. "But I believe there is a very real possibility that the whole concoction was spun not from solid facts but from the vaporous breezes of wishes, dreams, fears, desires. Eileen's mind, operating independently of reality, went about its business of collecting ambiguities and inconsistencies and wrapping them up into a sensible package, revealing to her in one blinding moment of insight a coherent picture of the past that was nevertheless completely and utterly false. Eileen's story is her truth, but I believe it is a truth that never happened."

Loftus's flight from California to West Virginia for Beard's retrial got delayed by a bad storm, and she had to be driven through the night in a taxi from Washington, DC, to Braxton County—a change of venue motion was also granted for the retrial—to make it in time to testify. Franklin's deposition was read into evidence.

On the stand, Weiford prompted Bill McCoy through his movements on June 25, 1980. McCoy finally gave Weiford the statement the prosecution had long been seeking—that he was there in the blue van when he, Fowler, and Walton had picked up Vicki and Nancy and driven them to the mountain, and that he'd seen Fowler cleaning out the inside of the van later that night and noted bullet holes in its side.

Farmer rose to cross-examine McCoy.

"Did you see Jacob Beard?" Farmer asked, of the day in question.

"Don't know. Don't think so," McCoy said.

"Did you see these girls?"

"Definitely not."

McCoy had gotten addicted to heroin in prison and was hallucinating and vomiting from the withdrawal when Alkire contacted him again, McCoy told the court. He agreed to testify when Weiford offered to get him into a methadone program, and he took the information in his testimony from information Weiford and Alkire told him.

"I was just wanting to get out to get what I needed," he admitted.

Alkire took the stand for the prosecution, once again carrying his large black binder.

Weiford asked Alkire a few preliminary questions, establishing the early years of the investigation, and then turned the witness over to Farmer. Weiford thought he would have the opportunity to ask Alkire many more rebuttal questions once Farmer was finished, as had been the case at the first trial. But Farmer did not even rise. "I have no questions for this witness," Farmer said. Both Weiford and Alkire were stunned. The judge had to repeat that Alkire was excused several times before he stood to leave the stand.

The morning of closing arguments, May 30, 2000, Weiford was getting ready in his hotel room with his wife when he collapsed. He was rushed to Charleston Area Medical Center with one of the worst cases of walking pneumonia physicians there had ever seen; he also suffered from severe dehydration and kidney problems. The jury was sent home for the day while a solution was found. Weiford's young assistant Steve Dolly agreed that if given the afternoon and all night, he could be prepared to act in Weiford's stead. He and Stephen Farmer delivered closing arguments the following day.

In under three hours' worth of deliberations, the jury of nine men and three women found Jacob Beard not guilty. Again, Beard sat stock-still when the verdict was read, but this time his eyes did wet with tears afterward, and he turned to look at his wife, Linda, who winked at him.

Interviewed by Susan Strong, one juror said that the prosecution's case lacked sufficient evidence—"We looked at all the points of contention. We went on the basis of the evidence. We felt the defense was correct and certain things were not convincing enough from the prosecution to merit a guilty verdict."

"Truth wins in the end," Beard told Strong. "I don't know that this will prove it to everyone, people who know me know I didn't do this. My conscience is clear."

"The system we have is the best system in the world," Alkire said. "You've got to accept what the jury says. There's still one more judge Mr. Beard has to go through." But Alkire was also relieved, he told reporters. The case was finally over.

"Over for Beard," wrote Strong, "but not for two families still grieving after 20 years and still looking for answers about the brutal murders of their daughters and sisters." Nancy's mom and sister Kathy had come again, but only for the first week of this trial; Vicki's sister Mary and cousin had declined to return.

And perhaps it was not over for Walton or Lewis, whose memories had been the subject of much testimony. "Some things you just don't forget," Steve Dolly told the *Charleston Gazette*. "Some things live on in our minds long after the event has passed."

Strong called her boss, the aging McNeel, at the office of the *Pocahontas Times* and reported the verdict. It was Wednesday, too late to get the story into the paper—it would have to wait. The *Gazette* would scoop them—their own hometown saga.

But the following week, people in every part of Pocahontas County read Strong's news: "The 20-year-old Rainbow Murders are once again officially unsolved."

PART VI:
JESSE IN THE QUIET ZONE

I believe that the normal human heart is born good. That is, it's born sensitive and feeling, eager to be approved and to approve, hungry for simple happiness and the chance to live. It neither wishes to be killed, nor to kill. If through circumstances, it is overcome by evil, it never becomes entirely evil. There remain in it elements of good, however recessive, which continue to hold the possibility of restoration.

—Pearl S. Buck

Beard, West Virginia, 2016

1

THAT WINTER OF 2009, IT snowed more than any year on record, and the Director sometimes called to tell me her dreams. She dreamed of making Mountain Views a boarding school so girls could opt out of the public school system if they wished and roll into classes at the Mountain Views office in smiley-faced pajamas, even in snow.

I had moved again and was living in a historic one-room schoolhouse that sat right off 219 on the crest of Droop Mountain. The schoolhouse had belonged to a long line of VISTAs before me, most of them women, most of them also placed with Mountain Views. It had beige carpeting and faux wood-paneled walls and furniture that previous girls had plucked, plopped, and left. One such item was the phone. It was pale and square with a ringer so powerful it vibrated the plastic shell and shocked me awake. There was no cell reception here, so to talk to the Mountain Views girls or anyone else, I sat in the small office and held the phone's spiral cord.

My landlords were an elderly couple who treated me more like a guest to take care of than like a tenant with whom to transact business. They lived a little ways down 219 in a neat ranch house and were retired, though they still worked every day tending their chickens and sheep. They stopped in to check on me, invited me over for Sunday dinner, and showed me how to cook ramps, that flavorful cousin to the onion that grows only in patches of shade in the Appalachian mountains. After a particularly big snow, the husband got his John Deere out of the shed and moved a white mountain from in front of my house so I could see the road and feel a part of the world again. The orange cat, whom I'd brought with me from the farmhouse, tread and retread the windowsill when I kept him inside, and courted death by writhing around in the middle of 219 when I didn't.

Peter and Dan, a DMHB recently back from living abroad, hitchhiked occasionally, just from Droop to Lewisburg if they were short on cash, and my house was a good place to park and catch a ride or to leave a truck in favor of a carpool. They knocked sometimes on my storm door to ask permission or tell me of their plans, to ask for a glass of water or see what I was baking. Trey was rarely with them; he and I had split, and several months passed without me seeing him.

Then one night, he and I both ended up in a ten-person crew of DMHBs and friends who were squatting in an abandoned house after a night of drinking in the Lewisburg bars. Everyone seemed to be pairing off, but I found a quiet upstairs room and went to sleep in a sleeping bag on the floor.

I woke to a heavy weight bearing down on my chest. It was Trey. My sleeping bag was down around my waist and he was lying on top of me, kissing my mouth. I can't be certain what I said; the word or words, if I said any, are gone now, but I feel sure I made some sound, something low and wincing.

What? Trey said, pulling his face back from mine.

I looked at his face in the light streaming in through the window, and I saw that he knew what, and his face changed from looking outward to looking inward, reflecting a kind of fear—fear of himself I think, and of what he had been doing. He rolled himself off of me.

It wasn't a huge boundary crossing—for that, I suppose, I should count myself among the lucky—but it felt like a crossing nonetheless and the first one, and something in me was never quite the same again. There was the person of before this night and there was the person I became after it.

When I woke in the morning, I saw that the hardwood floor we had slept on was covered in black ash. It was in my sleeping bag, my hair, my eyes. Trey was curled up against a wall in the fetal position. I left him there.

* * *

Deeper into winter, I was supposed to meet Ruth, a VISTA worker from Kentucky and the best friend I had then, at the restaurant in Hillsboro for a special Valentine's Day dinner and movie event, but she didn't show. I looked at the walls, which Ruth and Trey and Peter and I had painted in exchange for pizza and beer, until the lights in the restaurant began to flicker, and the waitress who'd given me extra mashed potatoes on the house came over to say they were closing early. When she and I stepped outside, I could hardly see the café's wooden steps before me—the wind was blowing the snow sideways. I was stalling in the parking lot with the heat on, hoping the storm would let up a little, when I heard a honk. I rolled down my window. It was the waitress.

Where do you live? she called.

Top of Droop, I said.

Follow me, she said. You can follow my lights.

I was thankful for her then and even more so as we wound our way up the mountain going five, maybe eight miles an hour. It was a total white-out, impossible to tell which lane I was in or if I was even on the road at all. When we finally passed the sign for Droop Mountain Battlefield State Park, she honked again, accelerated into the snow, and was gone.

The light was on at my house—odd. When I opened my front door, Ruth leapt into my arms in her snow pants, and we hugged each other and danced, rejoicing in the other's safety. Thus set up with bowls of Corn Chex and something stupid on TV, we killed that blizzard and several more. Ruth was living in a house at the end of a two-mile road on land that its owners had turned into a Christmas tree farm, but when it snowed, it was a half-hour walk to her front door. She lived with me for most of that winter. She was still dating Peter, who lived with his parents, so soon Peter was there most nights too. My house was so close to the road that there were only two places to park, so Peter usually parked his truck across the road by the mailboxes, annoying the mailwoman and leading to some speculation about what the doctor's son was doing with two VISTA girls every night up on Droop Mountain.

I gave Ruth and Peter the small back bedroom that had a door you could close. My own bed was separated from the yellow kitchen by a curtain only, and the cat, still a kitten really, had a habit of waking me once an hour with his nose and claws. When pushing him off the bed gently with my hands failed and doing the same with my feet only turned the volume up on his madness, I grew frustrated and then enraged. One night, I threw him across the room so hard and fast that when he scrambled to his feet on the carpet, he spent several minutes looking at me and cocking his head from side to side, stunned. On more than one occasion, I locked him in the cold laundry room away from his food for hours, prompting whimpers of betrayal or hunger or both.

Sometimes, particularly when Ruth and Peter were out, a feeling came. It wasn't a new feeling, but I was surprised at its return, so soon, here in this new landscape. In college, I'd be getting dressed in some kind of shirt contraption that tied behind my neck, and I'd feel fear and energy surge up like two dolphins rising in sync and know that a tide of alcohol was coming and that I'd lose the night tomorrow.

I tried to put this feeling into shoveling snow. It snowed continuously, so I had ample opportunity. I dug my car out in the morning before work, and again in the afternoon to drive to a meeting, and sometimes again after the meeting, or again in the evening to make the drive home. I had been catching rides to Mountain Views with a coworker who had a four-wheel drive, but even still we were obliged to park at the foot of the steep driveway and hike the rest of the way up on foot. Somewhere around the twenty-second school day missed, the Director called and told me not to come to work until spring.

I had already read all the books I had and watched every even slightly gay television show available on the internet. Some evenings I stood at the living room window with the cat and counted the number of individual revolutions made by the tires of cars driving carefully over the fresh powder. They honked sometimes if they knew me, just to say hello. Sometimes I talked to people from my old life on the beige phone—my college roommate, my mom—but the once-cute question "Where are you again?" became aggravating and then intolerable. I let that phone ring and ring.

* * *

One white Friday afternoon, when winter's volume had gone down, I was just finishing up digging out my car when a squat black Honda hatchback I had often seen at pool night slowed on 219, then stopped near where I was sweating. I knew the driver; we'd chatted and laughed together. He was the one who'd worn shorts with wool socks even into late October. He rolled down the passenger-side window.

Need help?

Actually, I just finished, I said. Perfect timing.

The driver laughed. He said his name, then my name, then thumbed toward his passenger.

This is Jesse, he said, and Jesse bobbed his head in acknowledgment. His shape was familiar. I knew he too had been there some Friday nights, but I couldn't place him in the center of any particular scene, couldn't call up any joke he'd made or song he'd played.

Six hours later, I was back at my house, only this time it was dark, and I was looking at it from the other side of the road as I passed, seated inside a white sedan with dark tinted windows driven by a man who played the mandolin. There was bluegrass music every Friday night at the restaurant in Hillsboro, and while there I'd run into the driver of the black hatchback again and this mandolin player. We stood around together, having a few beers, and they asked me if I'd like to come to Lewisburg with them to keep the music and the fun going. My old landlord and coworker Sam's stepfather, Don, was playing a show there.

Ever since Sam had knocked on my door one day the previous summer, I'd been going to all of Don's shows. Don was a banjo player and the front man for a band that was sort of famous around the county, Sam had told me. Later I would find out this was an understatement—Don's band was notable throughout West Virginia and many other places where bluegrass music is revered.

The first time I'd seen him play, his band had stood on the wooden portion of a flatbed truck, shaded by a white pop-up tent. He tapped the microphone and smiled. He did not pander, but the crowd paid attention.

I didn't know the songs yet, but I knew they were being played very well. The sound a bluegrass banjo makes when it repeats itself—metal up, metal down. They seemed to throw the song around to each other. Don would sing the verse and then step back from the mic. Then all five men would lean together for the chorus.

When you encounter for the first time a thing that will change your experience of living, something like an alarm bell goes off. The tall woman who did not love me was like that. Her shaved neck and the backs of her ears and how she turned them to me when she danced and the light that bounced off the skin there—very pale. Also, bluegrass.

I sat in the back of the sedan. The mandolin player was driving, and a man who worked as the chef in the gourmet cafeteria that served the scientists who worked on the famous Pocahontas County telescope sat shotgun. He drank from a can of Nattie Light nestled in a yellow coozie.

So you're gonna DD? he said to the mandolin player.

Well, the mandolin player said, within reason. He made a gimme gesture, and the Chef took a beer from a twenty-four pack at his feet and handed it to the mandolin player, who opened it with one hand and plopped it into the driver's cup holder. I had been around the proverbial block long enough by this point to know that drinking in a moving car was a thing not infrequently done here and not necessarily cause for extreme alarm, but not long enough to let my sense overcome the thrill.

We stopped at a green double-wide set back from the road. The thin man from that afternoon—Jesse—got in the back with me. He had to fold himself to fit, then hunched low and forward. He took off his bright yellow West Virginia Mountaineers hoodie to reveal a T-shirt that bore the name of Don's band. The faces of its members hung loose on his body.

You're a big fan, then? I said.

Yeah, Jesse said. They're cool as shit. Don's my uncle.

The Chef passed back two silver beers, and Jesse and I took them and opened them in twin pops. Jesse fished an Altoids box from his deep jeans pocket, opened it, and withdrew a joint. He lit it and passed it around without hitting it himself. When it returned to him, Jesse pulled on it a long time, then slumped back against the sedan's leather seat. When the mandolin player prompted him to pass it forward again, Jesse snapped to attention. He had been somewhere else.

We wound our way down the south side of Droop Mountain. The mandolin player talked. I learned he had a male roommate he took care of and that he drove race cars. It showed—he drove the curves of 219 with a speed I'd never known and let the car drift over the center line into the other lane to keep from braking, even when we went around a blind curve.

If someone's coming, I'll see their lights, he said.

Route 219 widened and flattened as we cruised into Lewisburg, where I went every week for Kashi cereal and fresh grapefruits, purchased with food stamps issued to me by the US government. Buoyed by funding for the nearby women's prison and the osteopathic medical school, Lewisburg had been recently reborn as a prosperous college town, drawing cool young Appalachians and DC summer people. There was an Irish pub for craft beer and folk music. Teenagers stood on corners sipping smoothies from bubble-topped plastic cups, and young men in khaki pants and institution-bearing sweatshirts held glass doors open for their skirted dates.

The mandolin player turned the car down a little side street, then maneuvered it through an alley, where we parked in a special, semi-legal spot behind the bar where Don's band was playing. My companions scooped ice cubes into red Solo cups and fixed themselves Old Crow and Sprites. I accepted mine with thanks. I appreciated that drink, the way it fizzed and popped carbonation into my nostrils, the way I appreciated the whole night—it was free, something gotten for nothing.

Don's band stood with their backs to the bar's plate-glass front window, so that a passerby outside would get just the butts of their baseball caps. Inside we were luckier. If old-time music is sweet, all strum and pluck, bluegrass is salty. A banjo made for bluegrass has a metal resonator and is played three-finger style with metal finger picks so that its sound is one hundred times louder than a drum skin alone, either plucked or strummed.

The sign above the liquor bottles behind the bar was red, the tips of the crowd's cigarettes were red, and Don's Converse sneakers were red. The sparked ends of fifty cigarettes went down every time Don thunked on a melody note with his thumb pick, then up again with every whirring of his index and middle fingers over the drone notes. This happened freaky fast—cigarettes twitched to keep up; people jangled their limbs with the same energy they might use to appreciate a rangy electric guitar solo. I perceived the low-down power of the upright bass, played by a billiard bald man in a Hawaiian button-down shirt, almost subaudibly—felt in my throat more than heard in my ears.

This is good, I said aloud, to Jesse apparently, as he was suddenly the only person within spitting distance I knew.

Jesse had a beer to his lips, but he was looking hard at the band over its rim. His eyes were open. He barely moved, but he did move. His breath filled his small chest and then left it; his throat, white beneath a puff of goatee, glugged. Little whiffs of vitality—he emitted them like a star, first in blasts, then in a steady, gentle pattern to match the song's rhythm. He seemed to plump, turn redder, perhaps trying to match the bar's color. Jesse let the beer can fall and looked down at me. I arranged my face to show him that I was serious about what I had said about the music, that it was meant to be truer than a thumbs-up. Jesse lifted his eyes back to the band, but I felt him see me too, felt him register my greeting and reply in kind. The extra fabric of his jeans, loose on his body, tented ever so slightly in my direction.

Jesse was a frequency you had to tune into. Once I tuned in, I started noticing things. If you asked him a question, he'd say, "Ummm," or "Hmm," and think about it—really think about it—a long time. He asked me questions and listened to my answers. Questions! It's such a small thing, the construction of a sentence and its intonation, ending high instead of low, but it was huge to me, a quiet and obedient child; it created a space for me to move into. What did you study in college? Jesse asked me. Do you miss your family? Why did you come here?

I bought Jesse a shot. He went down to it instead of lifting it up to him. He bought me a shot and a beer. I drank them. Girl can drink, he said. I could; I had the genes for it—an alcoholic's tolerance and ability to stay upright even when blitzed. We went back to the sedan and made ourselves another drink, except with less Sprite and more Old Crow. We sat on two cement parking barriers. He told me that he had grown up listening to his uncle play, but that now he had his own band, in which he played the upright bass.

They don't want to practice like I want to practice, he said.

I think I might be a writer, I said.

I remember coming back up Droop Mountain, Jesse's hand up my shirt, the lights of an oncoming car lighting up his neck, his mouth on my neck, the Chef turning around to look at us, the mandolin player watching in the rearview mirror. I remember waking, dry-mouthed, naked, and on my back, as I never slept, my big breasts lolled out across my stomach, Jesse's spine to me, his white ass, my white comforter, my cat trotting around the bed wanting to get fed. The light shifting; Jesse shifting to face me.

He got up and rooted around in my cupboards until he found the coffee. Sitting stock-still in bed, I listened to him place the filter, scoop the grains, and pour the water. He brought me some in a yellow mug.

Jesse pointed to a cowboy hat hanging from a peg on the white wall, another thing left by a previous VISTA girl.

You'd look good in that cowboy hat, he said.

Yeah? I said.

Yeah, he said.

We talked like that from the beginning—easy.

I drove him back to his parents' house, which had a pretty wooden fence I hadn't noticed when we'd picked him up the night before. He kept his neck slotted through my open passenger-side window a long time before he said good-bye. He told me about what he was going to do that day—help his mother around the house—and asked what I would do.

Work, I said. I had girls to call, and I wondered what I could possibly say to them now. I felt damaged, unfit for consumption or dispensation of counsel. I knew I had a prescription for Plan B somewhere in my house, in one of the boxes of books I'd lugged from Philadelphia. Finding it would take some time, a couple hours maybe. I drove away, turned onto a side road, opened my car door—*ding ding ding*—bedded down in the snow like a deer, and sat there for a long time.

Jesse began inviting me to the Tuesday music nights he hosted at the white board-and-batten house near the Greenbrier River that his grandmother had roamed until she died. At first, I used the truth that Tuesday nights were tutoring nights at Mountain Views as my excuse; the way that night had gone down with Jesse gave me an unsettled feeling I didn't want to linger over. The red-haired girl continued to struggle over the algebra problems I gave her. She was razor smart, that much was clear; she just got the order of operations mixed up.

When tutoring was over, I drove my Nicholas County charges up to the crest of Cheat Mountain, battling snow or rain as the altitude rose, to where their parents would meet my car. There was often comedy in those rides—How old *are* you? one girl would ask cheerfully as she scrolled through my iPod looking for Rihanna or Lady Gaga, anything but the pop country played by the only reliable radio station—and there was often joy: snacks and pumping the music loud against the cold night and just being together, people of not so different ages but very different origins, swapping stories of fish not caught and insults not internalized. There was sometimes something else—what is it about being in a moving car at night with music playing that makes questions that have long been burning in silence finally break into speech?

Usually after the students slammed my doors and climbed into their parents' cars, I turned around and drove the curves back down to 219 and then to my home on Droop. But one Tuesday night there was only one girl for me to drive up the mountain, and she told me a story so long and so good about how generous she and her parents had been to each other through a medical situation involving the failings of so many people who are not supposed to fail you, and then we sat in silence listening to Rihanna for the rest of the ride. Her resilience and her ambition and the weight of her responsibilities rolled off of her in waves, a smell I could have kept smelling forever. That night when I got back to 219, instead of cruising on into Hillsboro toward home, I took the left at the church with the slender white steeple and parked beside Jesse's house.

That house was kitchen—ancient black cast-iron stove, washing machine that served as counter space, Tweety Bird highball glasses—and it was living room—pink couch, ruffled curtains, trays of cigarette or weed ash stuffing the air. It was always the mandolin player, Jesse on bass, the Chef on guitar, and a bearish, good-natured blond man on banjo—clawhammer for old-time, not three-finger for bluegrass, but he was Jesse's friend, and even the wrong kind of banjo was better to Jesse than none at all. Other people often stopped by—Ruth, Peter, the boisterous DMHB brother, the driver of the black hatchback.

The mandolin player would call a song—"How Mountain Girls Can Love" or "This Weary Heart You Stole Away" or "Little Maggie"—and they would all sing. *I wait for you dear all night long, It seems you never do get home, I fall asleep at the break of day, Just to drive these awful blues away.* These songs are mostly about heartbreak, cheating on someone and being cheated on, leaving home, or death. *Oh yonder stands little Maggie, With a dram glass in her hands, She's drinking away her troubles, She's a courting some other man.* There was almost always longing, there was almost always sorrow. I recognized myself in them.

Music nights were long. They began for the men around 7 or 8 o'clock with dinner, usually hot dogs or a pot of sautéed meat that Jesse would fix on the cast-iron stove and that he and the band would eat together around the darkened TV. I usually arrived during the beer phase, Budweiser or Nattie Light in twenty-four-packs that sat front and center in Jesse's fridge and that I sometimes brought myself, stopping first at the Marathon gas station. Playing music and drinking were yoked together, and if in the pause between one song and the next there was not a beer ready and waiting, the men and I turned around looking at each other, confused, until someone—usually Jesse—got up to toss another round.

Generous does not approach what Jesse was—he would give you a ride home and a can of Natural Light and thank you for it. He put in ten-hour days hanging drywall with Peter and Trey, and then liked to sit quietly watching television or drinking a beer. I believe he was happiest in this way, when he could be quiet, when he could look out from behind his eyes at a room full of people and watch them and not be expected to do anything. He liked for the party to be big; he liked for people to have a good time.

Unlike many bass players who lean into the mammoth instrument and work it over with bopping shoulders, when Jesse played, only his fingers moved. His left hand went high, fretting the chords, and his right hand went low, plucking at the bass's great ropes. He didn't hit the string with the long sides of his fingers, but rather hooked each string with his fingertip and pulled it, with insane gentleness.

Liquor came later in the night—plastic handles of Old Crow mixed with soda. A certain mood took over then. We might make necklaces from Froot Loops and licorice strands, or duct-tape beer cans together like scepters and pronounce each other knights. It was delight; it was camp— the sensibility that Susan Sontag wrote about.

There was no end to how long I could sit and listen to Jesse and his friends play. More, I would say at midnight, when I had to be at work at nine the next morning. Then, later: More, I would say at four in the morning, when I had to get up at eight to take the girls on a college trip to North Carolina.

Eventually, they would all put down their instruments, too drunk to play. There was a feeling at that point in the night of approaching a tight rope and choosing, masterfully, to walk across it. You could begin to feel triumphant, like a victor in your own life, a victor in your own story. Perhaps it was the Quiet Zone or perhaps it was the quiet hills around this electric white house, but there was a sense here that whatever you did could not possibly count, that no one was watching and no one was keeping score. No one in the life I'd known before knew where I was or could imagine it.

One evening in May 2010, Jesse let me and Ruth host a full-on, flowered-hat-wearing, mint-julep-drinking, Kentucky Derby party at his grandmother's house. It was Ruth's idea—she was from Kentucky and knew all the real things to do. We came to Jesse's house early, and Jesse played sous chef, watching dutifully as Ruth demonstrated how to crush the fresh mint with powdered sugar into each glass for the perfect julep, then repeating her instructions with his own hands in glass after glass.

I felt glad to see Jesse in a new way that night: something was growing there, but I didn't know what. It wasn't sexual exactly or romantic; after Jesse and I had slept together, I'd told him it was a onetime thing. He said he understood, that being friends was fine with him.

I had the sense that some of his friends thought Jesse was, on the whole, a weak man. They teased him a good bit and sometimes spoke over him, but it was his usually gentle demeanor, I think, that drew me to Jesse. We could sit next to one another on a couch on a porch and talk all night about nothing in particular. We had no shared experience like these words might suggest, but we shared something else—a drive, maybe, or an obsession, deep down at the bottom of our quiet selves. We both wanted to say something, I think, something we had each long been keeping inside—but what?

Peter came that night, and his sister who was in town did too, and a few VISTA girls who were new, working at sites in Marlinton and Lewisburg. Trey and Bill and the other DMHB pulled up in their Subarus and Tacomas and hatchbacks. After we'd bet on our horses and watched the races and lost, we sat on the roofs of our cars in floppy hats. As the light died across the field behind Jesse's house and the clouds moved fast over the valley, we flew kites and played ultimate Frisbee. The Chef and the mandolin player showed up, and the men of music night played outside in the cool May air, and we drank the last of the mint julep syrup. When that ran out, we drank straight bourbon, and when that ran out, Old Milwaukee, and when that ran out, Natural Light, and when that ran out, we piled into Bill and Peter's pickups and drove the miles down to the Greenbrier River, where the drivers turned the trucks around and backed them straight down the embankment, and we fell out into the water and floated on our backs in the dark.

My clothes were wet, and my throat was dry, and it was maybe two in the morning. Several couples had already taken the bedrooms on the first floor, and I knew there would be more Frisbee and fun in the morning. Jesse told me I could stay in the attic—there was an air mattress there—so I made my way up the narrow stairs to the stuffy attic and climbed aboard. Before I closed my eyes, I saw a pink tube jutting out of the attic closet, and I stood to see what it was. It was an inflatable blow-up doll of a woman with voluminous breasts that fell out of her string bikini top. Her mouth was open, and her eyes were dumb. I put her back in the closet.

I woke to the sensation of the sheets moving, and the blanket being lifted.

Can I sleep here with you? Jesse asked.

Okay, I said, and turned away from him onto my side. I fell asleep again. I woke.

Sweetie, he said. It was the name my mom had called me as a child. Jesse ran his hand down my arm, then onto my hip and thigh.

I just want to sleep, I said.

Come on, he said.

We continued. An hour, two. I'd fall asleep, wake, say something neither encouraging nor clearly rejecting, fall asleep again. Eventually, the sun was nearly up, and the attic filled with heat.

I had power in that moment, and I didn't. Jesse had power in that moment, and he didn't. I wanted to want to have sex with him—I liked spending time with him and being in community with him and getting to sit in his house with his friends and his music, and I knew that sex with me would make him feel good, physically and generally—but I did not want to have sex with him. I looked through the window to Jesse's back field and the mountains beyond it and knew already that I was bound to this place with a ferocity I had no words for and that I likely would be all my life. I could hear our friends downstairs already, clinking spoons in coffee cups. Someone, the Chef maybe, turned on the boom box releasing rock music, fast and bright.

Jesse's hand moved lower. Come on, he said again.

"When you are twenty-two or twenty-three," writes Joan Didion, "you figure that later you will have a high emotional balance, and be able to pay whatever it costs."

2

THE GIRLS OF MOUNTAIN VIEWS were disappearing. One week they were there at Tuesday night tutoring, and the next they weren't. I'd see them at the Marathon gas station getting into a Chevy S-10 with a bear dog rack in the bed and a guy with a beard in the driver's seat. I'd see them at Rite Aid, adorned in that franchise's signature blue vest, in the middle of the day. Or I wouldn't see them for months, and then I'd catch sight of them in a group of bodies by the low-water bridge, stomping an empty beer can into a disc, as I drove home from some party of my own.

What happened to Tina? I'd ask. To Cecilia? To Heather? To Ashley?

The other girls would shrug. Haven't seen her in school, they'd say.

Feeling this specter of loss, I felt myself clutching at the girls who continued coming to our programs ever more tightly. I wanted the red-haired girl to answer the math problems I gave her. She could do them, I knew, so why wouldn't she?

Come on, I said, one Tuesday night, then repeated the phrase.

I don't want to, she said finally.

Why?

You make me feel dumb, she said. No one's ever made me feel like that before.

My whole body felt jerked; I flushed and flubbed out a sorry reply. But later that night, I drove faster than I'd ever driven to Jesse's house, flooring the gas along the straight stretch of 219 just to see if I could.

I kept going to Tuesday night music nights at Jesse's house, and Jesse and I went to other parties too—parties at the low-water bridge, parties at his cousin's house, parties in the woods. At one such party, there was a metal band who wore black T-shirts with neon green writing and wore glow-in-the-dark necklaces. Jesse got two paint buckets from a nearby basement and set them on the ground for us to use as seats. I told him I was queer and that my most recent relationship had been with a woman. That's cool, he said. He asked me what kind of girls I liked. I told him. He held my hand. He broke open one of the necklaces and rubbed the glowing chemical liquid between his finger tips. When it began to rain, we ran to my truck with its snug-fitting camper shell. In the muddy field, we maneuvered Jesse's bass out of the truck bed and into the cab. It fit, except for the bass's curled head and tuning pegs, which Jesse covered with plastic bags and cranked the driver's-side window up to hold them in place. The sound the rain made on the aluminum camper top, as Jesse and I lay inches underneath, was tremendous. It can't possibly rain any harder, I thought, and then it did.

But the best parties were always at the Homeplace, a big square house where Jesse's uncle Don had grown up. Fourth of July fireworks, Labor Day picnics, birthday Scrabble parties. Always there was pepper jelly and hugs and croquet; always there was the music. I brought my banjo but, afraid to bring it into the Homeplace, usually left it in my car. Eventually Don spotted it and began cajoling me to play. He wanted me to learn and wanted me to play it well. You have good rhythm, he told me at one of those parties, when I was strumming along quietly and trying to catch the chords being played. Come by the house sometime, and I'll teach you a few things.

I did, and he did. He told me how there was a very small canon of music he considered "real" bluegrass—Bill Monroe, Ralph and Carter Stanley, Earl Scruggs and Lester Flatt, also known as the Foggy Mountain Boys, end of list—and how he had learned to play bluegrass by listening to Flatt and Scruggs on the radio during the years his family had been forced to leave Pocahontas County to find work. Later I would learn that this had also been the way of so many of the musicians—the Stanley Brothers chief among them—he considered real.

I had gone to some parties at the Homeplace before as Sam's tenant and friend, but now I came with Jesse as his girlfriend. Family members smiled at us, patted my knee, made comments about what it would be like when Jesse and I married, and I let their comments, sometimes made in front of Jesse himself, stand without correction, though I knew such a thing would never come to pass. These were acts of cowardice, and they were acts of cruelty. I felt for once in my life that I'd been taken into something more than a family—this was a clan; this was a tribe. If we can give back real meaning to the word, instead of its general usage as a platitude, this was a community—to make common, to share. Yet my membership in it felt predicated on me being Jesse's girlfriend and on me performing that role in specific ways.

Jesse's favorite song, his trademark and the one that the other men would look to him to sing, was "It's Just the Night" by the Del McCoury Band. Jesse had a good voice made for bluegrass, tenor and nasal, but he was shy about using it; it usually took him several beers to get there. Once at a party, when everyone else was calling for him to sing and he was demurring, the wife of one of the other musicians leaned over to me and said, "He hasn't got good confidence, does he?" "No," I said, "not too good, I don't think." "Aw well," she responded. "My husband used to be the same way, but he's better when I'm here. That's what we women are for." I said nothing, a thing I'd found myself doing more and more in moments when I felt judgment or fear or sadness surging up against my own discomfort and shame that I was feeling those things in the first place. I remembered the words I'd read in college about not imposing your own culture and values on a different place.

My membership in this community I loved now also came to feel predicated on sex. I know that I had to get very drunk to have sex with Jesse, but I did have sex with Jesse, most nights, for about five months. This was not something that Jesse did to me, nor something I did to him, but a complicated stew of both of our fumbling actions and ambivalent needs. Alcohol came to be like the third member of our relationship, the center crux without which our connection would have shattered. In her report back from the field on the ways alcohol abuse and sex became intertwined for her, Sarah Hepola writes that the consent issues at stake in these moments are anything but simple. "I knew why the women writing on these issues didn't want to acknowledge gray zones. Gray zones were what the other side pounced on to gain ground," she writes. "Activism may defy nuance, but sex demands it. Sex was a complicated bargain to me. It was chase, and it was hunt. It was hide-and-seek, clash and surrender, and the pendulum could swing inside my brain all night: I will, no I won't; I should, no I can't. My consent battle was in me."

Jesse and I saw each other alone now and on nights other than Tuesdays, sometimes at his grandmother's house, sometimes at my house on Droop Mountain. He'd fix me a drink, and we'd watch a little television, and then I'd fix myself another drink. He would take off his shoes and line them up neatly at the foot of his bed, then his shirt and pants, and hop into bed. "Sweetie," he'd say, pushing the hair away from my ears. I made sure all the lights were off, and in the dark, he touched me the way I liked to be touched. Sometimes it was a great relief not to be seen, to pretend to be just a body devoid of any feeling but nerve sensation, a pink plastic skin made up of nothing but breasts and air.

I felt caught in a bind—I wanted to belong to a place, really and truly, for the first time in my life, but I felt that these nights with Jesse were the tax I paid for it. I never told Jesse this. There were many other things we did not speak about. I had a credit card that I could swipe anytime I wished and fly away from there. I had a four-year education and a privileged upbringing in New York. Jesse would not have called himself poor, and I don't think I would either—he always had the cash he needed—but I know he thought and worried about work and money most days that he was alive. Neither of us had what wider America would consider real jobs, but for me this was a choice.

There was another way to belong to this community: to do the job I was brought there to do, to "alleviate poverty" as per AmeriCorps VISTA's proclaimed mission, and to do so via "empowering" the girls of Mountain Views, but I was failing at it. I could not empower myself, and yet I was expected to be a role model for others, for girls from a completely different context. The Director seemed to have endless confidence in me to do everything from organize a meeting with parents to talk about college access to set up and staff a community drop-in center for youth, and sometimes her confidence did lift me and give me strange and magical fortitude. There were moments of triumph—a full sign-in sheet of names and phone numbers of parents who wanted to talk more about how to fill out the FAFSA—and there were nights at Mountain Views when I was able to sit down at a long table of teenage girls and be that person for them, a powerful adult woman with hope in her heart and wild laughs in her stomach.

The red-haired girl did eventually stop coming to Tuesday night tutoring, too, but she did not disappear. She lived with her family in a trailer just down 219 from the schoolhouse where I lived, so I'd see her each day as I drove past their house on my way to work and again as I drove home. Sometimes she would be jumping on the trampoline that sat in their yard or riding a four-wheeler with her sisters. Nothing seemed wrong. And yet, when she'd wave to me as I drove past, something felt wrong.

Then one day I saw her gun the four-wheeler toward a pile of extra doors and drywall her dad was using to build an addition on their house and lean into the crash, her eyes still open, and I realized what was wrong, if you can call a sensible response to a senseless state of affairs wrong. She was enraged, I think. Enraged at me and at Mountain Views and at her family and the whole town, that whole swath of land, at a state of affairs in which she had a few different options, but none of them seemed liable to give her a good outcome.

I was getting better at the music, but I still wasn't good. I learned to watch the Chef's fingers move over his guitar's neck and learned to take my chord from him. Jesse was always kind to me, asking if I needed help following the chords and encouraging me to take my banjo out of its green case and play it. But often, and especially later in the night as we all got drunker, I mostly sat and watched the men play.

I thought I was being respectful of the bonds these men had built and their artistic process—after all, these nights were ostensibly band practice, for Jesse's band was booked every now and then to play at a festival or anniversary party. Intimacy with women is my literal lifeblood now, but even though I worked with women and girls all day, it was hard for me then.

The only kind of closeness I saw was closeness between men, and I wanted to be inside it.

I see now how much of my free time "and a great amount of time that was not free," as the writer Claire Vaye Watkins puts it, I spent prizing the movements of men over those of women, and how much time I spent watching men do stuff that I could have spent moving my hands or my mouth or getting to know the Chef's girlfriend.

I'm so bored, the Chef's girlfriend said to me one night when we were the only two women in the room. Aren't you? She motioned me to follow her outside and pointed to the sky. She taught me constellations beyond the Big and Little Dipper, and told me how she and the Chef had met— in a college poetry class—and why they had never bothered to marry until now—who cares? But even then, I was itching to get back inside.

Peter and Ruth split; the blond banjo player and the VISTA girl he had been dating split. The blond banjo player had a special love for the word "faggot," and one night I got fed up or brave enough to say something about it. We had what I thought was a tough, deep, good conversation about it on the screened-in porch of Jesse's grandmother's house, me on a wicker chair and him sitting in the doorway, smoking into the night. Why can't I say "fag" if hatred isn't what I mean? he asked. You just can't, I said. The word carries so much pain. I get it, he said. I won't say it ever again. He was mostly true to his word. Then one night he wasn't. Uh-oh, he said, laughing, when he saw my face.

I got a part in the county play that required me to kiss another actor onstage, and when Jesse and his friends came to see it, they got loud during and riled up afterward, pointing at my costar and yelling at Jesse to "simmer down" and "let it go—he isn't worth it." For his part, Jesse didn't seem to care much, but the message from his friends was clear: Jesse owned me.

The mandolin player looked roughly at my body but wouldn't meet my eyes. One night at my house, the beige phone clanged, and it was for Jesse. It was the man who booked shows up at Snowshoe Mountain, asking after Jesse and his band. They would put him and the band up overnight, the guy said, plus dinner, drinks, whatever.

The day of the show was sunny and clear, one of the first bright days of summer when you can sit outside without a jacket, and everyone looked rumpled and surprised at their own bodies. The guys—Jesse on bass, the mandolin player, Jesse's cousin on banjo, and the Chef on guitar—took the stage.

Don't they look handsome?, Jesse's mom leaned over to me and said. They did. I felt a twinge of pride, a good feeling that spread knowing that Jesse, a person I loved in my way, though the exact nature of that love was unclear, was doing the thing he loved most in the world.

The mandolin player and the Chef switched off singing lead, but the mandolin player did most of the banter between songs. He called Jesse up to sing, "It's Just the Night," and after introducing Jesse to the crowd, he leaned into the microphone: Now, don't embarrass this guy, okay, because his girlfriend is here today, the mandolin player said. He's never had a girlfriend before, so it's extra important. That's her, right back there. The mandolin player pointed at me then and kept his index finger in the air, and though surely they did not, in my memory all three hundred people seated in lawn chairs turned to look at me. Isn't she pretty?, the mandolin player asked. And then they played.

That night after dinner, the band, minus the Chef, who had gone home with his girlfriend, and I went to our hotel. I'd wanted to go home, but Jesse had asked me very sincerely to stay; he was on a high after the day, I think, and wanted to hold my hand all afternoon and I cared for him and wanted him to be well. We sat around the white box room drinking for a while and telling jokes. It was fun at first, then less so. The mandolin player stumbled into the bathroom, then stumbled out of it. He made a joke, I think, something about wondering what kind of underwear I wore and how only Jesse would know the answer. I went into the room where I thought Jesse and I were to sleep, then closed the door. Soon Jesse was there too, and we lay together in bed with our clothes on, just talking over the day.

The mandolin player began to pound on the door. His speech was slurred.

What's he saying? I asked Jesse.

Ignore him, Jesse said, rolling onto his back.

But the pounding continued. He wanted this room—Why had we taken the only good room? Then, unmistakably, through the door, the mandolin player said, Fuck her good for me.

Something broke in me then that was about the mandolin player and not about the mandolin player, that was about the girls at Mountain Views and not about them, and like a character in a movie, I turned to Jesse and said, That's it.

I got up and hurled open the door and can't say what I might have done had Jesse not leapt up after me and gotten between us. Jesse was not like the mandolin player—I know that now, and I knew it then. But what kind of man has that kind of man for a friend? In such a small community and with ties that run deep and in every direction, every person is bound to every other in ways that may or may not feel optional, I know, and it is more difficult than it may seem to avoid or cut ties with someone. Yet we never spoke of that night again, a thing that pointed to the fact that both Jesse and I would rather let the lies we were telling ourselves stand than grapple with the specific facts of that situation.

Jesse knew the mandolin player's behavior was fundamentally unacceptable, but he felt bound to the mandolin player and also to each of the DMHB, Trey included, in a way that was stronger than he felt bound to me. And why not? He was. I knew continuing our relationship meant keeping quiet about a great deal of what I thought and felt to be true and that I would not be able to stay quiet forever.

If I began my relationship with Jesse feeling like I was a victim of some violation, I did not end up that way. It became clear to me that what we had in common, underneath our quietness, was an ambivalent relationship to power, influence, mattering. We both wanted these things, I think, and were afraid of them.

I came to have a power over Jesse, a different kind than is the inevitable result of loving connection. There came a point when whatever power we had been playing with fumbled, flopped, and then finally flipped. It happened one night, one ordinary Tuesday night, when I was standing in the middle of Jesse's living room leaning on his dead grandmother's curio cabinet. The Chef took a guitar break, a bluesy run that didn't quite fit with the song and then somehow did, and then they sang the chorus again—*everybody I met, everybody I met, everybody I met, seemed to be a rank stranger*—and the song ended, and Jesse sat down on the pink couch and looked over at me out of the bottoms of his eyes in this way, this troubling and electric way. The look seemed to say, *Take my life and do anything that you want with it*. I let my gaze creep through the alcohol in my blood and down the bridge of my nose and over the space between us and then up Jesse's baseball cap and onto the crest of his head. Something very old in me, something that had been kept down too long, some desire to dominate and win in a struggle, boomed alive.

I sat down next to him.

What was the name of that song? I asked.

Rank Stranger, he said. It's real.

Will you stay?, the Director asked me. We were on her porch, she in one wooden Adirondack chair and me in the other, twin glasses of Diet Coke and Old Crow in our hands, and passing a cigarette back and forth between us. We'd been talking about work and all the things we had left to do that week, and about a Mountain Views girl who had called to tell us she was pregnant.

She wanted to be a lawyer, I said, and she won't get to do that now. It's just too bad.

Not necessarily, the Director said. I've seen kids for whom getting pregnant was the thing that really helped them ask the deep questions and make the big, good choices. There are all kinds of ways to live a life, you know.

I know, I said. But I didn't.

As we drank, the talk turned to Jesse and Trey and the other DMHB. The Director said that she had another dream. She'd dreamed that we had started a Mountain Views for boys and her son had gone to it.

That would be so beautiful, I said, because it would.

We could do it, she said. And you could help run it!

I don't know, I said.

Why not?

I wanted to tell her that I was failing with men like I was failing with girls and I was failing to bridge the space that seemed to separate them like a river that was running very fast. I wanted to tell her that masculinity, as we have traditionally conceived of it, was a disease that was killing people. Mountain Views was an important part of treating it, but it was not enough. You cannot treat women only for a disease of which men are the main carriers. Nor, I knew, could you punish every man who fell ill.

I passed the cigarette back to her and drank from my glass.

I need you here, she said. I need you to stay.

More and more young people, I knew—the DMHB and their sisters, the Mountain Views girls who were graduating—were staying in West Virginia on purpose or coming back after years away to build lives for themselves. They were joining organizations and starting organizations and trying to do all the things that would make staying possible.

I felt the old urge—comply comply comply—and its opposite—flight that would make me free free free.

I'll try, I told her.

The end of my one-year term came and went, but I stuck around, racked with indecision and guilt about whether I should renew for a second year. If I left after only one year, I would be a quitter, I knew, a stopper through Appalachia, another VISTA girl from somewhere else who didn't stick around.

I went as Jesse's date to the wedding of the Chef and his girlfriend. The ceremony was quick and without extended vows or testimonials from the couple's friends; they had been together so long and loved each other so well that the wedding itself was a foregone conclusion. The redheaded girl was there, and I watched her face change as she realized that I was there as Jesse's date. She looked at me hard and directly. "You have lipstick on your teeth," she said, in a hostile way I still don't understand—did she know something about Jesse and his friends that I didn't? Did she know something about Jesse and his friends that I did?—then walked away toward the buffet.

At some point late in the night, Jesse and the Chef danced, arms around each other, the Chef dipping Jesse nearly to the floor. Jesse was so happy all that night and even into the next day. They're married now, he said, taking my hand. I'm so glad.

A darker side to Tuesday night music nights began to show itself, and so did a darker side to my character. The boisterous DMHB brother and the blond-haired banjo player came to blows one night, then hugged and cried and called each other brother. My drinking got bad, then worse, then dangerous. I matched the men shot for shot and asked for more. Sometimes we drank and threw up and kept drinking. One night, a VISTA girlfriend of mine wanted to go out, and we did. On the way back from Lewisburg, I made an illegal right turn on red, and the lights of three West Virginia State Police cars whirled to life behind me, pulling me over into the Walmart parking lot.

Blow, one of them said to me, shoving the hard plastic Breathalyzer in my mouth. I can't, I said—I have a natural distrust of authority and a hustler's instincts for crime and evasion—but I really couldn't; the machine was too far down my throat, and I kept gagging on it. Blow, the policeman said again, the light reflecting off his gun. It took twenty minutes for them to get a reading from me, minutes that may have been crucial—I blew a .07, just .01 from the legal limit to drive, and a hair away from losing my license.

At a local music festival that summer, I had sex with Jesse in his car while it was parked in a parking lot that was not dark enough nor far enough away from a gathering of community members, Mountain Views girls among them. To the array of pictures of their futures as young women from which the girls could choose, I added this one: the searcher who had gone too far.

One night not long after this, I worked late, and Jesse said he was coming over, and we ended up entering my house from my dark porch together. I asked him to turn the light on. He didn't, and I didn't reach for the switch either. He took off his sneakers and lined them up by the door and then sat on the couch. Every so often a car passed my house lighting up the room, and I could see Jesse, his eyes open, one hand on the armrest and the other on his knee. I was down on my knees on the beige carpet, though I do not remember why I was down on my knees on the beige carpet. I want to say it was because I was making a fire, but that can't be right because my landlords didn't install that woodstove until after I moved out.

Every so often I said, What do you want?, and he said, I don't know. After a while he started saying, What do you want?, and I started saying, I don't know.

I was asking him to want anything—the music, a job, school, his life.

I want you, he said.

Something else.

Then it was winter again, 2010. I sat with Ruth in her car in a dark field, car lights on, windows rolled up, taking a quiet moment away from a party that pumped in a nearby house. Ruth used her thumb to slide the heat to its highest notch, but it did little good. We watched people stand in the window of the house or dance past it; inside were young people who were both from and not from West Virginia. It was such a good party—there was cider and a jukebox and everyone I cared for—that I couldn't stand to go to it.

I loved Jesse in a way that I knew was doing damage both to him and to me, and I knew I could not be to the Director or to the Mountain Views girls what they wanted or deserved; these things had been revealing themselves to me slowly but with increasing gravity, and I felt them now as a sudden image of revelation, the red velvet Broadway curtains of my childhood drawing back fold by fold.

The last object I touched before I drove away from Pocahontas County was the phone. I pulled my truck over onto the shoulder of 219 a few meters down from Jesse's family's mailbox, put the phone in, and closed the little tin door. It had belonged to Jesse's mom, it turned out, and it was time she got it back. I put my truck in drive and stepped on the gas. I could drive now, with confidence and trust and with my back touching the driver's seat and only one hand on the wheel. My landlord, parked by his sheep pen, honked his powerful horn as I went.

It's strange that we talk about leaving a rural place as happy, a bursting forth from black and white into color, though for some this may be the truth. "Why don't they just leave?" many of my friends from cities had asked me of the DMHB and the Mountain Views girls and their families. But here is what they don't know: Pocahontas County was the color. The world I was seeing now—I-64 heading west—and that I would be seeing for a long time was the gray.

That first night in Asheville, North Carolina, I tried to insert slices of gourmet pizza into my mouth, but they would go in only as far as the back of my throat, then stop. I could not bite or chew or swallow, on account of all the crying. I drank the beer that was set before me—markedly more hoppy than the American lite beers I'd grown accustomed to—and I watched the college kids in their prosperous backpacks and the artists busking in their feather caps. My cell phone made satisfied little beeps, reveling in all the service. I had come back. I was a citizen of society now, I supposed, with all its proper tools.

I found the little green house that belonged to Tim's daughter and Peter's sister, a woman who lived here in this cool and prosperous town. The house had dark wood floors and light wood walls, and I got into her bed with my clothes on. I looked up then and saw, pasted to the underside of a shelf, several small lithographs of the mountains of Pocahontas County. For years, I knew, this woman had been trying to get home.

3

MILES PASSED. I DROVE MORE than ten thousand of them in three months in my white Toyota Tacoma with the wooden platform bed in the back. Years passed. Philadelphia, with trips back to West Virginia. Virginia with trips back to West Virginia. Philadelphia again. I took jobs and did them. I bought books and read them. I drove up and down I-95 and I-76 and I-81 in every season and in every kind of weather. This was living.

I could hear voices talking calmly on the radio and voices yelling, trying to convince one another of something. I could eat and I could sleep and I could fuck and I could dream. I could look but I could not see. Not the orange cones, not the lawns that ended in softly sloping curbs, not the paved brick pedestrian malls or the wood and chrome coffee bars, not the classrooms in which I sat and then in which I taught. I focused my eyes on a point in the back of the room, safely above every human head.

One June, on my way back to Pocahontas County to work a few weeks at Mountain Views, an SUV collided with the corner of my tailgate, and my truck did two complete revolutions on I-76 going eighty miles an hour before colliding with the concrete median. I'll always hold the sensation of spinning in my body, how strangely slow it felt, and the ripping sound that rubber makes when it is dragged. The truck with its West Virginia wildlife plates was totaled, but aside from bad whiplash, I was not harmed. Then the West Virginia barn cat that had adopted me when I lived on Lobelia Road was run over by a passing car during one of his romps outside. He'd died as he lived, I felt—hard. I did not know what, if anything, these things meant.

In the winter of 2013, the Chef called down to the restaurant of the observatory where he worked, gave the menu for the following day, hung up the phone, and put a bullet through his brain. He had separated from his wife, or he was a sensitive person with depressive tendencies, or there is never any reason.

Not long after this, the boisterous DMHB called a friend. He didn't have much money, he told the friend, but he could pay fifteen dollars plus a carton of cigarettes in exchange for the heroin. The friend did as he asked and came to the house. The younger brother, the quieter DMHB, was there too. The three men ground the heroin and injected it. I found a vein, the boisterous DMHB reportedly said, then dropped to the ground. His brother and the friend drove him down I-77 to the nearest hospital, where they left his body outside the emergency entrance.

I felt ruined by my time in Pocahontas County—no other place would ever be so good. I felt harmed and also that I had harmed others with my weakness and my silence and my actions, and I didn't know how to make those two feelings stay together. Every time I grasped one of them, the other seemed to fade away.

Things kept returning to me and knocking, demanded to be heard. For one, I remembered that when I lived in the farmhouse on Lobelia Road with Bill, calls came in for him at night from men, older men who lived along the road and had known him since birth. Man, they would say, sometimes slurring his name into our answering machine. It would be 3:37, 4:28, 1:11 am, and I'd sit up in the night, disoriented, listening to their voices roll in downstairs. Man, I'm hurting real bad, they'd say. I never knew exactly what kind of hurt they meant, only that they had to wait until it was 3:37 and they were loaded to talk about it.

For another, the waitress at Hillsboro's only restaurant who had helped me home that night of the whiteout had likely participated in the spray-painting of "NIGGER LOVER" across the restaurant's north-facing wall. I thought a lot about the kindness in the waitress and also the cowardice and cruelty it took to write those words—both.

And then and always, Jesse. I'd see a station wagon that looked like his making a wide turn around the statue of Lewis and Clark and Sacagawea in the Virginia town where I now lived and be smacked again: What had happened to me in Jesse's house, where we played music all those nights and drank until we could no longer feel the parts of our bodies that were most private and the blow-up sex woman peeked out from the closet?

And what had I brought into or out of being for other people? The withholding of true feelings and information from people with whom you are intimate can be its own kind of weapon. The redheaded girl's words: *you make me feel dumb.* I was most haunted by my own actions, the ways I let my appetites for belonging and alcohol get out of control, for I was not just a witness but a part of all of it, a person who wanted oblivion for my own reasons.

What did it mean that I had been employed to better the lives of girls, and all around me it seemed, grown men were dying? Could women and girls and men and boys truly be together in mutual community, or could they only hurt and wound each other? And how did poverty and class play into all this? Didn't know.

I reread my journals from my time there and found the entry about the writers' group and about how Tim, Peter's father, had found two women's bodies up on Briery Knob. What had all that been about? I had camped with Jesse up on Briery Knob, I remembered.

There we were, Jesse—rail-thin and gentle in a West Virginia University hoodie, pale hands on the wheel of his station wagon, and me, the feral girl from somewhere else sitting shotgun. We were on our way to camp with Ruth and Peter, a new VISTA from California and her boyfriend—a boy from the northern part of the county—and the blond banjo player.

Briery Knob was a reclaimed surface mining site. We knew it had been reclaimed because plants were growing there again, but they were gray-green, spongy, and all the same height. We might have been on the surface of the moon. When we stuck our tent poles into the dirt, it wasn't dirt but chalky ash. The poles went in an inch, hit rock, wouldn't budge.

It was June probably, because the VISTA girl from California has already gotten her dog from the pound, a brown mutt who kept sniffing the perimeter around their tent, but Jesse and I hadn't had our joint birthday party yet, the one where we wore newspaper hats that looked like boats and the Director and her husband got a babysitter and came and danced with Jesse and me, holding our hands. It could be July if it were early.

We pitched our tents in a flat spot surrounded by steep wooded embankments. Maybe fifty feet away, someone had dumped a blue corduroy couch. It looked strange in this moon place, but it was less foul than you might think, just damp. Some of us touched it; some of us didn't. I touched it; Jesse touched it. When I climbed the embankment to the ridge, I could see the white wind turbines over in Greenbrier County turning slowly. On the way back, I found a pair of sunglasses in the shaded path. Bear hunters, Jesse said, and put them on.

Later, we lit the fire, and the banjo player played a few tunes as the dark shrank the space. Jesse hadn't brought his upright bass and kept looking around for it, his fingers twitching. When the temperature dropped, Jesse and I and Ruth and Peter chickened out and slept in our cars. But the girl from California and her boy stayed out, perhaps comforted by the noises her dog's paws were making as he did slow circles in the dark. I thought for sure she was the tough one who would last—she wore brown Carhartt pants and thick knitted caps and learned how to change the oil in her car—but that isn't the way it turned out. She went back to California, took some other man's name, and I don't know her now.

I remember being cold, the cold that moved across that plateau, and then being warm from the heat coming off Jesse's body. I remember drinking water from a jar we filled at a spring on the way up, taking a bite from a block of white cheddar cheese in the night when I woke up starving, wearing two pairs of thick Smartwool socks, Jesse's hands on my face. Laughing—*roll over, roll over, three in the bed and the little one said, roll over.*

I hadn't known that Vicki and Nancy died in that spot when we camped there; now I did. Story speaking, nothing happened; it was just another night we slept in the woods as men and women from there and elsewhere. But I began to think about it all the time. I felt if I could understand what we had done up on Briery Knob and what had happened to the two dead women up there and if these things were the same thing or different things, I could answer some of the big questions that were choking my life and blocking my eyes.

I started staying in my car a long time after returning from getting groceries or seeing a friend. I looked through the windshield out at my dark Virginia street and left the engine running so I could listen to bluegrass. Before I'd left Pocahontas County, Jesse had made me three CDs: the Foggy Mountain Boys, the Stanley Brothers, and his own pick, Jimmy Martin. There they sat in their neatly layered CD case, labeled in Jesse's black Sharpie hand.

I knew I'd have to turn the car off and go back to my apartment and my life eventually, but there was nothing in me that was ready to do it. The car was an in-between space, a temporary container, and I could put my most curious and strange feelings into it. I did my best thinking and messaging and Googling there.

I read the 1992 and 1993 coverage of the arrests of the seven men and about the first trial of Jacob Beard in the *Pocahontas Times* and elsewhere. I read the words "culture clash" and "they weren't the slimmest, trimmest little things" and "hicks versus hippies" and "he goes to parties with axes and chainsaws" and "culture of silence," and I smelled something off, something wrong. Something false had hardened into a story, I suspected, that people both from the county and not had heard over and over and then began to tell. I wanted to know how and why.

Jesse's parents, I learned from messages I was exchanging with people in Pocahontas County, had been friends with Ritchie Fowler, the alleged driver of the blue van, and had believed strongly in his innocence. The redheaded girl was a relative of Fowler's too, and Bobby Morrison was tied to a Mountain Views employee by marriage and friendship. Jesse had recently taken a job at the hardware store in Marlinton, a job that allowed him steady hours, a good paycheck, and colleagues he liked—including Pee Wee Walton.

If I had been harmed by Jesse or some other invisible force in Pocahontas County, and if I had harmed him or Mountain Views in turn, what did I want now? I wanted justice. And what was that? Didn't know.

"A crime creates a debt; the criminal becomes a debtor, the victim his creditor," writes Lacy M. Johnson. "One primary meaning of the word redemption was the sense that one could buy that debt back—every injury has some equivalent of pain or sacrifice."

The idea that I might buy back my debt to Pocahontas County and to myself by writing about the deaths of Vicki and Nancy on Briery Knob did not come all at once. It came on hot afternoons when I fell off my bike and my knees ground against loose asphalt. It came at night when the light through the bars on my window fell in stripes across the face of some kind sleeping woman or man. It came in the morning when I woke looking at how those iron bars stood between me and the hostas I had just planted in my backyard, and it stayed with me, even after I had finished graduate school to become a writer and moved back to Philadelphia. Why did it make sense to put the story of Vicki and Nancy and the nine local men who had been implicated in this crime over the years up against the story of me and Jesse and the Mountain Views girls and the DMHB? Didn't know. But it made sense.

The idea to write about both the Rainbow Murders and my own time in Pocahontas County, together, came most perhaps when I found out about Liz—a woman who was both a part of this story and not a part of it. I cared about the women who died, I knew, and I cared about the men who suffered because two women happened to die where they lived, in a place America prefers to forget exists. Writing this story became real to me when I realized a story could—must—encompass both.

PART VII:

THE THIRD RAINBOW GIRL

Have you had enough darkness yet?
No, I haven't had enough darkness.
Have you had enough fire?
Maybe…
Enough water? No, not nearly enough.
Enough dirt to walk on?
No. Never, never.

—Irene McKinney

Liz Johndrow, 2017

I DIDN'T KNOW WALT WEIFORD when I lived in Pocahontas County, but I knew his daughter. She was married to a man Jesse had grown up with, and sometimes she and her husband would come to Tuesday music night. She played the bass—acoustic for when she was playing bluegrass, electric for when she wasn't. Jesse showed me videos of her from high school—head banging, hair swinging, T-shirt riding up, her face—rocking out. Girl can play, he said.

I saw Walt Weiford's back before I saw the rest of him. It was August 2013, and he was waiting for me at Marlinton's gourmet coffee shop that doubled as a bike shop in a Shaker-style wooden chair; his back a beige square, his hands clasped on the café table in front of him. He was bald-headed and khaki-panted.

"There was a time probably not terribly long ago that I would've said, 'No, that's in the past for me,'" he said, smoothing his hands over a knot in the table's wood. His dress shirt looked like his face—pale peach, soft, and a little shiny. "At some point I let the Rainbow case go. I was retired for Christ's sake, and the case was done. But then, I don't know how, but recently it all came back. I started wondering about it again. And then you called."

An oval of men on their third refill were klatsching in the cushioned seating area near the front window and spilling out the door into the sunny afternoon. It was the tourists who mostly took advantage of the bike-shop part of this business, renting cruisers or mountain bikes to take down the gravel rails-to-trails route or up into the Monongahela National Forest. The food was wheat wraps and health cookies but also pizza and milkshakes, a solid compromise. It was the only place to get a latte in forty miles, but you could still pay for the self-serve house blend in quarters if you wanted.

"It was a lot like putting a jigsaw puzzle together," Weiford said as we ate our Reubens and potato chips from yellow plastic netted baskets. His eyes were small and quick; he smiled with his mouth closed. "You couldn't put it down."

I agreed, and said that I felt that already. I'd been staying up most nights reading all the case documents available online or making arrangements to get the ones that weren't. I said that I thought part of the case's puzzle quality came from how many stories have been told about what happened to Vicki and Nancy that night—all the statements that contradict each other, all the confessions that contradict each other, all the testimony. "None of the facts seem to be facts," I said. There was hardly anything that everyone agreed on.

"That's true," Weiford said. "There were so many people there. And of course everybody is drinking, and all that. You can't fit what Franklin says around the facts that we know. But the same is true with our theory. All the cogs don't meet exactly, in places. That's why we build courthouses."

I envied his certainty in Beard's guilt. I asked him to convince me. Weiford took another bite of his sandwich, then rubbed his hands together to wipe off any traces of Thousand Island dressing, and when he did so, I saw the drive for this case in his face, the energy that had propelled him through the twelve-day murder trial in 1993 and then the eleven-day retrial in 2000. For him, he said, Beard's guilt came down to that phone call.

"If [Beard's] intentions had been sincere," Weiford said, "why didn't he say, 'Mr. Durian, this is Jake Beard, and I'm really sorry about what happened to your daughter, and in my opinion they're not working on it, and I wish there was something I could do to help you'? But why do that anonymously and then follow it up with another call? It was almost like Jake was taunting [Mr. Durian], and the police."

"And why would he do it if he were guilty?"

"I think there was a part of him that kind of wanted the notoriety, wanted to be caught. You know you read about that all the time and see it on TV—same kind of thing. Though I can't say I'm completely comfortable in saying that's why he did it."

And what of Bobby Morrison and Gerald Brown?

"I think Gerald Brown may have been there," Weiford said. Morrison still lived in Pocahontas County, Weiford said, though he and his ex-wife had run into some legal trouble, he for drinking and driving, she for selling drugs. "[Morrison] was very young then, just kind of an itinerant farm worker, that would go from one farm to another putting up hay and things like that. The older Bobby got, the more courage he had....He got a little more gumption, eventually accusing Jake Beard right to his face."

Morrison's statement incriminating Brown was so detailed, I remembered, full of precise details that set the scene and were immaterial to a criminal statement—"we talked about partying and how much we used to drink." Why, then, all those details?

"He wanted you to believe him?" I asked Weiford.

"Yes," Weiford said.

"But he confessed!" I want to say. My attachment to the idea of confession may be a function of the word—religious, flavored with morality; the stakes of talking about murder seem so high that my first thought is that everything people say in relation to it must be factually correct. "False confession" feels like a contradiction in terms, a paradox that undermines the whole idea that what people say can be believed.

But Weiford made his living inside this paradox. "It's not uncommon," Weiford said, unfazed, and he was right. It turns out that false confessions are not uncommon at all, especially among people under eighteen; Morrison was seventeen at the time. Children, or adults with the mental capacity of children, are at the highest risk for professing responsibility for crimes they did not commit. Police misconduct, wishing to please authority, or the misguided belief that going home in the short term is better than sticking with the truth and waiting in jail in the long term are all factors. In 2013, 38 percent of exonerations for crimes allegedly committed by people under eighteen in the last quarter century involved false confessions.

Richard Fowler is dead today, but he was still alive when I met with

Weiford. I'd called Fowler from my house in Virginia, but his wife had answered. I told her who I was and my aim.

"We're never talking about that again," she said, growing heated when a few moments before she'd been bright. "Never, never. Not him, not me. That Rainbow thing. It ruined our lives."

Pee Wee Walton was still alive, living in Pocahontas County, too. I had begun to develop a feeling about him, a feeling that he was the key to understanding this whole case, and said so to Weiford at our lunch.

Weiford allowed that Walton could have been wrong about certain things in his testimony.

"I think Pee Wee tried really hard to remember this event," Weiford said. "And of course one of the problems I later had to deal with was that he was abused by Sergeant Estep, the police officer who interviewed him. And of course Pee Wee's take on that was what I told you was true. It wasn't voluntary, but it was the truth."

Weiford claimed that he wasn't at the state police barracks until after Walton's interview had concluded.

"I can remember Alkire telling me something about it—Estep was getting it out of Pee Wee now. Finally getting it out of him."

I nodded. "I suppose I can guess what you think about the Joseph Paul Franklin theory," I said.

"Well, you know, anytime somebody says, 'I done it,' you got to pay attention to that," Weiford said, leaning back in his chair. He told me about DiFalco's trip to Marion, Illinois, in 1984 and how Franklin denied any knowledge of the murders at first. "DiFalco was a really pretty girl. She was a,…she looked kind of like, well, kind of like you. Olive skin, dark hair, dark eyes, very shapely. But she was hard as nails too; she could kick the ass of any guy," Weiford continued. "Franklin sort of took a liking to her, and Franklin liked attention—a lot. I've talked to Franklin myself a couple of times. He called me collect and just wanted to talk."

"From death row, you can just make a phone call?"

"Yep. But I think I pissed him off the last time he called me. Maybe the last several times he called me. I haven't heard from him in a while. I thought about getting in touch with him again and just saying, look, whenever they give you the shot, I'd like to be there just to see if you change your mind. Of course, now it's not that important to me."

Why, I pressed Weiford, could he not believe in Franklin's guilt? What was it about Franklin's story that felt fundamentally not believable?

Weiford told me that he thought Franklin was "an attention seeker" and that the holes in his initial story were too hard to overlook. "Nothing was right about it. It just didn't conform with what we knew had to be true." Weiford felt Franklin's statement became more believable as time passed because of all the investigators from different states who interviewed him over the years.

Our conversation drifted back to 1980 and the Gathering itself. He told me how the arrival of the Rainbow people, the run-ins between local people and Rainbow people, and the county making national news, set a somber mood.

I asked him what the source of the feeling toward the Rainbow people was. Just a knee-jerk human reaction to difference?

"I think initially it was just suspicion—these folks are so different; we don't know them from a load of coal." For the most part, the people who came were peaceful and law-abiding. "But there were also some who were traveling so light they had no money and nothing to eat. They stole. They were right here at the Greenbrier River, yet made no attempt to clean themselves. They were pretty unappealing to a lot of folks. It seemed like some of them would take some pleasure in the shock value associated with them, nudity and things like that. People just didn't get that, couldn't understand it."

My experience as a person from somewhere else coming into Pocahontas County was so different, I said. I felt deeply taken in.

But it was a different time then, more than thirty years ago, he reminded me. "And the fact that the Rainbow people were here, and that they've been here three or four times since the murders actually," Weiford said, "and the murders themselves may have opened some doors for folks. And you may have gotten some benefit from that."

I let that sink into the air a moment.

"There's a lot of things about this case that I would like to know that I don't know," he went on. "There's a lot of suspicions that I have that I'm not really happy to have."

The impartiality of Judge Charles Lobban, who presided over both trials, for one thing, Weiford said. Before the first trial, Weiford felt that Lobban wasn't convinced by the state's theory and was not pleased to be presiding over such a high-profile case. "When the jury came back [and delivered the guilty verdict] and before I left the courtroom, he called me up to the bench and said, 'Walt, you made a believer out of me.'"

Yet Lobban granted the motion for a new trial, a thing that Weiford had never understood. He felt it had something to do with politics, optics, and all the publicity surrounding the case in the years 1998–1999, particularly the *60 Minutes II* special. "There were CBS cameras right up in his face when he made the ruling. I always thought CBS had something to do with getting Jake Beard a new bite at the apple."

He paused then, rubbed his hands again, then put them back on the table. I asked him what was on his mind. If I had known then that he would die of a sudden heart attack at age sixty-one just months after this meeting, I would have asked him much more.

Weiford stumbled over the starts of a few different sentences, paused, then spoke again. The friction around the Gathering and then ultimately the murders and the immediate suspicion that the killer had been local, he said, the whole sequence of events that began before the Gathering and lasted more than twenty years cast a shadow on the county that was larger than the facts of the case—it was emotional in a way he couldn't quite name.

"It all created a sense of foreboding and just—something wasn't quite right," Weiford said. He needed to set it right. That's what his prosecution had intended to resolve.

"I was a big hero at one time," Weiford said. "But I gave it away."

When West Virginia police sergeant Robert Alkire retired from investigating crimes and being the sheriff of Pocahontas County, he turned to making art. He built chairs with dark square legs, benches with curlicue-shaped holes, dressers with star designs ripped into the grain. His glassed-in showroom sat just off Route 219, surrounded on two sides by a defunct motel and on the third by a field that in the summer became sprawling seating for a DIY drive-in movie theater. His hours were few and changeable; he traveled often with his wife to see his grandchildren. I had been calling his unlisted number and shoving letters under the showroom door for a year. But after Weiford and I finished our lunch and stepped out into the street, he told me to try Alkire one last time, and I did, and—whammo—there he was. His Ford truck was parked in the gravel by the door of his showroom, and the lights were on.

Alkire didn't get up when I came in, but he called to me from a corner, where the wall was wood paneling and the light was dim. He sat in a straight-backed chair next to a stone fireplace—cool, empty, and swept out. His hair had turned pigeon white but was still thick and swooped. On his desk sat a clamshell phone, a large calculator, and his hands—fingernails very clean, knuckles smooth. He wore a snap-up shirt like a cowboy.

"Oh well," he said, when I told him why I was there. He took his hands from the desk and put them on the knees of his dark jeans. Outside on Route 219, a car with a loud muffler passed, clanking.

"They'll sue you, and I'm too old to be sued again," he said. "I feel I gave that case what I had to give it. Thirteen years. That's a long time."

Alkire still had all his notes in two binders and a book in which he kept a clipping of every newspaper article ever written about the killings. He had the Court TV tapes. But when I asked to see them, he was vague, noncommittal. He preferred to tell me about how long it takes him to make a table—six months because he's slow.

He pulled over a small bench with a rhododendron—West Virginia's state flower—carved into its face. The price tag read $250. "You can sit there," he said, "if you like."

"I can see them right now," Alkire said then, "just as good as I could when I went in there. The thing that got me the most was both of them had their eyes open. No matter where I walked around the table, it looked like they were looking at me. Never had that feeling before."

I asked him about the Franklin theory of the crime and why he didn't believe it. He said that he didn't get "tunnel vision," as Beard and others have accused him of having; he was open to the possibility that Franklin did it. He listened to DiFalco read from the report of her investigation, and he listened to the tape she had made in the Illinois prison.

"I could hear DiFalco say on the tape, 'What we want to talk to you about is the death of two girls in Pocahontas County.' Then there was a silence. And then Franklin said, 'I don't know nothing about that.'"

Alkire did his own investigation and was willing to have his mind changed. "I still hadn't gotten Franklin out of my mind. I wasn't going to be satisfied until I talked to him myself." He drove to Chattanooga, where Franklin had been transferred to stand trial for slaughtering the black man and white woman outside the Pizza Hut. "If you can't prove that somebody did something, then you can back up and prove that he didn't do it."

But Franklin wouldn't see Alkire. He tried to call Franklin, but Franklin wouldn't take his calls. He listened to tapes of interviews other law enforcement agencies had made of Franklin. "He would just ramble," Alkire told me, "like I am doing now."

Alkire asked me if I minded if he chewed a little tobacco, that he knew it was gross but that it was his only vice, and when I told him I didn't, he loosened the pouch, pinched a tuft, and inserted it into his cheek with a finger.

"I got the right guy," Alkire said, after a while, of Beard. "I presented all the facts that I had. I presented them to the grand jury. They indicted him. They found him guilty. To me, I did my job."

Alkire was still calling Beard "Jake," I noticed; there was still that chain that connected them. It's important that I understood who Jake Beard was, Alkire said, many times. How involved, how changeable, how mean, how strange. If Jake hadn't been that way, if he hadn't been who he was, Alkire said. But there was no end to that sentence, and Alkire would refuse to talk to me anymore after this interview.

"I guess there's still some people around here who don't think Jake did it. But I want to tell them about how he was. That third-girl thing." Alkire stopped, chewed, smiled. "It was 2 o'clock in the morning, and the phone rang," he remembered, though the official report has Beard calling the

Marlinton office rather than his home directly. "And it was Jake Beard. He said, 'Bob, I got some information for you.' He said, 'I know what happened to that third girl.' I said, 'Jake, there is no third girl.'"

Bobby Morrison's ex-wife was on house arrest but serving her community-service hours that night at the Pocahontas County Animal Shelter office. She'd dealt weed and later heroin, she told the *Pocahontas Times,* as a way to support her children as a single parent because she did not qualify for government vouchers at the time. She started using opiates after her doctors prescribed them for a spinal injury she suffered in childbirth that dislocated several of her vertebrae. "I don't blame any of the doctors for me being an addict by no means," she said, "but it certainly didn't help."

The shelter was in a corner of a Marlinton warehouse the size of a cruise ship that held secondhand furniture and antiques. I could hear the river running just on the other side of the parking lot. There were two boys skateboarding in the rain near the door and I walked around to the back corner, where I could see cages of animals. They barked and jumped in the air all at once, a forest of dog sounds. The door opened, and a man's head stuck out. "Get in here!" he called. "I heard you coming."

Inside, the walls were also concrete, and the only light was coming from a rectangular fluorescent panel. Most of the cages inside were empty. In a small clearing in the center of the room was a foldable table with two chairs, one of which the man took again. In the other was a tall woman with dry, tan skin. Powerful shoulders, indigo denim, and white sneakers. Hair worn up in a ponytail with short bangs. She raised her hand when I said her name—Teresa—then said we could talk in the back.

We settled into the back room, which was a bathroom with two stalls. "Oh Beard did it," Teresa said, "there's no doubt in my mind." I leaned against a scrub sink; she stood next to a metal shelf of towels and detergents. She lit a cigarette and ashed it into a red plastic cup that sat on the shelf for this purpose.

She said that Beard would come to the house where she was living with Bobby after he separated from his child's mother just to scare them. "That guy Franklin, he doesn't know what he's talking about. He's never been here. It sounds convincing to you when you read about him, but I know. We lived through it."

I'd already called all Morrison's numbers and written letters to no answer. I gave Teresa the newest letter I'd written and asked her to give it to him. She said she would try to get Morrison to talk to me, but she didn't know. He was in his early fifties; they'd been divorced for years but were still good friends. "For a long time he wouldn't talk to anyone. So mad, so mad, so mad," she said. "I think, also, ashamed."

"Why?" I asked.

"I don't know," she said. "That's what I asked him."

In the cage room, the phone rang. The voice of the man who let me in the door, then his footsteps. He appeared and handed the cordless to Teresa.

"I'll be there, sweetie," she said into it, "anything you need. Just as soon as I'm off work. But what did they say about the follow-up? Which medications? Shit."

Past the Little General store and straight through the intersection is the building supply store where Jesse and Pee Wee Walton worked. The building supply store was low and wide but too small for the vast acre of wet gray pavement on which it sat. Mine was the only car in the parking lot; Jesse's wagon was probably parked behind or somewhere special. The automatic doors slid apart, and the entryway to the store was wide and decked with straw tiki torches. I wandered down the center aisle, then turned left at the paint and paintbrushes, and followed the aisle all the way to the wall. A few aisles down, there he was, filling a shelf on the end of the aisle with rolls of duct tape.

Whoa hey, Jesse said. He wore his navy West Virginia Mountaineers hat as usual. He had filled out a little, and looked more solid somehow. I knew about his recent wedding, had heard that his wife was a cool outspoken woman his family loved.

I asked him about music night, if it was still that night, Tuesdays. No, he said. They had to move it because the mandolin player was racing cars again.

Oh yeah?

Yeah, he said. You should come by.

I will, I said.

Cool, he said.

It was very quiet in the store—no music.

Well, he said. I've got to go check something outside, but you can come if you want.

Jesse got to work in his sweatshirt, moving boxes around underneath the cover of a small outbuilding, but the rain was coming in sideways. He never did own a rain jacket. Or rain boots. Always only those gray sneakers.

I was afraid, I noticed. But of what? Of myself and my own desire to know. And yet something pushed me forward—a smell, or a Spidey sense perhaps, that what there was to know would hurt but in a way that was necessary.

I'm writing about the Rainbow Murders, I said to Jesse then. I think I need to talk to Pee Wee Walton.

He's not here today, Jesse said. It's his day off.

Another time, then, I said. Will you help me?

Jesse looked straight ahead at the corrugated tin walls of the store. For once he kept his head still, no bobbing. I wanted to reach through everything that had happened—my sudden departure, the Chef's death, the boisterous DMHB's death, every mile and every minute—and say something that wasn't an apology and wasn't an accusation, something that was just true. But my language was language, and his was living. I saw that he had survived, not just growing up in a place where the roads and the trees and the weather can become weapons, but also growing up in a place where his form of masculinity was often reviled, and that his survival, though complicated, was no small feat.

Hmm, I don't think so, Jesse said, rain dripping down the brim of his hat and onto the ground. He doesn't want to talk about all that mess.

Jesse had never refused me anything before—not a drink, not a ride, not anything. I was, almost, proud.

* * *

Pee Wee Walton's mother had answered the last few times I'd called, but this time it was Pee Wee himself. I told him who I was, and we spoke for a few minutes about the weather and the roads I'd lived on when I lived in the county.

Then I told him that I knew the truth was more complicated than what had been reported and that I suspected he had been caught in the middle of two versions of events, neither of which were exactly true. I told him that so much time had passed and no one could be prosecuted anymore, and was there anything he could tell me, anything he wanted to say?

Pee Wee Walton was silent on the Hillsboro end of the line, but he was there, breathing.

Then he said one word—"No"—and the line went dead.

I returned to Pocahontas County many more times after that and asked many more questions. But before I drove away that time, I went down to the low-water bridge to see how it was faring after the 2016 flood. During the flood, it had been under feet of water—mud marks on the concrete and the grass showed how many. But the small beach of pebbles was beginning to show again, and there was a black pickup parked there and a few young people having a small party. One of them was the redheaded girl.

She was just as thin as she had always been, but now she was taller and more elastic, as if her whole body had been stretched. She wore a black string bikini top and a jean skirt and had her hair in a low ponytail. I slowed and watched her open the door to the pickup, pull out a hoodie, and put it on. Our eyes met, and I waved and tried to decide whether to slow enough to speak and if so what to say, when she turned and picked her way over the rocks to the water. I watched her drink from a can of beer, and I watched her get picked up and tossed over the shoulder of a tall tan man who wore nothing but shorts and a West Virginia Mountaineers baseball cap.

I drove away, through the state park and past Jesse's grandma's house to the place where the road comes to a T with 219. There was a time when seeing her that way would have made me think that she had disappeared, was disappearing from women and from herself, heading for things that would bring her mostly pain. Also, there was a time when I would have told myself no—think nothing, say nothing, *be* nothing.

But this time I thought: both things were possible and were likely happening at the same time. I had made a mistake thinking I knew what it looked like for myself to disappear or what it looked like when someone else did, and I had made a mistake thinking that hiding my truths from other people could keep me from doing harm.

This woman—she wasn't a girl anymore, I saw—may have just been a person who was loving the taste of a beer and the feel of her own body with many twisty years left to make the important mistakes and stay alive.

2

DEBORAH DIFALCO—DEBBIE, AS SHE signed her emails to me—was waiting for me outside a Starbucks at the end of a brightly lit shopping plaza in a suburb of Washington, DC. Her Frappuccino was half empty before her on the slatted iron table, and she was older than I expected her to be, softer and more blurred, in a blue rain jacket and jeans. I understood her neck and her shoulders before I understood her face—dark eyes, dark eyebrows, dark thick hair past her shirt collar that looked as if it had been straightened, today or recently, and then frizzed. It was going to storm. I'd promised not to make her late for her daughter's basketball game, where she was the coach.

DiFalco had left the state police and began working for US Customs doing special investigations. "If anything other than people was crossing the border, it was ours." Drug smuggling, weapons, fraud, cargo ships. "Eventually we got into investigating child pornography, or cybersmuggling," which is what brought her to northern Virginia and this Starbucks landscape. She worked on drug cases and spent three months in Bulgaria enforcing sanctions against Serbia Montenegro; she became the deputy director of her task force and the director of the cybersmuggling investigation. She was retired from law enforcement, now, though she still did investigative work.

"There is no doubt in my mind that Franklin did it," DiFalco told me bluntly.

I'd like to have what she has—no doubt. I told her about my sense of being caught between two stories, each with their believers. I asked her how she could be so sure.

"Emma," she said, "there was no evidence that ever pointed to Jake Beard. That's the bottom line." Whereas when it came to Franklin, "the evidence matched."

She rejected the idea that Franklin might have read about the case in newspapers or a true crime magazine, as Alkire and Weiford have alleged over the years. I had spent hours myself on this line of thinking, even engaging the services of a professional archival researcher and research librarian to try to find a detailed article on the Rainbow Murders published before Franklin first confessed in 1984, but to no result.

"He could not have read about it," DiFalco said. "Everyone always says, 'Oh he read that,' but where, I would like to know? He was locked up right after the murders." She also disputed the notion that the police made details of the crimes available to the public and that his story changed over time. Every agency that interviewed him—the Wisconsin State Police, the Illinois State Police, the FBI—believed him, she reminded me, except the West Virginia State Police.

I didn't know Alkire, I said, but I knew Weiford a little, and I believed he was a good person. If Weiford was good, how did he go so wrong?

"You can't put blinders on," DiFalco said. "You can't believe one thing absolutely."

The wind picked up, and the umbrella in the middle of our metal table threatened to take off.

"Emma," she said, "show me some evidence against Jake Beard."

"Well," I offered, "there are the eyewitnesses—Walton, Lewis, and also all the citizens who gave testimony about that day. Why would they lie?"

"They were talked to so many times," she said. "When you're talked to so many times, you develop a story; you develop a story with the police who talk to you."

"Beard simply made a mistake, albeit a big mistake," she said, in calling Vicki's father.

"Beard made a lot of mistakes," I said, reminding her of the false statement he had given to police implicating Arnold Cutlip for killing the "third Rainbow girl."

DiFalco dipped her head, agreeing. "I'm not sure anyone will ever truly know what happened with that." She was quiet another moment. "In a community like that, you have to understand. We would get calls all the time. On a rainy day, we would get calls. 'Trooper, the TV man says it may rain, but I trust you more than I trust him. Should I take an umbrella?'"

"Wow," I said. I had been thinking of Pocahontas County in 1980 as a community that did not trust the police much, but this may not have been so.

After Beard's conviction, DiFalco said, she was trying to help the Beard family. She says that Beard seemed like a normal guy with a family; he didn't creep her out.

"I was a police officer. I took that serious. An innocent man was sitting in jail."

After his conviction was overturned, she went out for coffee with him. "I said to him, 'Nothing can happen now, you can't be retried, so did you kill those girls?' And he said to me, he said, 'Debbie, I absolutely did not.'"

So she did doubt, I think. To ask is to doubt.

"And you believed him?"

"It is one of the things I have prized in myself over the years," Di-Falco said. "I have developed a way of knowing people, of judging their character. And what's the motive? If it were Beard, what would be the motive?"

No motive, I conceded. I asked if she had other cases before where there was no motive.

"Never," she said. "There was always a motive. Franklin had the motive; he had the means, and he had the opportunity."

DiFalco said that Alkire had insisted over and over that it had to be somebody local, that people just don't come through Pocahontas County. "Well, they do."

Further, the case had divided the state police, officer against officer, she told me.

"People were on one side of it, the Beard side, or they were on the other side of it."

If I really wanted to know about how much the state police was split,

DiFalco said, I should talk to Michael Jordan, who served with her. Then she rose and wished me luck. She looked toward her silver Toyota minivan, an older model but well kept. "The traffic here," she said. "I never wanted to end up in a place like this."

I looked back at the index of witnesses for Beard's trial and found him, as Weiford noted, testifying for the defense: Corporal Michael Jordan—his real name. I called him.

He spoke well of Alkire, which surprised me, called him Bob, and seemed to feel the loss of their friendship acutely. "I have had no contact with Bob whatsoever since the early '90s," Jordan said into his landline phone and then his cell phone on his way to work security with the college near his home in Elkins. "When this case kind of blew up, I went my way, and he went his."

In the mid-1980s, Jordan worked in the plainclothes division of the West Virginia State Police out of Elkins. His boss was Alkire. This was during the time when Alkire had been assigned away from the Rainbow Murders in order to pursue other cases but had, according to Jordan, never truly stepped away. Jordan, alongside DiFalco, worked under Alkire in the major crimes division, and their load was mostly drug cases. They were discouraged from socializing with the officers in uniform, so they often hung out with each other. Dinners and picnics and the Fourth of July.

"Everybody got along," Jordan said. "The wives got along well; the men got along well. It was kind of like a little clique. The ladies would cook; the men would play cards, smoke cigars, do what guys do."

Jordan described Alkire as a mellow, even-tempered officer and boss who didn't micromanage and always signed off on Jordan's investigation reports and receipts with a joke or two. Jordan's then-wife was close with Elaine Alkire, and Jordan watched Alkire be a caring and present father to his two sons. "That's what also made this very hard," Jordan said.

Sometimes when there was a significant crime, such as a murder that wouldn't solve, detectives from their twelve-county area could request major crimes officers to come in and assist. "That's how I got involved in the Jake Beard aspect of the Rainbow case," said Jordan. In the hallways and over the coffeepot, officers told each other that Alkire was holding stead-fastly to the idea that local people had killed Vicki and Nancy.

Alkire got a promotion in the late 1980s to sergeant and then first sergeant and took a transfer back to Pocahontas County. One day in the early '90s, after they had already arrested the "relevant necessary people," Jordan said, "Bob came to me and said he wanted me to help him put this case together."

"When we sat down initially, the Franklin issue came up, and I said, 'What are you going to do about this?...It's discoverable, I mean, you know it's gonna come up.' And he said, 'We're going to investigate this case to the fullest, and if Franklin did it, then Franklin did it....If you want to look at the Franklin aspect of that, that's fine.' And he gave me full leeway to do that. And I did."

Jordan retreaded much of DiFalco's investigative territory from the early 1980s, and was involved in many of the actions in 1992—taking statements from the witnesses who still lived on Droop Mountain as well as interrogating Pee Wee Walton and Johnny Washington Lewis.

He reported on his work daily to Alkire. "To me, the further the case went, the more the Jake Beard aspect of the case fell apart, and the further the case went, the stronger to me it looked like Joseph Paul Franklin had committed the crime," Jordan said. He was persuaded by the sum of the facts in support of Franklin's guilt. Plus, simply, that Franklin was an es-tablished killer with a modus operandi and Beard was not.

"I think Jake is a detective wannabe. I think he wanted to be the hero of the case and crack the case—he has an ego thing going. I think he wanted to be some sort of little local hero."

In contrast, Jordan said, "[Franklin] is a psychopath. I get that part. Not everything that comes out of his mouth is truthful. But when you look at Jake Beard, you take a man that has no real criminal history...to brutally murder two girls in cold blood and not just kill them, but shoot them to pieces for apparently nothing. Then you have Franklin, who has all kinds of issues and upwards of thirty confirmed kills [*this number is in dispute*], and I mean just that within itself....I believe [Alkire] is sincere in his belief [in the Beard theory]. But I personally don't see it, and didn't at the time, and made that known."

Jordan cited one incident in particular that precipitated his split with Alkire—the interview of Johnnie Lewis on June 12, 1992. Lewis had just been brought in to sign an agreement that offered him immunity in exchange for his testimony against Beard, and there was, Jordan said, a plan to interview Lewis the following day to hear whatever information he could offer now that he was legally protected. Jordan was supposed to be part of the interrogation team. He was still living in Elkins at that time and commuting the nearly two hours back and forth to Pocahontas County every day and was in his car heading to the Buckeye West Virginia State Police office when a radio operator contacted him and told him there was no need to come to Pocahontas County that day—the meeting with Lewis had been cancelled.

"I find out that that was the day that they *did* interview Lewis, and I personally believe they intentionally did not want me there," said Jordan.

That night Alkire and Jordan spoke on the phone, and Alkire delivered this news. Jordan said he understood but asked if Alkire would mind if he interviewed Lewis himself, in the presence of Lewis's attorney. Alkire agreed, and Jordan did so. "I started asking [Lewis] some very direct questions. In his original statement [to Estep and Alkire], there were things that I thought were very strange. He described the girls as 'the tall one' and 'the short one' and if you look at it I think there was a one-inch difference, a very small amount of difference in [Vicki and Nancy's] heights. And when I started asking [Lewis] some very direct questions, and which one was which? And which one had on this clothing? And which had on that clothing? This guy *maybe* had a first-grade education. I mean, he was very, very not smart. Very. I don't know if you would consider him—whatever. So when I'm asking him these questions, he eventually just kind of gave it up and said, 'I didn't see any girls,' he began to say, 'I didn't see any girls. I was threatened; I was throttled; I was assaulted.'"

At that point, Jordan alerted his boss, who alerted others higher up in the state police. Then Walton told his attorney he'd been assaulted too.

A great deal happened very quickly after that. Weiford was forced to dismiss the charges against all of the arrested men that summer, and the state police brass called a meeting to discuss the whole mess of a situation at the state police headquarters in Charleston with all the involved players—Alkire, Weiford, Estep, and Jordan. The superintendent himself presided over the meeting.

"And that was the last contact I had on the Rainbow case," Jordan said.

"So did they say to you, 'Thank you very much, you're no longer assigned to this case'?"

"They didn't say, 'Thank you very much,' no." Jordan laughed. "They said that they were going to continue to investigate the case against Jacob Beard but that I was not going to be involved in it."

"Did you feel that you were a whistle-blower and they were mad at you for having spoken up?"

"Very much so," he said.

I told Jordan I couldn't believe that any person, and definitely not Alkire, who made that wooden bench I loved sitting on and was a friend and card player to Jordan, meant to put an innocent man in prison for six years. Jordan didn't either.

"I don't think [Alkire] was that type of a person [to get violent]. I don't think he was that type of person in this case.... He's a good person. To me, good people make mistakes. I do it every day. I am a good person, but I make mistakes. I think with this case...it got personal. Everybody wants to protect their beliefs and their interests. I believe that Bob will go to his grave believing that he had the right person."

I wondered aloud what made Alkire so convinced of Beard's guilt. Did he give Jordan any sense of that, or any sense of why he truly couldn't believe in Franklin's guilt?

Jordan went silent on the phone for the first time. "No," he said after a time. "He felt like they still had a provable case, like they had the right people. Sometimes police are just like anybody else: they get blinders on. They get tunnel vision. I'm not accusing him of that; I'm just saying that sometimes—I probably did it at some point with Franklin. My belief was that he committed the crime, and maybe I began not to be able to see the Beard theory any longer. I don't have any evidence of [Franklin's guilt]. I don't think there'll ever be any evidence of that."

Jordan continued, "I'm not saying he's a perfect witness; I'm just saying compared to the Jacob Beard aspect, I thought there was a lot less holes in the Franklin stuff than there was with the Jacob Beard stuff."

"We want the story to be perfect," I noted, "and the minute it's not perfect, we're like, it's a lie!"

"Right."

3

THE STATE OF MISSOURI SOUGHT the death penalty against Franklin for the murder of the Jewish man outside the St. Louis synagogue, but first it would have to prove that he was sane enough to stand trial.

Malcolm Gladwell's 1997 *New Yorker* article "Damaged" depicts the 1994 hearing to determine this very issue. In Gladwell's words, the object of the hearing was whether Joseph Paul Franklin "embarking on a campaign to rid America of Jews and blacks was an act of evil or an act of illness."

No one disputed that Franklin had suffered astounding physical abuse at the hands of his mother, and many signs pointed to mental illness, but his crimes were so many and his hatred so extreme. To gain insight, the defense brought in Dorothy Lewis, psychiatrist to the criminal stars, who had consulted on the trial of Ted Bundy among others, and her colleague, the neurologist Jonathan Pincus.

Lewis, a doctor at New York's Bellevue Hospital, is the pioneer of a theory that brain injury, when combined with psychosis and physical abuse as a child, results in a superstorm that is an almost sure predictor of becoming a repeat murderer. According to research she and Pincus conducted on scores of America's most violent offenders, when the frontal lobe of the brain, which houses impulse control, is damaged, the consequence is that the person cannot tell the difference between an everyday mishap and a threat to life. When your car is cut off in a parking lot, for example, you might perceive it as a fatal attack requiring a defense of lethal force.

Lewis spoke with Franklin for six and a half hours and concluded that Franklin was a paranoid schizophrenic unable to determine what was real and what was not. He had also suffered head trauma and likely traumatic brain injury as well, though Franklin refused to let Pincus examine his brain. Taken together, these truths meant that in Lewis's opinion, Franklin was not responsible for his actions. In short, wrote Gladwell, "she didn't feel that Franklin's brain worked the way brains are supposed to work."

"I just don't believe people are born evil," Lewis told him. "The deed itself is bizarre, grotesque. But it's not evil. To my mind, evil bespeaks conscious control over something. Serial murderers are not in that category. They are driven by forces beyond their control."

Franklin represented himself at his 1994 capital trial and lost. He then asked the judge to give him the death penalty. If the judge demurred, Franklin threatened, he would kill again inside prison.

Franklin was put to death in Missouri in 2013, but in the intervening time he'd changed his mind and launched a series of bids for stays of execution. In the last years of his life, he liked to read the Bible, as well as the Koran and the Bhagavad Gita and other Hindu writings. He meditated. When he had exhausted the prison library's supply of meditation tapes, he sent away for more. He had also profited from the effects of antipsychotic medication to treat his schizophrenia. When interviewed weeks before his death, he seemed profoundly changed from the man Melissa Powers had spoken to in 1998.

"I was so mentally ill and crazy," Franklin told a local Missouri reporter. "I was like a totally different person. You would think it was somebody else except for the name."

He said that when he read *Mein Kampf*, he was a child, impressionable and starving for words that would help him. "I would get a real funny feeling after reading [that book]," he said.

At the end of the interview, the reporter asked Franklin if he thought he deserved to die for everything he'd done. Franklin thought about it a long time before he answered: "I do, yeah."

Franklin had one child, a daughter—a fact I did not know until she contacted me on hearing about this book. Her name is Lori, and in several online profiles she favors a quote from Jane Austen: "I was quiet, but I was not blind."

Franklin met Lori's mother in 1978 in Chisholm, a community in the northern part of Montgomery, Alabama, and Lori's mother raised her there. Lori was a year old when Franklin went to prison in the fall of 1980, but she was always in close touch with him, sending letters and pictures back and forth and talking on the phone. "He acted like my daddy," she wrote to me in a series of emails, "always telling me things I needed to do. Stay in school. Go to the library, study, no boyfriends, learn karate, self-defense."

Since Lori was old enough to know she had a father, she also knew that he was a person who had killed many people, most of them black people. At school, she was scared someone would find out who her father was and what he had done, especially her black classmates. Whenever anyone asked about him, Lori would lie and say he was a businessman in Chicago.

Her mother and maternal grandmother talked about Franklin all the time—how he had seemed like such a nice guy, how it had all come as such a surprise—and later would echo these sentiments about the other men who came into Lori's family.

"I had an alcoholic and physically abusive stepdad," Lori wrote to me. Her messages were short and staccato, the result of a liberal relationship with the return key.

When Lori was fourteen, her mother remarried, but the new choice was no better, she said. As is often the case when girl children are abused by adult men, she said she was not believed when she tried to tell her mother about the abuse, and her mother kicked her out later that year. "I was glad to go."

She lived with aunts and cousins until she got pregnant, and then she moved in with her boyfriend, whom she later married, and his parents. But trouble—family, legal, emotional—seemed to follow her. Lori, too, had been through the criminal justice system, for drug possession and public intoxication. At last contact, her child was not living with her.

"I'm pretty much a lone wolf," she told me. "I stay to myself most of the time. I tried hard to interact with society around me. It didn't and usually doesn't work out too good....My mind stays busy. It never stops."

On social media, Lori was partial to posting full-screen pictures of quotes written in white script on black or pink backgrounds. Another one she liked was from the Dalai Lama: "If human society loses the value of justice, compassion, and honesty, the next generation will face greater difficulties and more suffering."

"I feel cursed in a lot of ways, for his sins," Lori wrote of Franklin. She felt there were dark parts of him that were also in her. He struggled with addiction; she has struggled with addiction. Other things too, she said, but did not elaborate. I could not help but think of the story of Beauty and the Beast again and the idea of intergenerational trauma, that the wounds of the parent are transmitted to the child through the way the parent presents what the world is, what a person is, what is safe and what is dangerous. "Surviving," writes social worker and researcher Sue Coyle, "does not mean coming away unscathed."

Lori never told her father about the abuse she says she suffered at the hands of the men in her mother's life or about her own run-ins with the law because she felt it would drive him crazy. After all, he was stuck in prison for life, and there was nothing he could do about it. But Lori harbored fantasies that he would get out and return to her.

"I've always loved him. I needed him out and taking care of me. I knew he would never be. I never had false hope on that. I wished. But I knew better."

In the northwest corner of Liberty Park in Salt Lake City, equidistant from the two stocky oak trees that face the crosswalk, there is a small brass marker engraved with the names of David Martin and Ted Fields.

In the late 1970s, if you walked anywhere around the southeast side of Salt Lake City and heard music, it was usually coming from Liberty Park. This was the poor side of town, and the park was a favorite with teenagers, black and white. When the sun went down, they came out on foot and on bicycle and on roller skates, and they talked and skated and danced together.

Martin, eighteen, and Fields, twenty, were friends and neighbors who decided to go out for a jog on the evening of August 20, 1978, with two girls—both fifteen—whom they knew from the park. Martin had just graduated from high school and was taking some time that summer to think about what he wanted to do next. Fields was about to begin his sophomore year at the University of Utah studying chemical engineering. His father was the pastor of the Baptist church where Martin's family also went, a ritual that made the Martins feel closer to Mississippi, where they were from; they had moved to Utah when Martin was in elementary school because they feared the effects their home state's virulent racism might have on their son's future.

Earlier that night the boys, both black, had played a prank on the two girls they were jogging with, both white: they jumped out from behind a bush to scare their friends, who had fallen behind. But at around 10 o'clock, when they were crossing the street to return from the park, the friends were four abreast, and all keeping the same pace. Cracks of gunfire came fast then—*pop pop pop*. Martin was shot first and fell into the street. Fields tried to drag Martin from the crosswalk to the safety of the park, but he was shot before he could do so. "Run," Fields told the two girls, one of whom was Terry Mitchell. She did.

Mitchell is not exactly white, it turns out—her mother is Mexican American—but she passed. The night her friends were killed was the first time she had ever been jogging in her life. She was not hit by Franklin's bullets but was hospitalized for shock and wounds from shrapnel that passed through Martin's body, and scarred her arms, legs, neck, and stomach.

Martin and Fields were handsome young men with bright futures and churchgoing families. No one appeared to have any motive for killing them. Later that year, when Joseph Paul Franklin was arrested in Florida, he said that when Martin and Fields came around the corner with two white girls, he decided to shoot them just because they were black and white people together, moving their bodies in the same space.

Mitchell quit school after the murders—she was getting beat up and jumped; people were writing "NIGGER LOVER" or "RACE TRAITOR" or

"SPIC" on her locker. Eventually she got her GED. She worked long hours at many different jobs to provide for her mother and sisters, married, and had children. In the decade after the murders, she returned to a classroom a couple of times, but it didn't stick until she earned her degree at forty-eight. It was that stint in college that gave her the language to talk about race and gender and trauma that she didn't have before.

She began to look back at Franklin's crime and the ways her life had been shaped by it. Newspaper articles after the events had printed her home address, accused her of setting her friends up to die, and questioned why she had lived when they had not. Inspired by a class assignment that asked her to create a mask about the parts of herself that people don't normally see, Mitchell put on her own art exhibit in June 2013 and decided to create a piece that would have a component in which she drove to the mountains outside Salt Lake City and recited words forgiving Franklin. "I did this meditation, and I just said, 'May his suffering be eased,' because I understood that in his childhood there was nothing else that he could be but what he was. Nobody showed him kindness. Nobody tried to help this child," she said. "Because this whole village saw his suffering. They didn't help him, so he took vengeance on the village in his own way. And I got it. There was nobody who could get it that deep like I got it."

When Mitchell left the mountains that day, she said, she felt completely at ease. Then the next week, she saw an article on Facebook chronicling how Franklin had denounced racism and was asking for his victims' forgiveness.

"Seeing that was so shocking....I just couldn't stop crying; I couldn't breathe. I couldn't believe that he was finally going to be released from his suffering. And maybe I would be too."

At Franklin's request, one of his lawyers contacted Mitchell. "Everybody's saying, 'He wants to talk to you.' And I'm like, 'I don't want to talk to him; I forgave him; let's just leave it at that and be done.'" But Franklin was insistent—he wanted to be forgiven before he died, and he wanted to be forgiven by Mitchell. Eventually, she agreed to speak to him by phone.

When we talked, we had two conversations, that one and one the day before his execution. It was one of the most intense experiences of my life because I never expected to deeply forgive him. He wanted me to fight for him not to be executed, and I told him, 'No, I think you should be executed. You've been a prisoner from womb to tomb, let it be done.' He was trying to avoid accountability in the first conversation, like, 'Oh sorry about what happened with your friends and all,' so I knew he wasn't sorry.... To this day I feel strongly about this, that when he dies his energy goes somewhere. And I did not want it to bind with more dark energy; I wanted it to bind with light.

I talked to him again, and it was very different. He was a very different person at that point. The day before the execution, they put him right next to the room where they were going to kill him. And he goes, 'So what are you doing?' And I go, 'Nothing, what are you doing?' And he goes, 'I'm watching TV....I turned the TV on and the very first thing I see is the KKK rally. With these two blond girls holding this banner.'...and I go, 'What do you think of that?,' and he goes, 'Those poor girls don't know how they're ruining their lives. I wish I would have known how much I would ruin my life.'...He told me the only people that ever were good to him were black people, and I'm like, 'I don't understand why you hated them so much,' and he was like, 'Terry, I was really messed up.' He described when he was accepted into the KKK, and he said there were a thousand hoods. I could smell the smoke. I could see the fire, the way he was describing it to me.

Mitchell told Franklin to stop. She could not bear to hear any more.

I brought up the white supremacist rally in Charlottesville, where I had lived during graduate school, and the ways racist hate seemed to be ever-growing lately. "Yes," Mitchell said. "Everything [Franklin] once wanted to come true is coming true now."

I asked Mitchell what it was like to speak to someone she knew was about to die and if she felt called to offer him anything.

"I said, 'When you die, choose light, and then come to me, and let me know you chose light.' And he did. I swear to God, it was incredible."

The day Franklin was executed, Mitchell said, she woke early to go to class and was protected all day from reporters by her fellow students. "And then I came home that night after class, and I told my husband, 'It's so weird—I feel like this weight has been lifted off my chest; I can breathe a full breath.'"

Later, Mitchell was in bed, and her husband was in the living room, but she says she felt a presence in the doorway. "You're looking at your child sleeping like, 'Oh my God, she's so beautiful—I can't believe that's my child,' and you just can't not look at them. You just stare at them and lose time? It felt like somebody was doing that with me." In that moment, she felt a burst of energy, more full of gratitude and joy than any other feeling she'd had in her life. "I know it was [Franklin] choosing light. There's no doubt in my mind....And I slept for the first time in months all the way through the night."

The morning of the execution, Mitchell had received two emails confirming that Franklin had been executed. The emails were signed "from the Honorable R. Roberts," a name that Mitchell recognized but could not immediately place. "And I'm like, who is that? I swear I know that name. And then I remembered."

Utah had come early in the list of states that wanted to prosecute Franklin, and he was scheduled to stand trial for the murder of Martin and Fields in the winter of 1981. Utah's attorney general decided to prosecute Franklin for the additional crime of "depriving Martin and Fields of their civil rights"—a charge that reflected Franklin's motive to murder them specifically because they were black. But Utah local law enforcement was inexperienced in prosecuting a federal civil rights hate crime case. To help, they asked the US Department of Justice to send in a seasoned attorney who could take over the civil rights trial against Franklin, due to begin in February 1981. Twenty-seven-year-old Richard Roberts, a young black attorney and rising star in the department's Washington, DC, office, soon landed in Salt Lake City.

It was Roberts's job to prepare Mitchell to testify that she had been with Martin and Fields and seen them get gunned down by Franklin. She testified. Franklin was convicted and given multiple life sentences. This seemed like justice, and the families of Martin and Fields gave statements to the press saying they were satisfied with the outcome.

In 2014, Terry Mitchell reported allegations of criminal misconduct about Richard Roberts, by then the chief US district judge for DC appointed by President Bill Clinton, to the Utah attorney general's office, alleging that Roberts sexually abused her many times while he was prepping her as a witness for Franklin's trial.

"I did whatever he said because he told me Franklin would be let out on a mistrial and he would be free to kill again and it would be my fault," Mitchell said.

Roberts admitted he had a sexual relationship with Mitchell in 1981— his sixteen-year-old witness—but called it "a consensual affair, a bad lapse in judgment."

After Mitchell received Roberts's email about Franklin's death, she started having nightmares. "And I'm thinking to myself, *I'm going crazy. Right? This can't be real; this didn't happen; that was my fault.*" A few weeks later, Mitchell formed a plan to kill herself with the gun her husband kept in his bedside drawer. "I was going to go drive up to the mountains and just be done because I couldn't take the pain anymore and I didn't want to be a burden to my family.... I'm gonna add this too and tell everybody? And who's gonna believe me?"

Mitchell found some solace in her community, and her will to be alive returned. But the investigator for the Utah attorney general recommended that their office not take any steps toward a criminal prosecution. Sixteen was the age of consent in Utah in 1981, and so much time had passed.

"In some theoretical sense, [Mitchell's] description of the events... could arguably fit the elements of the crime of rape," reads their report, "but in terms of a real world criminal prosecution, the case would be impossible to prosecute."

Roberts has never been arrested or charged for any crime in relation to Mitchell. She decided to file a civil complaint against Roberts, the outcome of which is, at the time of this writing, still pending. Roberts announced his retirement because of an undisclosed illness on the same day Mitchell's civil complaint was filed, and he will receive a generous pension from the US government until he dies.

Trauma is cumulative, argues Lovie Jackson Foster, an assistant professor at the University of Pittsburgh. "You don't get through one trauma and then it dissipates. They just keep building on top of each other."

Foster specifically studies the effects of American slavery and racism on mental health in the black community and is part of a broader conversation about the idea of "historical trauma," a kind of extension of the familial intergenerational trauma logic.

"Historical trauma is related to a genocide of a people, where some major event is aimed at a particular group because of their status as an oppressed group," says Mary Ann Jacobs, chair of American Indian studies at the University of North Carolina at Pembroke. "It could be a war; it could be cultural, such as when a people's language is banned and they are not allowed to speak or print it. It could be the desecration of monuments, such as graveyards and other sacred sites. Any of those events that have to do with ignoring the humanity of a group and having that part of social policy, be it formal or informal." When a traumatic event is inflicted on a community or social group, the descendants of that group will always carry its effects.

In the middle of Liberty Park in 1980 was a long wide street, and in the middle of the street all the teenagers would park their cars and play their music, and everybody would dance or roller skate. But after Franklin murdered Martin and Fields, the city closed that street and filled it in.

4

Jerry Dale's father had just taken a bad fall when I reached Dale on his cell phone. As we talked, he looked for, located, and then offered his father painkillers. In addition to being Pocahontas County sheriff from 1985 to 2000, Dale has been teaching college students since 1983 at Marshall University and elsewhere. He told me he has taught many Mountain Views students over the years and has nothing but respect for that organization. It was Dale who arranged for the judge to order that the Mountain Views land be cleared so that it could become the campground.

He is years younger than Jacob Beard, and the two didn't grow up together, but he has formed an opinion of him over the years through the interviews he conducted with people who did grow up with Beard. It was Dale—who told me he studied behavioral science along with criminal justice—who offered the comparison to Dr. Jekyll and Mr. Hyde: "Split personality. The psychologist in me looks at him too as someone that was born later in his parents' life and did not have any siblings that were close to his age. He kinda ended up being almost like an only child, somewhat pampered and somewhat spoiled." One side of Beard was kind, attentive to his family, and successful in business. The other side was, Dale said, "crazy. He abused alcohol a lot, and I don't have to tell you how people who use alcohol to the extreme can be unpredictable and somewhat violent."

Along with Weiford and Alkire, Dale was still sure that Beard had been the person who killed Vicki and Nancy. His confidence was mostly based on the ballistics evidence—he believes that one of the women was killed as she sat on the bumper of Ritchie Fowler's blue van, and the other was shot as she ran along the lane that sloped sharply downward. The idea that Franklin might have shot them from above as they sat in his Chevy Nova seems preposterous to Dale—there would also be a great deal more paraffin, or gunpowder residue, if that were the case, Dale said, since a car is such a small enclosed space and they were shot at such close range with such a high-powered gun.

Dale felt that Beard was found innocent at his second trial in large part thanks to Walt Weiford falling ill. Assistant Prosecutor Stephen Dolly did his best, as Dale sees it, but he didn't understand the case from the inside as Weiford had.

"We lived and breathed that [case] for years, and we knew more about it than anybody.... When you work a case as long as we did, there wasn't anything that the three of us weren't knowledgeable about."

This knowledge could feel like too much at times, Dale said, like a pressure bearing down on his body and those of Alkire and Weiford. When Franklin confessed again and again to the crimes, it upset Dale, who felt that he knew what had happened to Vicki and Nancy, and Franklin's version of events wasn't it; when Beard was acquitted, the whole world seemed to believe it.

"But that's the way it is—that's the way our criminal justice system is," Dale told me. They had gotten six years from Beard, and that was pretty good for a case that so many had thought was cold. "The criminal justice system is never absolutely ideal; it's usually a compromise someplace in between."

I asked Dale to expand on the pressure that he, Alkire, and Weiford had been under. What was the source of that pressure? Politics, as had been suggested in the media over the years?

"No," Dale said. "It was the pressure of being a human being and knowing what was right and wrong." Dale strongly disputes the idea that he pursued a conviction for Beard so he could get reelected or that there was any pressure in the other direction from locals telling him to stop putting so many resources toward the investigation of two "hippie girls."

"I know this is hard to believe in this day and age with as corrupt as our politicians are, but all we wanted to do was put the person responsible for this crime behind bars," Dale told me. "It wasn't right what happened to these girls."

Years after Beard's retrial, Dale lost his youngest son, and he felt that now he truly went to the place where the Durians and Santomeros had been. "I thought I knew what it was like to deal with death, having a parent die or a cousin," Dale said. "But you lose a child—that's an altogether different thing."

I put off calling Jacob Beard many times. When I finally called him in April 2015, he answered just like any other human person, but my name in his mouth, which he uttered often at the beginning of a sentence like a man trying to sell you a car, felt threatening in a way that was hard to articulate, perhaps portending something he might want in return. In those first phone calls, I still thought he might be guilty, and he sensed it, and it made him pushy—he had an evangelical drive to convince me. By the time I was arranging to meet him in person, I believed he was likely innocent, but that didn't mean I liked him. I booked a flight to Gainesville.

I was already late, and he was frustrated with how long it took me to find his apartment complex, which looked identical to all the other apartment complexes in that vast asphalt development soaked in sun. He wore glasses, a gray T-shirt, khaki pants, and orthopedic black sneakers. His head was bald and sunspotted; his back was large as a pillow. He wrinkled his face into the light and shook my hand.

When I asked to use the bathroom, I found it was equipped for the needs of both the very old—Preparation H—and the very young—bath toys; he and Linda often watch their only granddaughter. I was surprised when he said that he and Linda had been renting this apartment for eight years. The walls were white and bare but for the most perfunctory decorations. A hard sculpture of apples decorated with red berries floated precariously on the wall above his head when he took a seat at the small round table.

I could see his den/office, where there was a computer and a shelf of plastic John Deere tractors. He used the computer to go on Facebook (he had gone through all my Facebook friends, he told me, to see which side I was on) and make what little money he needed brokering deals for farming equipment online.

"Farming is my first love," he said, clasping one hand with the other.

He told me that shooting groundhogs, as Pee Wee Walton and Bill McCoy were doing on the day Vicki and Nancy were murdered, is in Pocahontas County not just a way to pass the day but in fact highly utilitarian. "There's nothing I'd rather shoot than a groundhog. They root up the fields."

Beard filed a lawsuit against the West Virginia State Police, the Pocahontas County Sheriff's Department, as well as Alkire and Weiford specifically, alleging malicious prosecution and police misconduct, and in 2003 he was awarded nearly $2 million to be paid by the West Virginia Board of Risk—supported by the state's taxpayers. Most lawyers take a third of this, Beard told me, but Beard and Stephen Farmer agreed that Farmer would take 50 percent, since he'd been handling Beard's appeals pro bono for so long. After taxes, Beard ended up with $640,000, of which he used $140,000 to pay off his debts and buy a new pickup. He estimated he paid about $600,000 in total defending himself against the charges of having killed Vicki Durian and Nancy Santomero; $7,000 alone went to purchasing the transcript of his own first trial. The remainder of his settlement remained in a complicated annuity, which pays him $2,174.75 a month for the rest of his life. If he died tomorrow, which was possible since he was fresh out of the hospital for a heart attack, Linda would receive his payment in his stead until the year 2023. Linda declined to participate in the interview, even calling Beard several times to see if I was still in the apartment or if it was safe for her to come home.

Beard jumped right into talking without many pleasantries or gestures of hospitality.

"They weren't the kind of people I ran around with," he said, of the men with whom he was arrested. "I didn't want to be friends with them. And I didn't have to. I'd speak to them if I saw them, but they weren't people I'd sit down and have a drink with." Beard attributed this to a difference between him and these men, a difference in "quality." "You might say that there was a little bit of a socioeconomic difference....I didn't go around telling people that I was better than them. I just avoided them." As for the Rainbow people and the Back to the Landers, Beard said he got along with them. "It didn't matter to me one way or the other."

The day heated up, and Beard's air conditioner blasted. I could ask a single short question, and Beard would talk for many minutes uninterrupted.

"I don't think Gerald Brown did it," Beard said. "And there's two reasons to this. Where the darn backpacks were found. Gerald Brown would have never driven all the way over there. If he'd have driven on Briery Knob with them, he'd have thrown them over the hill and thrown their backpacks over the hill and nobody would have probably ever found them."

I reminded him that Brown would go around saying, "I'm a hippie killer," and that he took his girlfriend up on Briery Knob and cried, even gave her a necklace that he claimed "belonged to one of his Rainbow friends."

"[Brown] was just like that," Beard said. "When he was sober and hadn't had a drink all day, he was just fun-loving and hardworking, hard at work at his logging business. When he and Drema lived there on the mountain, he got to drinking real bad and started losing his equipment. And she left him. It was bad. But other than that, he was just a happy-go-lucky somebody who would show up at dinnertime, eat supper, and then go on to somebody's house to party."

I told Beard that I found a lot of the ways the nine men talked about women in their statements very ugly. "Brown, Walton, McCoy, Morrison. It seems like they didn't like women very much."

"No," Beard said. "I don't think they did."

I asked him about the comment he made to *Newsday* in 1992 that most shaped my impression of him. When confronted with pictures of Vicki and Nancy as they would have been before they died, he had looked at the pictures, and, as a way of denying that he had been the one to kill them, he said, "They were definitely not the type of women I'd want to have sex with. They weren't the slimmest, trimmest little things."

What did he mean by that? "Well, if you said I said it, I said it," he said, and left it at that.

Beard, too, thought the perpetrator was most likely Franklin. "There's two or three things that Franklin said that are absolutely true, as far back [as when he first confessed in 1984]. I-64 wasn't finished [west of Pocahontas County]; you'd get back on Route 60. When he describes it in one of his interviews, he said, 'I was on the interstate, and I found myself on a two-lane road going through town,' and he got worried about having [the women's belongings] in his car."

He told me that he also saw on Facebook that I was friends with Susan Strong, former editor of the *Pocahontas Times*.

Beard thought Strong's articles, which made a stronger case for his guilt than his innocence, were a part of why everyone believed he was guilty over the years and why some believe it still. "She was biased before the trial ever began," he said. "All through the first trial, she tried to get ahold of me in the evenings for comment, but I always told her no."

I asked Beard about his life now, his life in Florida, and what it was like to live in America within the law after, for six years, being unfairly punished by it. "I am more skeptical when I see police," he said, and extra careful driving. "It's a shame that there's a few people like Alkire out there. And I know there are."

Beard, too, is bound to Alkire, forever probably, in his anger and his contempt. In Beard's opinion, Alkire is fundamentally evil and made unethical choices in order to implicate Beard to the exclusion of other suspects. "He had this cocky little smile that he would give you," Beard said. "It just irritated the hell out of me. It made me feel like, 'I'm your best friend; you can tell me the truth.' You told him the truth, but if it didn't line up with what he thought was the truth, he'd disbelieve it."

Steve Farmer, too, said that he believed Alkire was "a deeply dishonest person" who was motivated by a profound desire to matter, to be at the center of things. "He wanted to be part of the story," Farmer told me of Alkire's insistence that the killer was local. "That let him be a starring character instead of a bystander."

Farmer says he didn't continue to represent Beard over the years because he felt he had to, but rather because he felt Beard was innocent of the murder charges, and Farmer was young and had the space in his life to listen to his convictions. He felt that Beard was a vulnerable target because he was a figure about whom people had strong opinions, even if those opinions often didn't agree. Some knew him as a heavy drinker and partyer; some knew him as an exceptionally skilled mechanic who had fixed a piece of their equipment. "There were two stories about Jake," Farmer said, "and the story you got depended on who you asked."

To Beard, I wondered aloud about the years he spent in prison at Moundsville and then Mount Olive. I asked how he coped with the feelings of anger and despair, if he ever thought about killing himself.

"A few times in the beginning there, yeah. I would call [his lawyer, Robert Allen], and he just said, 'You can't call in here every day like this!' I had no idea what the appeal process was and how long it was going to take. I thought, You do an appeal, and you'll be out in two months. No. I was angry, and I was hurt that the justice system could do that to me. But I always believed in the justice system, or I'd have slit my throat when I was sentenced."

Reconciling with Linda helped. Mount Olive was only an hour away from Beard's old house in Greenbrier County, and Linda decided to move back there and take an apartment to be closer to her family and to Beard, but their daughters—one grown, one almost grown—made their own choices; one moved with Linda, and the other stayed in Florida.

Beard teared up when he described the second trial and the moment he knew he was free.

"Judge Lobban did this little speech after the jury gave their verdict," Beard said. "He said, 'And you may go forth hence!' I went over to him, and he turned around in his chair, and he shook my hand. He was smiling ear to ear. And I said, 'Can I go back into your office and call my daughters?' We were both crying now. And he said, 'You go back and call whoever you want.'"

He flew back to Florida, tried to find work on the land, and moved into a two-bedroom apartment that belonged to his older daughter, Teresa, where his younger daughter, Tammy, was also staying.

In newspaper articles covering Beard's successful wrongful prosecution suit, Beard was quoted as saying that there was no amount of money that could make up for what had happened to him and that he planned to live out the rest of his life far away from Pocahontas County. But he didn't. After he was liberated, Linda remained in West Virginia. She was close to retirement at her nursing job and didn't want to leave it until she reaped the benefits. Before long, Beard moved back there to join her.

Beard had little to say about his drinking, calling the period after his father's death in 1983 "the only time I ever drank much." Beard was arrested outside Lewisburg in the fall of 2006 for yet another DUI, just blocks away from the courthouse where he had been convicted of murder. The sheriff's deputy "observed the defendant cross the center line several times and observed the defendant run at least five vehicles off the roadway and drive 15 mph to 30 mph in a 55 mph zone." Beard blew a .204, almost three times the legal limit. When he was asked to get out of his car, he could not stand and had to be assisted in walking the line by a state police officer.

Why did he keep coming back? Why did he continue to live in a place that had so wronged him? He was silent a long time.

"It's the place," he said. "The land. I can't explain it."

The worst part of Pocahontas County is "what happened to me," he said, "the way people who know each other so well and don't have nothing else to do make up stories. The worst part is people that don't want to work that get tied up into the situation of being on welfare, drink their welfare money up or whatever they do, they just hang around. You'll see them on the streets. You see them up on the sidewalk in Marlinton one day, and you go back a day or two later, and they're still there. I think the area is so depressed on the one hand, for a certain segment of people."

"Why is it so depressed?"

"Well, right now the lack of work. If you give those people a job to go to, a lot of them would go. For young people, there's nothing for them to do. In the summer you can get out there and swim in the creeks. You can hunt and fish, but those things are limited, time-wise. Kids now, they get out of school or quit high school as soon as they turn sixteen. There's the feeling that 'I gotta get out of here; there's nothing for me to do; Mom and

Dad are stuck here.' Unless they can make a living doing what they love, they don't stay."

And the best part?

"The mountains, and the change of seasons, and the good, hardworking people that I knew and still care for up there."

I drove around a long time after I left Beard, through one development and into the next, which all had the same beige construction and identical storefronts selling smoothies and pancakes. I didn't know how to hold him or his story. I couldn't seem to fit him into the box marked "martyr" in my mind; I neither admired nor pitied him. He was only who he was— an old man with a heart condition developed and exacerbated during six years of incarceration for a crime he probably did not commit.

Neither was he an innocent exactly. He had probably done "the cat thing," though we'll never know for sure. He had created stories that harmed people—"the corn chopper man" and "the third Rainbow girl." He was a misogynist and kind of a jerk, it seemed to me. But that is not the same thing as being a murderer, however much they may sometimes feel like the same thing.

5

MEIGHAN HACKETT, THE DAUGHTER OF Nancy Santomero's sister Jeanne, was born eleven months after her aunt's death to a family reeling from loss. As she grew up in Long Island, everyone saw Nancy in her—in the hippie outfits she wore, the way she braided her hair, her hunger to walk and sleep outside, and the way she was always moving and looking around. She was camping in upstate New York, or she was taking TGV trains through Italy, or she was moving to San Francisco and driving into the mountains on the weekends. Her aunt Patricia worried about her—they could never have watched their own kids take such adventures. In addition to Patricia losing Nancy, Patricia's husband, Paul, had lost his brother in a car accident. "I think we held onto our kids a little too tight," Patricia said. "We made them afraid. They got it from both sides." One time Jeanne came to pick Patricia's kids up in a little Honda. "You can have a nice ride by yourself," Paul told her, "but you're not taking our kids in that." The following year, he bought Jeanne a Chevy Suburban.

For her college admissions essay, Hackett wrote about her aunt who had been murdered. She said that she experienced Nancy as a spectral presence in her life, one not of grief but of unconditional love, similar to how some people describe God. There was a wild weeping willow tree in Caumsett State Park on Long Island that everyone called Nancy's tree because she had gone there often when in junior high and high school. Later, Hackett went there too.

Hackett had grown up in a family shaped by women—her mother and two aunts, as well as her grandmother—and the family shared openly with each other everything they knew about Nancy's death, but the Durian family was different. Brittney Durian, who is studying social work at the University of Iowa, said that she and her cousin Victoria Lynn Durian grew up knowing that their aunt had been murdered but little else. No one in their family would talk about it. To obtain admission to the social work major, Brittney, too, wrote an essay about her aunt Vicki's murder and the ripples it began across her life and the others in her generation. "I would love for you to read it," she wrote to me, "so maybe then you can understand why it is so important to me and my siblings/cousins that we know the truth about what happened."

"Instead of coping with grief, my family failed to acknowledge the pain," her essay continues. "They believed that if you ignore it, the pain will disappear. Consequently, my father's side of the family never received the full closure they deserved. They were never able to properly heal, or open up to each other. After I took 'Death and Dying: Issues Across the Lifespan,' I learned about the concerns of death, dying, and the grieving process. I realized my family struggled with accepting death. Additionally, I discovered more about myself by witnessing my family's unhealthy way of coping. I aspire to help others recognize that death is 'okay.'"

The Mountain Views student with the scar is a trans man named Jordan. He, too, left southern West Virginia for college but stayed in the state, finding a school he liked in the eastern panhandle near Washington, DC. There, despite the college ignoring the fact that he had checked the box marked "transgender" on his housing placement form and a six-foot penis spewing sperm that was graffitied on his dorm room door, he thrived, finding queer friends and mentors, majoring in psychology and minoring in Appalachian studies and catalyzing the implementation of a policy to better serve transgender students as well as the founding of the institution's first LGBTQ center.

Upon graduation, Jordan had several job offers in the Maryland area and had gotten accepted to a five-year doctorate program in DC. But his mother, back home in southern West Virginia, had recently been diagnosed with a brain aneurysm, and his stepfather had little to offer in terms of her care. Plus, "a lot of my heart and soul is here," he said. "There is something in me that needs to be here, in the mountains, in a place that is familiar. It was hard, hard to explain what it felt like to be away from home. Just existing in a world that I didn't recognize felt very hard."

So he came back. He found a job with a health care company that provides physical and mental health care services to the people of Pocahontas County. Every Sunday he drove more than an hour to see his mother in the house she lived in with his stepfather to refill her medications, restock her groceries, and leave cash for her to give to the woman he had hired to clean her house. Sometimes her illness meant she became nearly fully paralyzed, so Jordan began paying out of pocket for a home health aide. Then one of his male colleagues at work refused to use the same bathroom that he did, so the company gave Jordan a private bathroom, but across the building from his desk. "If he has a problem peeing in the same room as me," Jordan told the company, "*he* can use that bathroom in the boonies."

During the nine months that Jordan was unemployed, he looked diligently for another job, the kind of job that would value his education and experience and compensate him appropriately, but it simply did not exist within two hours' driving distance. His college degree meant he was told time and time again by restaurants and gas stations that he was overqualified. Many times he wondered why he had bothered to go to college at all.

In June 2016, southern and central West Virginia were hit by a rainstorm that quickly became a catastrophic flood that killed twenty-three people; destroyed homes, schools, infrastructure, and businesses; and left five hundred thousand US citizens without power. The event barely registered in the national media, and it took bureaucratic channels nearly two years to release the funds that would drastically improve the lives of survivors and repair the damage. I was working at Mountain Views that summer and was the person on call the night the storm rolled in. The rain on the tin roof of the staff shelter made a sound so intense and continuous it felt physical, as did my anxiety over the well-being of the minors under my charge in that campground. Then there was a sound in the sky that I knew was thunder but could best be described as a gun put to my ear and then fired.

Somehow we made it through the night. In the morning we took our students down to the sturdier Mountain Views office building and built a fire. All of our roads were washed away; the area by the mailboxes and the culvert there had become a rushing river. But this was nothing, we would learn, compared to the state of affairs in the counties neighboring Pocahontas to the south and west. In Nicholas County, the county to which I had been assigned to make those calls, their middle school and high school, their Mountaineer Mart, many homes—gone. Someone in Greenbrier County posted a video to Facebook of their neighbor's house catching fire and floating down the river.

Jordan was living with a friend at the time of the 2016 flood, a young woman who had also been a Mountain Views student. They watched the water approach their house and then submerge it up to the second story. Both Jordan's and his roommate's cars were fully underwater.

"We thought the house was gonna go," Jordan remembered. "The house was shifting—I could see it rocking on the foundation. So we made the decision to leave."

They tied a rope to the back porch, then threw it to a nearby tree, and by pulling themselves on the rope were able to reach dryer ground on the high side of a nearby mountain. They had taken shovels from the house and were able to use them as walking sticks as they shimmied across the side of a rock wall. At one point, Jordan fell in the water, and his friend pulled him out. They did a first-aid assessment to make sure Jordan could go on—he had hurt his knee in the fall but was otherwise unharmed.

"How did you know to do all that?" I asked, incredulous.

"Mountain Views, man!" Jordan said, laughing. But he was serious. "If you all hadn't thrown us out into the woods and taught us how to get back, we would have died that day, I feel sure."

He lived now with his best friend, another trans man who had also gone to Mountain Views and his friend's wife and four beautiful cats in a neat trailer on some land in Greenbrier County. The steps leading up to their house were lined with rocks and crystals that his roommate had found on his hikes all over southern West Virginia. Even as a Mountain Views kid, that student loved rocks—all he wanted to talk about at lunch was his rock collection and how much it would be worth some-day. The two friends liked to hike together or walk the river trail and talk or go to flea markets. Jordan did eventually find another job at a company that provides services to adults with developmental disabilities in crisis, which means his days are spent talking to and touching the bodies of people experiencing some of the most difficult moments of their lives. But he was proud of the work. "I know the people. I know that this Dollar General has peanut butter and that one doesn't like our clients. I know this place."

Romantic love was something he would like in his life eventually, he said, but he was not in any rush. Jordan was still somewhat guarded when it came to his body and being trans in Greenbrier County, but he found he felt comfortable wearing fewer layers of clothing than he thought he would—"just a T-shirt is fine, no need for the seven sweatshirts. I'm not hiding here nearly as much as I thought I would be," he told me. In a fact that shocks many of my friends when I tell them, West Virginia has the most transgender teenagers per capita of any American state.

"I have found a lot of acceptance," Jordan said. "I've been able to share my story and be out there in the community here in ways I didn't expect.…Greenbrier County has opened up a lot. It's a mix between the old life and the new—it has that farm life still, and agriculture, and familial culture. But we are also seeing this surge of cultural diversity. We have a Jamaican restaurant now, and a fry bread restaurant is coming in. Our access to technology is changing. The high school gives their students net-books and laptops now."

But, he acknowledges, the price of living at home is sometimes high.

"The bad side of coming back is that you're consistently fighting those Appalachian values of closed-mindedness, man and woman, God is the word.…No matter how much women work, they're still expected to come home and take care of the kids. Men do the physical labor, and that's considered enough."

It was Jordan who, super in love with his high school girlfriend at the time, changed Greenbrier East High School's policy on queer couples attending prom together. He considers himself a natural-born fighter with a knack for standing out but understands that not everyone wants to live like that. The questions Appalachian young people must ask themselves, he said, are these: "Are you willing to put your heart and your soul into changing a place that you love? Are you strong enough to withstand the barricades that you will come up against?"

6

AT SOME POINT IN THE process of writing this book, I became concerned that I was going to die. I became concerned that I was going to die because I was thinking, more and more often, about killing myself. These are two separate states, are they not—the faraway fear and the longing, so nearby.

The image that rose and would not leave me during this period was of my chest as a puzzle missing a central piece that was shaped like a gun. After my meeting with Debbie DiFalco, I'd driven west on I-66, then south on Route 29, and pulled off the road at a collection of red buildings with a sign that advertised "GUNS ALL KINDS & SHOOTING RANGE." On top of the roof of the largest red building was a plastic statue of a brown bear, its mouth open in anger.

I pulled in ostensibly for research, to learn about how Franklin's gun, a .44 Magnum, would have felt in the hand. The gun felt much lighter than I had expected, and once pressed up against the right temple, the trigger much easier to pull.

I say Franklin because I believed then, as I do now, that though we'll never know for sure, the evidence supports the conclusion that Franklin killed Vicki and Nancy better than it supports the conclusion that Beard did. I say Franklin additionally because the violence and death this book cares about is also that which began before Vicki and Nancy were killed and which was visited upon so many others after they died: Walt Weiford, Bobby Lee Morrison, Gerald Brown, Arnold Cutlip, Pee Wee Walton, Johnnie Washington Lewis. David Martin and Ted Fields in Utah, Darrell Lane and Dante Evans Brown in Cincinnati, and all of Franklin's other victims and their families. Lori Franklin and Terry Mitchell, and so many more whose names I will likely never know.

At the darkest point in this process, I felt that if I could go back to the gun store where they had let me hold that .44 Magnum in my hand, I would get the relief I needed. The puzzle piece would fall into place, aglow, and the cracks would heal. I was dreaming often of death, though like Pee Wee, death was appearing so often in my waking life that I was not always sure if I had written it or dreamed it. I could understand how the distinction could be confusing, as I could understand everyone in this story, how one might lose whole nights to alcohol, waking in the weak light of the morning to the sight of your car in the field but having no memory of how your car might have gotten to the field, meaning you drove it from the restaurant in Hillsboro to the party at the Homeplace at Mill Point and then back again, some thirty minutes of driving executed in the apparent absence of my mind. In the presence of such actions and feelings, I could understand how one might begin to pray, not just for a gun, but for a pile of white pills in a repurposed bottle, the entrance to a building marked "EMERGENCY," which you can drive your brother to but cannot, yourself, enter.

It turns out that disappearing yourself does not allow you to shed your privilege off like a skin, nor does it create any meaningful crack in this already broken system. It means only the final and irreversible death of your body.

In the white schoolhouse on the top of Droop Mountain, I had a small office with not just a phone but also a desk where I wrote my first real words. I wrote them because I felt safe there and I had time. Something about Pocahontas County opened up a space in me for unknowing, for that thing some call magic, some mysticism, some God—that which cannot be held in the mind but only be felt elsewhere and which not only allows contradiction but demands it. I wrote them because I was confused, baffled, bonkers, and I wanted to know why. Something had begun; it was my life.

I wrote to Trey not long after I realized I was writing this book, to ask about including him in it. "I think that sharing truth is important, and everything is relevant," he wrote back. "I hope you will understand that with me it is often my consideration that is most offensive." I don't know what that means. I think we believed in each other. I know we did.

Telling a story is often about obligation and sympathy, identification and empathy. With whom is your lot cast? To whom are you bound?

When I first began looking into the Rainbow Murders, I thought the relevant necessary people of Pocahontas County were guilty of the murders and the general crime of misogyny and that, by proxy, so were Jesse and Trey and Peter and many others. I thought that it was to Vicki and Nancy to whom I was bound and by proxy to their daughters and the girls of Mountain Views. Then, as I investigated more deeply and saw the state's theory about Jacob Beard and the relevant necessary people begin to unravel, I thought the opposite—that Joseph Paul Franklin was guilty and the relevant necessary people were innocent, and that I was actually bound to them and by proxy to my friends, their sons and godsons and coworkers, that it was these voices I was really supposed to hear.

I thought that there was only ever a thing and its opposite, and nothing in between. In writing this book I have come to believe in this far less than I did when I started. Unraveling and unlearning this split logic is crucial to justice, I think, and it is crucial to love—loving a person, community, or most of all perhaps, a place, which may turn out to be the same thing. It is possible to be a victim and a perpetrator at the same time. Most of us are. We are more than the worst story that has ever been told about us. But if we refuse to listen to it, that story can become a prophecy.

7

IT WAS TWILIGHT IN AUGUST 2016 when I pulled up to the Putney
General Store in Putney, Vermont, a solid red building with a slatted
porch lined with hanging plants, with two of my best friends in tow. After
a few minutes, a white Toyota Previa van with one bike attached to the
back of it drove into the small front parking lot, shrieking as if its timing belts were about to go. The driver's-side door opened, and Elizabeth
Johndrow got out.

She took her driving glasses off and put them in the pocket of her
shorts, which seemed to be made for hiking—they looked soft and
moisture-wicking. Her hair was long and gray and down. She wore a blue
V-neck shirt, which looked extra blue against her tan skin, and open-toed
hiking sandals with many straps. She hugged me and then gave me a tour
of the store's offerings, saying, "What do you want to eat? Here are some
sandwiches—they are labeled, but sometimes they're wrong. You never
know what you're gonna get!"

Liz was fifty-five. She and I sat down in wood-cane rocking chairs on
the porch of a square white building across from the general store and next
to a steepled church. It was all very Vermont and very pretty. As we sat,
from about 7 to 9:15 in the evening, the sun set, the street got dark, the
moon rose, and the clouds cleared, exposing the moon. The cicadas were
loud that night, and the cars too, which went by every so often, going fast
down the street, and then turning onto Route 5.

In one photograph of Liz from 1968 I'd found, she and her brothers
stand in hazy sand at Indian Lake, New York. Her brothers wear matching
red-and-white-striped T-shirts and look straight at the camera, but Liz is

staring off intensely at something low to the ground. She wears a blue top that looks like a sports bra and drawstring shorts, the closest a little girl in the late sixties could get to gender-neutral swimwear.

In another, she and her older brother stand in a sprawling yard in front of a gray shingle house with a great brick chimney. She is seven, dressed in a high-necked flower-print dress and matching headband, and her brother stands next to her in a clip-on tie, but there's so much space between them you could drive an eighteen-wheeler through it. Her pale freckled face is screwed up in an expression that is more than squinting, that is maybe rage—as if the camera clicked just as her mouth was opening to scream.

She and I had been talking on the phone and Skyping while she was in Nicaragua, then while she was biking in Colorado. She answered all of my questions without ever avoiding or moving away from them, even when they were painful.

The daughter of a schoolteacher and a factory foreman, Liz grew up to be an honors student, but at night and on the weekends she and a friend got the hell out of suburban Connecticut. They hitchhiked. They hitchhiked to Vermont and to music festivals all along the East Coast. She didn't like where she lived; her home life was really not good. Hitchhiking was free magic. You got in a car and got out somewhere better.

Liz turned seventeen in 1979. A semester shy of graduating high school, she dropped out and took off west. Her plan was California, too. The second ride she caught in Vermont was a van going west and all the way—the guy said he was traveling cross-country for work. But then he started getting weird, looking at Liz too long—she could sense he would expect sex at some point. Liz was tall, wore a baseball cap over her rectangular sheet of blond hair, and carried nothing but a backpack. When the guy stopped the car near the Food Conspiracy co-op in Tucson, she grabbed her pack, opened the door, and strode off into the heat.

When I sat with her in Vermont, Liz was living mostly in Nicaragua, where she had started an organization teaching and working with women to exchange knowledge of natural building techniques. But Vermont was where she had made her life for a long time and where she had raised her son, so she returned often to visit and work.

She'd already told me the truth about the moment that she changed her mind about going to the Gathering in West Virginia. It wasn't because of her father's wedding; her father drank a lot, and their relationship was difficult. When it started raining, she and Vicki and Nancy left the South Carolina beach. Back on the mainland, an empty Trailways bus pulled over on the road's shoulder. Vicki talked to the guy as he drove them up into North Carolina. Nancy dozed. But Liz couldn't. She was watching the rain run down the windows in diagonals and the wet trees flick by when something began to gnaw, something began to bother.

"I had a very strong feeling then," Liz had said. "It seemed to be, like, some dread and uncertainty." Premonition? Gut feeling? "I don't think I know the difference, even though maybe I should. I just had a very strong feeling that led me away from continuing traveling with them."

At a rest stop, Liz called her brother collect and learned that their father was getting remarried that very weekend in Vermont and that there would be a big party. Liz said she would think about it, that she'd try to make it.

Three women in a field just below Interstate 95, near Rocky Mount, North Carolina. Cotton. Long-haul trucks on their way south and north.

I'm not coming with you to West Virginia, Liz finally said. Vicki and Nancy were shocked—we haul all the way across the country, and a few hours away you quit?

So Liz lied.

"I was like, 'Things are weird, but also my dad's getting married, and I'm gonna go.' [And they said] 'Okay? Wow.' But at the same time they were like, 'Okay. It's your journey. We wish you'd come, but okay.'"

She caught a single ride almost straight through from the truck stop in Richmond all the way up I-95. "I got there that night at like 11. I remember I was out in a lawn chair, and my mom came home with her boyfriend, and they got out of the car and I was just like, 'Hi Mom!'" She spent the night, then took off the next morning, hitchhiking to Vermont for her father's wedding bash. The party was huge; her brothers were there; she was glad to see them. Sometime later that week, Liz decided to go back down to her mom's for a night on a whim and was standing in her mother's kitchen when the phone rang.

It was a friend of Liz's from Eugene, Oregon. Vicki and Nancy were dead, she told Liz. The friend had heard the news from a friend of Vicki's who was living in the area. Everyone thinks you're dead, the friend told Liz. They were looking for her body.

Liz slumped down the kitchen cabinets to the floor. Her friend kept talking, talking of how she had recently broken up with a boyfriend and how sad it had made her. Liz just kept listening, holding the phone. She sat on the floor a long time. Eventually her mom came home from her Al-Anon meeting; Liz saw the car pull into the driveway. *Soon my mom will be with me,* Liz thought. But the car kept idling, and her mom kept talking to her friend and not coming inside. After a long time, Liz let the phone fall on the floor, propped herself up against a cabinet, stood, and went through the screen door. Her mom looked at her through the car's passenger-side window, then rolled it down.

Liz told her the news. Liz's mom helped her use the operator to get the number for the West Virginia State Police. My name is Elizabeth Johndrow, she told Alkire when she was connected to him. And I'm alive.

Well, Miss Johndrow, Alkire told her. I'm really glad to hear your voice. We've been looking for you for a while now.

Vicki and Nancy's families both wanted to meet with her that summer, but Liz didn't want to. Her mom urged her to do it, saying they probably just wanted to know her and share with her and be comforted.

"I can understand now, if my son was killed, I would want to find who was with him last. So I feel bad that I wasn't able to do that, but I didn't have the support. I was eighteen and nearly on my own with no money and no support and no car, and I didn't think they would have bought me a ticket, and I just felt like, 'No, I can't do that.' I just couldn't imagine [facing them]. It sounded really scary. But if somebody had been like, if my mom had been like, 'I'll go with you.' But she didn't. I kind of feel like maybe there should have been an adult in my life who had a better understanding of the suffering that was happening all around me.... All I could imagine is that they would hate me for having survived."

Most of that summer after she found out Vicki and Nancy were dead, Liz sat by the creek down from where her brother and sister-in-law were living, and she drank until she did not know who or where she was. "I was eighteen, I was definitely traumatized, you know, but I wasn't harmed. I felt like maybe I should have been. 'Why am I alive and they're dead?' I had a lot of survivor's guilt for a while."

She had two friends who had just come back from traveling through Mexico; they'd been gang-raped there. "We were just like, I don't know. They didn't want to talk about it; I didn't want to talk about it. But if we were partying, like, down by the river, and somebody got a little drunk, truth would come out. There just wasn't a lot of support. I remember my one friend, she didn't want to feel *anything* about it at all. Yeah. And then I remember one time we were doing mushrooms, and a bunch more [of what happened to her] came out." They watched the sun die behind the gray trees, threw sticks into the water, and watched them move. Six-packs, whole plastic handles of shitty vodka. Sometimes they pitched tents and just lived there by the river.

In the fall, she and her two drinking buddies and a few other friends went to Key West. She had dropped out of high school and had no idea what she would do with her life. "My people that I respected were homesteading and growing food, and that's like all I really knew. I had gotten all this stuff—I had a backpack full of drop spindles and wool and beads. I was just like a handcrafty person. I think I was just looking; I was searching for something that had deeper meaning. I was looking for circles, communities, a lifestyle that was me."

But Key West didn't last long, and soon Liz was back in Vermont, where she would be, mostly, for the next thirty years.

"I got really paralyzed by my feelings," Liz said. "I wasn't able to make good decisions about things for a long time if I started to have that feeling again. Like I had been missed, or somehow I slipped through."

She sewed hippie clothes and sold them to friends and at farmers' markets and school festivals. She got involved in street theater and activism for women's liberation, particularly a demonstration during the Gulf War called Breast Fest, for which she organized people to think about what was obscene and what was not—women's bodies were considered obscene, but killing Iraqi children and showing their bodies on the news was not.

I asked her why she hitchhiked, if it was pure economics or something else. As the writer Vanessa Veselka points out, we tend to condemn women who travel alone much more harshly than we do men, allowing them only the slimmest of acceptable stories.

"You can go on a quest to save your father, dress like a man and get discovered upon injury, get martyred and raped," Veselka writes, "but God forbid you go out the door just to see what's out there."

Liz thought for a moment, then answered.

"Well, there was adventure to it too. There was something back then: hitchhiking was like falling forward into the universe that you wanted, in a way. It was very much putting yourself in the hands of others and going where you serendipitously landed. It was a little bit like sloppy Buddhism. We were putting our faith in humanity. For me, there's something important in that. I still do it. I know where my car keys are because they're always in the ignition." She did note, however, that she now has a car from this century and does sometimes take her keys out and lock it.

I told her I knew what she meant—I made choices when I was in West Virginia that came from that place, and I make them sometimes still. There's a beauty in living that way, I told Liz, and you can also get hurt that way.

After Vicki and Nancy were killed, she promised her mother that she would never hitchhike again. But she did, and in February 1981, she was attacked while hitchhiking.

"Yeah. It was a pretty typical fucked-up scene where, like, it's February in Vermont, and in the deposition they are grilling me like, what was I wearing? And I was like, 'Umm, you know, Sorels and a parka? Many layers.'"

Liz got pregnant in the spring of 1984, when she was twenty-three. After having a short relationship with a man in Vermont, she took off for Glacier National Park in Montana, where she had gotten a job doing river rafting and trail maintenance. "About eight weeks into it I was like, 'This elevation is not working out for me at all,' and then I figured out I was pregnant. So I was definitely like, 'What am I doing with my life?'"

"Did it ever occur to you to have an abortion?"

"I think if things had been different. I think I was meant to have him because I was living in Glacier, where I couldn't figure out what was going on, like I literally thought I had altitude sickness for weeks and weeks and weeks. And it's really common to not get your period at high elevations. So by then I was so bonded with the spirit in me. I was kind of far along at that point too." She went back to Vermont and got an apartment; a few friends who were working nearby as apple pickers would sometimes party and then come back to her apartment wanting to crash there. Liz gave birth to her son at home, but there were complications. She began hemorrhaging badly and had to be rushed to the hospital and given three blood transfusions.

"It was a pretty intense start as a parent. Pretty heavy-duty. And then he met his dad when he was three. So it was just like everything else went out the window except, like, protecting him and being the best mom I could. I was like, 'Oh, it's not all about me anymore.'"

Liz was eighteen when Vicki and Nancy died and thirty-one when she was called to testify at Beard's trial in 1993. "Their families got pretty messed up," Liz said. The intervening years had been terrible for all the parents; the Durians had divorced since their daughter's death.

"Vicki's mom was like, 'I've forgiven—whoever, in the eyes of Jesus....' She was done. Nancy's dad, he was just pretty torn up still."

Over the years, to take care of her son and for her own fulfillment, Liz became a massage therapist, worked at a bookstore, trained to be a midwife and an herbalist, worked at a wilderness school, did landscaping, and cooked at a natural foods restaurant. She also went to the Rainbow Gathering eight times after she skipped the one where Vicki and Nancy died.

I would not have predicted this and told Liz so. She said the fact that it was a Rainbow Gathering that Vicki and Nancy were headed to when they died didn't matter that much to her. She brought her son to several Gatherings as well, and some of her best friends' children were conceived at Rainbow Gatherings over the years.

Today, though she is the director of a nonprofit, she still doesn't make much money. When back in Vermont, she fund-raises for her organization, and lives out of her van or house-sits for friends. "I have a big skill base," she said, "but I always kind of steered away from conventional pathways."

"How do you cope with all that uncertainty?" I asked.

"Being this age and letting things be this uncertain, it's been a huge practice—it's like surfing or something. Like, 'That wave knocked me over.' It's like, 'Wow, that wave was fun.' You know, 'What was I doing to make that wave work?' It is a little bit about timing; it is a little bit about being a little older."

"That really works?"

"I don't know—my friend says it's some hard wiring in me. I find I get a little depressed when I'm not honoring that part of myself. But maybe that's also why I haven't been in a relationship in, like, six years. I don't really have a lot of intimate relationships."

Liz told me that she allows herself to say yes to opportunities that present themselves and participate in conversations in vulnerable ways. "I mean, what do I got to lose?…It might sting a little or something, but I'm not gonna die."

Near the end of our time together, Liz asked me only one question about Vicki and Nancy—what I had found out about Franklin. I told her I had found out a whole lot, that it had changed my mind, and that I now believed more likely than not that it was Franklin who killed her friends, not Jacob Beard. She sat for a while and rocked back on the rockers of her chair. "Wow," she said after a while. "That's a mind-fuck. It's such an elaborate thing for them to have constructed with all those guys and all that, if none of that actually happened."

I agreed that it was.

"Wow," she said again. "But I don't have any attitude of like…I can't believe you're bringing this up again," Liz said. "I'm definitely not one of those people who's like, 'Well, you're invading my comfort zone.' I'm like, 'Well, what's out here outside the comfort zone?' That's pretty much where I live. And like you were saying, a lot of amazing things happen there."

"You didn't close in after all that happened to you," I said. "That is hard. That is the tendency. When there's a lot of grief. You didn't do that."

"Yes," Liz said. "I try to breathe. In and out."

Liz filled her lungs and then emptied them, and I did the same.

"Where are your friends?" Liz asked me then, and I told her they had walked down the road a ways to check out a Mexican restaurant with a sign advertising "BEST SANGRIA."

"Yum," she said. "It's a beautiful night."

"It is," I said, because it was.

Vicki Durian, 1978

ACKNOWLEDGMENTS

To write a book that is the story of events that are painful to so many at the same time that it is the story of my becoming was at times a strange and terrible undertaking. I'm grateful to everyone who was able to hold both things in the mind at once and celebrate its making with me, even as it is also not a celebration.

Thank you to my agent, Jin Auh, for your steady support, your patience with me over the twisty years, and for the brilliant feedback that helped me see the core enterprise of this book more clearly. Thank you to Alexandra Christie of the Wylie Agency for being my advocate and steward, and for always treating my work like a precious thing you can't wait for the world to see.

To the team at Hachette—my editor Paul Whitlatch, as well as Mollie Weisenfeld, Joanna Pinsker, and Lauren Hummel—my deepest gratitude. Paul, thank you for believing in the importance of this story and in my abilities to execute its telling even when my own belief faltered or my resolve left me. Your sharp eye, for narrative structure and the rhythm of a sentence both, shaped this book in ways I continue to appreciate.

Thank you, Maia Hibbett, the smartest, most detail-oriented, and fastest fact-checker in the world.

Jerry Dale, Steve Farmer, George Castelle, Jaynell Graham, Pam Pritt, Jillian Lacasse, Blair Campbell, Judy Cutlip, Gerry Morrison, Landon Sheetz, Jerry Kauffman, DeAnn Bowersox, Twyla Donathan, Melissa Bennett, JoAnn Orelli, Catherine Shea, Tim Sheerin, and Ralph Echols provided essential information, assistance, documents, and media. Naomi and Harvey Cohen gave me a place to stay while reporting the Greenbrier County sections.

This book benefited from the generous support of the Millay Colony for the Arts, the Elizabeth George Foundation, the Carey Institute for the Global Good, the Turkey Land Cove Foundation, and the Literary Reportage program at the Arthur L. Carter Journalism Institute. A million hearts and flowers to Barbara Moriarty at the University of Virginia MFA program. To the program: though our relationship was not easy, you gave me my first big gifts of time and confidence, for which I will always be grateful.

Theresa Tensuan, Dan Torday, and Kim Benston of Haverford/Bryn Mawr, Alden Smith of the Mountain School, and Karen Luten of Dalton: you were my most important teachers of writing and ideas, and you are all over these pages. Likewise, Elizabeth Richards, Susan Buksbaum, and Susan Avino, who are missed. Thank you, Carmen Maria Machado, Kelly Link, and Justin Torres for your friendship and for helping to get me here.

To those who believed in this material in its earliest forms, read early drafts, or offered invaluable insights—Chris Tilghman, Robert Boynton, Stephanie Reents, Sara Tandy, Alyssa Songsiridej, Sam Allingham, Matt Jakubowski, Ben Goldstein, Amanda Korman, Andrew Martin, and Alison Penning—I'm very grateful. Thank you to the best book bridesmaids— Elizabeth Catte, Sarah Marshall, and Jacqui Shine—for the time you spent developing, encouraging, and interrogating this manuscript. An especially glittery thank-you to Sarah, my partner in doing this strange work, who answered my calls and texts with joyful and hard truths each and every time. I can't wait to do the same for you as you write your books.

To my chosen family—Chelsea Alsofrom, Megan Goestch, Lindsay Mollineaux, Jules and Elissa Martel, Shira Cohen, Emma Bergman, Fay Strongin, Cara Tratner, Sarah Peterson, Jeff Frankl, Sonia Williams, Anna Krieger, Joshua Demaree, Julie Lipson, Alisha Berry, Emily Newton, Kim Rolla, Corey Chao, Julia Greenberg, Anastasia Aguiar—you made it possible to venture into the unknown and return to love. Dana Murphy, Annie Liontas, Sara Sligar, and Hilary Leichter—your support in the final hours made all the difference.

Thank you to my parents: for teaching me what books do, for making sacrifices in order to put me in the way of beauty, and for taking me over and over again into the Residency for Wayward Artists & Orange Cats. Forever and always, thank you to my sister and co-resident, Mollie Eisenberg. We've made a way together when there was no way.

Put plainly, neither these pages nor the person who wrote them would exist without the relationships I made in Pocahontas County. To those who educated me and called me in and pushed me deeper, thank you for your labor. It was generous in ways I will keep trying to deserve.

Kathy Meehan, Jeanne Hackett, Jeanne Santomero, Patricia Porco, Meighan Hackett, John and Robin Durian, Howard Durian, Brittney Durian, Ashley Durian, Terry Mitchell, Lori Franklin, Deborah DiFalco, Michael Jordan, Walt Weiford, and Liz Johndrow: I am more than grateful for your time and your trust. It was the honor of my life.

FURTHER READING

Agnew, Eleanor. *Back From the Land: How Young Americans Went to Nature in the 1970s, and Why They Came Back*. Chicago: Dee, 2004.

Baldwin, James. *The Evidence of Things Not Seen*. New York: Holt, Rinehart and Winston, 1985.

Barret, Elizabeth, director. *Stranger with a Camera* (film). Whitesburg, KY: Appalshop, 2000.

Berry, Chad. *Southern Migrants, Northern Exiles*. Urbana: University of Illinois Press, 2000.

Bolin, Alice. *Dead Girls: Essays on Surviving an American Obsession*. New York: William Morrow, 2018.

Catte, Elizabeth. *What You Are Getting Wrong About Appalachia*. Cleveland: Belt, 2018.

Engelhardt, Elizabeth S. D. *The Tangled Roots of Feminism, Environmentalism, and Appalachian Literature*. Athens: Ohio University Press, 2003.

Giardina, Denise. *Storming Heaven: A Novel*. New York: Norton, 1987.

Harkins, Anthony, and Meredith McCarroll, eds. *Appalachian Reckoning: A Region Responds to Hillbilly Elegy*. Morgantown: West Virginia University Press, 2019.

hooks, bell. *Appalachian Elegy: Poetry and Place*. Lexington: University Press of Kentucky, 2012.

Isenberg, Nancy. *White Trash: The 400-Year Untold History of Class in America*. New York: Viking, 2016.

Lewis, Helen M., Linda Johnson, and Donald Askins, eds. *Colonialism in Modern America: The Appalachian Case*. Boone, NC: Appalachian Consortium, 1978.

Loftus, Elizabeth F. *Eyewitness Testimony*. Cambridge, MA: Harvard University Press, 1979.

Maren, Mesha. *Sugar Run: A Novel*. Chapel Hill, NC: Algonquin Books, 2018.

McKinney, Irene. *Vivid Companion: Poems*. Morgantown, WV: Vandalia, 2004.

McNeill, Louise. *The Milkweed Ladies*. Pittsburgh: University of Pittsburgh Press, 1988.

Monroe, Rachel. *Savage Appetites*. New York: Scribner, 2019.

Nelson, Maggie. *The Red Parts: Autobiography of a Trial*. Minneapolis: Graywolf, 2016.

Niman, Michael. *People of the Rainbow: A Nomadic Utopia*. Knoxville: University of Tennessee Press, 1997.

Null, Matthew Neil. *Allegheny Front: Stories*. Louisville, KY: Sarabande Books, 2016.

Sonnie, Amy, and James Tracy. *Hillbilly Nationalists, Urban Race Rebels, and Black Power: Community Organizing in Radical Times*. Brooklyn: Melville House, 2011.

Veselka, Vanessa. "Green Screen: The Lack of Female Road Narratives and Why It Matters." *American Reader* 1, no. 4 (February–March 2013).

Wilkerson, Jessica. *To Live Here, You Have to Fight: How Women Led Appalachian Movements for Social Justice*. Urbana: University of Illinois Press, 2019.

Wilkinson, Crystal. *The Birds of Opulence*. Lexington: University Press of Kentucky, 2016.

Ammonites and Leaping Fish

Penelope Lively is the author of many prizewinning novels and short-story collections for both adults and children. She has twice been shortlisted for the Booker Prize: once in 1977 for her first novel, *The Road to Lichfield*, and again in 1984 for *According to Mark*. She later won the 1987 Booker Prize for her highly acclaimed novel *Moon Tiger*. Her other books include *Going Back*; *Judgement Day*; *Next to Nature, Art*; *Perfect Happiness*; *Passing On*; *City of the Mind*; *Cleopatra's Sister*; *Heat Wave*; *Beyond the Blue Mountains*, a collection of short stories; *Oleander, Jacaranda*, a memoir of her childhood days in Egypt; *Spiderweb*; her autobiographical work *A House Unlocked*; *The Photograph*; *Making It Up*; *Consequences*; *Family Album*, which was shortlisted for the 2009 Costa Novel Award; and *How It All Began*. She is a popular writer for children and has won both the Carnegie Medal and the Whitbread Award. She was appointed CBE in the 2001 New Year's Honours List, and was made a dame in 2012.

Penelope Lively lives in London.

By the same author

Ammonites and
Leaping Fish

A Life in Time

PENELOPE LIVELY

FIG TREE
an imprint of
PENGUIN BOOKS

JACK – in memory

FIG TREE

Published by the Penguin Group
Penguin Books Ltd, 80 Strand, London WC2R ORL, England
Penguin Group (USA) Inc., 375 Hudson Street, New York, New York 10014, USA
Penguin Group (Canada), 90 Eglinton Avenue East, Suite 700, Toronto, Ontario, Canada M4P 2Y3
(a division of Pearson Penguin Canada Inc.)
Penguin Ireland, 25 St Stephen's Green, Dublin 2, Ireland (a division of Penguin Books Ltd)
Penguin Group (Australia), 707 Collins Street, Melbourne, Victoria 3008, Australia
(a division of Pearson Australia Group Pty Ltd)
Penguin Books India Pvt Ltd, 11 Community Centre, Panchsheel Park, New Delhi – 110 017, India
Penguin Group (NZ), 67 Apollo Drive, Rosedale, Auckland 0632, New Zealand
(a division of Pearson New Zealand Ltd)
Penguin Books (South Africa) (Pty) Ltd, Block D, Rosebank Office Park,
181 Jan Smuts Avenue, Parktown North, Gauteng 2193, South Africa

Penguin Books Ltd, Registered Offices: 80 Strand, London WC2R ORL, England

www.penguin.com

First published 2013
001

Set in 13.5/16pt Dante MT Std
Typeset by Palimpsest Book Production Ltd, Falkirk, Stirlingshire
Printed in Great Britain by Clays Ltd, St Ives plc

A CIP catalogue record for this book is available from the British Library

ISBN: 978-0-241-14638-5

www.greenpenguin.co.uk

Contents

Preface

This is not quite a memoir. Rather, it is the view from old age.

And a view of old age itself, this place at which we arrive with a certain surprise – ambushed, or so it can seem. The view from eighty, for me. One of the few advantages of age is that you can report on it with a certain authority; you are a native now, and know what goes on here. That, and the backwards glance – the identifying freight of a lifetime.

A lifetime is embedded; it does not float free, it is tethered – to certain decades, to places, to people. It has a context; each departure leaves a person-shaped void – the absence within a family, the presence lost within a house, in a community, in society itself. We go, but hang in for a while in other people's heads – something we said, something we did; we leave a ghostly imprint on our backdrop. A very few people go one further and are distilled into a blue plaque on a building.

I began on a spring morning in the Anglo-American Hospital in Zamalek, which was a residential suburb on Gezira, the island in Cairo's Nile; 17 March 1933.

3

Elsewhere, things were going on that would lead to turmoil in North Africa in a few years' time; my parents' lives would be affected, and mine, but they were comfortably oblivious that morning, and I was tucked up in a crib, the feet of which stood in tin trays of water, because there had been instances of ants getting at newborn babies.

Towards the end of my own stint I find myself thinking less about what has happened to me but interested in this lifetime context, in the times of my life. I have the great sustaining ballast of memory; we all do, and hope to hang on to it. I am interested in the way that memory works, in what we do with it, and what it does with us. And when I look around my cluttered house – more ballast, material ballast – I can see myself oddly identified and defined by what is in it: my life charted out on the bookshelves, my concerns illuminated by a range of objects.

These, then, are the prompts for this book: age, memory, time, and this curious physical evidence I find all around me as to what I have been up to – how reading has fed into writing, how ways of thinking have been nailed.

There can be a certain detachment about it; the solipsism of writing about oneself tempered by the more compelling interest of general concerns – what it means to be old, what the long view does to us, or for us, how we mutate with our times. But a report from the front line has to be just that; this is my old age, so I have to get personal, as well as consider the wider implications of where I am now. Which is something I have not done before; like, I think, most people, I have not paid too much attention to old age. To individuals, yes – family, friends. But the status has not been on my radar. Give up my seat on the bus – of course; feign polite attention to some rambling anecdote; raise my voice, repeat myself with patience. Avoid, occasionally, I fear: that hazard light worn by the old – slow, potentially boring, hard going. Now that I wear the light myself, I am nicely aware of the status. This is a different place. And since I am there, along with plenty of my friends, the expedient thing seems to be to examine it. And report.

We are many today, in the western world: the new demographic. I want to look at the implications of that, at the condition, at how it has been perceived. And then at the compelling matter of memory – the vapour trail without which we are undone.

And my own context – the context of anyone my age. The accompanying roar of the historical process. I want to remember what those events felt like at the time, those by which I felt most fingered – the Suez crisis, the Cold War, the seismic change in attitudes of the late twentieth century – and see how they are judged today, with the wisdoms of historical hindsight.

And, finally, some pure solipsism: one person's life as reflected by possessions. Books; and a selection of things. Mine. But a story that anyone could tell; most of us fetch up with an identifying cargo – that painting, this vase, those titles on the shelf. I can give eloquence to mine – I know what they are saying. Not so much detachment here; more, a flicker of memoir proper – a voyage around the eighty years by way of two ammonites, a pair of American ducks, leaping fish . . . And a raft of books.

Old Age

Years ago, I heard Anthony Burgess speak at the Edinburgh Book Festival. He was impressive in that he spoke for an hour without a single note, fluent and coherent. But of the content of his talk all I remember are his opening words: 'For me, death is already sounding its high C.' This was around 1980, I think, so he was in his early sixties at the time, and died in 1993. I was in my late forties, and he seemed to me – not old, exactly, but getting on a bit.

Today, people in their sixties seem – not young, just nicely mature. Old age is in the eye of the beholder. I am eighty, so I am old, no question. The high C is audible, I suppose, but I don't pay it much attention. I don't think much about death. I am not exactly afraid of it, though after reading Julian Barnes's book *Nothing To Be Frightened Of*, with admiration, I felt that I had not sufficiently explored my own position on the matter but have perhaps arrived at the state of death-consciousness that he distinguishes with the argument that we cannot truly savour life without a regular awareness of extinction. Yes, I recognize that, along with the natural human taste for a conclusion: there has been a beginning, which proposes an end. I am afraid of the run-up to death, because I have had to watch that. But I think that many of us who are on the last lap are too busy with the baggage of old age to waste much time anticipating the finishing line. We have to get used to being the person we are, the person we have always been, but encumbered now with various indignities and disabilities, shoved as it were into some new incarnation. We feel much the same, but clearly are not. We have entered an unexpected dimension; dealing with this is the new challenge.

The extent of the challenge depends on when and where you experience old age. Social context is crucial. You don't want to be old when circumstances mean that anyone who doesn't contribute but requires support is a drag, and there is therefore a grim logic in failing to sustain them. Nomadic groups existing at subsistence level did better without the encumbrance of anyone who couldn't keep up. The district nurse in Ronald Blythe's *Akenfield* talks of the Suffolk cottages in the last century where a decaying grandparent was stacked away somewhere and nudged towards the grave. The anthropologist Colin Turnbull has given a horrific account in *The Mountain People* of the Ik, a Ugandan tribe whose flexible way of life was curtailed, forcing them to live in one area with insufficient resources, at starvation level. The effect was the erosion of any care or concern for others, with the old forced to starve first, and children also (further stark logic: keep the breeding group alive, you can always make more children if things improve). But the old, in this corner of Uganda in the mid-twentieth century, were around forty; 'old' is never a fixed feast.

There is anthropological evidence from elsewhere that in a hunter-gatherer society the old are valued simply for experience – they have a bank of hunter-gatherer knowledge. That again makes sense; you may not be all that fond of Granny, but she knows where to find those roots you need. Elephant groups also depend on the matriarch, it seems, to know where to head for water and for food; I like this elemental link with animal behaviour.

Things aren't quite like this in a world powered by technology; just as well that increased affluence means that nobody disposes of the aged just because they can't cope with a computer or a mobile phone. Rather the contrary; at the time of writing there is a heated debate about the quality of care for the elderly in hospital, and a scandal about conditions in a failing group of residential homes for old people. Things can go wrong, but it is beyond question that society assumes a responsibility towards the old; you don't leave them by the wayside, you don't push them into a cupboard and forget to feed them.

This may not be due entirely to a more enlightened attitude. Old age is the new demographic, and you can't ignore the problems created by a group that has been getting steadily larger – alarmingly larger if you are in the business of allocating national expenditure. The poor have always been with us, and now the old are too.

We have not been, in the past, and we are not so much around still in some parts of the developing world. But in the West we are entrenched, bolstered by our pensions, brandishing our Freedom Passes, cluttering up the surgeries, with an average life expectancy of around eighty. But our experience is one unknown to most of humanity, over time. We are the pioneers, as an established social group gobbling up benefits and giving grief to government agencies. Before the early modern period, as historians like to call it, before the sixteenth century, few people saw fifty, let alone eighty. Scroll back, and average life expectancy diminishes century by century; two thousand years ago, it stood at around twenty-five. That said, the old have always been around – it seems that perhaps eight per cent of the population of medieval England was over sixty – but not as a significant demographic group, rather as noticeable individuals. And sixty today is not seen as old.

The Bible blithely allowed for threescore years and ten – where on earth did they get that from? You'd be lucky indeed to make that in the Middle East in Roman times. Life expectancy is of course a slippery concept. The trick is to get through infancy, then the next four years; notch those up, and you're in with a fighting chance, your statistic rockets – if you are a medieval peasant (or in much of sub-Saharan Africa, or Afghanistan, today) you may well hang in there till forty or beyond. But chances are you won't leave toddlerhood; the underworld is a teeming sea of tiny ghosts, with, dotted amongst them, out of scale, inappropriate and incongruous, the exhausted figures of the old. Think Sparta (babies exposed on hillsides), think Coram's Fields (London hospital for foundlings), think Hogarth, think Dickens. Think *Kindertotenlieder*.

Archaeology recognizes old bones as likely to have been powerful bones. If you survived the demands of warrior culture and managed not to get picked off while leading the tribe into battle, then you got the lion's share of resources: food, creature comforts. Bones are intriguing, illuminating – this extraordinary surviving evidence of a life, for those who know how to read it. A recent television series did just that; an erudite expert homed in on a skeleton, and from it lifted the story of a Roman gladiator in first-century York, of the mother of triplets dying in childbirth, of the Iron Age sacrificial victim. Bones found in neolithic Orkney tombs indicate that people in their teens and twenties had osteoarthritis, brought on presumably by some repetitive physical activity (hauling all that stone around for the tombs, maybe). And I wince – arthritic young are an affront. But I am making the mistake of assuming a twenty-first-century perspective; these were not young, in their terms, or, rather, a lifespan was not long enough for the luxury of the seven ages of man – just an instant of childhood, a brief flare of maturity, and then into the chambered tomb with the ancestors.

A recent survey by the Department of Work and Pensions, which is somewhat obsessed with the question of old age, for good reason, found that most believe that old age starts at fifty-nine while youth ends at forty-one. People over eighty, on the other hand, believe sixty-eight to herald old age, while fifty-two is the end of youth. Of course, of course – it depends where you happen to be standing yourself. And youth has expanded handsomely since Charlotte Brontë wailed, 'I am now thirty-two. Youth is gone – gone, – and will never come back; can't help it.' It still won't come back, even after a century and a half of scientific advance, but there is plenty of remedial work on offer by way of nipping and tucking for those feeling a bit desperate. The rest of us settle for the inevitable sag and wrinkle, and simply adjust our concept of the climactic points. Actually, I'd step out of line and go for seventy rather than sixty-eight as the brink of old age; I have too many vigorous and active friends in their late sixties and anyway the round number is neater.

By 2030 there will be four million people over eighty in the United Kingdom – out of a population of around sixty million. No wonder the Department of Work and Pensions is getting rattled on behalf of its successors. I will have handed in my dinner pail and my Freedom Pass by then, I sincerely hope, though I can't quite count on it. I come from a horribly long-lived family. My mother died at ninety-three; her brother made it to one hundred; their mother reached ninety-seven. I look grimly at these figures; I do not wish to compete.

Suffice it that we are too many. That's one way of looking at it: the administrative point of view, the view perhaps sometimes of the young, who have inherited the world, quite properly, and may occasionally find themselves guilty of the ageist sentiments that are now proscribed. Actually, I haven't much come up against ageism, myself. There was an occasion, I remember, a few years ago, when a teenage granddaughter was advising on the acquisition of a mobile phone and the salesman's enthusiastic attention turned to disdain when he realized that the purchase was not for her but for the old granny, who had no business with any mobile, let alone the latest Nokia. But more usually I find that age has bestowed a kind of comfortable anonymity. We are not especially interesting, by and large – waiting for a bus, walking along the street; younger people are busy sizing up one another, in the way that children in a park will only register other children. We are not exactly invisible, but we are not noticed, which I rather like; it leaves me free to do what a novelist does anyway, listen and watch, but with the added spice of feeling a little as though I am some observant time-traveller, on the edge of things, bearing witness to the customs of another age. I am dramatizing, of course – I am still a part of it all and most of what I see and hear is entirely familiar because as society mutates – language, behaviour – so have I mutated, in assumptions and expectations. This is something I want to talk about in a later section – the way in which you change your skin, over a lifetime, change and change again. The point here is that age may sideline, but it also confers a sort of neutrality; you are no longer out there in the thick of things, but able to stand back, observe, consider.

The other view, the counter-view to the administrators and the ageists, is that this is the human race adapting again, and how interesting. How significant, how challenging that there is now this new demographic, this hefty group of people who have notched up seven or eight decades and counting, many of whom are still in good nick, with all their marbles, able to savour life.

Up to a point, that is. I am a diarist. It is a working diary, mainly, in which I jot down stuff that might possibly come in useful at some point. This means that I can never find anything I think I may once have

noted, but during a trawl recently I came upon my
visit to a specialist in 1994, around the time the spinal
arthritis first struck that has plagued me ever since.
"Anno Domini, I'm afraid," says the man kindly.
"Whoever designed us didn't make sufficient allowance for wear and tear." Which chimed nicely with
my view of the Great Designer in the Sky – a piece of
malevolent sabotage to ensure that when the human
race gets to the point of discovering penicillin and
sanitation and generally prolonging life those prolonged won't find it worth living anyway.'

I beg to differ, eighteen years on. One does; today,
and for a while, perhaps. Most of my friends of my
age group would agree, I think, and most of them
have been slammed with something: hips, knees,
teeth, eyes . . . We do indeed wear out before our
time. The science of ageing is complex and intriguing. The gerontologist Tom Kirkwood gives a technical but lively account in his book *Time of Our Lives*.
He quotes John Maynard Smith's dry definition: 'Ageing is a progressive, generalized impairment of
function resulting in an increasing probability of
death.' Quite. But what is going on? Why do we age?

The short answer seems to be: because we are disposable. And we are disposable because our own genes
have decided this; their interests in keeping us going do
not coincide with our own. The maintenance of certain
cells most affected by the ageing process takes many

resources. If this is reduced, then energy is released for growth and reproduction, so natural selection favours such a mutation. This is called the 'disposable soma' theory; my digest of it is inadequate – please go to Professor Kirkwood for a proper account. There is a cool rationality to the process (of course, natural selection is always rational) and while this is not exactly a palliative (it remains a natural response to 'Rage, rage against the dying of the light') at least you can see what it's all about. And what would be the alternative? Swift's Struldbrugs in *Gulliver's Travels*, born to immortality, were condemned to an eternity of senile decay and estrangement from society. They presumably suffered from some genetic derangement; I think we must prefer genetic normality and accept the consequences.

Society is stuck with us, I'm afraid, and it will get worse. In countries with high life expectancies, a third of today's children may reach one hundred. In 1961 there were just five hundred and ninety-two people over the age of one hundred in this country; by 2060 there will be four hundred and fifty-five thousand. Consider those figures, and gasp. Old people were of interest in the past simply because there weren't that many of them – the sage is a pejorative term suggesting that old age necessarily implies wisdom. That view may have changed radically towards the end of the twenty-first century, I'd guess, when the western world is awash with centenarians. Goodness knows what that will do for attitudes towards the elderly; I'm glad I shan't be around to find out. I am concerned with here and now, when I can take stock and bear witness.

One of the few advantages of writing fiction in old age is that you have been there, done it all, experienced every decade. I can remember worrying when I was writing at forty, at fifty, that I didn't know what it was like to be seventy, eighty, if I wanted to include an older character. Well, I didn't know what it was like to be a man, either, but you have to stick your neck out – use empathy, imagination, observation, all the novelist's tools. But it is certainly a help to have acquired that long backwards view; not only do you know (even if it is getting a bit hazy) what it felt like to be in your twenties, or thirties, but you remember also the relative unconcern about what was to come.

You aren't going to get old, of course, when you are young. We won't ever be old, partly because we can't imagine what it is like to be old, but also because we don't want to, and – crucially – are not particularly interested. When I was a teenager, I spent much time with my Somerset grandmother, then around seventy. She was a brisk and applied grandmother who was acting effectively as a mother-substitute; I was devoted to her, but I don't remember ever considering what it could be like to *be* her. She simply *was*; unchangeable, unchanging, in her tweed skirt, her blouse, her

Shetland cardigan, her suit for Sunday church, worn with chenille turban, her felt hat for shopping in Minehead. Her opinions that had been honed in the early part of the century; her horror of colours that 'clashed'; her love of Tchaikovsky, Beethoven, Berlioz. I never thought about how it must be to be her; equally, I couldn't imagine her other than she was, as though she had sprung thus into life, had never been young.

Old age is forever stereotyped. Years ago, I was a judge for a national children's writing competition. They had been asked to write about 'grandparents'; in every offering the grandparent was a figure with stick and hearing-aid, knitting by the fireside or pottering in the garden. The average grandparent would then have been around sixty, and probably still at work. When booking a rail ticket by phone recently, I found myself shifted from the automated voice to a real person when I had said I had a Senior Railcard, presumably on the grounds that I might get muddled and require help – which was kindly, I suppose, but I was managing quite well. We are too keen to bundle everyone by category; as a child, I used to be maddened by the assumption that I would get along famously with someone just because we were both eight.

All that we have in common, we in this new demographic, are our aches and pains and disabilities – and, yes, that high C evoked by Anthony Burgess. For the rest of it, we are the people we

have always been – splendidly various, and let us
respect that. The young are in control, which is as it
should be, and mostly we wouldn't wish to be out
there now taking the flak, though there have always
been majestic exceptions, with politicians the high
fliers: think Churchill, Prime Minister at eighty, think
Gladstone, think Bismarck. But we do not wish to be
arbitrarily retired, or to have assumptions made about
our capacities and our tastes, and since we are likely in
years to come to make significant demands on national
resources, then it would make sense to make use of us
for as long as we are fit, able and willing to contribute.
How you set about this I wouldn't care to say – I am a
novelist, not a think tank; some sharp young minds
could surely apply themselves to the matter.

'Go West, young man, go West.' The second part
of that exhortation usually gets left out: '. . . and grow
up with the country.' I sometimes think of that when
noting the influx of young foreign males in my part
of London – the Polish builders busy making over my
neighbours' houses; the teams of two, shoving fliers
through the doors, chatting away in some language I
can't identify; those loud on their mobiles as they pass
me in the street (is that Bulgarian? Czech? Russian?). I
have had many an interesting conversation with minicab drivers, apparently arrived in this country a month
ago and already whisking around the city: 'Where are
you living?' 'I am in Lewisham. There is house that is

all Afghan mans. Pity is no Afghan womans.' 'What
do you think of London?' 'Is pity is so many old building, but they put up new I see, perhaps in time the old
go.' 'How did you get here . . .' No, best not to pursue
the matter.

These resourceful young are not going to grow up
with a new country, but are cashing in on an old one,
and you cannot but admire them. That takes courage,
determination – and sometimes desperation. And, of
course, youth. You don't plunge into an alien city, you
don't stow away in a container lorry, unless you have
that panache, that as yet unstifled optimism, that
ingrained sense that the road ahead is there, still there.

'The party's nearly over,' says a friend and contemporary; she says it a touch ruefully, but gamely also.
We have had a party; we've been luckier than many.
And we are attuned to the idea of life as a narrative –
everyone is. Just as the young Afghan knows his story
has only just begun – and he is hell-bent on seeing
that it continues – so we take a kind of wry satisfaction in recognizing the fit and proper progress, the
shape of things. The sense of an ending.

The trajectory of life, the concept of universal death,
conditions our thinking. We require things to end, to
mirror our own situation. The idea of infinity is impossible to grasp. When I am invited to do so, watching one
of those television programmes about the expanding

universe, with much fancy computerized galaxy performance on the screen, and sober explications from
Californian astrophysicists, I can't, frankly. And what is
intriguing is that they too, while evidently accepting the
concept in a stern professional physicist way, seem also
to have an ordinary human resistance. Last time, two of
them said 'mind-boggling', reaching helplessly, it
seemed, for that most jaded cliché to account for something that is beyond language. They couldn't find words
for it; neither can I.

I have had much to do with endings, as a writer of
fiction. The novel moves from start to finish, as does
the short story; at the outset, the conclusion lurks –
where is this thing going? how will I wrap it up? how
will I give it a satisfactory shape? You are looking to
supply the deficiencies of reality, to provide order
where life is a matter of contingent chaos, to suggest
theme and meaning, to make a story that is shapely
where life is linear. 'Tick-tock': Frank Kermode's
famous 'model of what we call a plot, an organization
that humanizes time by giving it form'. The need to
give significance to simple chronicity: 'All such plotting presupposes and requires that an end will bestow
upon the whole duration and meaning.' This is the
satisfaction of a successful work of fiction – the internal coherence that reality does not have. Life as lived is
disordered, undirected and at the mercy of contingent
events. I wrote a novel recently which mirrored this

process but tried also to make a point about the effects of the process, which seemed like having it both ways and was fiendishly difficult to do, and that served me right, but it was a chance to explore the alarming inter-dependence that directs our lives.

We have this need for narrative, it seems. A life is indeed a 'tick-tock': birth and death with nothing but time in between. We go to fiction because we like a story, and we want our lives to have the largesse of story, the capacity, the onward thrust – we not only want, but need, which is why memory is so crucial, and without it we are lost, adrift in a hideous eternal present. The compelling subject of memory is for another section of this book; the point here is simply that we cannot but see the trajectory from youth to old age as a kind of story – my story, your story – and the backwards gaze of old age is much affected by the habits of fiction. We look for the sequential comforts of narrative – this happened, then that; we don't care for the arbitrary. My story – your story – is a matter of choice battling with contingency: 'The best-laid schemes o' mice an' men . . .' We are well aware of that, but the retrospective view would still like a bit of fictional elegance. For some, psychoanalysis perhaps provides this – explanations, understandings. Most of us settle for the disconcerting muddle of what we intended and what came along, and try to see it as some kind of whole.

That said, it remains difficult to break free of the

models supplied by fiction. 'The preference for progress is a basic assumption of the *Bildungsroman* and the upward mobility story, and an important component of much comedy, romance, fairy tale,' writes Helen Small in her magisterial investigation of old age as viewed in philosophy and literature, *The Long Life*. 'It is also an element in the logic of tragedy: one of the reasons tragedy (certain kinds, at least) is painful is that it affronts the human desire for progress.' We are conditioned by reading, by film, by drama, with, it occurs to me, long-running television soaps being the only salutary reminder of what real life actually does – it goes on and on as a succession of events until the plug is pulled; we should note the significance of *Coronation Street* and *EastEnders*. We want some kind of identifiable progress, a structure, and the only one is the passage of time, the notching up of decades until the exit line is signalled.

Helen Small has written also of the debate – usually between philosophers, it seems – about the concept of eternal life. Is death in fact desirable? A moot point indeed, and of course it depends on what sort of life you suppose – some kind of imagined eternal youth or the inevitable decline we all know and do not love but recognize. Swift's Struldbrugs seem to me to have had the last word. And the very euphemism we use for death – an end – seems to reflect our fictional conditioning, our sense of an ending. It is appropriate, that end.

Appropriate in theory, though we view it without enthusiasm. The thing that most vexes me about the prospect of my end is that I shan't know what comes after, not just – in fact, perhaps least of all – in the grand scale of things but on my own immediate horizon: how will life unroll for my grandchildren? What will they make of it? I shall be written out of the story (like disposable actors in *Coronation Street* – back to the sagacity of the soaps), and my story is hitched to many other stories. Every life is tangled with a multitude of other lives, again in a perverse mix of choice and contingency. You choose partners and friends; you don't choose those you end up working with, or living next door to. Either way, your story has wound in with theirs, and because of this you can be wrong-footed by your own existence. There is existence as it has seemed to you, and there are those other versions served up by other people. You think it was like this; your parent, child, discarded lover, professional rival, says no, the view from here is subtly different.

I shall never know the view from my grand-children, which may be just as well. And the discordant aspects of any life are of course the stuff of fiction – the ambiguities, the contradictions. When it comes to reality, plenty are anxious to get in a pre-emptive strike by way of autobiography and memoir, espe-cially those who have been on the public stage and are well aware that they are going to get a good

going-over in due course; there can't be many politicians who have not spent their declining years honing
their version of things before it is too late.

There is a vogue for 'life writing' at the moment,
both for publication and as private endeavours. I am
all for it, partly because I gobble up other people's
lives, as a reader, but also because it seems to me a
productive personal exercise – to stand aside and have
a look at your story and try, not to make sense of it,
which may be too taxing, but to trace the narrative
thread, to look at the roads not taken, to see where
you began and where you have got to. An exercise
also in solipsism, perhaps, but we are all solipsistic,
and actually the exercise itself demands as well a
measure of detachment.

There is one thing missing, of course, from personal
life writing: that requisite ending. Tick without the
tock. I would find that most unsettling, were I to
attempt any sort of conventional memoir (which I
shan't do); the novelist in me requires that tension
between start and finish, the sense of a whole, of a
progress towards conclusion. But I am quite at home
with the idea of my life – any life – as a bit-player in the
lives of others; that is the stuff of fiction, again, and the
challenge of any novel is to find a balance for the relationships within the cast list, to make these interesting,
intriguing, to have them shift and perhaps unravel over
the course of the narrative. So that side of things is

fine; fact and fiction nicely reflect one another. It is the search for an ending that is the problem.

Which takes me back to the prompt for this digression: the parabola between youth and age, and the way in which it conditions the view in winter. The winter of old age is not going to give way to spring, so the term is inept, but it suits the static nature of old age, the sense that things have wound down, gone into suspension. The party's nearly over, yes, and that euphemistic ending is somewhere just over the horizon, but in the meantime there is this new dimension of life – often demanding, sometimes dismaying, always worth examining.

Am I envious of the young? Would I want to be young again? On the first count – not really, which surprises me. On the second – certainly not, if it meant a repeat performance. I would like to have back vigour and robust health, but that is not exactly envy. And, having known youth, I'm well aware that it has its own traumas, that it is no Elysian progress, that it can be a time of distress and disappointment, that it is exuberant and exciting, but it is no picnic. I don't particularly want to go back there.

And in any case, I am someone else now. This seems to contradict earlier assertions that you are in old age the person you always were. What I mean is that old age has different needs, different satisfactions, a different outlook. I remember my young self, and I am not essentially changed, but I perform otherwise today.

There are things I no longer want, things I no longer do, things that are now important. I have no further desire whatsoever for travel. What? No further desire? You who crossed the Atlantic twice a year or so? Who left Heathrow twelve times one year? Who was happy to hop off pretty well anywhere at the behest of the British Council or on book-related business? Who went on holidays? That's right; absolutely no further desire, and that includes holidays. I never want to see another airport. And, furthermore, I don't miss it. Maybe I wouldn't feel like this if I had not done so much – been there, seen that – if I didn't have it stashed away in my head, though the random retrieval system means that only some of it floats up. A sudden glimpse of those ring-tailed lemurs in Melbourne Zoo, and the publisher's office in Ljubljana where I was given the Slovenian translation of 'Jabberwocky'; the audience member at a reading in New York Public Library who had brought me a red rose from her garden. The summers with friends in Maine and Massachusetts. I have it – at least, I have shreds of it – and that will do nicely.

All right, this is the diminishment of old age. I don't want to travel any more because I know I couldn't do it now, and perhaps there is some benign mechanism that aligns diminished capacity with diminished desire. Though I'm not sure – contemporaries have disputed this: they do miss travel, they resent being grounded. And some of them are not – still braving Terminal Four, still sitting squashed in a metal canister with hundreds of others for hours on end, still, I suppose, getting that adrenalin rush. Perhaps I have just given in to diminishment, or, I prefer to think, I have simply made a choice. I don't want to do it any more.

Homeland travel is another matter. I am still around and about in this country, but I don't regard that as travel – that is simply checking out the territory, discovering, revisiting, crossing my own path, and I wouldn't be without it. A number of years ago the railway authorities, with a sudden rush of indulgence, decided that senior citizens should be allowed tickets to anywhere at non-peak times for a fiver, I think it was. I remember finding myself on an east coast train surrounded by jubilant grey heads, busy notching up all the mileage they could. That offer was withdrawn, in a panic, after a month or so. That'll teach them.

So, homeland travel only for me now. I am nicely smug, where my carbon footprint is concerned. What else do I not want to do any more? Go to anything about which I am unenthusiastic. Time was, I attended hither and thither, frequently out of compunction: I really ought to show up. Or I thought: come on, give it a go, you never know . . . Not now. It is pure self-interest, today. I attend only when I think I will probably enjoy this. Out with all those speculative sorties to some event or gathering; far more alluring is the evening with a couple of hours reading and maybe some telly if there's anything with promise. I can – just – remember how it was to be twenty with the horror of a blank evening ahead, nothing to go to, no company lined up – help! I can remember what that felt like, I can remember myself feeling, but this is the sense in which I am someone else now.

This someone else, this alter ego who has arrived, is less adventurous, more risk-averse, costive with her time. Well, of course – there is the matter of the spirit and the flesh, and that is the crux of it: the spirit is still game for experience, anything on offer, but the body most definitely is not, and unfortunately calls the shots. My mind seems to be holding out – so far, so far. My poor father had Alzheimer's; that shadow lies over all of my age group, with the numbers of sufferers now rising all the time – but that is of course a factor of the new demographic. Dementia is irreversible and you can't fend it off, though it seems that exercise and a healthy balanced diet can help to do so, along with regular brain activity such as crosswords and sudoku. I am not a crossword addict and sudoku defeats me entirely; I must put my trust in writing novels and, maybe, this.

Writing is not a problem, thanks be. The language

arrives, the word I want. I have never much used a thesaurus, and don't do so now. But here's an odd thing – words remain biddable, but names do not. Names drop into a black hole – the leader of the opposition, that actor I saw last week, the acquaintance who comes up at a party. After a while Ed Miliband will surface, and I dance around the problem of the acquaintance by avoiding introductions. I'm not worried, because I know I'm not alone – my contemporaries all have the same complaint. But why names and not words? Nothing that I have yet read on the operation of memory or the function of the brain in old age has yet offered an explanation; answers in comprehensible detail, please. A friend says: it's because we've known, and known of, so many people – we have name overload by now. I am aware that there is a condition which makes sufferers unable to remember the word they are after – aphasia; Kingsley Amis had some wry fun with it in his novel *Ending Up*. But the name difficulty seems to be generic, and I'm sceptical about my friend's explanation.

Writing survives, for me – so far, so far. Other pleasures – needs – do not. I was a gardener. Well, I am a gardener, but a sadly reduced one, in every sense. I have a small paved rectangle of London garden, full of pots, with a cherished twenty-year-old corokia, and two pittosporums, and various fuchsias, and *Convolvulus cneorum* and hakonechloa grass and euphorbia and heuchera and a *Hydrangea petiolaris* all over the back wall (well, some of you will be gardeners and might share my tastes). It gives me much pleasure, but is a far cry from what I once gardened – a half acre or so that included a serious vegetable garden: potatoes, onions, all the beans, carrots, courgettes, you name it, the lot. All I can do now is potter with the hose in summer, and do a bit of snipping here and there, thanks to the arthritis; forget travel, what I really do miss is intensive gardening. Digging, raking, hoeing – the satisfactory creation of a trench for the potatoes, deft work with the hoe around a line of young French beans, the texture of rich, well-fertilized soil. Pruning a shaggy rose: shaping for future splendour. Dividing fat clumps of snowdrops: out of many shall come more still. And that was – is – the miraculous power of gardening: it evokes tomorrow, it is eternally forward-looking, it invites plans and ambitions, creativity, expectation. Next year I will try celeriac. And that new pale blue sweet pea. Would *Iris stylosa* do just here? And what about sweet woodruff in that shady corner? Gardening defies time; you labour today in the interests of tomorrow; you think in seasons to come, cutting down the border this autumn but with next spring in your mind's eye. And I still have something of this, in my London patch; twice a year, my daughter takes me to a garden centre for the seasonal splurge – the summer geraniums, the pansies for winter.

An addiction to gardening is genetic, I believe. My grandmother gardened to the exclusion of almost everything else; my mother had the gene, and now my daughter has it too. A working musician, she acquired Royal Horticultural Society qualifications in spare time that she did not really have. I wish I had done that – I admire and envy her more informed way of gardening.

All the discussion of how to confront old age focuses on physical and mental activity. We must not subside into the armchair and pack up; we should go for a brisk walk every day (hips and knees permitting), we should reach for the crossword, pick up a book. There is much said about attitude, too. Those who had a positive attitude towards old age when in their fifties and sixties have been found to display a more sprightly outlook when it arrives. Well, I dare say, and that is really just a matter of diversity; some of us are like that, others are not. You are exhorted to think positive when you have cancer, with the underlying suggestion that if you don't your chances will be that much worse. Hmmm. A positive view may well do much for the state of mind, but I doubt if it affects the disease.

Something of the same applies to old age – condition not disease. A positive attitude is not going to cure the arthritis or the macular degeneration or whatever but a spot of bravado makes endurance more possible. Not everyone can manage this – diversity again. And bravado comes a great deal easier to those cushioned by financial security; I am intensely aware of this. There's something else, though, and that is not so much state of mind as what the mind in question is up to, indeed, whether it is up to anything at all. Friends in my age group who are successfully facing down old age are busy; several are hampered by hips, knees, etc. but still pursue their interests and activities. I know I have a fairly left-field range of friends, nearly all of whom have earned their bread through brain work, and nobody forces a writer into retirement (except incompliant publishers), but there does seem to be some staying power bestowed by . . . what? Curiosity? Mental energy? Perseverance? A surviving drive to seize the day? Any, I think – and all.

Can't garden. Don't want to travel. But can read, must read. For me, reading is the essential palliative, the daily fix. Old reading, revisiting, but new reading too, lots of it, reading in all directions, plenty of fiction, history and archaeology always, reading to satisfy perennial tastes, reading sideways too – try her, try him, try that, Amazon and AbeBooks would founder without me; my house is a book depository – books in, books out (to family and friends, to my daughter's Somerset cottage where there is still some shelf space, to wonderful Book Aid which sends English language books to places where they are needed).

I buy; I am sent. Publishers send what my husband used to call bread-upon-the-waters books to people like me: 'We'd love to know if you enjoy this book as much as we have . . .' I can't read each one, but I always have a good look. Any book represents effort, struggle, work – I know, I write them myself – every book deserves attention, even if that ends with dismissal. And occasionally there is gold: today the postman hands over Robert Macfarlane's latest, *The Old Ways*. Ah – discerning editor! I have devoured and reread Macfarlane's earlier books.

Reading in old age is doing for me what it has always done – it frees me from the closet of my own mind. Reading fiction, I see through the prism of another person's understanding; reading everything else, I am travelling – I am travelling in the way that I still can: new sights, new experiences. I am reminded sometimes of the intensity of childhood reading, that absolute absorption when the very ability to read was a heady new gain, the gateway to a different place, to a parallel universe you hadn't known was there. The one entirely benign mind-altering drug. Except of course for those who ban or burn books, in which case benign doesn't come into it, but the power of books is all the more acknowledged.

So I have my drug, perfectly legal and I don't need a prescription. Over the last few years, I have considered nature and nurture with Matt Ridley, explored

Hengeworld with Mike Pitts, enjoyed centuries of British landscape with Francis Pryor, discovered France with Graham Robb. Plus a raft of novels and an expedient injection of poetry. More later on a lifetime of reading and the way in which reading has powered writing. My point here is to do with the needs of old age; there is what you can't do, there is what you no longer want to do, and there is what has become of central importance. Others may have a game of bowls, or baking cakes, or carpentry, or macramé, or watercolours. I have reading.

Writing this chapter, I have sometimes felt that I am eerily attuned to the thought processes of 10 Downing Street, where clearly some are much exercised about the new demographic. This morning the paper tells me that one of David Cameron's advisers says that elderly people should be encouraged to go back to work and move into smaller houses. It is not their welfare alone with which he is concerned; he wants their family-sized houses for the next generation, while to advance the retirement age would of course have an impact on the ever-increasing pension bill, though he masks this by insisting that the elderly need the social contact supplied by work – many of the old complain of isolation. True enough, I'm sure, and apparently the Swedish Prime Minister has floated the idea of seventy-five as a potential retirement age. The prospect of a future in which a great swathe of a nation's resources has to be ring-fenced for the sustenance of an entirely inactive slab of the population is indeed challenging. But seventy-five-year-old refuse collectors? Seventy-five-year-olds digging the roads, erecting scaffolds? I don't think so. Office work, maybe, and indeed all those occupations without an element of physical labour. Many septuagenarians might well welcome that. I hope the Swedish Prime Minister has thought this through, and indeed our own, who has apparently said that he loves the idea of an automatic 'life expectancy based adjustment' to the state pension age – which is already due to go up from sixty-five to sixty-eight over the next three decades. This is all very well, and I've advocated finding a means for those elderly who are able and keen to be useful to continue to be so, but the increased expectancy will have to be accompanied by increasingly robust hips, knees and everything else.

Professor Tom Kirkwood has written: 'There is a little progress with age-related diseases.' But he went on to say that in his study of a group over eighty-five not one had zero age-related disease, and most had four or five. Doctors' surgeries and hospital waiting-rooms are well stocked with those over sixty-five; it is the old and the young who demand most attention. On a trip to University College Hospital Accident and Emergency a couple of years ago my companions in the waiting-room were seven elderly men and women, and three mothers with babies or toddlers, all of us supervised by a stern-faced security man in case we started causing trouble. My visit was purely precautionary, insisted on by my doctor: I appreciated the resources and the efficiency but felt very much that I was indeed cluttering up the system.

Well, we do, and we can't help it. Over the last years, I have had surgery and treatment for breast cancer; hips and knees are holding out so far but my back gave in long ago: I have been in intermittent pain for fifteen years – discomfort always, tipping into real pain. My sight is dodgy – myopic macular degeneration, which may get worse (but also – fingers crossed – may not). There is a shoulder problem – a torn tendon. The worst was a cracked vertebra, four years ago, which required surgery – balloon kyphoplasty – which left me in intense, unrelenting and apparently inexplicable pain for three and a half months. Pain that had the specialists shaking their heads, baffled, passing me around like the unwelcome parcel in that children's game – and I am sorry, apologetic, through the miasma of pain, sorry to be such a challenge, but sorrier still for myself. I want my life back. I want to be able to sit, stand, walk to the supermarket, watch the telly, meet a friend. Write my novel. We have run through the entire repertoire of pain-killers, starting with kindly and ineffective paracetamol and ibuprofen, moving through flirtations with co-codamol, Voltarol, the fentanyl patch . . . We are on to the hard stuff now; morphine turns me into a madwoman, so we don't go there again, but pethidine gives temporary relief. Pethidine is – or was – used in childbirth; I remember it under different circumstances. But it works for about an hour and a half, and you can only take it every four hours. So, the blissful float into a hazy pain-distanced zone, and then back to reality, and watching the clock. Over those dreadful months, I wanted to see, talk to, only my children, and two friends. And my physiotherapist – superb professional, practical, breezy, funny, convinced that we'll beat this: 'You *will* get better.'

I did. At last.

I have sometimes wondered if an experience like that has some salutary value for any of us: it puts into perspective subsequent distresses. As for the rest of my continuing ailments, they seem more or less par for the course for an eighty-year-old; of those I know in my age group, most can chalk up a few, or more, with only one or two that I can think of maddeningly unscathed.

You get used to it. And that surprises me. You get used to diminishment, to a body that is stalled, an impediment? Well, yes, you do. An alter ego is amazed, aghast perhaps – myself in the roaring forties, when robust health was an assumption, a given, something you barely noticed because it was always there. Acceptance has set in, somehow, has crept up on you, which is just as well, because the alternative – perpetual rage and resentment – would not help matters. You are now this other person, your earlier selves are out there, familiar, well remembered, but you have to come to terms with a different incarnation.

'In seventy or eighty years a Man may have a deep Gust of the World. Know what it is, what it can afford, and what 'tis to have been a Man.' Reading Sir Thomas Browne, today, on a winter London afternoon, I'm in touch with a former self, who was discovering *Urne-Buriall* in Jack's set of the Works, in Oxfordshire in the 1970s: 'The treasures of time lie high, in Urnes, Coynes and Monuments, scarce below the roots of some vegetables.' Today, I am warming to Browne's discussion of the long view: '. . . such a compass of years will shew new examples of old things, parallelisms of occurrences through the whole course of Time, and nothing be monstrous unto him, who may in that time understand not only the varieties of Man, but the varieties of himself, and how many Men he hath been in that extent of time.' Yes, yes – exactly. And how strange, how exciting, to find an echo of what I have been thinking about myself in that wonderful seventeenth-century mind. Back in my forties, I was responding to Browne's archaeological interests, being that way inclined myself, and relishing, always, always, that language – the cadences, the flourished word, the music.

'. . . the varieties of himself'; perfect phrase. And it is of the varieties of myself that I am aware, seeing how today's response to Browne links me to that Oxfordshire self, in mid-life, busy with children, but essentially the same person. The body may decline, may seem a dismal reflection of what went before, but the mind has a healthy continuity, and some kind of inbuilt fidelity to itself, a coherence over time. We learn, and experience; attitudes and opinions may change, but most people, it seems to me, retain an essential persona, a cast of mind, a trademark foot-print. It is not so much that we simply get more like ourselves, as has been said, but that the self in question may expand, mutate, over time, but retains always that signature identity. A poet's voice will alter and develop, but young Wordsworth, Tennyson, Larkin are not essentially adrift from their later selves. There is this interesting accretion – the varieties of ourselves – and the puzzling thing in old age is to find yourself out there as the culmination of all these, knowing that they are you, but that you are also now this someone else.

Simone de Beauvoir confronted the problem in her extensive study *Old Age*: 'Old age is particularly diffi-cult to assume because we have always regarded it as something alien, a foreign species: "Can I have

become a different being while I still remain myself?"'
What is at issue, it seems to me, is a new and disturbing relationship with time. It is as though you
advanced along a plank hanging over a canyon: once,
there was a long reassuring stretch of plank ahead;
now there is plank behind, plenty of it, but only a few
plank paces ahead. Once, time was the distance into
which you peered – misty, impenetrable, with no discernible landmarks, but reassuringly *there*. In old age,
that dependable distance has been whisked suddenly
behind you – and it does seem to have happened suddenly. Not long ago, there was some kind of balance –
a fore and aft, as it were. No longer; time has looped
back, regressed, it no longer lies ahead, but behind. It
has turned into something else, something called
memory, and we need it – oh dear me, yes, we need
it – but it is dismaying to have lost that sense of expectation, of anticipation. Not only that, but we are aware
of the change in ourselves – we are the same, but different, and equipped now with a comet trail of
completed time, the memory trail.

The mind does not always keep up – the subconscious, rather. In dreams, I am not always the self of
today; I am often young, or younger, and if my children are present they have often become children
again, obligingly – we have all jumped backwards.
The mind cannot bear too much reality, it seems; in
the same way, Jack is nearly always present in my

dreams – it is twelve years since he died, but at night he returns, not always recognizably himself, but a shadowy dream companion figure that I always know to be him.

When Simone de Beauvoir published *Old Age* in 1970 she was sixty-two, so from my viewpoint she was barely even on the approach road to the status itself. And, indeed, her own life experience is hardly cited at all in her long, densely researched, somewhat impassioned and rather wonderful book, which remains an illuminating investigation of the subject. She embarked on this, she says, because she saw a conspiracy of silence about old age, as though all were in denial, refusing to anticipate their own future, and, in consequence, choosing to ignore the situation of the old. She cited the appalling poverty and state neglect of the old in France and in the United States. But the book goes far beyond indignation. She wanted to explore the way in which old age is not just a biological but a cultural fact, and to that end she delved into ethnology. She ploughed through history to see how the old had got on, from classical Greece to the present day, she pursued evidence of attitudes towards old age. She searched out the voices of the old. The book is laced with references from art and literature, from sociology, psychology, philosophy. It is compendious, exhaustive, extremely serious – there's no light touch, with de Beauvoir – and impressive. She died at seventy-eight, so she got there herself – in 1986 you would certainly be considered old at seventy-eight.

Whether or not she turned the analytic eye on her own old age, she eventually had a grim experience of it, managing the care of Jean-Paul Sartre in his wretched decline into infirmity and blindness. A harsh diminishment, for these two intellectual heavyweights, and nicely reflecting all that she had written of the alienation from oneself that is the condition of old age.

I am sharing old age with friends, but not with a partner. In that, my situation is entirely average: three in five women over seventy-five in this country live alone. The men go first. Jack knew that, and expected it; after his retirement, he spent much time organizing our affairs, and would talk routinely of a future that excluded him, to my irritation. I would remonstrate, and he would smile amiably: 'Statistics . . .' Well, he was right – though cheated, statistically, since he died at sixty-nine. The world is full of widows – several among my closer friends. We have each known that grim rite of passage, have engaged with grief and loss, and have not exactly emerged but found a way of living after and beyond. It is an entirely changed life, for anyone who has been in a long marriage – forty-one years, for me: alone in bed, alone most of the time, without that presence towards which you turned for advice, reassurance, with whom you shared the good news and the bad. Every decision now taken alone; no one to defuse anxieties. And a thoroughly commonplace experience – everywhere, always – so get on with it and don't behave as though you are uniquely afflicted. I didn't tell myself that at the time, and I doubt if it would have helped if I had, but it is what I have come – not so much to feel as to understand.

A common experience – like old age itself, for those fortunate enough (if that is the right word) to get there. Here we are – the eighty-somethings – around 1.4 million of us in the UK, most of us with nothing much in common except the accretion of years, a historical context, and a generous range of ailments from which we have probably been allocated two or three. For each of us the experience is different, each of us endures – or challenges – it differently. Both endurance and challenge will of course be more successful from the vantage point of financial security, and if you are not too encumbered on the ailment front. My own mood can vary from day to day – glum if it is a bad back day, buoyant the next if that is better, there's something interesting to look forward to, and the new tulips are out in the garden. But none of us escapes the daily challenge of the condition – so often newly surprising. However did I get like this? What happened?

Age-and-infirmity; portmanteau phrase, like law-and-order. But apt, unfortunately. We are indeed infirm, and the main reason for that is loss of balance. You lose your sense of balance in old age. It came on slowly, but the day arrives when you are always conscious of it. I don't at all care to be at the top of an escalator; any flight of stairs is a matter of expedient attention. In the street, kerbs have become unreliable; they seem to shoot up or down unexpectedly, to vary in height, and require stern treatment. The possibility of a fall grins and glares every day; what would have been a mere indignity twenty or thirty years ago could be catastrophic now. We fall about, we old, not because we are careless but because we no longer float around with easy balance, and a fall, for many, is the prelude to incapacity. I watch rugby players and footballers with wonder, as another species. And children – that glorious pliancy, which one knew, and has forgotten.

Kingsley Amis fell over a great deal, in his later years. In his case, this would seem to have been on account of drink taken, more often than not; Martin Amis's acute memoir *Experience* wryly records heaving his father up from the road, and the overhead crashes heard by his mother, living in the flat beneath. I have fallen twice in the last five years (drink not at issue); once on the pavement near home, having apparently slipped on a squashed tomato, and once on a treacherous staircase in France ('Une chute d'escalier,' I heard the A & E nurse say, in a bored tone – they were shunted in daily, I suppose). I was lucky both times – no broken bones, though the staircase had my back raging for many weeks. And in neither case was balance the root cause, I think; those particular tumbles could have happened to a thirty-year-old. But both events shook me up, and made me realize that from now on any kind of fall was potentially disastrous. After seventy, stay vertical if you possibly can, is the rule.

My artist aunt, Rachel Reckitt, fell off her horse when she was eighty-two. She was a few miles from home, on the edge of the Brendons, in west Somerset, and the horse, finding himself riderless, simply did what horses do, and headed for his stable. A neighbour spotted him, a search party was organized, and found Rachel on her way down from the hill, slightly bruised and annoyed about all the fuss. After that, we persuaded her to wear a whistle when out riding. She objected strongly, and had to be reminded that this strategy had saved the day for her own elderly uncle, many years before, who had come off his horse up on Exmoor and lay for hours in a bog with a fractured leg.

Rachel died at eighty-six, working daily in her studio until her last illness. That horse survived her, the last of many she had owned, in this case an irritable pony called Fury ('A tiresome creature,' she used to say, but she could no longer get up on to the big hunters she preferred). Fury himself was fifteen, which is a ripe age for a horse, and in the sad and onerous dispersal process after her death he became a central problem: nobody wanted him. Eventually, someone with field space was bribed to provide an expensive retirement.

Fury was true to form, in this; he was all set to cost. Old age costs; it costs the nation, it costs those going through it. We contribute nothing, but require maintenance – a winter fuel allowance, free TV licence, bus pass, free prescriptions, all the kindly state indulgences. Those don't add up to luxury, for anyone, any more than the state pension does other than provide basic subsistence. And old age has its needs, its greeds. You may not yearn for a Caribbean cruise – I don't – but certain comforts have become essential, the accustomed perks that make daily existence a bit more than just that. I can't start the day without a bowl of the right kind of muesli topped with some fruit and sheep's milk yoghurt; I can't end it without a glass (or two) of wine. I need the diversions of radio and television. I want flowers in the house and something tempting to eat – these are greeds, I think, rather than needs. And – high priority – there is reading, the daily fix, the time of immersion in whatever is top of my book pile right now. As demands, requirements, all of this is relatively modest. Much of it – the reading, the flowers – goes back to prelapsarian days before old age. The difference, though, is that then there were further needs and greeds, and those seem to have melted away, to have tactfully absented themselves as though to make things a bit easier because they would indeed be an encumbrance now.

I am no longer acquisitive. I was never exactly voracious, but I could fall prey to sudden lust: one simply could not live a moment longer without that sampler spotted in an antique shop, or that picture or rug or chair. No longer. I can admire, but I no longer covet. Books of course are another matter; books are not acquisitions, they are necessities.

I don't need or want excitement. Pleasure, enjoyment – yes. But that restless feeling that you must have something happen, you must look ahead, anticipate, you need a rush of adrenalin – that is gone, quite gone. Thanks be. Something to look forward to – yes. Seeing family, friends. Outings – a theatre, a gallery, a jaunt. Time in Somerset with Josephine. But I no longer want that dangerous edge to things – anticipation heightened by risk, the sense of venture. I am done with venture.

I was going to write: I am no longer aspirational. But that is not quite true. I do aspire in terms of wanting to do what I do as well as possible. I would still like to write a good book. But I don't have that ferocity for achievement that I can remember from early writing days: write a good book or bust. I have never been particularly competitive – and writers can be competitive, a trait fostered by the spectator sport of literary prizes; nowadays I find that it is other writers who are providing me with my greatest pleasures, as I pounce on a new work by Julian Barnes, Ian McEwan, Adam Thorpe, Matthew Kneale, Lawrence Norfolk, Anne Tyler, Jane Gardam, a bunch of others . . . Or as I light on one of the newer, younger writers, with the recognition that – yes, here is the sort of thing I want. I suppose that this is the reader in me taking command. But it is also, I think, a writerly satisfaction in seeing it done by others as I would wish it done – in seeing the show kept on the road. Maybe elderly athletes enjoy watching the hundred metres in the same spirit.

Out with acquisition, excitement, and aspiration except in tempered mode. And, on another front, I don't in the least lament certain emotions. I can remember falling in love, being in love; life would have been incomplete without that particular exaltation, but I wouldn't want to go back there. I still love – there is a swathe of people that I love – but I am glad indeed to be done with that consuming, tormenting form of the emotion.

So this is old age, and I am probably shedding readers by the drove at this point. If you are not yet in it, you may be shuddering. If you are, you will perhaps disagree, in which case I can only say: this is how it is for me. And if it sounds – to anyone – a pretty pallid sort of place, I can refute that. It is not.

Certain desires and drives have gone. But what remains is response. I am as alive to the world as I have ever been – alive to everything I see and hear and feel. I revel in this morning's March sunshine, and the cream and purple hellebore just out in the garden; I listen to a radio discussion about the ethics of selective abortion, and chip in at points; the sound of a beloved voice on the phone brings a surge of pleasure. Yesterday, I rejoiced in the David Hockney exhibition at the Royal Academy (for the third time) – that singing colour, that exuberance (and he is seventy-five); I am reading John Lanchester's *Capital*, slowly because it is the sort of capacious novel I like and I don't want it to end. I think there is a sea-change, in old age – a metamorphosis of the sensibilities. With those old consuming vigours now muted, something else comes into its own – an almost luxurious appreciation of the world that you are still in. Spring was never so vibrant; autumn never so richly gold. Maybe that's why Hockney is painting like this, now. People are of abiding interest – observed in the street, overheard on a bus. The small pleasures have bloomed into points of relish in the day – food, opening the newspaper (new minted, just for me), a shower, the comfort of bed. It is almost like some kind of endgame salute to the intensity of childhood experience, when the world was new. It is an old accustomed world now, but invested with fresh significance; I've seen all this before, done all this, but am somehow able to find new and sharpened pleasure.

On a good day, aches and pains in abeyance. On a bad day – well, on a bad day a sort of shutter comes down, and the world is dulled. But I know that it is there, the shutter will roll up, with luck, the sun will come out.

The stereotypes of old age run from the smiling old dear to the grumbling curmudgeon. In fiction, they are rife – indeed fiction is perhaps mainly responsible for the standard perception of the old, with just a few writers able to raise the game. Muriel Spark's *Memento Mori* is a black comedy, with a group of elderly plagued by sinister phone calls: 'Remember you must die.' No stereotypes, but a bunch of sharply drawn individuals, convincingly old, bedevilled by specific ailments, and mainly concerned with revisions of their pasts in terms of will-making and the machinations of relationships. Kingsley Amis also went for comedy, in *Ending Up*, with a group cohabiting in a cottage and busy scoring points off each other – funny, but with a bleak undertone. Saul Bellow's *Ravelstein* is neither comedy (though not without humour) nor stereotype, but strong writing about the view both of and from old age. And he was old – eighty-four – when the book was published, whereas neither Spark nor Amis were – Muriel Spark was forty-one when *Memento Mori* came out. Just three examples; they spring to mind simply because memorable and effective writing about old age is rare, though there are of course other instances. My point is that old age seems to be a danger zone for many novelists, somehow even more of a challenge than the universal problem of writing about and from the point of view of a man if you are a woman, and vice versa; we all have to deal with that unless we are to be left with a very curiously populated novel. But the old and the young are, somehow, the elusive element; equally, few novelists are good at children.

'What do they think has happened, the old fools, / To make them like this?' Any reference to Philip Larkin's poem in this context is almost a cliché. The poem marries perception of age with stark truth: 'Well, / We shall find out.' He never did, of course, dying at sixty-three. And the perception is of drooling, confused, incapable old age – not a stereotype so much as an evocation, both harsh and reflective.

Those of us not yet in the departure lounge and still able to take a good look at what has made them – us – like this can find some solace in doing so. What has happened is such an eccentric mixture of immediate and long-drawn-out, the arrival of a condition that has been decades in the making but seems to have turned up this morning. The succession of people that we have been – Sir Thomas Browne's 'varieties of himself' – are suddenly elided into this – final? – version, disturbingly alien when we catch sight of a mirror, but also evocative of a whole range of known personae. What we have been still lurks – and even more so within. This old age self is just a top dressing, it seems; early selves are still mutinously present, getting a word in now and then. And all this is interesting – hence the solace. I never imagined that old age would be quite like this – possibly because, like most, I never much bothered to imagine it.

My attitude towards these earlier selves – varieties of myself – is peculiar, I find. It is kindly, indulgent – as though towards a younger relative, sometimes impatient (you idiot . . .), occasionally grateful. I'm grateful for all that work done – a bunch of other people wrote my books, it can seem. I feel kindly towards those recognizable former incarnations, in whom I can see my present self – reading Sir Thomas Browne in the 1970s, digging our first garden in Swansea in 1961, entranced when my first baby laughs – spring of 1958. I'm angry about the mistakes, the deficiencies, the times I should have done differently.

This book is to be about the context of a lifetime. Some of this context lies within my own head – the shape-shifting backdrop of memory. There is a rich population here, all those people in the mind, my own previous selves, and alongside them so many others – transient encounters and, most vividly, family and friends.

My old age friends go back a long way. Twenty years, thirty, sixty – Susan and I were twenty together – and even seventy-five years, two were known in my Egyptian childhood. And now here we are sharing this new incarnation. Or is it new? Because they all seem to me much as they ever were. We behave towards each other much the same, except that we enquire after health in a way that we never used to – really wanting to know, not that casual perfunctory 'How *are* you?' But, I suppose because we have kept up with one another all along the way, we are not taken aback by the metamorphosis, the way we look now. When I was on the other side of the Atlantic a few years ago staying with my best friend in America, she produced a photo she had found of the two of us taken in the early 1980s. We gazed at it with surprised respect; 'Weren't we young!' said Betty. Actually, verging on middle age, but never mind – our reaction was in perfect accord: an acknowledgement of those other selves. Steve, next-door neighbour of my childhood, seems remote today from the six-year-old in my head, with whom I am still playing a messy game by the garden pond involving ships made of pieces of plank, but there is a resonance. He became a sculptor, and back then he was in charge of plank construction: talent will out. I go back thirty years and more with Ann and Anthony; they are layered in my head, saying and doing over time, a collective with a concertina effect that compresses to the known people of today. Several decades again with Joy, and it is sometimes a familiar younger self of hers who surfaces – a turn of phrase, a mannerism.

And others . . . The point of all this fossicking with my contemporaries is a tribute to the way in which we are each of us the accretion of all that we have been. You see this in yourself; you see it in those you have long known. Nothing new here, no fresh perception, but something you appreciate to the full in old age. I am aware of invisible ballast, on all sides, the hidden body of the iceberg.

I cherish the company of my contemporaries, but I want – need – also to touch base elsewhere. Two of my closest friends today are considerably younger than I am, and I value that; the great stimulus over the last twenty years has been watching, and knowing, my grandchildren, four of them now grown up. To be corralled with one's own age group must seem like some kind of malign exile, a banishment from the rich every-age confection of society. To walk along the street and see a toddler in a buggy, a bunch of teenagers, business people on their mobiles, middle-aged women with their shopping, someone else elderly like me, is to feel a part of the natural progression of things, to be aware of continuity, replenishment. And it is, quite simply, of consuming interest; a novelist is anyway a people-watcher – an old novelist is still in the business but in less forensic style. There is a kind of benign observation now; the street scene mutates from season to season, year to year. New adornment; different style. How on earth does she get into those skin-tight jeans? Tattoos *all* over *both* arms – you may get tired of that, you know. *Three* matching pugs with matching collars and leads?

We old are on the edge of things. Or are we? Yesterday was budget day, and the airwaves are full of outrage at the so-called 'granny tax' – the phasing out of tax concessions for those over sixty-five. Unfair to penalize those who have worked and saved, is the cry, but there is also threatening mention of the 'grey vote'. We might bite back. No doubt all this has been taken into consideration by those whose job it is to crunch the numbers, but the fact remains that there is an uneasy tension today between proper concern for the old, and a nervous apprehension about this exponential growth of a new demographic. We are many, and will be more; on the edge, perhaps, but unignorable.

The day belongs to the young, the younger. I feel overtaken, and that is fine. I don't like finding myself usually the oldest person in the room, and I am afraid of being boring. The old carry around the potential to bore like a red warning light; I know, I have shied away from it myself. But I wouldn't in the least want to reoccupy the centre stage, which is I suppose that mid-life period around forty, with youth still apparent and middle age at arm's length. I don't remember being any more appreciative of life then than I am now. More energy, yes, of course – vigour, capacity – but plenty of doubts and anxieties. Well, there still are those, but tempered somehow by experience; you don't fret or waver less, but you have learned that time will sort it out, for better or for worse.

Experience. What is it? The employer's question: 'What is your experience?' Mere existence is experience; being here, exposed, involved, no choice in the matter, get on and make what you can of it. At eighty, you have a war chest of experience – euphoric, appalling, good, bad, indifferent. You may have learned from it, you may put down to it – the clichés crowd in. The stark truth is that you know rather more than you did at twenty. Or at thirty, or forty. But don't go on about that; they will find out for themselves.

We old talk too much about the past; this should take place only between consenting contemporaries. Boredom hovers, for others – unless by special request for purposes of information or instruction. We must beware that glassy smile of polite attention: they are searching for an exit strategy. Fold up the past and put it away – available for private study. This is now, and while still present and a part of it, we do best to remember that that is where we are. This may sound a touch brutal; it is simply that I have become conscious of the need – for me, at least – to stay tuned in.

Memory is crucial, memory is everything, but to retreat there would be a fatal detachment.

Memory is the subject for another section – the crutch, the albatross, the defining story, all the things that it is for any of us. I remember (see?) getting interested first in the operation of memory when in my forties – mid-life, or thereabouts. Today, old, I am conscious of it as definition (shadow of the dreaded dementia) and, above all, as that essential setting. What has happened to me, but also what has happened while I have been around, which is where I go next – an examination of my own historical context both as it seemed at the time and how it seems now, with the wisdoms of analysis by others.

Life and Times

I was a wartime child. There were millions of us, and for many the experience was hideous. I was growing up in Egypt, where I was born. For me, the Libyan desert campaign of the early 1940s was simply the state of the world, the way things were; it sent us for a while to Palestine, then it receded, vanished. War continued, of course, but more distantly; it rumbled on, it was a condition, no more and no less.

Children do not question their circumstances. You are you, in this place, at this time, with these people – how could it be otherwise? I was required to say my prayers, every night: 'Please God, help me to be a good girl, and make the war end soon.' A mantra repeated without interest or conviction. War was a word; it was language, first and foremost, language that swirled around me, above my head, language that did indeed create the times, the place, that has lodged, that can still – just – turn then into now.

Tobruk. Benghazi. Mersa Matruh. Alamein. Monty. The Auk. Churchill.

Before the war. After the war. For the duration.

Peacetime. Shrapnel. Destroyers. Depth charges. Searchlights. Battledress. Armoured cars. Jeeps. Tanks. Spitfires. Hurricanes.

War was The War – this single commanding inescapable fact that so occupied grown-ups. It was constant, like the Egyptian sun. It was there, as far as I was concerned – as abiding as sunshine, as unremarkable.

'I have to tell you that no such undertaking has been received and consequently this country is at war with Germany': I know those words because I have heard and read them many times. But I heard them first when I was six – a thin, dry voice coming from the wireless in my grandmother's drawing-room in Somerset, 3 September 1939. They were language that I did not understand, and to which I did not listen; I had been told that I must sit still and keep quiet, this required all my attention. But The War had stalked into the room, and into my life. It would shortly send me on a helter-skelter journey down through Europe, clutching a gas mask which I must not lose (why? what is it, anyway?), back across the Mediterranean to Cairo, home, and the garden that was the haven of my childhood, with its eucalyptus and casuarina trees, its poinsettias and lantana, zinnias and plumbago, the banyan, the bamboo, the bougainvillea, the arum lilies. More language, defining language, language that provides a child with that other crucial dimension – what you see is expanded into what you hear.

I am trying to see *then* against the wisdoms of *now*, to look at the climactic points of the last century, to fish out what it felt like to be around at that point, if possible, and set that against the long view, the story now told, the arguments and the verdicts.

The experience of childhood presents the greatest challenge. It is in one sense crystal clear, in another sense irretrievable. It is the smell of crushed eucalyptus leaves, the crash of waves against the stone rampart of the Corniche in Alexandria, the shrapnel trophy gathered at an air raid there, the cool grip on my finger of the chameleon I have found in the garden. But it is also gone, it cannot be recovered. It is swamped, drowned out by adult knowledge. That child self is an alien; I have still some glimmer of what she saw, but her mind is unreachable: I know too much, seventy years on.

That war – The War – is packed away into books, and I read with fascination. It is history now, and not packed tidily, laid to rest, because there is nothing tidy or restful about history. The battle of Alamein has been differently fought, decade by decade. Did Montgomery simply take over plans originated by Auchinleck? Had Auchinleck intended a withdrawal of the Eighth Army to Khartoum and Palestine, if need be? The subsequent analyses chew over reputations, strategies, who said what to whom, why this happened, why that did not. Language illuminates, once more: 'I am fighting a terrific battle with Rommel,' writes Montgomery, sidelining a few hundred thousand others, '. . . a terrific party and a complete slogging match.' And, for me, I hear again the Cairo chatter of 1942: so-and-so is in the bag, someone else bought it when his tank brewed up.

The battle – or battles, depending on the analysis – of Alamein turned the tide of the desert war and stopped Rommel's advance into Egypt; that much is generally agreed. If it had not – well, at the most extreme estimate, the entire course of the war might have run differently, and possibly disastrously for the Allies. The Axis forces could have swept up through Palestine into Syria, Iran, Iraq, the oilfields there that must have been Hitler's target. If it had not – at a purely personal level, we would have lost our home, and my father, who stayed in Cairo when my mother and I went to Palestine along with other British women and children as Rommel advanced, would have been interned. It was said that our house a few miles outside Cairo had been earmarked for Rommel's retreat. So it would have been the German commander and his staff officers sipping gin and tonic on the veranda of an evening, instead of my parents and their friends, and diving into the large, raised concrete tank that was grandly called our swimming pool, and fraternizing with our dog, which was, conveniently, a dachshund.

I have written elsewhere of those years, of how it seemed to a nine/ten-year-old. I can still see it thus – eyes screwed up, peering backwards – but the effect is refracted now by time and discussion. The language that was once normal seems archaic; the clipped upper-class diction of the day startles me – the voices of news bulletins, of old films – can that really once have been familiar? The background clamour of the Libyan campaign – the army convoys on the desert road to Alexandria, the searchlight battery in the fields near our house, the soldiers on the streets of Cairo, the talk of the next big push – is reduced now to the cold print of the books on my shelves. I can read about what happened; about what they say happened.

Keith Douglas, soldier poet who fought at Alamein and was killed in Normandy, aged twenty-four, wrote his memoir *Alamein to Zem Zem* soon after the campaign, probably in 1943: 'I observed these battles partly as an exhibition – that is to say that I went through them like a visitor from the country, going to a great show, or like a child in a factory – a child sees the brightness and efficiency of steel machines and endless belts slapping round and round, without caring what it is all for . . . The dates have slipped away, the tactical lessons have been learnt by someone else . . . Against a backcloth of indeterminate landscapes, of moods and smells, dance the black and bright incidents.' And he makes them dance in that brief and vivid memoir, which is furnished with his own arresting, dashed-off sketches: the contorted corpse of a Libyan soldier, a tank crew cooking on a sand-filled petrol can. He gives the view from a tank (he was a tank commander, at twenty-one, fresh out from England, after a few months' training in the Delta), like that in a silent film, since the noise of the engine drowns out all other sounds, he gives the camaraderie and irritation of the officers' mess, he gives fear and exhilaration and the abiding, impervious presence of the western desert. It is a masterly piece of writing; when I reread it, I think with wonder that this life, his life, all those lives, were running thus just a hundred miles or so from where my child self was in animistic communion with the eucalyptus tree in our garden, or reading *Tales from Greece and Rome* under the banyan, or surfing the glorious waves of Sidi Bishr, in Alexandria. Seventy years on, that young man seems locked into that time, smiling out from the photo in the memoir, khaki-clad, moustached, looking rather older than he actually was. I read his poetry as a message from another world. There should have been more of it.

Wartime Cairo steamed with poets. Bernard Spencer, Robin Fedden, Terence Tiller, John Gawsworth, John Cromer, Gwyn Williams, Robert Liddell – none of these names would be familiar today to anyone outside the arcane world of mid-twentieth-century poetry studies. G. S. Fraser, a leading light, did have a post-war role as a prominent figure in London literary life; Tiller worked for the BBC and produced a radio adaptation of *Lord of the Rings*. Lawrence Durrell is known now as a novelist, for *The Alexandria Quartet*, but was working mainly as a poet in the early 1940s, and was one of the Alexandria gang of poets, with Robert Liddell and Gwyn Williams, exchanging insults and jokes with the Cairo crowd – Fedden, Spencer, Tiller. Keith Douglas was published in *Personal Landscape*, the literary magazine launched by Spencer and Tiller, and can fairly be said to be the only one of those wartime Cairo poets regarded today as a significant voice of the Second World War.

All were young – very young – as was most of the febrile, hectic Cairo society of those years, marvellously described in Artemis Cooper's *Cairo in the War*. Parties, drinks on the terrace at Shepheard's, drinks by the pool at the Gezira Sporting Club, more parties, expeditions to Luxor, to the Fayoum, yet another party. The Eighth Army officer buccaneers were at the heart of it; they came and went, and some went entirely – in the bag, or bought it. There were various planes of society – the Embassy circle, the bankers, the cotton magnates, the British Council, the universities – coteries and groupings but plenty of overlap in an overcrowded, centralized city. Lawrence Durrell was Foreign Press Attaché at the British Embassy, so with a foot in that camp as well as the more informal world of the Anglo-Egyptian Union and the Victory Club. Robin Fedden was a lecturer at Fuad al Awad University; I remember him at my mother's lunch parties, and that he taught our cook to make a dish I hated involving highly spiced lamb, apricots, nuts and garlic. Our cuisine was sternly English (rice pudding, cottage pie) and this injection of what sounds like pure Claudia Roden, and very good too, affronted me – the only brush with the esoteric world of the Cairo poets of which I am aware.

I came to England in a troopship in early April 1945; seven thousand de-mobbed soldiers and a hundred expatriate women and children, going home. Except for me, who was leaving home. It was a transition from the Middle Eastern world of warmth and colour to the chill grey of England, and wartime England at that, with its own hectoring vocabulary of coupons and points and identity cards and shortages. The war was not yet over; the V2 rocket offensive in London had reached a new intensity in February, the last weapon did not fall until the end of March. It was not until 7 May that the war officially ended, and the VE Day crowds surged through central London, dancing, singing, a sea of faces in front of Buckingham Palace, Churchill up there on the balcony with the royal family, flourishing V-sign and cigar.

No, I did not see that. Reaching back for that summer, all I can find is an array of personal concerns, the problems of a traumatized teenager uprooted from what had seemed a homeland, whose parents had just divorced, and who had now fetched up in an alien society where the social codes were mysterious and the climate defied belief. I was so cold. Well, so were most, back then, with coal the equivalent of black gold and central heating a concept of the future. Forget dancing in the streets; I was being kitted out for my first school, a dire establishment on the south coast. I met Chilprufe vests for the first time, and liberty bodices, and navy wool knickers. The war might have ended, but another had begun, for me.

But there is a landscape, in my mind – the eloquent landscape of London in 1945: the city fingered by the blitz, then again by the V1s and the V2s. I did surface enough from my own distresses to notice that: the houses with gaping façades, the floors gone, the ghost of a staircase snaking up, a fireplace clinging to a wall, the shape of a picture or mirror. The sudden absence in a street, like a tooth socket, a space filled with rubble and weeds. Someone took me to see the annihilation at the heart of the City; whenever now I come across that iconic photo of St Paul's rising above the wasteland I have my own clear, complementary vision – the acreage of low walls fringing lakes of purple willowherb, the cathedral enormous, startling, restored to its original dominance, everything else shorn to the ground. The willow-herb rampaged, birds sang.

My artist aunt, Rachel Reckitt, was in London throughout the blitz of 1941 and 1942, working at Toynbee Hall in Stepney, where she was one of those helping to organize the evacuation of women and children. Whenever she could, she made sketches of the bomb-blasted city, sketches that she would later – much later, in some cases – use as the basis for oil paintings and for the wood engravings for which she is distinguished. These hang on my walls today, and I look at them constantly. London of today is reminded of London then: *House in Fulham*, in which the shattered building serves as backdrop to a great pile of rubble from which, at the base, peers a Union Jack; *House in Berkeley Square*, three tiers of exposed doors, fireplaces, patches of wallpaper. And *Demolition*, where men with sacking hoods shift basket-loads of rubble; jagged walls, a fallen ladder, a flight of steps that go nowhere. The subject matter has become a display of the engraver's craft: the minuscule hatching and cross-hatching, the intensity of detail that becomes a kind of patterning, the subtle shadings to darkest black, the flares of white light. These are masterpieces of engraving; you study them for the intricacy, the effect. But they are also works of art about something once observed; she had sat sketching, back then, in front of a scene like this – that smashed house, those striving demolition workers. The engravings remember.

As do I, just. Such sights were commonplace, you did not much stop and stare. The demolition men were gone, but the scarred landscape was there. I did not wonder at it, particularly; it was just another strange feature of this foreign world in which I found myself. The war had been here too, as in Egypt, if differently. I took note, but my immediate concerns were offensive underwear, and how to conform with new requirements. London had an etiquette, it seemed; I was no longer a child, they told me, I must wear gloves, and lisle stockings, learn the procedures of the day. This was the class-ridden society of the mid-century; people were defined by speech and dress. I too must be defined, and understand the definitions. For one who had grown up amid the cosmopolitan exuberance of Cairo these were indistinct and baffling. Londoners all looked and sounded the same to me.

I can sympathize with that, inspecting photos of street scenes of back then: the queuing housewives, uniformed in coat to just below the knee, felt hat on head. All women seem to wear hats – they indicate neither age nor class; most men wear raincoats. But all, now, are lodged in an unfamiliar past; I don't recognize them as people who must once have furnished the world I knew. Along with wartime idioms, and the clipped speech of the day.

Does anyone identify with the age in which they were young? I don't. It seems to me more that we slide accommodatingly along with the decades, adjusting plumage as we go – dressing accordingly, thinking accordingly, or up to a point. I don't feel out of sympathy with today, by no means, though it has aspects that I deplore; I can play the grumpy old woman at moments. But there is far more that is alien and unappealing about 1945. And if I were again to feel nostalgic for polyglot and cosmopolitan Cairo – well, I have only to get out into London of today. A stroll round my own area this morning, and I hear Russian, Chinese, French, an eastern European language I cannot identify, ditto African. As for neutrality of dress, or being able to tell what sort of a person you are looking at – forget it. There are dress codes, yes – the urban hoodie, young fashionistas – but by and large I can have very little idea of a person from their dress or how they speak.

I am a Londoner now, of many years standing. I am not sure that I love London – countryside feels more like home – but I am acclimatized. I can appreciate organic London, the metamorphosis of a city, the shape-changing city, the way in which it moves with time. That is what I most like about London – its eloquence, long story, the sense in which it is of the moment, this year, these mores, but is also a permanence, a solidity that outlives the racy window-dressing of new bars, new restaurants, new shops, new talk, new ways of living, a different layer of people.

Some windows of my house in an Islington square have early glass – that beguiling, irregular glass beyond which trees ripple and change shape, a passing aircraft quivers and dissolves. These windows must have survived the blitz; indeed, the square appears to be unscathed, but the London Bomb Damage map for the area makes a silent comment: one house, a few doors from mine, is coloured dark red – Seriously Damaged, Doubtful if Repairable. A direct hit, presumably, but the building seems to have been put together again. These fascinating and eloquent maps show the city, street by street and house by house, with the colour coding that plots the extent of damage, from Total Destruction to Blast Damage, Minor in Nature. Large and small circles pin-point the strike of a V1 or a V2. Islington is liberally picked out in every colour – black, purple, dark red, light red, orange, yellow – each neat colouring-in of a house or street remembering some night of carnage, the maps becoming a strange and rather beautiful testimony. Much of Islington is early Victorian, houses that are a thin skin of brick. They always seem to me, now, to be holding each other up. Beneath the bombs, an entire street could go down like ninepins. My own house must have shuddered under the blast of that bomb a few doors away; the bricks remember. A few hundred yards away a land-mine fell on the corner of Ritchie Street, obliterating a large site, now rebuilt. The whole borough is pock-marked like this, the post-war new builds inserted into the Victorian infrastructure, replacing the rubble and the willow-herb. Islington knew the V2s; a pub on the corner of Mackenzie Road and Holloway Road was flattened on Boxing Day 1944, along with twenty houses and shop premises: seventy-one dead and fifty-six seriously injured. Another Islington rocket on 13 January 1945 killed twenty-nine and seriously injured thirty-six.

So the blitz has a legacy; it is still here, its manipulation of the city is visible, as though a giant hand swept through the place, knocking this down, plucking that out. And then other hands rebuilt, steadily, doggedly, just as they always have done, century by century, the place reinventing itself, expanding, responding to new requirements, new populations. And the real blitz, the actual thing, the *Sturm und Drang*, has slipped off into history, into the books, into the documentaries and the fictional reconstructions. It has spun its own legends of chirpy Cockney courage, of the King and Queen picking their way through the ruins of the East End, of heroism and stoicism. And the darker stories of those who seized the day: the black-marketeers, the looters who kept people camping out in their bomb-damaged homes in case they lost everything, the opportunists who snatched rings and watches from the bodies of those killed in the Piccadilly Café de Paris bombing.

My aunt Rachel, on the front line as it were, recorded her own vision in letters to her mother – brisk, factual letters that reflect her own vigour and energy (she was thirty-two at the time). She was giving an account of what she saw and did, of the behaviour of those with whom she was dealing (September 1940): 'It was exciting starting out this morning to view the damage. The first I saw was the Science Museum, all the large towers still standing, but the centre all gone. Up in Central London there was a big fire in Holborn, and various small craters to see, and then a big crater bang in the middle of the roadway between the Bank, Royal Exchange and a public shelter. It couldn't have missed more important targets if it had tried! . . . The people . . . really are wonderful. Lots were wandering, homeless, towards the City this morning, with suitcases, all they had saved, but they seemed quite resigned and unmoved . . . None of the homeless people I had in were grumbling; they were all determined we must stick it out . . . There seems to be only one billeting officer for refugees, so, naturally, he can never be got hold of by anyone; no canteens seem to function and of course all the gas, etc., is off, so people can't get hot food. They are still sticking it wonderfully well . . . I can have up to £30 to use for travelling expenses of intending evacuees who have an address to go to and don't come under any scheme. So I have got one or two off today in this way. Generally when they ask to be evacuated I ask, "Has your house been demolished yet?" and if it hasn't I have to tell them to wait until it has, as then we can do something. So later they come in with broad grins to announce that now it has been blown up and they can get away . . . There was an exciting air battle today – a big lot of Germans ran into a barrage of AA fire, one could see them scatter and rock in it, all very high up. Then they met our fighters, but came right over us so we had to stop watching. The sky seemed full of them for a few minutes. They came in the evening to drop incendiaries to start fires to guide them later . . . there is no evacuation scheme for old people, the blind, cripples, etc., who are too infirm to get to the shelters and have to lie and wait to be bombed. They don't matter so much as the children, of course, but something might be done . . . The *Evening Standard* carried a front page article on how the old and infirm are able to be evacuated, but are not availing themselves of the opportunity. It is cruel as of course it is entirely untrue and merely raises their hopes. The poor old things are dying to go in hundreds of cases.'

'Exciting . . .' she says, more than once. And I imagine that in an eerie way it was, to a young woman whose life hitherto had been led in the rural tranquillity of west Somerset. The experience affected her deeply; not only did it provoke an artistic response, but the revelation of urban poverty turned her into a lifelong socialist. She voted Labour thereafter, to the bewilderment of my grandmother, an entrenched conservative.

The blitz – the war in general – has taken on a sepia quality today, and, indeed, a sense of romance has taken hold. You don't get any fictional slant on the 1940s – on the page or on screen – in which young love does not take centre stage. For many, those years probably did have that flavour; certainly, hasty war-time marriages were a feature. I was the wrong age for the war, I realize; a child is a bystander. Ten years older, and you stood a good chance of getting killed, or you might have the time of your life.

By 1945 I was no longer a child, perched now on that perilous interface between childhood and adult life. There weren't teenagers back then; the status had not been invented. We were apprentice adults, very much on sufferance; our clothes were bought to last (oh, for Primark . . .), we must not smoke or drink or go to X Certificate films, we must behave ourselves and mark time until admitted to the real world. Most of us left school at fifteen, and were pitched into adult work; relatively few made their way into the privileged holding-pen of student life.

My university years seem to me now to have been lived in a sort of mindless trance. Not in an academic sense – I was reading history, and I know that those reading years have coloured my thinking ever since – but in absence of response to what was going on in the world. This was the early 1950s; plenty was going on, but it was not a time of student activism. Membership of the Oxford Union – the student debating society – was open to men only; those with political ambitions spoke there, and jockeyed for office. I have a vague memory of Michael Heseltine, a youth with floppy golden hair, and impeccably cut suits at a period when most male students wore grey flannels and duffel coats. I must have voted for the first time, but I don't remember the event.

The autumn of 1956 woke me up. The Suez crisis. I was in Oxford still, working as research assistant by then to a Fellow of St Antony's College. St Antony's was – is – a graduate college, specializing then in Middle Eastern and Soviet studies. It was international, a hotbed of young intellectuals. The group with which I became friendly included Americans, a Frenchman, an Israeli, a German, and Jack Lively, from Newcastle, my soon-to-be husband, who had come over from Cambridge to a research Fellowship at the college. The unfolding drama of Suez, and the growing possibility of British/French intervention after Nasser's nationalization of the Canal, polarized opinion throughout the country; Oxford was in a ferment of discussion, with those opposed to Prime Minister

Anthony Eden's increasingly belligerent stance in a majority. Jack, along with a colleague at St Antony's, set about a campaign to co-ordinate a response by senior members of the university, immediately after the first bombing raids on Cairo. I remember cycling round from college to college delivering personal letters summoning sympathizers to a meeting at which a statement was drafted, signed by three hundred and fifty-five members of Senior Common Rooms and ten heads of colleges, led by Alan Bullock of St Catherine's. The statement read: 'We consider that this action is morally wrong, that it endangers the solidarity of the Commonwealth, that it constitutes a grave strain on the Atlantic Alliance and that it is a flagrant violation of the UN charter.' I couldn't be at the meeting, not being a senior member of the university, but I remember vividly the heightened atmosphere of that time, the urgency of the newspapers, the climate of discussion, of argument, and eventually, for many of us, of outrage. For me, what was happening had a personal dimension – here was my own country dropping bombs on the country I still thought of as a kind of home. The Suez crisis was a baptism of fire, a political awakening, the recognition that you could and should quarrel with government, that you could disagree and disapprove.

Over half a century ago now, Suez, and nicely consigned to history: my granddaughter Izzy 'did' it for

her A level. I too can read about it, and set what I read
against what is in my head still – those autumn days
in Oxford, when the talk was all of the names now
packed away into the books: Eisenhower, Dulles,
Ben-Gurion, Hammarskjöld, Gaitskell, Bevan. And,
dominating all, Eden and Nasser. There was a
sequence of events – dismaying, startling, often inexplicable events – and plenty of judgements, applause,
condemnations, warnings. History has tidied it all up,
to some extent – what happened when, and why, the
inexplicable is explained. The judgements of history
are of course equally various, but one thing does
seem clear: there are not many today who defend
Britain's – Eden's – handling of the Suez crisis. Peter
Hennessy has written: 'It is rare to be able to claim,
historically, that but for one person, the course of history would almost entirely have been different. In the
case of Suez, one can.'

On 26 July 1956 Gamal Abdel Nasser, President of
Egypt, declared Egypt's nationalization of the Suez
Canal, seizing control of the Suez Canal Company
and proclaiming military law in the Canal Zone. Since
the conception of the Canal by the French diplomat
Ferdinand de Lesseps, its construction under his aegis,
and its opening in 1869, it had been administered
under largely French management but with Britain
owning forty-four per cent of the Company's shares.
The Company never owned the Canal; it owned the

concession to operate this crucial waterway that was on Egyptian territory, a waterway that united the Mediterranean and the Red Sea, vital to international shipping – the passage to India, to southern Africa, to the Far East.

There was a background to Nasser's action. He was angered by the withdrawal of the Anglo-American aid offer for his Aswan Dam project; Eden had initially favoured this, anxious to pre-empt Soviet influence with Nasser, and in the Middle East generally, but his attitude towards Nasser had hardened, as he came to see him as an enemy of the West. Eden acceded to US withdrawal from patronage of the Aswan Dam. Nasser reacted immediately and conclusively in the one way that he could, by taking over the Canal. Egypt's Canal would be managed by Egyptians – a step that vastly increased his popularity at home but challenged the West.

Over the Suez crisis lay the shadow of the Cold War. There was always the fear that Russia would make a move – exploit the situation to exert control over Middle Eastern oil supplies; it is always about oil, then as now – Suez, Iraq – the bulk of European oil supplies came through the Canal in the mid-century. And, more local and immediate, the simmering hostility between Israel and her Arab neighbours. The complexities of the situation have fattened the history books; to distil the international commotion of

1956 into a simple narrative is to leave out most of the surrounding clamour, but I am not writing history – I am trying to sort out what I now know happened and think of it against what seemed at the time to be happening. Now, I have all the advantages of hindsight, and the wisdoms of Peter Hennessy, Keith Kyle and others who have considered 1956 and drawn conclusions. Then, I was a twenty-three-year-old who, thanks to higher education but what now seems a deficient interest in current affairs, knew perhaps more about certain historic periods than what was going on in her own world. The Cold War was a term, merely; I would become more alert to that, grimly alert. The United Nations was a concept, and a good thing, but I was barely aware of it. I had never much listened to the battle cries of politicians, the cut and thrust of the House of Commons. That October, I paid attention, and about time too.

So, what happened then, shorn of surrounding clamour? Immediately after Nasser's seizing of the Canal on 26 October Eden set up a Cabinet committee – the Egypt Committee – to oversee the crisis. Its aims were uncompromising: to get rid of Nasser and see the Canal entrusted to international management. The expression 'regime change' was not yet around, but Iraq must spring to mind. With a colossal difference: Nasser was – in Eden's eyes at least – a threat to the West, but he was no Saddam Hussein.

He was not a vicious tyrant; Egypt's skirmishes with Israel did not compare with the invasion of Kuwait. Nasser had laid hands on what was seen as a Franco-British asset; his action might jeopardize the West's oil supplies. And Eden had become paranoiac about him.

The next weeks and months saw the clandestine manoeuvring that has become, in retrospect, the most significant feature of the Suez crisis: the Sèvres Protocol. This, in a nutshell, was a secret agreement between Britain, France and Israel by which Israel would invade the Sinai peninsula – Egyptian territory – whereupon British and French troops would intervene under the guise of peace-keeping, and thus occupy the Canal Zone. The details, and the agreement, were hammered out at a meeting hosted by the French in a Parisian suburban villa that had once been a safe house for the Resistance; the leading participants were Guy Mollet, the French Prime Minister, Israel's leader Ben-Gurion, and British Foreign Secretary Selwyn Lloyd, who seemed both at the time and subsequently to have wished he wasn't there. The Israelis were persuaded of their role as the pretext for intervention; the Franco-British objectives were clear – destroy the Egyptian army, bring down Nasser and occupy the Canal.

The British Cabinet was never informed about the Sèvres meeting; only a few of Eden's associates were in the know, the Foreign Secretary's presence was to be hushed up in perpetuity, any record was suppressed where possible. We know about it all now because there were records, people have talked. At the time, as things rushed ahead in October, unfolding precisely according to the Sèvres agreement, there were some suspicions. But only now has the great collusion become the essential – and shameful – aspect of the Suez crisis.

On 29 October Israeli paratroopers were dropped into Sinai twenty miles east of Suez, and a light division began to move in order to join up with them. At the same time an Anglo-French convoy with warships and supporting craft set sail for Port Said. On 31 October the first British bombs fell on airfields around Cairo, the idea being to neutralize or disperse the Egyptian air force so that it would not be a threat to the Israelis – which was what was done. By now, the United Nations was taking an active interest and calling for a cease-fire between Egypt and Israel – Egyptian forces were resisting in Sinai. On 5 November the British Cabinet decided that a cease-fire had not been achieved and that therefore occupation of the Canal Zone should take place. On 6 November there were sea-borne landings of British tanks and commandos. Fighting took place; seven hundred and fifty to one thousand Egyptians are thought to have died, British and French killed amounted to twenty-three. And then, later on the 6th, in response to the United Nations and to American pressure, Britain and France agreed to stop their action.

It was all very quick – a few days. There had of course been weeks of preparation; the stationing of the sea-borne force in Malta and Cyprus, the devising of an elaborate campaign of advance, *Musketeer*. Much of this had been all too apparent; you don't move aircraft carriers and cruisers around the Mediterranean without someone noticing, in particular the American Sixth Fleet, which had been acting as an interested shadow, and reminder of Eisenhower's displeasure at what was apparently brewing. But, when it all happened, it was done within a week – a week of newspaper headlines, mass protest meetings, furious exchanges in the House of Commons, argument in households up and down the land. Was this Britain standing up for our rights or an outrageous and illegal exercise of power?

For me, it was certainly outrageous, and also disturbingly evocative. The place-names – Suez, Ismailia, Qantara, Port Said. I had never been to Suez, which is the southernmost point of the Canal, where it joins the Red Sea. But Port Said was entirely familiar; the bustling harbour, presided over by the statue of de Lesseps. There, not that long ago, just over ten years earlier, I had stood on the deck of HMS *Ranchi* as the ship sailed past the statue, and had thought in a rather self-consciously grown-up way that this was the end of something. I was leaving Egypt for ever. The year 1956 was to be the end for de Lesseps: on 24 December the statue was blown off its plinth to the jeers of an angry crowd; apparently only his shoes remain, embedded in the concrete. As for Ismailia and Qantara, both were part of my childhood, the points at which you crossed the Canal when going to Palestine, whether by train or by car, in which case the car was driven on to a ferry, an exciting and hazardous process. At Ismailia my mother had had a row with an Egyptian customs official over two Palestinian tortoises I was importing in a shoebox: contraband, according to him. At Qantara I had inadvertently dropped my sandwich lunch into the Canal, leaning too far over the rail of the ferry. I knew the Canal; it was part of the landscape of the mind – a great reach of water, ships, the dockside commotion of shouting porters, people selling oranges and fizzy drinks, skulking pi-dogs, little boys begging for baksheesh. And here it was today the centre of world attention and, right now, apparently, out of action entirely, blocked by wrecks the Egyptians had sunk to that end.

In April 1957 the Canal reopened, under Egyptian management. The Suez crisis was over, except of course for the repercussions. It was a long time before Anglo-American relations recovered; for some, the crisis marked the end of Britain as a Great Power. Eden resigned in January 1957 (though he lived for another twenty years). The truth was that he had been ill throughout the crisis, following a gall-bladder operation some while earlier, and was heavily dependent on medication. It does seem that his condition may have had some effect on his state of mind, and his actions, during the crucial months of 1956. Certainly a number of his associates were surprised by his responses, their bewilderment expressed in their language at the time: 'gone bananas', 'bonkers'. His reputation never recovered – a tragedy for a man who had been a politician of integrity and a distinguished Foreign Secretary.

The Senior Common Rooms of Oxford settled back to more parochial matters of disagreement, except perhaps for St Antony's, which had always been concerned with the wider world. Jack and I got married; his Fellowship came to an end, we were expecting a baby, there were not many jobs around for young academics. In retrospect, we seem to have been extraordinarily unworried – no money, our home a two-room rented flat. As it was, Jack got a job – a Lectureship at the University of Swansea – we moved to Wales and the next stage in life began.

In November 2006, a conference took place at the School of Oriental and African Studies: 'Fifty years since Suez: from conflict to collaboration'. There were

British and Egyptian contributors, papers were read on political and economic relations and on cultural relations – the section to which I was asked to contribute. I talked about 'cultural confusion', about what it had been like to grow up knowing myself to be English, but identifying with Egypt, and feeling an alien when eventually I arrived in my own country. And I spoke also of my feelings at the time of the Suez crisis, about my sense of outrage at what my country was doing to the country with which I still identified, about the way in which the crisis made so many of us young sit up and take notice of a political climate. I felt rather out of place amid some distinguished academics and commentators, and was surprised to be warmly received – rapturously, indeed, in some quarters. Middle-aged Egyptian men came up afterwards, putting an arm round my shoulders, fixing me with those liquid, emotional brown eyes: 'Oh, Mrs Lively, you spoke to my heart!' I basked in brief undeserved glory, and went home thinking of how then had folded into now, the clamour of 1956 distilled into analysis and opinion – and my twenty-three-year-old self become an elderly woman whose mind she still tenuously inhabited.

Suez did not so much politicize me as join me to the times. Before that, I had not been paying attention – did not much read newspapers, was blithely cruising in a solipsistic world of my own. Plenty of the young do this; public affairs are not their concern, leave that to the oldies. At the other end of life, I look back at myself with surprise, and a certain impatience. How *young*. How – not innocent, but ignorant. And how judgemental I am being now, groomed by decades of newsprint, radio, television. We are indeed in, or of, the world, there's no escaping it, why should there not be a time of prelapsarian freedom?

Because I wouldn't want it now, I suppose I am saying. I can't do without the world. And perhaps that need is a characteristic particularly of later years. I want to know – must know – what the world is up to for as long as I am still a part of it, I feel – unsettled – without one ear cocked to the clamour of events. Wake up to the *Today* programme, on–off attention to that for an hour or so, read the paper, check in at one o'clock for the news, again at six, probably, and of course the television on at ten, before bed. Some of this was caught perhaps from Jack, for whom foreign travel was a torment unless he could lay hands on an English newspaper. But he was extremely concerned with politics; it was print he was mostly after – analysis and comment. For me, it is the narrative – the many narratives – the sense of an unstoppable progress, the march of time, everything going on everywhere, and because of the miracles of communication it is possible for me to know, sitting here thousands of miles away. Not a spectacle, but an abiding interest. How can you not be involved? These are your times, your world, even if those events are on the other side of it. And as for the narrative – you are a part of that, for better or for worse, whether the grey inexorable economic inevitabilities – recessions and recoveries and having less money or more – or the grand perilous global story.

That story was at its most perilous – or so it seemed – by the time I was a sentient adult. The Soviet invasion of Hungary exactly coincided with the Suez crisis. A deliberate coincidence, perhaps, and certainly one that meant the eyes of the world were focused elsewhere. But a reminder that the central matter of the day was the Cold War.

From the first test explosion of a Soviet atom bomb in 1949 to the Test Ban Treaties of the 1960s and the 1972 Anti-Ballistic Missile Treaty many people lived in a state of nuclear angst. I did. Not initially, not perhaps seriously until after the Korean War, not until there were constant reminders – the first thermonuclear tests, the stark assessments of what a hydrogen bomb could do, the crises, Khrushchev's threats, the constant lurking menace behind everything, over and beyond anything else. You got on with life – of course – you managed to put it all aside, and then it would come slamming back at you from the newspapers, from some new turn of events. It was always potentially there, that tight knot in the stomach.

I looked at my small children, on a beach in Swansea, and thought that there was a real chance they would never grow up. I have that moment still: the sand, the sea, them with their buckets and spades, and the sense of apocalypse. I have the moment, it is still there, but I can't now believe in it. Post-apocalypse – if that is where we are – it is hard to recover that abiding shadow, the spectre that stalked the days. Again, I go to the books, to find out where it went, what really happened.

Put at its simplest, this happened: because in any war between the Soviets and the West nuclear weapons would have been used, no such war took place. The Cold War was precisely that – cold. Mutually Assured Destruction saved the day, which was what was being gambled at the time, but when you were living through the gamble, that was all that you were aware of – the rolling of the dice, the arms race, the ratcheting-up of manic firepower, the concept of retaliation, tit for tat, city for city, Armageddon.

Jack and I did not join CND, go on Aldermaston marches. I can remember being uncertain, undecided, and then persuaded by his doubts about unilateral disarmament. In those early days of the bomb, Russian bombers could not reach the United States; the United Kingdom, with its American bases, would be likely to be the primary target. Discussion raged, always, accentuating that knot of fear.

And then, in 1962, there came the nine days of the Cuba crisis. Jack went to the university each morning, and I would wonder if I would see him again. My neighbour drove our five-year-olds to the school a mile away; the plan was that she would dash to fetch them if the four-minute warning went, while I minded our younger ones. You read in the papers of those who had retreated to the Highlands, or the west of Ireland. At one o'clock, at six o'clock, I would switch on the TV – those pulsating concentric rings that heralded the news back then, I can see them still – and I would watch the footage of the Russian missile-bearing ships, the faces of Kennedy, of Khrushchev. Waiting. Waiting.

Khrushchev backed off. It was over. It hadn't happened, but by a whisker, or so it felt. And still does, to those who have analysed that time, and those who were at the heart of events. And we know now, as we did not back then, of the elaborate preparations for a nuclear holocaust. The government – around four thousand people from various government departments – would have holed up in a bunker close to Box Hill near Corsham in Wiltshire, sixty miles of tunnels that had been used in the last war as an ammunition depot, a factory and an RAF operations centre. Assuming that there had been sufficient warning, sufficient build-up to a nuclear exchange, for them to get there; assuming that people agreed to go, leaving any surviving families to the mercy of radiation and the anticipated breakdown of any kind of social order. Ten Soviet hydrogen bombs on Britain would have killed nearly a third of the population and left a swathe of others seriously injured. With the government festering beneath Box Hill, the police and the military would have assumed control. Not that control seems a feasible term; thinking about this scenario, you move at once into fiction, as plenty have done, since: the absence of all facilities, a free-for-all where food was concerned, marauding gangs, violence, the rule of law a distant nirvana. It has been imagined many times, in print and film, and chills the blood.

Peter Hennessy has written graphically of the Cuba week, of how, if Khrushchev had not changed course at lunchtime on 28 October 1962, Prime Minister Macmillan would have set World War III drills in motion – the Transition to War Committee was nearly called that weekend. But it wasn't, the world breathed again, and one reads now with astonishment, and a kind of nervous hilarity, Hennessy's description of the arrangement whereby, should the Prime Minister have been in his car, on the move, at a moment of crisis, he would have been reached by way of the Automobile Association's radio network, whereupon his driver would have sought a phone box from which the Prime Minister could make the essential call: '. . . only the Brits . . . could have dreamt up a system whereby the Prime Minister is envisaged making a reverse-charge call from a phone box to authorize nuclear retaliation.'

Indeed, one reads of all these meticulous, bureaucratic preparations with a certain incredulity. They had to, of course, that is what civil servants are for, what a government has to do. But it is eerie now to think that all this was going on – the discussions, the paperwork – while the rest of us were listening to the Cold War rattling of sabres, understanding what thermonuclear meant, looking with fear at our children playing on a beach. The plan for removal of art treasures before nuclear attack – eleven pantechnicons with military escort to quarries in Wales and Wiltshire; the Corsham bunker with its bedsteads, its ovens, its cups and saucers, equipped for post-holocaust government. Government? Who, or what, would they have governed?

Escalation: the word that haunted, all through the sixties, the seventies, until at last the Vietnam War came to an end. Would the Russians come in? Would there be a direct Soviet–United States confrontation, spiralling up from that distant, localized conflict? It was as though the Cold War was already starting to smoulder, the embers poised for a conflagration if the wind blew the wrong way.

Again, it didn't happen. The history of the late twentieth century seems like a sequence of reprieves, until the one great, startling positive of the fall of the

Berlin Wall, the collapse of communism. I remember Jack, a political theorist, watching the events of 1989 and the end of the Soviet Union with amazement, almost with disbelief. And with exhilaration. He was the author of what is still seen as a seminal work on the definition of democracy; he had an interest.

Thirty years earlier – the summer of 1959 – there had been a summer school in Oxford for a party of Soviet academics and their students – quite a radical departure at that point, surprising that the Russians agreed to it. Jack was one of those giving lectures and leading seminars. I think that the general theme was Britain and its institutions, so he must surely have given them a run-down on democracy, but what I remember is his wry amusement at the appreciative reception of Harold Nicolson, a visiting lecturer whose subject was the monarchy, and the irritation of the Oxford organizers at the KGB man – ostensibly a professor of something or other – who sat through all sessions reading *Pravda* and smoking a cigarette. Jack did everything he could to make contact with the small group of students, who were under draconian supervision but occasionally managed to break free. I remember Vanya, a particularly charming and exuberant boy, vanishing into the garden with the hostess's Italian au pair girl at one evening party, and being hauled back by the KGB man. On the last night, at another party, everyone fairly tipsy, we hugged

Vanya and said we hoped, we really hoped, we'd see him again. His exuberance fell away; he pulled a face – 'No, no, you will never see me again.' He was well aware of the system under which he was living, would continue to live.

In 1984 I had my own glimpse of that system, as a member of a delegation of six writers sent by the Great Britain–USSR Association (which was sponsored by the Foreign Office) to have talks with representatives of the Soviet Writers' Union. We were there for ten days, first in Moscow having conference-style talks (immense long table, everyone wired up to microphones and headphones for simultaneous translation) and interminable toast-punctuated evening banquets, and then a few days' rest and recreation at Yalta on the Crimean coast as guests of the Ukrainian Writers' Union.

My diary of that visit is in a separate exercise book; we had been warned that if we were keeping notes we should have them with us at all times – our rooms and our luggage would undoubtedly be searched. They were; I found the contents of my suitcase slightly rearranged. Reading those scrawled pages now, I am at once taken back to the baffling, frequently tense, always inscrutable practices of that encounter with Soviet life. I wrote of the initial speech by their spokesman: '"We know a great deal about you all," says Kuznetzov after his remarks of greeting. Which was somehow unsettling rather than flattering.' And of Red Square: 'an eerie place, that rippling scarlet flag in the black night, hushed religious atmosphere in the small group in front of Lenin's tomb, people standing in silence or speaking in quiet voices. Statuesque policemen facing each other at the entrance, which was a crack open – a suspended feeling as though someone might come out – Lenin? The mausoleum is a monolithic slab-like structure. It – and the posture of the policeman – made me think of Pharaonic tombs in Upper Egypt.'

We were shepherded throughout by two minders – a middle-aged woman called Tatiana, who was a translator, we were told, and Georgy, head of one of the state publishing houses, specializing in English translation, and both of them, we had been warned back in London, members of the KGB. My experience of Georgy veered from bizarre to chilling, when he accompanied us to the Crimea: 'Somewhat odd to hurtle through the Crimea [in the coach from the airport] with Georgy, emitting the vodka fumes of his last three heavy evenings, bellowing an exegesis of the early works of Evelyn Waugh into my ear (apparently he is very popular here). It is really hard to credit that a Siberian public library he recently visited had copies of *Vile Bodies* and *Black Mischief* so heavily read as to be physical wrecks, but so he said.' On another

occasion, though, walking with him along the Yalta
seafront, from which one gazed out over the Black
Sea towards an empty horizon, somewhere beyond
which, way beyond, lay Turkey, I commented (deliberately, provocatively) on the total absence of sailing
boats or power boats off this coast, that would be a
usual feature of resort shores: '"No, here there are
not. People are just not interested, you see, Penelope,
it is a thing they do not much like to do." Shrugging.'

Some of the Soviet delegates did their best to drag
politics into the agenda: 'an address on the function
of the critic was for the most part a diatribe about the
arms race, the evil forces of violence and a denunci-
ation of capitalist greed and irresponsibility'. We
were aware that all of them were necessarily figures
acceptable to the regime, and some of them out and
out apparatchiks: 'People keep vanishing and being
replaced by others in the Russian delegation. On the
first day a woman scientist was there who appeared
to have been drafted in at the last moment to refute
our provocative item on the agenda about the paucity
of Russian women writers [initially there had been
no woman member of their team; we were fielding
three]. She appeared from her remarks to be a bio-
chemist but said she also wrote novels and claimed
this was a mass phenomenon – "the unity of the artists and the scientists".'

They all disregarded the agreement that none of

us, on either side, would speak on any topic for more than four minutes – this, we soon realized, was simply not compatible with Russian style: 'I have learned never to take at face value the expression "a short comment upon the last speaker's remarks".' Simultaneous translation meant that relays of translators staggered exhausted from their booths, and produced some interesting renderings: 'We cannot throw away a baby with the water from the basin.' And each evening there were those formal dinners: eat, a Russian rises to make a toast, a Brit rises to respond, eat a bit more, repeat the ritual. London had told us sternly that, while it would be all right for the women to take a token sip of each vodka toast, offence would be taken if the men did not down the glass – they must drink for England. Much mineral water was consumed by the British delegation during the morning sessions.

We arrived at the final session to find that everything was set for it to be televised: 'As soon as the cameras were rolling Kuznetzov launched into an account of how our discussions had been of literature and writing but we had of course concerned ourselves with matters of the writer's commitment to society and especially the overwhelming question of international peace and how to counter the forces of aggression. Consecutive translation, so we had to wait a few minutes to get it, and then all froze with annoyance. Francis King splendidly countered with a sharp piece about how he couldn't recall that we had discussed any such thing, and we each said something to the same effect (which no doubt they will edit out of the programme).'

In the Crimea we stayed at one of the thousand-bedroom hotels built for the recreation of the Soviet masses, sat about on a 'skimpy pebbly beach littered with very fat Germans and Russians. Lukewarm completely inactive sea full of small jellyfish in which you loll wondering what to do next. Sat and listened to Georgy (wearing jockey shorts and a scarlet peaked cap) holding forth on his degree dissertation at Moscow University and the relative merits of Muriel Spark and Doris Lessing.' And it was in the Crimea that there was the curious episode of the man who fell into conversation with some of us as we walked on the promenade one evening. Speaking good English, he explained that he was a seaman who had worked on a Russian refrigerated container ship plying the Baltic that had stopped off frequently at Hull, where he had English friends. Next day we were taken by coach to a palace along the coast, a place amidst an immense park with a cliff path along which we walked to admire the view: 'And half-way along out from behind a tree appeared, incredibly, the seaman from the refrigerated container ship, clad only in diminutive shorts and dripping with sweat, whom we had met on the promenade in Yalta the night before. We could scarcely believe our eyes. The sense of paranoia and disorientation induced by this country is now complete. Anyway, he ambled along beside us, a very nice fellow, talking of his affection for the English and taste for English books, etc. with Tatiana, distinctly rattled, muttering, "I think this is a very boring man, we must get free from him."'

Coincidence? Or not? Had he wanted something of us? We speculated. We never knew.

Years later, I turned that episode into a short story, one that was to do with quite other things but was prompted by that time and place, an instance of the way in which, for me, short stories have always risen from some real-life moment but have then expanded into something quite detached from that.

And this was the abiding sense of opacity and ambiguity that made that taste of Soviet life so unnerving. You never really knew if things were as you thought they were, or quite other. Some people were genuinely open and friendly; others were opaque. The ten days were demanding, exhausting, intriguing; and occasionally hilarious. One evening, after a reception at the British Embassy, we managed to elude our minders and ended up in a restaurant where a large party of Romanians at a neighbouring table were singing national songs: 'Melvyn [Bragg] insisted we must counter so we belted out John Brown's Body,

Tipperary, etc. until the Romanians announced themselves defeated and departed with much flashing of teeth and hand-shaking.'

My Soviet diary ends: 'Things I never want to see again: a Russian bath towel, which is two feet by one foot and made of sandpaper; the lift at the Yalta hotel, full of large sweating people all pushing each other; the beach at Yalta; Georgy; the grey carcasses of cooked chicken offered for breakfast in the hotel canteen; a microphone; Georgy.'

A diary is an ambivalent reflection of memory. Much that is in mine I no longer remember; the diary is testimony but memory has wiped. And, conversely, stuff lies still in the head that apparently escaped the diary. From the Soviet visit, I have further shreds: our final hours before the plane home, when we spent our remaining roubles (a daily subsistence 'fee' which could not be changed into hard currency) on large bowls of caviar for afternoon tea; Tatiana, on the plane to the Crimea, ordering several rows of fellow passengers to their feet with a mere gesture and tilt of her head, in order to have us seated together rather than scattered around the plane and thus not under her eye – how did they know that she was a person you had to obey? And I remember a visit to Chekhov's house in the Crimea – a rare privilege, apparently, not generally open – small cluttered rooms with photos and personal possessions and I wanted to keep quiet, and had that sudden blinding recognition that the past is true, that Chekhov had indeed existed, had been here, once, where we now were.

I have never been back to Russia; the Soviet Union that we fleetingly experienced is now a historical phenomenon. Someone of my age, living there now, will have known an extraordinary social and political upheaval, in an incredibly short space of time. Born into one world, they live now in another – from totalitarianism to democracy, of a kind. Accelerated change, unlike the slow social metamorphosis of this country – indeed, of most politically stable countries in peacetime.

But change there has been, here, and when I squint back at my twenty-year-old self I realize that she would be surprised by two of the major ways in which assumptions and expectations have mutated, and would be startled, probably, to understand that she herself would shortly be a manifestation of a third. I want now to look at this: the three ways in which, to my mind, our society has revised itself during my lifetime – one seismic, one determined and by and large successful, one opaque and generating argument.

Opacity and argument first. The shifting ground of class and social distinctions. Is the twenty-first century any closer to achieving the classless society to which John Major looked forward in 1990? On the

face of it – no. That said, the social landscape of the
1950s looks very different from that of today – more
predictable, more rigid, you could place a person by
how they spoke, how they dressed. There is a flexibil-
ity today that is less to do with social mobility than
with a more open-minded approach; perhaps we are
just less bothered by apparent distinctions. But the
polarizations are still there – the violent apposition of
those who have and those who have not.

Any comments I make on social change come from
a single perspective. Not unusual – most people live
out their lives within a particular context of society.
Social mobility? Well, yes – there are plenty also who
have changed ground, hopped up a rung or three –
social mobility is usually talking about improved
rather than reduced circumstances. I have a friend my
own age who says, 'People like you and me have gone
down in the world.' What he means is that we live a
lot more humbly than our grandparents did, though
his were rather more amply situated than mine. But
that is to do with a general historical shunt rather
than families in decline. The middle class does not
live like it did in the early twentieth century: the servicing, the expectations. Well, some do, I suppose,
but none that I know. And there's the difference. The
middle class in which, and with which, I have lived is
not the same as the one my grandmother knew.

So I have lived on ground that was shifting, but it

did so rather suddenly, in the mid-century, before I was firmly enough established to notice. I never expected to live like my grandparents had. Just as well. We began married life on Jack's salary as a university lecturer, and academic salaries have never been other than frugal. But we could manage – just – the mortgage on an Edwardian semi in Swansea with a little garden; that is middle-class living, then or now. And he was in what would be regarded as a profession, if that is a defining feature of the middle class, even if he had arrived there from quite elsewhere.

What I am trying to say is that I have observed rather than experienced. My only swerve was to marry a young man from the northern working class, the two of us meeting up in the fresh air of the mid-century, both liberated into the social neutrality of higher education. But he had, and continued to have, the advantage of a dual perspective; if he were here still he would be looking over my shoulder at this point and making stringent comments.

However, to observe is to experience, in one sense. If those around you are behaving differently, if assumptions and expectations and opinions mutate then you are going to mutate with them, unless you are peculiarly intransigent or holed up in some fortress of religious or political belief. I have been formed in and by late twentieth-century Britain; I reflect my times. I can't think or see as my grandmother did. She was born when Disraeli was Prime Minister, died in the age of Harold Wilson. For her, class differences were not only inevitable but desirable; she seemed to be unaware of homosexuality and I never knew if this was genuine ignorance or tacit rejection; her view of gender distinction was that men were a different breed from women, you deferred to them in some respects and recognized that they had special needs – cooked breakfast and somewhere to go and smoke. Sex was unmentionable. And alongside all this ran an ingrained sense of obligation; you were more comfortable than most, it was therefore beholden upon you to help others. She did. A Christian ethic – and she was of course paid-up Church of England – and also a manifestation of the arbitrary system of gift aid inherited from the nineteenth century that the Welfare State was to supplant.

I imagine that my own grandchildren when elderly will cast a critical eye upon my own mind-set of today. How I would love to know in what ways it appears – will appear – archaic or perverse. Ours is on the whole a pretty tolerant and liberal-minded age; can tolerance be stretched yet further? Some would say, indeed yes. That there are still areas of ignorance and insensitivity. Or could there be a reversion – could we come to seem unprincipled, licentious, devoid of standards? Somewhere, at some level, the seeds of change will be starting already to sprout. Society does not support stasis.

My grandmother's house, and the sense in which its contents seemed to have become signifiers for the century, inspired a book for me – *A House Unlocked* – and I discussed there the shifting pattern of social expectations over her lifetime, and the way in which my perception of the world differed from hers. My own marriage had come to seem to me nicely symbolic of the reforms of the mid-century, which meant that two people who could not otherwise have met came together because of the Butler Education Act of 1946.

There is plenty of informed argument about the degree of social change in the last fifty years: the answers can be opaque, conflicting. But there are two areas of change that seem to me in one case indisputable and in the other seismic: the expectations of women, and attitudes towards homosexuality.

When I was a small girl, there was a teatime ritual. She – it was always a she – who took the last cake, bun, sandwich from the plate was entitled to a wish; you had a choice of wish – a handsome husband or ten thousand a year. Nobody ever chose the ten thousand. There were various related strictures, too: if you don't sit straight you'll grow up round-shouldered and no one will ever marry you; if you make faces the wind will change and you'll get stuck like that and no one will ever marry you. The central female concern was being made clear.

An atavistic concern. Marriage – partnership – is a natural and normal aspiration. Most people would prefer to go through life in alliance with someone they love, and most want children. But the teatime wish husband was about status, not inclinations. Unmarried, you would have reduced social status – the ancient social stigma, the heart of the matter in any Jane Austen novel. And, of course, in the past the spinster's position was precarious economically. But cashflow can't have much entered into the teatime wish choice, or more would have plumped for the ten thousand. Indeed, my recollection is that it was seen as ludicrous to do so, if not a touch disgraceful.

A recent television programme featured an organization that makes a packet out of running seminars for people who want to become rich enough fast enough to be able to live off their cash without ever working. The accumulation of a property portfolio was the scheme, and it was clear that most of those paying a wad in order to learn how to go about this were already in catastrophic financial debt to the organization. Many were young women, and their attitudes startled me. Not only did they feel they 'ought' to be millionaires, but they felt that they ought not to have to work; work was not their aspiration, what they wanted was a certain lifestyle, a nicely well-heeled lifestyle free of obligation.

Dupes, I fear, poor dears, and I hope there weren't

too many of them. But they did make me think about feminism, and what it originally meant, and to wonder what those girls would have thought about that. Feminist aspiration, back in the sixties and seventies, was all about work: equal opportunity in the workplace, equal pay, equality of esteem across the board. The feminist did not want to be a trophy wife, or a millionaire; she wanted respect and recognition for who she was, and what she could do.

Have we got what they were demanding? Today, it seems that two-thirds of low-paid workers are women, and that women in full-time work earn sixteen per cent less than men. So the answer would seem to be no, not entirely. And one hears constantly of women bringing claims against employers on the grounds that male colleagues were preferred for promotion, and for unfair dismissal when pregnant. The glass ceiling exists, apparently, and every woman has to balance career against motherhood.

But I am concerned with assumptions and perceptions, and it is impossible to deny that a young woman today steps out into a very different society from that of fifty years ago. Depending, of course, on what sort of young woman she is. The feminist movement was ever a middle-class movement, and there is a big divide today between the professional woman, who may well be earning the same as a man, and the vastly larger female workforce that is cleaning offices, stacking shelves and sitting at checkouts and mostly does not. Plenty of ground still to be gained, but the seminal matter is that a point has been made, slowly and inexorably, over the last decades: it is no longer possible to treat women differently from men and not be held to account.

There's more, much more. Women have surged into higher education. At my university, in the 1950s, we were one woman to ten men. This did give us a certain commodity value – ten chaps to pick from – but what I wonder now is why we didn't question this. Why didn't we look at that morass of males and think: they can't all be so much brighter than lots of girls who aren't here. Today, that university has near parity between men and women, actually tipped slightly in favour of women.

We were the pre-feminist generation. Long postsuffragette, but apparently not awake to the stillprevailing anachronisms. There were exceptions, of course, those already sniffing the air, but on the whole my generation now seems to me to have been somewhat inert. Ten years later the climate would be very different.

One thing above all, though, reminded us that it was hazardous to be a woman. We girls of the midcentury lived with one eye on the calendar. There was far less discussion of sex back then but it was quite as brisk a component of student life as it is today. We just made less fuss about it, kept it under cover, mindful of what was likely to happen to any girl who got pregnant. She would probably be sent down, dismissed from the university, quietly and conclusively. And the man? Oh, no. Those were pre-pill days; contraception was unreliable, and most of us were pretty uninformed about it. So girls brave enough to embark on a relationship lurched from month to month, eyeing the diary and hoping for the best. And this was going on up and down the land, of course. No difficulties back then for childless couples hoping to adopt; the relevant institutions were well stocked with babies discreetly unloaded.

Sometime in the early sixties Jack, who taught PPE – politics, philosophy and economics – was interviewing a candidate for a place at his Oxford college, a bluntly-spoken northern lad. He asked the boy which aspect of contemporary society he saw as most in need of reform. The answer bounced back without a moment's hesitation: 'Reform of the abortion laws and legalization of homosexuality.' The boy got a place, needless to say.

We all knew that you could get an abortion. We had all heard of someone who had. We knew that it involved furtive enquiries, a clandestine visit to a closely guarded address, the handing over of an envelope of bank notes – a couple of hundred quid, a fortune in those days, if the address was not in some back street but somewhere you stood a better chance of a medically qualified practitioner and, indeed, of survival. We all knew the myths about self-induced abortion: the glass of gin and a hot bath, the trampolining on the bed. And that they did not work, by and large. The shadow of that fate hung over any burgeoning love affair – just, frankly, as it always had done. We were in exactly the same position as the Victorian skivvy, or the medieval village girl.

So what a catalyst for change – the pill. And how quickly we have forgotten just what a revolution it heralded. Not just in giving women the power of choice, but in reshaping attitudes towards sex and sexuality. For the first time in human history a young woman – any woman – can enter into a sexual relationship without fretting constantly that she will be landed with an untimely baby. And it is openly acknowledged that sexual activity takes place, everywhere and all the time, which may sound an absurd statement, but set it against the paranoid reticence of much of early twentieth-century society, when someone like my grandmother – far from untypical – went through life avoiding all mention or recognition of that most basic human concern. And she had three children.

She and her like represented, I suppose, the last gasp of Victorian middle-class sublimation, soldiering on into the twentieth century and surrounded by an insidious tide of provocative new behaviour. Elsewhere, things were already different. Take that emblematic Bloomsbury drawing-room gathering when Lytton Strachey pointed a finger at a stain on Vanessa Bell's dress and announced: 'Semen?' Sometime in the 1920s. In most drawing-rooms the word would have been unfamiliar to many and unmentionable for all. Bloomsbury was ahead of the game, and even today Strachey might seem a touch candid. But the point is that the shift had already begun, the unstoppable slide towards entire permissiveness, to a climate in which nothing is unmentionable and most of it is mentioned all the time. And this has happened over sixty years or so – not unlike the reverse journey from the cheerful profanity of the eighteenth century to the constraint of the Victorian age. Maybe it will switch once more and my descendants will find themselves with pursed lips and averted eyes.

Feminism; the pill; sexual candour. But there is one aspect of change in assumptions and attitudes over my lifetime that seems to me seismic – so rapid, so absolute.

When I was nine, one summer in Alexandria, I fell in love with a young man. He was twenty-eight, and a sort of relative – his sister was married to my uncle, Oliver Low. Hugh Gibb was serving with the Eighth Army in the Libyan campaign, and on his leaves from the desert, he would visit us, often joining my mother at Sidi Bishr, Alexandria's prime beach, where she held lunch parties from a rented cabin. Hugh was popular, charming, and I was besotted. We surfed together; I was pretty good with a surfboard, and those moments are with me still – the careful choice of wave, and then the glorious slide down its flank, with Hugh a few feet away, head turned sideways, beaming encouragement as the wave broke and we rushed towards the shore.

A few years later, in London now, Hugh turned up for a family lunch at my grandmother's house in Harley Street. Uncle Oliver was there – various others. And Hugh – still charming, still everyone's favourite person, still being nice to me (who was by then perhaps fourteen). After he had gone, I remarked to Oliver, complacently, that Hugh was not married (could he be waiting till I was old enough . . .).

Oliver laughed: 'My dear girl, Hugh's queer.'

Queer? *Queer?* In what way?

Did I ask for an explanation? Was one given? I don't know – and actually Oliver was being quite risqué, talking like that to a fourteen-year-old, but he was the bohemian end of my father's family, my favourite uncle, and he liked me, as a seemingly bookish sort of girl with whom he enjoyed a chat. Suffice it that, somehow, I knew from then on that there were men who weren't interested in women, and if Hugh was one of them then that was that. I fell out of love at once, sensibly enough, though

I continued to like Hugh and to bask if he noticed me.

When my granddaughter Izzy was not much older than I had been then, I took her to a production of *The Importance of Being Earnest*. She knew little of Oscar Wilde, so on the way to the theatre I filled in with some facts – the life, the scandal, the trial, the imprisonment. When I was done she exploded: 'I don't believe you! He was sent to prison because he was *gay!*'

A fifty-year gap, or thereabouts. One adolescent who had never heard of homosexuality; another who didn't realize that it had once been illegal. A chasm of understanding and assumption.

So by the time I was grown-up I was well aware of homosexuality. There was the occasional scandal – some high-profile figure arrested, some peer or actor whose misfortune was relished and prolonged by the newspapers. But it seems to me that my student generation was still wonderfully naïve. Looking back, I can identify contemporaries both male and female who were undoubtedly gay, but this was never spoken of, or at least not in the circles in which I moved, and in some cases I wonder if they themselves recognized their own nature. And this was the early 1950s; legalization 'between consenting adults' was only just over ten years off.

Within half a century the most abiding sexual taboo has vanished. Yes, there are still pockets of homophobia, but by and large same-sex relationships are accepted as a norm. The 2011 census asked if you were in a same-sex civil partnership or, indeed, a registered same-sex civil partnership (along with your ethnic group, if mixed/multiple: White and Black Caribbean, White and Black African, White and Asian . . . one imagined households up and down the land puzzling over their correct definition). The census is the status quo made manifest, or rather, the bureaucratic drive to identify the status quo. In 1951 they were exercised about the fertility and duration of marriage, the dates of cessation of full-time education, and how many outside loos the nation still had; a question compiler of back then, fast-forwarded to 2011 and confronted with registered same-sex civil partnerships, would have gasped in disbelief.

But the census tells it as it is, an unblinking social snapshot, and this is the way we live now, by grace of the extraordinary tidal wave of change unleashed by the legislation of 1967. Change not just in what people may do now, but in how others view them, which seems to me the most remarkable aspect – the overturning of an entire history of prejudice and denial. An upheaval neatly slotted into my lifetime, so that I grew up to the backdrop of one set of assumptions and sign off in a very different society.

Memory

A couple of years ago, Izzy yearned for an old-fashioned manual typewriter: 'Vintage!' A Smith Corona was found off eBay, and she rejoiced in it until a new ribbon became necessary, and then no one could work out how to change the ribbon. I was summoned: 'I can't believe we're going to Granny for technical support.' I sat at the machine, looked, did not know how it was done, but lo! my fingers did. They remembered. You lifted out the old reel, put the new one on, thus, you slotted the ribbon through there, and there, pushed that lever, wound the end of the ribbon round the empty reel and caught it on that prong. There! My brain hadn't remembered, but my fingers had – veterans of manual typewriters. That was how it felt, anyway.

This is an instance of what is called procedural memory, that aspect of memory whereby we remember how to do something. How to ride a bicycle is the example frequently cited, but I prefer my typewriter experience, or Vladimir Nabokov's of pushing a pram, he being that most refined authority on memory: 'You know, I still feel in my wrists certain echoes of the pram-pusher's knack, such as, for example, the glib downward pressure one applied to the handle in order to have the carriage tip up and climb the curb.' Yes, yes – and a sensation alien to those who have known only the abrupt tilt required for a pushchair or the buggy of today. My first pram, as a very young mother, was one of those sleek majestic cruisers, and my wrists too respond.

There is procedural memory, and then there is semantic memory, which enables us to know that this thing with two wheels is a bike, and that object is a typewriter – the memory facility which retains facts, language, all forms of knowledge without reference to context. And finally, and crucially, there is episodic or autobiographical memory, which gives the context, reminds me that my student bike was dark blue with my initials painted in white, that the baby in the sleek pram once grabbed the shopping, and squeezed ripe tomatoes all over everything. Autobiographical memory is random, non-sequential, capricious, and without it we are undone.

Much of what goes on in the mind is recollection, memory. This is not thought – it is an involuntary procession of images, ranging from yesterday to long ago, interspersed with more immediate signals like: must remember to phone so-and-so, or, what shall I have for lunch? Pure thought is something else – it requires conscious effort and is hard to achieve. The Borges story about the boy cursed – not blessed, cursed – with total recall, with a memory of everything, demonstrates how punishing that would be, how he remembers 'not only every leaf of every tree in every patch of forest, but every time he had perceived or imagined that leaf'. And, crucially, he did not think: 'To think is to ignore (or forget) differences, to generalize, to abstract.' It is the mind's holy grail, thought, and the process hardest to control – erratic, and prone to every kind of hijack. What bubbles up most of the time is memory, no more and no less.

Memory and anticipation. What has happened, and what might happen. The mind needs its tether in time, it must know where it is – in the perpetual slide of the present, with the ballast of what has been and the hazard of what is to come. Without that, you are adrift in the wretched state of Alzheimer's, or you are an amnesiac.

Amnesia disrupts autobiographical memory. In retrograde amnesia, everything is forgotten that happened before amnesia struck; in anterograde amnesia, memories can no longer be stored, the past is kept, but the future – passing time – cannot become a part of it. In dementia, life takes place in a segment of time without past or future. For mental stability we need the three kinds of memory to be fighting fit – procedural, semantic, autobiographical. And never mind that autobiographical memory is full of holes – it is meant to be like that. There is what we remember, and there is the great dark cavern of what we have forgotten, and why some stuff goes there and something else does not is the territory of the analysts, where I cannot venture. We forget – we forget majestically – and that seems to be an essential part of memory's function, whether it is the significant forgetting of sublimation, or denial, or whatever, or the mundane daily forgetting of where the car keys have got to, or those elusive names that so challenge us. William James is elegant on that particular problem: 'Suppose we try to recall a forgotten name. The state of our consciousness is peculiar. There is a gap there, but no mere gap. It is a gap that is intensely active. A sort of a wraith of a name is in it, beckoning in a given direction.' I love the concept of the active gap, the wraith, and know them well: that evasive name of mine has a T somewhere about it, or possibly a P . . . And it is good to feel companionate with a brilliant thinker of a hundred years ago, irritably flogging his mind because he can't remember what that man he met last week is called. But he doesn't put forward any theory as to why it is names that are most vulnerable. I am still waiting.

The memory that we live with – the form of memory that most interests me – is the moth-eaten version of our own past that each of us carries around, depends on. It is our ID; this is how we know who we are and where we have been.

That, presumably, is why we spend so much time foraging around in it, in that unconsidered, involuntary way – we are checking it out, touching base, letting it demonstrate that it is still in good working order. This morning, while going about ordinary morning business – shower, breakfast, read newspaper – I have visited Seattle, where once years ago I was taken to the fish market, this memory prompted by an item on the radio about fish stocks – I saw those huge Alaskan salmon again, laid out on the slab; I have seen my aunt Rachel, and heard her voice, conjured up by a painting of hers that I pass on the way down to the kitchen; the orange in the fruit bowl there became the one through which I once stuck a skewer, trying to reproduce for four-year-old granddaughter Rachel the turning of the world, she having asked – inconveniently, while I was making the gravy for the Christmas turkey – why it gets dark at night. None of this is sought, hunted down – it just pops up, arbitrary, part of the stockpile. And each memory brings some tangential thought, or at least until that is clipped short by the ongoing morning and its demands. The whole network lurks, all the time, waiting for a thread to be picked up, followed, allowed to vibrate. My story; your story.

Except that it is an entirely unsatisfactory story. The novelist in me – the reader, too – wants shape and structure, development, a theme, insights. Instead of which there is this assortment of slides, some of them welcome, others not at all, defying chronology, refusing structure. The Seattle salmon, my aunt, that

Christmas orange are simply shuffled together –
make what you like of it.

We do just that, endlessly – it is the abiding challenge
and mystery, memory. I have to invoke Sir Thomas
Browne again: 'Darkness and light divide the course of
time, and oblivion shares with memory, a great part
even of our living beings; we slightly remember our
felicities, and the smartest stroaks of affliction leave
but short smart upon us . . . To be ignorant of evils to
come, and forgetful of evils past, is merciful provision
in nature, whereby we digest the mixture of our few
and evil days, and, our delivered senses not relapsing
into cutting remembrances, our sorrows are not kept
raw by the edge of repetitions.' Exquisitely put, but I'd
take issue with some of that, which seems to be letting
memory off rather lightly – the cutting remembrances
are around all right, I'd say, and the stroaks of affliction. It is the view of memory as we'd like it to be,
rather than as it is. Or is there a premature glimmer of
psychological theories far in the future – ideas about
suppressed memories? 'Forgetful of evils past . . .' –
denial? Suffice it that he is thinking about the operation
of memory, and with such style that you can't but mull
over the words, the phrases.

Joseph Brodsky thought memory 'a substitute for the
tail that we lost for good in the happy process of evolution. It directs our movements, including migration.
Apart from that, there is something clearly atavistic in

the very process of recollection, if only because such a process is never linear.' His own migration from youth as an active opponent of the regime in Soviet Russia, with accompanying punishments, to exile in America as a celebrated poet and commentator, gave him a striking memory trail, though he says, oddly, 'I remember rather little of my own life and what I do remember is of small consequence.' But he had considered memory: 'What memory has in common with art is the knack for selection, the taste for detail . . . Memory contains precisely details, not the whole picture; highlights, if you will, not the entire show.'

All the best commentary on the working of memory seems to me to share this emphasis on 'the knack for selection, the taste for detail'. Nabokov's 'series of spaced flashes' – and I want to get on to them later. Just as the most effective method of memoir writing seems to be to focus on that, to try to reflect the processes of memory itself rather than the artificial plod through time of routine autobiography. When I did that myself, nearly twenty years ago, in a memoir of childhood, it was because I realized that that childhood was there in my mind still, but in the form of these finite glimpses of that time, not sequential but coexisting, each of them succinct, clear, usually wordless, and conjuring up still those frozen moments of a time and a place. Most people remember childhood in that way, I think, and in old age these assorted shards in the head seem to become sharper still; they assert themselves when a conversation you had last week has been wiped, along with a friend's name and the whereabouts of your Senior Railcard. Childhood memories have a high visual content – I certainly found that, as Egypt surged up in bits and pieces – the buff and brown bark of a eucalyptus tree, the brilliant green of a praying mantis, the white of roosting egrets on a tree by the Cairo Nile. Coleridge noted this feature, thinking about the nature of memory, and wondered if the visual quality was enhanced because of the lack of a spoken element: 'I hold that association depends in a much greater degree on the recurrence of resembling *states of feeling* than in trains of ideas; that the recollection of early childhood in latest old age depends on and is explicable by this.' And also, surely, because of the novelty, the fresh vision of the physical world – Wordsworth's splendour in the grass – when things are seen for the first time, the imprint that remains.

This would seem to account also for the capricious nature of time. It accelerates, it has broken into a gallop by the time you are old – a day then has nothing of the remembered pace of childhood days, which inched ahead, stood still at points, ambled from lunchtime to teatime. And laid down, every now and then, one of those indestructible moments of seeing. William James described this effect: 'In youth we may have an absolutely new experience, subjective or objective, every hour of the day. Apprehension is vivid, the retentiveness strong, and our recollections of that time, like those of a time spent in rapid and interesting travel, are of something intricate, multitudinous and long-drawn out. But as each passing year converts some of this experience into automatic routine which we hardly note at all, the days and the weeks smooth themselves out in recollection to contentless units, and the years grow hollow and collapse.'

The collapsing years of old age are indeed a source of dismay. They disconcert. What has happened to time, that it whisks away like this? And such answers as the psychologists have come up with seem to home in on the idea that the experience of time is linked to what is going on in our consciousness. Intensity of experience is a factor: traumatic events appear to be more recent than they in fact are. Intense expectation can make time pass more slowly; I can still remember the agonizing crawl of a week when I was waiting to go to Oxford station to meet a young man I was in love with – four more days . . . three . . . days that were each a week long. Nearly sixty years ago.

When you are busy, time scampers – a truism, but one that we all recognize. 'A week is a long time in politics' – a cliché, but one that nicely suggests the flexible quality of time, its ability to expand, as it were, on demand. A political week can stretch to accommodate gathering events: more and more can happen, in obligingly baggy days, until on Sunday the Prime Minister resigns.

That is expansion of time. The old age experience is the opposite – the sense of having entered some new dimension in which the cantering days and weeks are quite out of control. In some ways this puzzles me. Intensity of experience is not lost – there are still the bad times and the points of great pleasure, but they seem to have lost their capacity to arrest time, to make it pause, hover. On the other hand, memory has acquired some merciful ability to close up, to diminish the worst passages of more recent life. For me, the awful summer and autumn of Jack's illness – the hospital months, the last weeks at home – are now not time but a series of images I cannot lose. My own three and a half months of pain, four years ago, are also not months at all, but just the memory of a state of being, of how it was.

In childhood, a year is a large proportion of your life. Not so when you are eighty. That must have a lot to do with it. We old are cavalier about years; they have lost the capacity to impress. When you are eight, to be nine is a distant and almost unimaginable summit; Christmas is always far away, it will never come. For the old, it is a question of time's dismaying acceleration; we would prefer it to slow up now, to give us a chance to savour this glorious spring – we may not see so many more – while anticipation is

now welcome and there's no rush for that next birthday, thank you. And maybe it is precisely because we
find ourselves on this unstoppable conveyor belt that
we are so much concerned with recollection, with
reviewing all those memory shards in the head,
brushing up time past, checking it out.

Much of my own childhood was spent in a garden,
and I find that – miraculously, it seems – I can, today,
seventy plus years later, draw a precise map of that garden, more or less to scale. Not only can I see it – the
eucalyptus and casuarina trees, the rose pergola round
the basin with the statue of Mercury, the water garden
with the arum lilies and bamboo – but I know exactly
how it was laid out. This was a very English garden, created by my mother, but in Egypt, a few miles outside
Cairo. And I spent so much time in it because I was a
solitary only child, and did not go to school. But what
surprises me now is not that I have all these images of it
in my head, but that I have also a map of it, which I can
reproduce on paper (I know – I've done it). I can make
a plan of this large garden – the drive leading up to the
house, flanked by the lawn and the pond with the weeping willow, the rose garden, the kitchen garden, my
secret hiding place in the hedge, the wild bit at the end
where there are persimmon bushes that the mongooses
raid – no uncertainties, no section uncharted.

Spatial memories are stored in that area of the
brain called the hippocampus, specifically the right

hippocampus. My eight/nine/ten-year-old hippocampus was at work back then, it would seem. Today,
I often watch a couple of young men on motorbikes,
consulting clipboards, outside my window. They are
trainee taxi drivers, who have teamed up to do the
Knowledge together, the repertoire of three hundred and twenty main routes within a six-mile radius
of Charing Cross, covering twenty-five thousand
streets, on which they will be examined before
receiving their licence as a black-cab driver. The
square on which I live is the end point of the first
'run' in the Knowledge. A study done in 2000 at University College London of sixteen black-cab drivers
who had spent two years doing the Knowledge,
showed that all had a larger right hippocampus than
control subjects, and the longer they had been on
the job, the larger the hippocampus. I find this fascinating – the thought that the intricate maps of the
city crammed into these heads could actually alter
the brain. And I am amazed that my own young
brain could operate in the same way, storing spatial
memory that I still have.

The hippocampus for spatial memory. Is there
some site in the brain dedicated to language, to sign
systems? It can certainly feel as though there is, some
memory cabinet in which certain knowledge is
stashed away, seldom or never used, its contents not
in good shape, but somehow easily available. When I

went back to Egypt for the first time, as an adult, I found that words and phrases of Arabic came swimming up, that I must once have known and had not forgotten but had put away somewhere, ignored for decades. Equally, I never speak French now, but because once, when I was young, I spent a long time in France and emerged with good French, I still have the language, after a fashion; I wouldn't be able to speak it as I once did, but the ghost of it is there in my head – I know how you say this, say that. Unused equipment, but not defunct. And because I learned Latin at school, I can make a bit of sense of a Latin text, not absolute sense, but some understanding comes smoking up – a word I know, and that is a noun, and that a verb, and also I can recognize all those connections to the language that I speak, the ancestral sounds and meanings. I wish I had some shreds of Anglo-Saxon as well.

More oddly, I have this system of shapes, too – Pitman's shorthand, if you please. I could write this sentence in shorthand – ponderously and pointlessly. I learned typing and shorthand for a few months well over fifty years ago; typing proficiency has been invaluable, my shorthand never got anywhere near the point where anyone would have employed me to use it, but there it still lies, in my head, indestructible and rather irritating.

★

When did I first become interested in the operation of memory? Slowly, I think, gradually – noticing its various manifestations. My daughter, aged three, referred to a place we had been to 'a long time ago not as long as all that'. The visit had been about a month before; I liked her first attempt to marshal time, to put it in context, to pin memory to time. Children under five remember all right, there seems to be no question of that, but at some later point most or all of these memories disappear – childhood amnesia, this is called, a phenomenon that has fascinated psychologists since Freud's obsession with it. Nabokov saw his own 'awakening of consciousness as a series of spaced flashes, with the intervals between them gradually diminishing until bright blocks of perception are formed, affording memory a slippery hold'. The 'flash' of his that I most relish is his memory of crawling through a tunnel behind a divan and emerging at the end 'to be welcomed by a mesh of sunshine on the parquet under the cane work of a Viennese chair and two game-some flies settling by turn'. Reading that, you realize that you are seeing through the eyes of a four-year-old in St Petersburg before the Russian revolution.

The psychology of childhood memory is complex and strewn with different theories – why we remember this, forget that. Fear and shock seem to play a part – most of us remember something nasty to do with a dog, or one's gruesome injury to a knee. But many childhood memories are simple and visual – a frozen moment that has for some reason become hardwired into the mind, there for ever. And this surely is related to the pristine experience of childhood, when everything is seen for the first time – those game-some St Petersburg flies, Wordsworth's glory in the flower. Spring is still a marvel, when you are eighty, but it does not have the electric impact of novelty. What happens, it seems to me – my own diffident theory of memory development – is that the laying down of vivid visual experience in early childhood shifts to the accumulation of scenes from life as lived, the patchy collection of what has been seen and heard and felt that will add up to autobiographical memory. Quite a bit still that is sharply visual, but with added soundtrack, and a freight of significance. The great stockpile on which we depend, perched upon that initial fragile structure of uncomplicated observation.

My own earliest childhood memories – those that have survived childhood amnesia – are either visual or tactile. I don't much remember what anyone said, or what I felt. Lucy, who looked after me, was admirable at creative play. There was little acquisition of toys or games; we *made* things. So I have the memory of what making papier mâché feels like: the shredding of newspaper, the mixing of squeaky, tacky starch with water to make a paste in which you soak the shredded paper, the careful layering of the result into a relief map – we were particularly keen on maps – which could then be painted: brown hills, green valleys, blue rivers. We made Christmas wrapping paper with potato cuts: a halved potato cut into a star shape, or a holly leaf, a Christmas tree, then dipped in poster paint and stamped on a sheet of brown paper. Enjoyably messy – poster paint everywhere. For dolls' tea parties a thimble was used to cut tiny tarts out of orange peel, with a eucalyptus seed stuck in the centre. The dolls themselves were made of card, drawn by Lucy, and then provided with a paper wardrobe made by me, extravagant creations that clipped on with tabs at shoulders and waist. Hours of intense application – the sleeve to go thus, the skirt like this, cut it out, and then reach for the paintbox and the final flourish of creativity. These memories of absorbed involvement are different from uncomplicated observation, but seem to me equally pristine, equally a part of the distant fragile structure of childhood in the mind.

There is individual memory and there is collective memory; our own locked cupboard and the open shelf available to all. What only I know, and what is known – or can be known – to anyone. This startling apposition between a myriad memories, available only to the owner, and the immense record of the collective past, which is incomplete, argued over, but of which a vast amount is indisputable and familiar to millions. Only I know that once I spoke certain words, misguidedly, and am sorry now; everyone knows that men once landed on the moon. The huge collective hoard is impersonal; certain items may prompt dismay, distress, sympathy, but the emotions are detached – there is not the creep of intimacy, that I did this and should not have done, that this was done to me and it still hurts.

There is the further apposition that personal memory is the same extensive larder for each of us, unless we are given to denial, or otherwise affected in some way, but collective memory is unevenly distributed: some people have a rich and deep resource, for others it is minimal. A matter of education, and also of inclination. But however minimal, however threadbare, it is ballast of a kind. We all need that seven-eighths of the iceberg, the ballast of the past, a general past, the place from which we came.

That is why history should be taught in school, to all children, as much of it as possible. If you have no sense of the past, no access to the historical narrative, you are afloat, untethered; you cannot see yourself as a part of the narrative, you cannot place yourself within a context. You will not have an understanding of time, and a respect for memory and its subtle victory over the remorselessness of time.

I have been reading history all my life, and am sharply aware that I know very little. I have an exaggerated respect for historians – certain historians; they seem to me grounded in a way that most of us are not, possessed of an extra sense by virtue of access to times and places when things were done differently. They have – can have – heightened perception.

History is not so much memory as collective evidence. It is what has happened, what is thought to have happened, what some claim to have happened. The collective past is fact and fabrication – much like our private pasts. There is no received truth, just a tenuous thread of events amid a swirl of dispute and conflicting interpretation. But . . . the past is real. This is simplistic but also, for me, awe-inspiring. I am silenced when I think about it: the great ballast of human existence. Archaeology appeals to me precisely because it offers tacit but tangible evidence – the pots, the weapons, the bones, the stones. Jack, as a political theorist, needed the legacy of thought – he needed the minds of Aristotle, Rousseau and Hobbes. I am fired more by the eloquence of objects – the pieces of seventeenth-century salt-glaze I used to dig up in our Oxfordshire garden that said: a person made this dish, people used this (and broke it), they were here and that time actually happened.

To be completely ignorant of the collective past seems to me to be another state of amnesia; you would be untethered, adrift in time. Which is why all societies have sought some kind of memory bank, whether by way of folklore, story-telling, recitation of the ancestors – from Homer to Genesis. And why the heritage industry does so well today; most people may not be particularly interested in the narrative of the past, in the detail or the discussion, but they are glad to know that it is there.

For me, interest in the past segued into an interest in the operation of memory, which turned into subject matter for fiction. I wanted to write novels that would explore the ways in which memory works and what it can do to people, to see if it is the crutch on which we lean, or the albatross around the neck. It is both, of course, depending on circumstance, depending on the person concerned. In *The Photograph*, Glyn's memory of his dead young wife is distorted and perverted by the discovery of a challenging photograph. In *Moon Tiger*, Claudia's version of her past is questioned by the conflicting evidence of others. I have learned to be suspicious of memory – my own, anyone's – but to accord it considerable respect. Whether accurate or not, it can subvert a life. And for a novelist, the whole concept of memory is fascinating and fertile.

In a novel, the narrative moves from start to finish, from beginning to end. But within that framework time can be juggled, treated with careless disregard – the story can progress, can dip backwards, fold up, expand. What matters is the satisfactory whole defined by Frank Kermode: 'All such plotting presupposes and requires that an end will bestow upon the whole duration and meaning.' For a novel to work, you want to come away from reading it with a sense that everything has gathered towards a convincing conclusion – not one that necessarily ties up every loose end, but one that feels an integral part of what has gone before. It must make sense of the space between the beginning and the end. You start reading a novel with no idea where this thing is going to go; you should finish it feeling that it could have gone no other way.

The novelist would like the writing process to be thus; it is not – or at least not for me. I do need to have a good idea where the thing is going – I won't have started at all until a notebook is full of ideas and instructions to myself. And I will have achieved the finishing line only after pursuing various options, wondering if this would work better than that. The reader should have an easy ride at the expense of the writer's accumulated hours of inspiration and rejection and certainty and doubt.

The novelist's problem is infinity of choice. It is also the privilege, of course. Time can be manipulated; so also can the operation of memory. You can make lavish use of it, allowing it to direct what happens, or simply evoke what has once happened in order to flesh out a character, or give added meaning to what a person does or thinks. It is the essential secret weapon, for a novelist. The novel itself occupies a particular framework in time – the period of the action – but there is also the hidden seven-eighths of the iceberg, known only to the novelist, which is everything that went before, that happened to the characters before the story began. In fact, I don't exactly know all of it – rather like personal autobiographical memory, the antechamber of the novel I am writing seems a murky place in which I can rummage around and pounce upon promising fragments: character A can suddenly remember this event, character B can challenge character A by evoking some long-ago behaviour. The infinity of choice is at work; I don't actually need to know everything that went before, just the things that are pertinent to the narrative in hand, that may affect it in the way that memory affects real life.

What does memory do to us? It depends on you, of course – what has happened to you, how you are disposed, whether you sublimate, foster, manipulate, reinvent, enjoy, regret, deny, do any of the stuff we all spend time doing. I imagine my own memory behaviour is pretty standard. I don't know about the sublimation because I have never been in analysis – the rest is familiar. There are memories that induce shame, guilt, where I wish I could tweak the record – behave differently; there are memories about which I am dubious – maybe I have invented or elaborated this; there are those that I return to, savour, but with a certain melancholy – gone, gone, that moment; there are those that I wish I didn't have. A mixed bag – much what anyone has. Some are highly polished, in frequent use; others are vestigial, surfacing only occasionally, and surprising me. Collectively, they tell me who I am and what has happened to me – or rather, they tell me an essential part of that, leaving much in the mysterious dark cavern of what has been forgotten.

They are in no way chronological, and patently I am not in control of them. They seem to appear of their own volition, and a concerted search for something specific is difficult and often unproductive. Let's try this: a search through my eight decades.

Childhood is at once a challenge, because most memories are among the highly polished, having been summoned up for the memoir I once wrote. But – rooting around – here's a neglected one: I am waiting for Lucy in our favourite garden space where we have a table and chairs. Abdul, the *sufragi*, brings our elevenses on a tray – orange juice and biscuits. I reach for a biscuit. Abdul says, sternly – or seems to say: 'Sit!' Puzzled, I sit. Only later does it occur to me that what he was saying was: 'Wait for the *sitt!*' – Arabic word for 'lady' – I should not start on the biscuits until Lucy arrived.

This memory has its own coda – my realization of a misunderstanding – which is unusual, but rings true: there would have been that childhood fascination with language and its ambiguities. Let's move on to adolescence.

Memory

I am staying with my aunt Diana and her family in
Kent. Winter 1947, and bitterly – famously – cold. I
remember going to bed with all my clothes on. I am
fourteen, only recently exiled from Egypt, shunted
between my two grandmothers during school holidays because my father is mainly abroad, with a new
job. Di has kindly taken me on for Christmas, a somewhat taxing guest, I don't doubt. There is a Boxing
Day lunch party to which come friends of theirs, with
a son my own age. And he is everything that I am not;
he is charmingly forthcoming with adults, charmingly playful with my three young cousins, entirely
comfortable with himself – *bien dans son peau*. I am
lumpen, too tall, tongue-tied, unable to relate to the
children, hideously self-conscious. I observe his performance, and swelter. He ignores me, except for
some token charming remarks.

That memory has left me with a lifelong sympathy
for adolescence, except that I think they have things
rather better now that it is an accepted status. And I
was an only child, who had been at a single-sex boarding school. That period was a Calvary; few adults
penetrated the miasma of gloom, except for my uncle
Oliver, who noticed a reading habit, and talked books
to me, and my Somerset grandmother, who simply
absorbed me into her routine.

But what about something more upbeat? Something
joyous, celebratory, properly young? Trivia float up

here: a lipstick called Paint the Town Pink; I am sixteen now and my father does not like me to wear lipstick. He had become a single parent after the divorce, my mother not having applied for custody. He is out at his office all day, so I have put on the lipstick anyway, and sail out feeling glamorous, sophisticated. And, later, at seventeen I think, I have been allowed a pair of wedge-heeled shoes, cutting-edge fashion of the day, and am obsessed with them. The most precious acquisition ever.

Also, around now, my father marries again and I have stepmother number one, Barbara, who has a son of her own, aged twelve, and is perfectly nice to me. We go to Italy for a summer holiday *en famille*, and Barbara has persuaded my father to buy me a sumptuous travelling vanity case for my birthday equipped with little pots of this and that, manicure set, lotions and potions. The sights of Rome I remember not; the vanity case is in my mind's eye to this day. I see now that Barbara was ahead of her time, attuned to the yearnings of a teenage girl. But the marriage lasted only a couple of years, and I never saw her thereafter.

The twenties? Oh, there's plenty here. Marriage, childbirth, becoming a rather young mother. We are in Kensington Registry Office, Jack and I, with our respective witnesses, a friend each, waiting in a sombre brown room, occasionally murmuring to one another. An official puts his head round the door and says: 'Would you mind making less noise, please?'

I am in the Radcliffe hospital, in Oxford, an emergency admission, having just given birth after a prolonged home labour that went wrong. I am aware that all is not well, because everything is going grey and I cannot speak. A nurse is doing something at a sink, at the far end of the room, but I cannot attract her attention. The baby is in a crib beside me; she has a little thatch of dark hair. At last, the nurse comes over, inspects me, and at once goes to ring a bell. I hear feet running.

We are off for a weekend excursion in our first car, a Ford Popular. The children are in the back, Adam in a carry-cot, Josephine alongside (no child seats in those days, or seat belts). We round a bend in a Welsh country lane (somewhere north of Swansea, where Jack has his first academic job), and at the same moment a cow dashes in front of us; we go slap into it. Amazingly, the cow is unhurt; equally, mercifully, all of us. But the car is immovable. The farmer in pursuit of the escaped cow calls for help; the local policeman discovers that Jack's car licence is out of date but – benignly – decides to take no action: 'You people have had enough for one day.'

Ordnance survey map in hand, I am making my way across Oxfordshire fields in search of the site of a deserted medieval village. Both children are at school now, and I am free to do this kind of thing, in my thirties – a heady liberation after the child-intensive years.

Lapwings lift up ahead of me, and, yes, there are the grassy lumps and bumps of what was once a village called Hampton Gay.

We are driving somewhere in France; a town looms, announced by the road signs – 'Sa cathédrale . . .' – and – 'Piscine!' shout the children. The deal is that if we take them to the swimming pool they will then without complaint do time in the cathedral. My next book is going to be a guide to the municipal swimming pools of central and southern France.

Josephine rushes into the house – breathless, distressed: 'They're going to drown little black puppies in a bucket!' She has been down at the farm, playing with the three boys there, as on most days. I consider, I take a deep breath, I say: 'All right, you can have one.' Dogs live for around ten years, I am thinking, Josephine will be eighteen or so and leaving home by then. The puppy was a *mésalliance* between a Jack Russell terrier and a poodle, and lived to be seventeen.

My forties – mid-life – and we are into the 1970s now, the age of long cheesecloth skirts (which I wore) and flares (which I did not). These are the Warwick years, when Jack has moved from Oxford to that university. We have come to a poetry reading by Dennis Enright – D. J. Enright – who is Writer in Residence, and we have got to know, and enjoy, him. He starts to read, and after a few moments a young man in the front row of the small audience rises and leaves the room. Dennis breaks off for a moment, sighs: 'You win some, you lose some.' And continues with the poem.

But there seems to be something awry with this mid-life period – the roaring forties, but mine do not roar, they have sunk largely into an oblivion from which Dennis Enright sneaks out. And, yes, here now is a pond in Massachusetts (in England we would call it a small lake) in which I am swimming with my best, my oldest friend, Betty, but a new friend back then, and we are swimming through stripes of hot and cold in this dark green water, and Betty calls: 'Look! Look!' and there all around us are large blue dragon-flies.

Massachusetts, where I would now go often. The travel years are just beginning, and will fling me hither and thither before long. But for the most part memory is tethered to Oxfordshire, where we live (though in a different elderly farmhouse) – a dim continuous present which sends up occasional images. I am digging over a disused section of the vegetable garden, and am seized with sudden botanical fervour: I decide to take a specific square yard and list every species of plant growing there – hairy bittercress, groundsel, couch grass . . . I am at my desk, working; Jack comes past the window carrying an armful of logs; I hear him open the kitchen door, stamp his wet boots on the mat – thump-thump – drop the logs into the basket . . . Jackdaws have tried to nest in our high seventeenth-century chimney; failing to get their dropped sticks to lodge, they have come down to investigate, and are unable to find their way back, flying around the room and desecrating the furniture . . . There is another mouse in the kitchen trap; I remove it, my pre-breakfast chore. We share this place with much wildlife.

Why do I remember so little about work? These are the work years, also, the early work years. Writing. But that is part of that vague continuous present, until the 1980s – my fifties – when books come to direct my life, determine what I do, where I go.

I am in Docklands, where the skeletal framework of the Canary Wharf buildings are rearing out of a vast and muddy building site. This visit is in the service of the London novel that I am planning, and I have wangled an introduction to an architect working there, who has given me a guided tour, and now points me over to the Marketing Suite. In this sleek reception area, I suspect that my novelist role is not going to cut much ice, and I make some profoundly unconvincing enquiries about office space.

Bicycling in upper Egypt, somewhere outside Luxor, with Jack, and Ann and Anthony. We are on a Nile cruise, disembarked; Anthony has made a sortie into town, and hired the bikes, and now we are spinning on dirt roads through fields of sugarcane and clover, pursued by pi-dogs and children. For me, this landscape is at once alien, and entirely familiar. Later, in Cairo, we will discover my childhood home, now part of a teeming suburban slum, but surrounded by such fields, back then.

New Haven, Connecticut. Yale, where Adam is doing postgraduate work. Josephine and I are visiting, and find ourselves taking part alongside him in a civil rights demonstration. Many of the faculty are on strike in protest against the university's treatment of women and blacks. Adam, who has teaching responsibilities, is on strike, which means he teaches, but not on university premises. We stand in the rain, demonstrating, and Josephine says, rather irritably, that she is not sure this is what she has crossed the Atlantic for.

University College Hospital. Josephine is holding Rachel, who is a day old; she has pink cheeks and a thatch of dark hair. My father appears, in high spirits; he is visiting at the same time this great-granddaughter, and a grandson, Oliver. Nicky, wife of my half-brother Marcus, has also just given birth here. Marcus and his brother Valentine are the sons of my stepmother number two, Daphne. My father – our father – is a wow with the nurses on the ward, who are much entertained by this jovial elderly gent and his complex genetic arrangements.

I wake up, and know at once that I am somewhere else. The birdsong. Outside the window there is birdsong, much birdsong, and it is wonderfully wrong. It is song such as I have never heard before. In fact, I am in Australia, at an idyllic country motel to which the long-haul participants in the Adelaide Literary Festival have been brought to detox after their flights, before the festival begins. I open the window, listen some more, see birds I cannot begin to identify, and realize that I am seeing and hearing that Darwin was right. This is another continent, where things are done differently.

We are into the 1990s here, and I have hit sixty. I don't remember feeling especially bothered about this – full of energy still, writing, living. The view from eighty says: huh! a mere slip of a girl – just you wait.

Slovenia. I have been sent by the British Council to British Book Week at Ljubljana. I am being briefed on the day's activities over breakfast by the British Council representative when one of the Slovenian officials rushes up to cry excitedly: 'Your Mrs Thatcher is fallen! She is no longer the government, she is gone!' We say: 'Oh! Great!' It seems to me now that the Council representative was a touch out of order here, with such openly expressed political commitment. 'You will need to go home,' continues the Slovenian. 'You will need to be with your families. There will be . . . disorder.' We say that no, we don't need to, and there won't be, and recognize the gulf between those who have lived always in a politically stable society and those who have not.

And I have to note here the curious conflict between what is remembered and what was taken down at the time, for a diarist. Wanting to check this exchange, I looked in the diary: nothing about it at all, nothing.

But several pages on other aspects of that week that only returned, vaguely, as I read. The conference on Contemporary British Fiction, for example, at which, apparently, papers were delivered on such subjects as 'The Macedonian response to the Movement poets', and 'The Serbo-Croat reception of the Sirens episode in *Ulysses*'. Really? However can I have forgotten that?

In fact, a short story eventually surfaced from that time – 'The Slovenian Giantess' – and the diary entries had come in useful here, along with that other, unrecorded, memory. That, essentially, is what it has been for, the diary. And, at the time of writing the story, in 1994, I was apparently bothered about 'the inexplicable shift between significance at the time and significance in recollection – the way in which memory evidently transmutes events . . . Now if you could lay a finger on why one moment is immortalized and another obliterated you would presumably have made a seminal discovery about the workings of the human mind . . . All a fiction writer can do is take note.' I quite agree, eighteen years on.

Recent memory – the last ten or fifteen years – seems reasonably well furnished. More grounded – less travel now – and much that is distressing: death, illness. The hospital years, Gore Vidal has called this period of life, and yes, indeed, there is plenty of hospital experience – Jack's, my own. Verdicts delivered by kindly, deliberate, consultants: 'We have a problem';

waiting-rooms; procedures; trolley rides to operating theatres, contemplating the building's internal pipe-work overhead; the unrelenting hospital pillow; 'How is your pain today – on a scale of ten?'

But much else, too. Isaac says: 'When you're four, *Horrible Histories* is good, but you don't really understand it. When you're five, you understand it but it isn't so funny.' He is five – Adam's fourth child, and my sixth grandchild. We have gone forth and multiplied.

Luxborough village fête with Josephine. There is to be a hawk and falconry display, but the hawks and falcons refuse to fly; they sit glowering on the grass, or on the handler's wrist. He points out the reason – a pair of buzzards circling overhead: 'My birds are saying no way are they going up there with the local thugs around.' We repair to the produce tent, for cakes and chutneys; it is heaving in there, it is Harrods sale.

Monksilver village fête. There are camel rides on offer, the camels a discordant sight against the tipping green hillsides of west Somerset. I win an extremely ugly teapot in the raffle.

Old Cleeve village fête. Minehead brass band is play-ing, and I send Adam a photo from my newly acquired mobile phone, proud of this technological achievement.

The village fête years also, evidently. Forget Aus-tralian literary festivals, Toronto Harbourfront, Chicago. And that is just fine. Nowhere have I been happier, more fulfilled, than in west Somerset.

But these are essentially the London years, where I am ending up, rather to my surprise – I am not at heart a city dweller, but it makes every sense: family, above all.

The banshee wail of police-car sirens. The yellow-white night sky, jewelled here and there with a creeping aeroplane. City snow – a brief miracle, dishevelled within hours. The subterranean past, glimpsed when I spot the stem of a clay pipe in a mound of soil thrown up by road works.

I am a bus person; I hate the tube. The spider web of the London bus system has hardly changed in sixty years; the 73 performs today exactly as it did when I was very young. One day a few years ago, I was on an Islington bus whose novice driver mistook the route and plunged off down a tree-hung road. Branches snapped off and cascaded down. The driver was heard to wail: '. . . I don't know where to bloody go!' A local lady rose and stationed herself beside him – brisk, authoritative, one of those natural crisis containers – and delivered crisp directions until we were back on course.

Minicab drivers have been an education: Turkish, Kosovan, Afghan, Iranian, Iraqi, Polish, Estonian, Albanian – these disparate people converging on London, resourceful, opportunist, often wanting to talk, and giving me in a half-hour drive an insight into lives flung around by circumstance. On the Holloway Road, an Iranian says: 'My father was a university professor. I am an economist. Now . . .' He shrugs, lifting his hands from the wheel.

City life: alone, and in a crowd. Just me and the book I'm reading, of an evening; within a few hundred yards there are dozens, hundreds of people, but I wouldn't know it. Passing the British Library, I see from the bus a face I know, a friend, and this familiarity – this personal resonance – is startling amid the anonymity all around.

City life: today, and a whole lot of yesterdays. I cross my own path, time and again – walk up the steps of the British Museum, and there is my own alter ego, doing the same, ten, twenty years ago. I meet myself at a particular seat on the Embankment, in Bunhill Fields, at the Soane Museum, in Tavistock Square – and remember what I was doing, who I was with. The city is collective memory, and every kind of personal refrain, for anyone. You are rich, in the city. Maybe not such a bad place in which to end up, after all.

So there it is – the random search through eight decades. There is selection here, obviously. But not a selection that I have mulled over, sorted with care. And there is no pattern that I can see, no particular revelation. This is just a trawl from the mass of lurking material, the moments that I have, that I have had for years. There are many, many others, of course; some I prefer not to share, others are so tattered, so incidental, that they would make no sense to anyone else. And others so prosaic, so dull, that they seem to have no content. This lot just looked like some of the more presentable.

We can make a choice from accessible memories, as I have just done, but we can't choose what to remember, and what not to remember. There is something disturbing about the thought that, if some other, hitherto unavailable retrieval system were activated, I might find myself with a series of entirely unfamiliar memories – an alternative past that happened, but of which I had ceased to be aware. I suspect that I am straying into the realm of analysis here, but I am looking at the idea more from a novelistic point of view, and while it is disturbing it is also fertile matter for fiction. A fictional character is equipped with a past that establishes and defines them, just as I am, and you are. But suppose that past – those memories – were to be supplanted by a different set; what then would happen to the personality concerned? I am conditioned by – cushioned by – what I remember, which tells me what has happened, or what I believe to have happened, and how I have behaved, or think I behaved. Pull the rug away, furnish me with a whole new set of memories which make things look rather different, which make me see myself differently, and what will happen to me? Do I go mad? Or emerge as someone else, a revised personality?

This is a fancy; for me, a possible prompt for a story, even a novel. A new way of exploring the significance of memory in fictional terms. But it is a meaningful fancy, too, because it points up the power – the defining power – of the memories that we have. We are who we are because we have that particular range of memories, which form our past as we know it.

When I pinch the leaves of the rosemary plant in my garden, and sniff, I am back on a hillside above Jerusalem, aged nine. I suppose there must have been wild rosemary there. This is an instance of what psychologists call the 'Proust phenomenon', in reference to the novelist and that now overworked madeleine. Smells, tastes, are famous memory prompts. Psychologists find olfactory memory interesting because there is an argument about whether the Proust phenomenon – smell and taste as memory triggers – exists at all, and if so whether it is always laid down in early life, and accessed best in later life. In old age the ability to distinguish smells is apparently much diminished, which may have something to do with it; back once more to the heightened response to the physical world when you are young. But in that case the distinctions are preserved: rosemary takes me back to the Jerusalem hillside, thyme and marjoram do not.

There is a sensuality about memory, then. And the heritage industry seems to have latched on to this idea. A London pub-cum-restaurant cultivating a nineteenth-century atmosphere used to smell authentically of coal fires, despite being centrally heated throughout and free of such things; an aerosol spray was available, apparently – canned nostalgia. And at Jorvik, York's recreation of the Viking town, to which you can return in a trolley-car that trundles back through the centuries and past scenes of Viking domestic and commercial life, the sights and sounds are augmented by pungent whiffs of livestock, cooking, and inadequate sanitation. The past can be conjured up by the appropriate aroma, much as supermarkets seek to induce a spending appetite with the smell of newly baked bread, and house agents urge us to woo prospective buyers with a waft of fresh coffee.

But it is not that memory is scented, rather – if the Proust phenomenon exists – that smells evoke a time, a place. That moment has not gone, can be recovered, because an experience in the present brings it back; my London garden is tenuously linked to what was in 1942 a Palestinian hillside. This is the sense in which memory is the mind's triumph over time. The same has been said of history, and I relish both concepts: it is as though individually and collectively, we succeed in seizing hold of what is no longer there, that which should be unavailable, and making it miraculously permanent and accessible because it matters so much, because we need it.

We are robust about time, linguistically, we are positively cavalier about it – we make it, we spend it, we have it, we find it, we serve it, we mark it. Last time, next time, in time, half-time – one of the most flexible words going, one of the most reached for, a concept for all purposes. Time is of the essence, or it is quality, or time will tell. We talk about it . . . all the time, I find myself writing. There. But when I think about time, I am awed. I am more afraid of time than of death – its inexorability, its infinitude. It is as unthinkable as space – another word we tame by making every use of it. And in old age I am time made manifest; sitting here, writing this on a summer afternoon, twelve minutes past three, the watch hand moving relentlessly round, my weathered body is the physical demonstration of passing time, of the fact that eighty years have had their way with it, that I ain't what I used to be. I have lived with time, in time, in this particular stretch of time, but before too long time will dump me; it has far to go, and we don't keep up with it. None of us, ever.

Fifteen minutes past three.

Impersonal, indifferent; it neither knows nor cares. It sweeps us along, the ever-rolling stream and all that, nothing to be done about it, but we do have this one majestic, sustaining weapon, this small triumph over time – memory. We know where we have been in time, and not only do we know, but we can go back, revisit. When I was nine, I was on a Palestinian hillside, smelling rosemary (and collecting a wild tortoise, but that is another story). Time itself may be inexorable, indifferent, but we can personalize our own little segment: this is where I was, this is what I did.

Reading and Writing

My house is full of books. I suppose that I have read all of them, bar reference books and poetry collections in which I will not have read every poem. I have forgotten many, indeed most. At some point, I have emptied each of these into that insatiable vessel, the mind, and they are now lost somewhere within. If I reopen a book, there is recognition – oh yes, I've been here – but to have the contents again, familiar, new-minted, I would have to read right through. What happens to all this information, this inferno of language? Where does it go? Much, apparently, becomes irretrievable sediment; a fair amount, the significant amount, becomes that essential part of us – what we know and understand and think about above and beyond our own immediate concerns. It has become the life of the mind. What we have read makes us what we are – quite as much as what we have experienced and where we have been and who we have known. To read is to experience.

I can measure out my life in books. They stand along the way like signposts: the moments of absorption and empathy and direction and enlightenment and sheer pleasure. Back in the mists of very early reading there is Beatrix Potter, who does not just tell an enthralling story but challenges the ear. Her cadences, her linguistic flights that I repeated to myself over and over: 'The dignity and repose of the tea party', 'too much lettuce is soporific', 'roasted grasshopper with ladybird sauce', 'The dinner was of eight courses, not much of anything, but truly elegant.' When eventually I came to write for children myself, an occasional pursy-lipped teacher would tell me that I sometimes used words that a seven/eight/ten-year-old would not know and I should stop it. Such letters were binned – beneath contempt; go and read Miss Potter, lady.

Later, much later, I met up with Arthur Ransome and was transported to an alien world in which unimaginably liberated children larked around in boats in some exotic landscape of hills and greenery and water. I was growing up in Egypt, and had known nowhere else; I would surface from *Swallows and Amazons* to my own mundane backdrop of palm trees, a string of camels beyond the garden hedge, the postman's donkey titupping up our drive.

That Egyptian childhood was book-heavy. I did not go to school, but books made me. I have written elsewhere, in a memoir of those Egypt years – *Oleander, Jacaranda* – of my home instruction, the Parents' National Educational Union system devised for expatriate families and administered, in my case, by someone

who had herself left school at sixteen. That was education, and I am concerned here with books in a rather
different sense. But there is an overlap, inevitably. The
Do-It-Yourself education method was focused entirely
upon reading: the child was read to, required to 'tell
back', and in due course to read and 'write back' – a
sustained exercise in the absorption of language. I am
grateful to it. The Bible – the King James Version, of
course – featured strongly. Palgrave's *Golden Treasury of
Verse*. And, above all, for me, Andrew Lang's *Tales of
Troy and Greece*, that late Victorian retelling of Homer.
The *Iliad* and the *Odyssey* spilled out of lesson time into
the rest of the day; I re-enacted the siege, the wander-
ings, as I drifted around our garden, because of course I
was in there anyway – Penelope – so this must be something to do with me personally. The solipsism of the
nine-year-old mind. Except that I was in there with the
wrong part; Penelope is not as beautiful as Helen, she is
described as wise and good, qualities that did not appeal.
And Ulysses – red-haired and crafty – is clearly not a
patch on brave Hector or glamorous Achilles. So I juggled with the narrative – true to the tradition of
reworking Homer, had I known it – airbrushed the tiresome Helen, and set myself up with Achilles. And, to
bring things more up to date, equipped him with a
Matilda tank and a Bren gun, instead of all that stuff
with chariots and spears – the Libyan campaign was
raging a hundred miles or so away, remember, in 1941.

Many of the books sent out from England by the PNEU failed to reach us. We fell back on our own resources, for reading matter. Dickens's *Nicholas Nickleby* and *David Copperfield* – immersed in the drama and tragedy of mysterious lives, reading as literary innocents, barely aware that the setting was the nineteenth century. Macaulay's *Lays of Ancient Rome*, with me learning great chunks by heart: 'Lars Porsena of Clusium, by the nine gods he swore . . .' I did much learning by heart, and some of it lingers, surfacing at unexpected moments, a shred of Tennyson, a whisper of Shelley: 'Break, break, break / On thy cold grey stones, O sea'. 'Swiftly walk over the western wave, spirit of night'. Deeply out of educational fashion now, learning by rote, but it was hanging on still when I did eventually go to school, aged twelve, and I accumulated more: Shakespeare speeches, Wordsworth, Keats – bits and pieces of which I still have and I wish there were more still. You can only learn by heart when young, unless, I suppose, you are an actor.

I think I was probably starved of fact – of nonfiction. The educational system's offerings were not enticing: Plutarch's *Lives*, and a turgid book on the history of Parliament which serviced the weekly period known as Citizenship Studies. I did relish our Natural History text, Arabella Buckley's *Eyes and No Eyes*, published in 1901, so not exactly up to date, and dealing with the flora and fauna of Devon – entirely inappropriate to our Nile-fed garden, but with its own exotic and vaguely scholarly charm. This paucity of fact may account for my passion for Hendrik Van Loon's *The Home of Mankind* – a treasured possession that still has a place on my shelves. When I open it now there is a whiff of that long-ago appeal; it is a nicely eccentric geography book with chatty text and the author's own pungent views to the fore: 'Poland suffers from two great natural disadvantages. Its geographic position is most unfortunate, and its nearest neighbours are its fellow-Slavs of Russia.' And the illustrations are a delight: the author's own quirky drawings, accentuating geographical features. He demonstrates watery Europe, fringed by its elaborate coastline, invaded by chunky rivers; if the Pacific ocean should run dry – with the land-masses perched on top of peaks; the Atlantic – a section of blue underwater mountains with a curved surface on which perch tiny ships.

By the time I arrived in England I was thoroughly book-addicted; socially inept, after that isolated upbringing, a floundering outcast at the fearful boarding school to which I was despatched, but an ace reader. Books became my retreat – anything, everything. My school holidays were spent going from one grandmother to the other. My London grandmother's Harley Street home was well equipped with books – short on creature comforts, in the late 1940s, but plenty to read, though reading that required a degree of perseverance.

I ploughed my way through Charlotte M. Yonge – *The Dove in the Eagle's Nest*, *The Chaplet of Pearls*, *The Daisy Chain* – and Harrison Ainsworth – *Old Saint Paul's*, *The Tower of London*, *Windsor Castle*. I cite these not as signposts along the way – I was reading what was available, not what I would have chosen – but as indicators of what a desperate adolescent reader will undertake if necessary. Charlotte M. Yonge seems to me now an extraordinary challenge for a mid-twentieth-century thirteen/fourteen-year-old – those long, dense, mannered historical novels. In her own day, she had published many of them in serial form in her *Monthly Packet*, which one commentator has called the first teenage magazine. Victorian adolescents must have been made of stern stuff. Commentary on Charlotte Yonge is something of an industry. There is a Charlotte Mary Yonge Fellowship, which holds regular meetings and publishes a twice-yearly *Review*, and indeed the writer herself was an industry, with about one hundred and eighty works to her name, mostly novels. And she was highly regarded by her peers – George Eliot, Gladstone, Tennyson, Trollope. But not much read today, except by the stalwarts of the Charlotte Mary Yonge Fellowship. I have several of her novels, 1880s editions but evidently not filched from my grandmother's shelves because they bear pencilled second-hand bookshop prices – 35p, 25p. So I must have acquired them in adult life, out of nostalgia, maybe.

William Harrison Ainsworth is an equally unlikely choice – but of course this was not really choice, it was a question of what was available in that high, chill, Harley Street house, where the main rooms had all been dust-sheeted for the duration of the war, and the books stared darkly out from within glass cases. Harrison Ainsworth was another prolific Victorian – thirty-nine novels, master of the popular historical romance, friend of Dickens in their early writing lives. I think I enjoyed him rather more than Charlotte Yonge; there is a memory of being fascinated by the atmosphere and action of *Old Saint Paul's* and *The Tower of London*, which probably chimed with a nascent interest in the presence of the past, its visible evidence – I would have been taken to both sites by my grandmother.

Where choice operated, I discovered Mazo de la Roche, Canadian author of the Jalna novels, and wallowed in this family saga – rich with romance and spiced with lurking sex. And there was a brief, alarming engagement with the London Library. The uncle who had observed my bookish tendency gave me temporary membership for a sixteenth birthday present – my first experience of a great library. You could order books there, back then; for some obscure reason I ordered Hakluyt's *Voyages Round the World*. It arrived on a trolley, in several volumes, and I sat stolidly reading for a week, unable to admit to a mistake.

At my Somerset grandmother's house there were fewer books, but there was a complete run of bound volumes of *Punch* from about 1890; many a long, bored afternoon was spent poring over one of these, mainly in pursuit of the cartoons, but sometimes tackling the text, and picking up something along the way about the social attitudes of the early twentieth century and what seemed the heavy-handed humour of the day. There was little fiction; I moved on from Charlotte Yonge to Charles Morgan (boring), A. J. Cronin (ditto), and other popular novelists of the twenties and thirties.

At last, a few years later, I plunged into the public library system and unfettered reading. Oxford Public Library, where the poet Elizabeth Jennings worked, and stamped your chosen books, and I observed her with awe – a few years older than me and a writer, a poet at that. And then the small branch library in Swansea, where Jack had his first permanent academic post at the university. I was coping first with a toddler, and then a three-year-old and a baby, and would trundle both in the pram to the library once a week, packing Iris Murdoch, Graham Greene, Evelyn Waugh around them for the return journey. It was not the best time at which to be servicing a reading addiction; I remember reading in snatches while feeding the baby, shovelling food into an infant mouth, minding them in the park or on the beach.

Early reading is serendipitous, and rightly so. Gloriously so. Libraries favour serendipity, invite it; the roaming along a shelf, eyeing an unfamiliar name, taking this down, then that – oh, who's this? Never heard of her – give her a go? That is where, and how, you learn affinity and rejection. You find out what you like by exploring what you do not. In the late 1940s, when I was first putting a toe into the waters of real grown-up books, the favoured authors of the day were the Sitwells – Edith, Osbert and Sacheverell (just to recite their names brings back the mocking refrain of a disrespectful number in some late night revue less doting than the reading public) – Norman Douglas, Lesley Blanch, the kind of writing that did not use one word where ten would do – florid, self-conscious, portentous. I read dutifully and thought that either the times were out of joint or I was. And then later, much later, I found Henry Green and Ivy Compton-Burnett, and realized that what I was after was economy and accuracy, the use of that just right, but startling language. Henry James and Elizabeth Bowen taught me that writing can be expansive and complex but still be accurate and exciting. I had no thoughts then of writing myself – I was reading purely as a gourmet reader, refining taste, exploring the possibilities. And now I think that a writer's reading experience does not so much determine how they will write, as what they feel about writing; you do not want to write like the person you admire, even if you were capable of it – you want to do justice to the very activity, you want to give it your own best, whatever that may be. A standard has been set.

The signposts sent me towards particular kinds of writing; these were what I wanted to read and, when eventually I came to write myself, these would be – not how I wanted to write but the majestic exemplars always in the back of my mind. But no one – writer or otherwise – reads in search of stylistic satisfaction alone; what is said matters just as much as how it is said. Where fiction was concerned, I had the basic needs of any fiction reader – I wanted to escape the prison of my own mind, my own experience, and discover how it may be for others, to see other people's lives distilled through an author's imagination. The variety, the disparity, of fiction, is a constant astonishment. How can it be that there is such abundant fertility – that so many people turn to and create character, and narrative – both extraordinarily difficult feats, as anyone knows who has tried to do it. Well, only a very few do it with real power and effect, of course. But many, many have a shot at it – even more so today, with universities up and down the land offering their Creative Writing MA courses, so that it begins to seem as though you need formal qualifications to become a novelist. My generation beavered away in solitude – whether for better or for worse, I wouldn't care to say.

Sixty years or so of fiction reading now, for me. A torrent of story poured in, much of it forgotten entirely, a good deal half remembered, some so significant that I go back again and again. I have had fitful relationships with some writers. At one time I could no longer read Lawrence Durrell; now, suddenly, he is again alluring. I can't abide Barbara Pym – enjoyed her once. Anthony Powell is irritating today, yet in the past I have revelled in Widmerpool and company. And there is the handful with whom each rereading is a new discovery. William Golding, who offers something you hadn't noticed before each time you go back, in every single book of his. Updike, Henry James, Willa Cather, Edith Wharton . . . others.

The stimulus of old age reading is the realization that taste and response do not atrophy: you are always finding yourself enthusiastic about something you had not expected to like, warming to some writer hitherto right off the radar. But, that said, there is by now that medicine chest of works to which you return time and again. And, if I had to whittle that down from a chest to a slim stash – the desert island books – there are three titles that I would pick, because, for me, they are perhaps the ones that have most elegantly demonstrated what the novel can do, when the form is pushed to its limits. And these are: Henry James's *What Maisie Knew*, William Golding's *The Inheritors*, Ford Madox Ford's *The Good Soldier*.

What Maisie Knew is a brilliant exercise in narrative technique, in which an entire tale of adult betrayal and duplicity is seen through the uncomprehending eyes of a child, a fictional discussion of evil and innocence in which the reader is eerily and uncomfortably aligned with the forces of darkness because recognizing the corruption which the child's vision simply records without the insight of experience. *The Inheritors* is a novel of ideas in which the ideas and the discussion of human nature are so effectively subsumed within the story that each new reading of it points up another layer, or shifts the emphasis. It is also the saddest novel I know. And *The Good Soldier* is another marvellous narrative tour de force in which the truth behind a pattern of relationships is revealed with such subtlety and guile that while the reader is never deliberately deceived, each new release of information changes the view of what has happened. All of these are books in which the apparently straightforward business of telling a story about some characters has been refined to its most delicate and allusive but at the same time to its most powerful. You are left with a feeling of astonishment, and of involvement, because part of the skill has been to draw the reader into the book, to make the reader a participant by inviting judgement and complicity. The reader becomes a confidant, as it were, and, like a confidant, may find that there has been an ambivalence. You are left with an insight into human behaviour, into your own.

Just as importantly, the signposts were starting to wave where non-fiction was concerned – they were dancing up and down, indeed. They pointed me towards landscape history, towards archaeology. 'Oh, there's a book you'd like . . .' said Jack one day, offhand – he was an academic political theorist, by trade, but seemed to have read everything and anything – '. . . W. G. Hoskins – *The Making of the English Landscape*.' I read, and my way of seeing the world was changed. *The Making of the English Landscape* was first published in 1955; I read it in around 1965, when we were living in Church Hanborough, a few miles outside Oxford. I devoured the book, put on my wellies and walked out in search of ridge and furrow, lost medieval villages, drove roads – all of which could be found within a radius of ten miles or so. Hoskins makes you see the physical landscape as a palimpsest, layers of time inviting interpretation; he lets you see it also as a challenging medley, where everything exists at once – today, yesterday and long ago all juxtaposed. For me, this vision was to become a driver for fiction – the presence of the past, whether in an

Oxfordshire field or in someone's life. We are all of us palimpsests; we carry the past around, it comes surging up whether or not we want it, it is an albatross, and a crutch.

The Hoskins approach to landscape history has come under criticism as 'Romantic' – harking back to the Wordsworthian tradition of landscape appreciation – and also too heavily weighted in favour of historical evidence rather than the archaeological record. The New Archaeology of the 1950s – processual archaeology – considered that the survival of a landscape in the present cannot and should not be used to infer past processes: Hoskins's interpretations had sometimes done precisely this. That said, those working in the field who have reservations about his approach readily admit that he has been an inspiration, to them and to many others.

'You might try Norman Cohn – *The Pursuit of the Millennium*,' said Jack. 'And Frances Yates – *The Art of Memory*.' I did, I did. I was finding the kind of history that had not been on offer during my three undergraduate years at Oxford. Not that I am ungrateful for that induction; those three years created a climate of mind, I am certain – they did not make me into a novelist but they determined the kind of novels that I would eventually write. But now, through with Stubbs Charters and the *Oxford History of England*, I could spread wings, discover different history. In 1971 Keith

Thomas published his magisterial *Religion and the Decline of Magic*. I was enthralled – here was the history I had been wanting, without knowing that I did. And there was more of it around: Peter Laslett, Christopher Hill, Alan Macfarlane. Jack had been a historian as an undergraduate, but had focused on the history of ideas for his postgraduate work, and thence became a political theorist. He had been unfashionable on the history scene, in the early 1950s, when the Namier school still dominated – the insistence that the course of events is directed by politics and personalities. But the Namierites and their study of ruling elites were soon to be shunted aside in favour of social history, the emphasis on people and how they have lived, behaved and thought. And, where Jack was concerned, the history of ideas had come in from the cold.

Subsequent reading – the reading of a lifetime – has been this marriage of the fortuitous and the deliberate, with the random, the maverick choices tipping the scale and serving up, invariably, the prompts for what would next be written. Books begetting books; intertextuality, of a kind. It has never felt like that – more that something read has sparked off a story idea that is owed to that subject but will eventually have nothing much to do with it. But if I had not read that book, the story might never have arrived, or not in that particular form. Elizabeth

Bowen, whom I admire and regularly reread – no falling in and out of favour there – has a short story called 'Mysterious Kor' in which a pair of lovers wander the night-time streets of blitzed London. Years after writing it, she herself wrote that her description of that moonlit, ruined cityscape must have been prompted, subliminally, by a memory of reading Rider Haggard's *She* in childhood – the eerie, imagined city in that novel. In that instance, a half-forgotten reading experience inspired and informed a story, decades later.

It has not been fiction so much, for me, but the random discoveries. Sometime in the 1970s I came across William Stukeley, probably in Stuart Piggott's biography; Stukeley, along with my abiding fascination with archaeology, would inspire *Treasures of Time*, a novel concerned indeed with archaeology, but that is also a love story and a take on the attitudes of the 1970s, and the title came of course from Sir Thomas Browne's *Urne-Buriall* – 'The treasures of time lie high, in Urnes, Coynes and Monuments . . .', a text that Jack had pointed me towards, long before, something that he had read in his voracious teenage reading years and returned to whenever he wanted to remind himself of the glories of seventeenth-century English prose-writing.

A decade or so later, the popular science writing of the day brought me Stephen Jay Gould's *Wonderful*

Life and the lightning struck once more; his account of the Cambrian fossils of the Burgess Shale, most of them evolutionary dead-ends except for the one from which we are descended, was the fuel for a novel about the apposition between choice and contingency, *Cleopatra's Sister*. A while later, the chance acquisition in Toronto's Royal Ontario Museum of a booklet about Martin Frobisher, the Elizabethan seaman, would be the trigger for a London novel, *City of the Mind*, a novel about time and the eloquence of place – and a further love story. And, later still, a rereading of Frances Yates's *The Art of Memory* made me see how I could make a house – my grandmother's house – speak for the century by way of its contents, a piece of non-fiction this time: *A House Unlocked*.

None of these books would have been written, or written in the way that they were, if I had not come across something that in some mysterious symbiosis inspired and wound in with what I was already thinking about, in a vague and inconclusive way. These readings lit a fuse. And from the point when first I recognized what was happening I have known that I have to read – mostly undirected, unstructured reading. Those of us who write fiction write out of much – out of what we have seen, and done, and heard, and thought, out of every aspect of experience – but as far as I am concerned books are a central part of that experience, the driver, quite as much as my own life as lived, with all its inevitable limitations and restrictions.

These have been books that were prompts, that triggered work of my own. But when I look along the non-fiction shelves there leaps to the eye a collection of titles that seem to be saying something about a need, a taste – no, something more than that, a pursuit, a cultivated hunger. They are fingered, reread. Here is Barry Lopez's *Arctic Dreams*, Hugh Brody's *The Other Side of Eden* and *Maps and Dreams*. And Colin Turnbull's *The Forest People* and *The Mountain People*, equally reading-worn. What are the Arctic and the Congo to me? Travel books? But these are not travel books; there is indeed a travel section, but these are something apart, with something in common. There is Peter Matthiessen's *The Snow Leopard*, and everything by Robert Macfarlane, and a row of Redmond O'Hanlon titles.

These books complement some adventurous streak in me? No. Rather, the opposite. I am not adventurous; I have enjoyed travel, but of the most cushioned kind. I relish the physical world, and liked to walk it, when the going was good, but knew only the well-trodden ways of my own country – Exmoor, the South Downs, Offa's Dyke. What these books and their like have done for me is tap into some roaming tendency of the mind; I know that I could never have done what these writers have done, been where they have been, pursued the interests they have pursued, but I want to know what it is like. We go to fiction to extend experience, to get beyond our own. For me, this kind of non-fiction writer is furnishing the same need – taking me out of my own comfortable expectations and showing me how it might be elsewhere. Armchair travel? Not quite. I have never believed that travel broadens the mind, having known some well-travelled minds that were nicely atrophied. Rather, these are books – experiences – that encourage a leap of the imagination. Hugh Brody invites you into the life of the Inuit; Barry Lopez offers a glimpse of the Arctic, richer and more vivid by far than any television documentary. Colin Turnbull is describing existence at its most harsh, in Africa, and is also showing you human nature. Redmond O'Hanlon – well, I would be alarmed to go for a walk along the Thames towpath with Redmond O'Hanlon but I want to go with him vicariously up the Amazon, or to the Congo, or Borneo, or the North Atlantic. Equally, Robert Macfarlane takes me to the places I could never have known, and sets me off on all manner of enquiry in the process. And from where I am today, in the tiresome holding-pen of old age, that seems all the more valuable.

My Somerset grandmother – to whom I was devoted – had reservations about reading as an activity. Definitely not in the morning: 'You should be out and about, my dear, not sitting there with a book.' Possibly after tea, a more relaxed time of day, but in moderation, always: 'You'll ruin your eyesight.' This was in the late 1940s, when Aldous Huxley's method of treating poor eyesight was much in fashion. My London grandmother was keen on that; I was made to sit for a quarter of an hour twice a day, elbows on a cushion placed on a table in front of me and the heels of my palms pressed lightly against my eyes. You were supposed to 'think black'. I had been wearing glasses since I was seven, but Huxley was apparently nearly blind, so one was tempted to say that the system clearly hadn't done him much good.

One-sixth of the world's population is myopic, but amongst readers the proportion is much higher – about a quarter. Habitual readers, that is – those who spend much time reading. Which raises the intriguing question of whether we book-addicted are thus because of some genetic conditioning or whether we have wrecked our eyesight through our addiction, as my grandmother would have claimed. Whichever, we are in distinguished company – Aristotle, Goethe, Keats, Wordsworth, Joyce. Samuel Johnson, shown in that iconic portrait both peering at a book and abusing it, wrenching the pages round the spine.

The ophthalmologist and writer Patrick Trevor-Roper looked at the way in which myopia may have affected writers and artists, citing as an instance the images in the poetry of Keats and of Shelley: short-sighted Keats often favoured auditory subjects – the 'Ode to a Nightingale', the sonnet 'On the Grasshopper and Cricket'– and his images tend to be within his focal range: the Grecian urn, the 'beaded bubbles winking at the brim', whereas Shelley, who had no sight problem, went in for the distant prospects of sky and mountain. And there is an identifiable myopic personality, it seems: myopic children don't flourish in the playground or at sports – they can't see what's going on and they miss the ball; but reading and writing are not a problem – within their field of vision – so they focus on that and tend to do better academically than their peers, though they may not be more intelligent.

In the past, to be seriously myopic must have been crippling; you would have had problems with all daily activities, many trades would have been out of the question. And who ever heard of a myopic warrior? As for hunter-gathering, forget it. Today, we are well taken care of, with contact lenses and varifocals and competing high street optometrists. Even the adage of my youth has rather lost its clout: 'Men seldom make passes at girls who wear glasses.' I gather they do, nowadays.

Myopia is a human disability; there are no myopic animals, except for some instances in domesticated dogs. And this makes perfect sense; natural selection would account for that – a short-sighted bird of prey wouldn't last long. So is a myopic hunter-gatherer conceivable? Common sense suggests not – the tendency would have been bred out, if it appeared. And this seems to be right; myopia is indeed a relatively modern condition. If so, why? Was my grandmother on the case, with her suspicion of reading?

Opinion is against her, it seems. A classic study of a hunter-gatherer society – an Inuit group – found a very low level of myopia amongst older members who had lived the traditional isolated lifestyle but a far higher level amongst their children who had grown up in a westernized community and had received schooling. At first the finger was pointed at books, until it was realized that the older Inuit group had always done close work in ill-lit igloos – the making and repair of clothes and weapons. Other studies of hunter-gatherer communities have confirmed this onset of myopia with the advent of western dietary habits, and this is now thought by some to be the explanation: carbohydrates. The cereals and sugars that are the basis of modern diet but unfamiliar to those accustomed to high levels of proteins and fats. An excess of carbohydrates can affect the development of the eyeball, causing myopia. As for those myopic domesticated dogs: dog biscuits?

So myopia is not genetic? I look around my own family, in which specs and contact lenses are rife, and doubts creep in. Surely there is something going on here? Patrick Trevor-Roper certainly thought there was, in his study, homing in on the Medicis; one Medici pope is on record in a portrait holding a concave lens, an early form of glasses, while other Medicis are referred to as having bad sight, and 'beautiful large eyes'; the myopic eyeball is large. Also, their dynastic success was based not on soldiery but on banking, scholarship and the encouragement of art – a nice display of the myopic personality. But it seems that there is as yet no identification of a specific gene responsible for the short-sightedness that appears to be endemic in some families; the favoured conclusion at the moment is that a combination of genetic predisposition and environmental factors stimulates the development of myopia. Your parentage may well have something to do with your life behind specs; equally, your circumstances – if you grew up with the emphasis on study rather than long-distance running. Reading may play a role, but is far from being the whole story. Myopia is a modern trend, but owed probably more to the availability of sugars and cereals than to universal education. Books are excused – for the moment, and up to a point.

But books and specs go together, no question. At the dire boarding school to which I went, where one of the punishments was to spend an hour in the library, reading (there wasn't anything much in the library, except for some battered reference books), the myopic amongst us were labelled 'brainy', a term of abuse. And we were probably bad at games too, a further social solecism. Ah! The myopic personality. Reading was seen as something you did only when you had to, an attitude connived at by the staff. My copy of *The Oxford Book of English Verse* was confiscated from my locker: 'You are here to be taught that sort of thing, Penelope. And your lacrosse performance is abysmal.'

I broke out into the clear blue air of higher education, eventually, and a lifetime of unfettered reading. And yes, my sight is pretty dodgy – cataracts and macular degeneration – but the splendid specialist who will do his best to ensure that I don't lose it further exonerates the books: I would have headed that way in any case.

Reading, for all of us, is fettered only by obvious restrictions. You can't own all that you want or need to read. There are, then, two kinds of books – yours, and the contents of libraries. There is the actual, personal library, your own shelves, which mark out reading inclinations, decade by decade, and the virtual library in the head – the floating assemblage of fragments and images and impressions and information half-remembered that forms the climate of the mind, the distillation of reading experiences that makes each of us what we are.

Let's look first at the actual library – the real, tangible books. My two thousand plus, which is nothing very much in personal library terms and requires no cataloguing system beyond crude subject allocations: Fiction in the kitchen, Poetry in the television room, some History upstairs, other History down. Alberto Manguel, in his lovely book *The Library at Night*, says: 'Every library is autobiographical . . . our books will bear witness for or against us, our books reflect who we are and what we have been . . . What makes a library a reflection of its owner is not merely the choice of titles themselves, but the mesh of associations implied in the choice.' His own library sounds awesome: many thousands of books in a converted barn somewhere in France, the amazing accretion that is the fruit of his tastes, his eclectic reading, his generous interest, his voracious curiosity. And his book is a homage to the very concept of the library.

My granddaughter Rachel, at the age of ten, was made library monitor for her form at school. She had all the proper librarian instincts; under her aegis, the form-room books were arranged by subject matter, and, within that, in alphabetical order. She was away ill for a week and came back to find that some interfering ignoramus had reshelved everything in height order; Rachel was outraged, quite rightly.

Had she known of it, she would have no doubt attempted an embryonic Dewey system. So would I – had I the time and the energy and rather more books than I have. When I was first raiding the public library system, I didn't know what those cryptic numbers on the spines meant, and was entranced when at last enlightened – the elegant simplicity of the Decimal Classification system whereby the field of human knowledge is divided, and then subdivided – theoretically ad infinitum. Dewey is under fire these days, it seems, but I still like the elegance.

Alberto Manguel does not use Dewey, it would seem; his library has 'no authoritarian catalogue' and the title of his book – *The Library at Night* – is intended to evoke that random, disordered quality that he feels so crucial to a library, that power to make connections, create echoes, cross cultures. A majestic collection such as his would do precisely that; it has the discipline of groupings, in some form, and further groupings within these, but its essential feature is that it is a private not a public library. The shelving system of a public library must be apparent to all users; a private library is *sui generis* – it has been assembled in response to the pursuits of a particular mind, a particular reading life, and is coloured by all the associations and connections of that particular reading narrative. It is not trying to be comprehensive; it is relishing selection. It is about time and space;

it tells you where this person has been, in every sense. Manguel records his pleasure, when unpacking his books and starting to arrange them in their French barn, at the coded references he found among the pages: the tram ticket reminding him of Buenos Aires, the paper napkin from the Café de Flore, the name and phone number scribbled on a flyleaf.

Exactly so. For any of us, with our humbler collections, the books have this archival aspect; they are themselves, but they also speak for us, for this owner, for you, for me. My books spill train tickets, invoices, pages of notes, the occasional underlining or swipe with the highlighter (though I don't approve of defacing books). A little copy of *Silas Marner* in a slipcase has my name in childish handwriting – Penelope Low – and a year, 1945. And there too is the printed sticker of the bookseller: Librairie Cité du Livre, 2 rue Fouad, Alexandrie. So I acquired it at the age of twelve, in wartime Alexandria. And it has followed me from there, and then.

Perhaps my most treasured shelves are those with the old blue Pelicans, over fifty paperbacks, including some seminal titles: F. R. Leavis's *The Great Tradition*, Margaret Mead's *Growing Up in New Guinea*, Richard Hoggart's *The Uses of Literacy*, Richard Titmuss's *The Gift Relationship*. And John Bowlby's *Child Care and the Growth Of Love*, which had us young mothers of the mid-century in a fever of guilt if we handed our under-fives over to someone else for longer than an hour or so lest we risked raising a social psychopath – even the father was considered an inadequate stand-in. Pelicans were the thinking person's library – for 3/6 you opened the mind a little further. And Penguin had of course their own flamboyant Dewey system – the splendid colour-coding: orange for fiction, green for crime, dark blue for biography, cherry red for travel.

I don't have enough old Penguins. The Pelicans have survived, but the rest have mostly disappeared – read until in bits, perhaps, or left on beaches or in trains or lent and not returned. And long gone are the days when a paperback meant a Penguin, pure and simple, let alone when a paperback publisher could confidently market a product with no image at all on the cover – just the title and the author's name, emphatically lettered. Beautiful.

Biography and autobiography and memoir are alphabetical by subject, for me, and I rather relish the strange juxtapositions – Edith Sitwell and Wole Soyinka, Kipling and Werner Heisenberg. Like a game of Consequences: He Said To Her . . . And The Consequence Was . . . This is Manguel's library at night – the library of thoughts and voices and associations. I was once taken on a tour of the stack at the Humanities Research Center in Austin, Texas, where the long shelves of that great literary archive reach away into shadowy distances, each run of boxes labelled – Hemingway, Joyce, Woolf – and one imagined it when the archivists were gone, a silent colloquy of all those voices.

The biblical story of the Tower of Babel has an apparently malevolent Deity creating a confusion of languages in order to foil attempts at the unity of mankind, the term Babel thus becoming a synonym for linguistic chaos. A library is indeed a Tower of Babel – multilingual, multicultural. Jorge Luis Borges was a librarian as well as a writer, a dual commitment which presumably accounts for that enigmatic story 'The Library of Babel' in which he proposes a library that is composed of infinite hexagonal galleries, in which each book is of uniform format – four hundred and ten pages – and amongst which librarians wander in interminable pursuit of some final truth, the book that will explain all books, many of whom have strangled one another, succumbed to disease, or committed suicide. It sounds more like life as lived than the ambience of the British Library, the Library of Congress or the Bibliothèque Nationale and indeed the story can be read as some sort of fable or allegory with the library as the universe: 'unlimited and cyclical'. But the image is a powerful one: the multiplicity of a library, the cacophony of voices, its impenetrability, unless you can read the codes. When I worked in the Round Reading Room at the British Museum, before the British Library moved to St Pancras, I used to have a fantasy – a short story that I never wrote – in which humanity has disappeared, all systems are down, for ever, and members of an alien race pad into the Reading Room, taking down the catalogues with their long green fingers, crack teams of scholars who have been set to work to penetrate the mysteries of this inexplicable archive, in which, now, all material is of equal significance: the Lindisfarne Gospels and *Beekeeping for Beginners*, the Koran and the *Guinness Book of Records*, *Hamlet* and *Asterix*. A great library is anything and everything. It is not for its current custodians to judge what the future will find to be of importance, and it is this eclecticism that gives it the mystique, that is the wonder of it. A private collection is another matter entirely: you or I have accumulated what we feel to be of significance to us, the books speak for what we have responded to or wanted to know about or got interested in and may include many acquisitions that have sneaked in for no good reason, like – in my case – that fat hardback *Collected Works* of Jane Bowles, whose work I do not care for, and plenty of other titles towards which I am indifferent but that I might need to check out at some point.

There has been plenty of checking out in the service of these pages. That is the other function of a private library – reference. Today we have the internet, and very wonderful it is, and I am getting better at Googling, but an atavistic urge still has me reaching for the Shorter Oxford, or Chambers, or *Brewer's Dictionary of Phrase and Fable*, or *The Oxford Dictionary of Quotations*, those reliable companions over the decades.

My first engagement with a great library was as a student. A vague memory of induction to the Bodleian is that it involved making some kind of ritual declaration in Latin – presumably that you wouldn't steal or abuse the books – and of the inimitable smell of Duke Humfrey's Library, the rich aroma of old book – very old book, in that case. I doubt if I ever went into it again. The Radcliffe Camera was the place for history undergraduates; you got to know it all too well, homing in on favourite desks, from which you could look around and see who else was there, the hunt along the shelves for the book you needed and the frustration when you found it was already taken, which meant a search for the reader and a negotiation about how long he or she would be wanting it. One man always achieved the book I was after before I could get to it by dint of arriving at the library the moment it opened, which I never managed to do. Years later I came across him again, by which time he was the distinguished historian Theodore Zeldin; it was somehow gratifying to know that he had put the books to better use than I had – one forgave that pre-emptive early rising.

In 1993 I was invited to serve on the Board of the British Library, and did so for six years, only too glad to give up some time and energy to an institution from which I had had so much. And what can be more important than the national archive? Here is the record of pretty much everything that has been thought, and said, and done over the centuries, not just in these islands but the world over – the Library thinks multicultural, it reaches out in space as well as time. As a reader, I was awed by the sense of that vasty deep from which you could conjure up not spirits, but the precise work you had noted in the catalogue, the sense of infinity of choice but also of order imposed, the idea of an immeasurable resource, a grand ideal, made available to individual enquiry. As a Board member, I was immersed, involved, sometimes baffled, occasionally panic-stricken.

Membership of the Board was quite a commitment: ten meetings a year of three hours or so, each meeting served by a batch of papers that certainly took me half a day or more to read. Some ancillary commitments. Board membership carried a modest salary; you had been appointed by the Secretary of State. In my day there were, I think, twelve members, who included the three senior executives of the Library. Eleven suits, and me; for three years I was the only woman on the Board. The sole advantage of that, from my point of view, was that my isolation made it virtually impossible for the Chairman to avoid my eye if I wished to say something: discrimination, that would have been.

I enjoyed those Board years – learning corporate speak, a language new to me, watching the St Pancras building rise from the rubble of its construction site, for this was the point at which the Library was about to leave its old home in the British Museum. We had conducted tours, wearing hard hats, being briefed about the problems with wiring and shelving. It was a dismaying process at times; you thought you had signed up for involvement with the running of a great library, instead we found ourselves presiding over the travails of one of the most elaborate and complex construction processes this country has known. There was plenty of white water – boardroom confrontations between our project manager and that of the Department of Arts and Libraries, responsible for the construction, angry letters flying from the Library to the Department. I listened to civil service speak, also new to me. But at last the new Library was there. I remember a triumphant completion tour: the acreage of shelving, the marvels of the book delivery system, the light-flooded reading-rooms. The safety measures: the sprinkler system, the steel doors that would close in the event of fire. One of these was demonstrated – the imposing shutter that inched slowly and remorselessly down. And I remember that

Matthew Farrer, a fellow Board member, looked at me and we both said 'Gagool!' – being of the generation that read *King Solomon's Mines*. A neat instance of cultural community, and nicely appropriate to the Library.

The technologies of today were relatively new, back then, but the Library was at the cutting edge. Turning the Pages became available, that enthralling process whereby you can wipe a finger across a screen and leaf your way through a virtual Luttrell Psalter or Sherborne Missal. The then Director of Information Technology gave a presentation on current innovations, and was asked by someone what he thought the most significant information development so far. Without hesitation he replied: 'The book – user-friendly, portable, requires no infrastructure, relatively non-degradable.'

Since then, the e-book. I don't care to read on an e-reader myself, though I would under certain circumstances – when travelling, or if in hospital – and I get bored by the exclusive defence of either paper or screen. Future readers will require both, I assume, but I can't imagine that many would wish to own a personal library that consisted of the Kindle on the coffee table, rather than some shelves of books, with all their eloquence about where we have been and who we are.

There is a devastating poem by Tony Harrison

about his mother's death, about love and grief, about the distance between him and his father:

> Back in our silences and sullen looks,
> for all the Scotch we drink, what's still between's
> not the thirty or so years, but books, books, books.

I can hardly bear to read that poem; it is so sad, and so true. Books can have a divisive power. They can estrange – but can also unite, of course. Great courtship material, books – that discovery of a shared enthusiasm, the exchange of gifts. We read to bond, to oblige, to discover how someone else reads. And read to persuade, to agree or disagree. Why weren't book groups around when I was a child-tethered young mother in Swansea in the 1960s? Why didn't we think of starting one up? They are a marvellous concept, combining a social and intellectual function: you spend time with like-minded others. You read something you might not otherwise have read and are provoked to defend, or criticize.

Cultural community is shared reading, the references and images that you and I both know. Books are the mind's ballast, for so many of us – the cargo that makes us what we are, a freight that is ephemeral and indelible, half-forgotten but leaving an imprint. They are nutrition, too. My old age fear is not being able to read – the worst deprivation. Or no longer having my books around me: the familiar, eclectic, explanatory assemblage that hitches me to the wide world, that has freed me from the prison of myself, that has helped me to think, and to write.

Six Things

My house has many *things*, too, besides those books –
the accretions of a lifetime. Not many of them are
valuable; some of them are eloquent. People's possessions speak of them: they are resonant and
betraying and reflective. When house-hunting, I
used to find myself paying more attention to the
furnishings than to the house one was supposed to
be inspecting. They spoke of the people who lived
here.

So in this last section I have picked out six of the
things that articulate something of who I am. This is
to plagiarize myself, in a way – I used a similar device
in *A House Unlocked*, making objects in my grandmother's house speak for a time, for the century. But
self-plagiarization seems to me permissible. And, at
this late point in life, I have seen these objects in the
house imbued with new significance – I have seen
how they reflect interests, and concerns, how they
chart where I've been, and how I've been.

I imagine them in a car boot sale, or an auction
room, mute, anonymous, though perhaps each might
be picked up, considered, thought to have some

intrinsic merit – or not. The bronze cat would be a snip – someone would bag that. The Jerusalem Bible might appeal, and the sampler. The leaping fish sherd and the ammonites and the duck kettle-holders are probably in a box of assorted junk, unwanted.

But before that happens let me give them each their story – theirs and mine. A sort of material memoir.

The duck kettle-holders from Maine

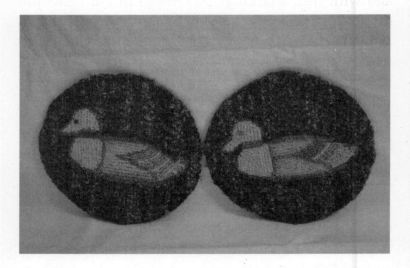

These are, strictly speaking, American folk art. They are a pair of circular kettle-holders, about nine inches in diameter, each with a duck worked in coloured

wools on sacking. They were sent me by my friend
Betty, many years ago, as an addition to our collection
of emblematic ducks which had accrued – inevitably –
when we lived in Oxfordshire at the seventeenth-century
farmhouse called Duck End. Decoy ducks, gift shop
ducks, small oriental papier mâché ducks.

These particular ducks had been made by an old
lady living at some rather remote spot in Maine; she
made such things for sale at local fairs and was working nicely in the American folk art tradition. The
ducks are closely woven in wool, simple, stylized,
and with their markings picked out in different colours. Betty breeds border collies and is a renowned
sheepdog handler and demonstrator at sheepdog
trials. She was on a trip to one such trial up in Maine,
had rather lost her way and was in desperate need of
water for her dogs. She stopped off at the old lady's
house to ask for water and directions. The old lady
invited her into her kitchen, filled a can, and Betty
spotted the ducks and exclaimed. It was apparent
that this was by way of a (very small) business, and
she asked if she could buy them. The old lady
demurred: trouble was, she needed something for
the craft fair next week, she was right out of burlap
so couldn't make some more, and if she let these go
she would have nothing to show. Okay, said Betty,
what if I drive to a store, get you some burlap – then
could I have them? That would be fine, it seemed. So

Betty sought the nearest store (some way away), achieved a yard of sacking, and the ducks were hers. And, in due course, mine.

The ducks are stitched on a mottled grey-brown background, and outlined in blue. They have brownish-buff sides, a blue band at the tail end, with some white, cream-white head and breast, short beak and rounded head. Precisely portrayed ducks. And it seems to me that this lady who had lived all her life in rural Maine, amid its wildlife, would not have adorned her kettle-holders with any old made-up duck. These would be some actual duck. So – I must turn to Peterson – *A Field Guide to the Birds East of the Rockies*.

American Peterson is lavish, compared to our own familiar European Peterson. We have five owls (British, that is – we can't claim European exotics such as Tengmalm's Owl); they have twelve, and that's east of the Rockies only. Eleven woodpeckers for heaven's sake, as against our own mingy three. A whole page of what we call 'little brown jobs': Confusing Fall Warblers. You can say that again – they look more like Indistinguishable Fall Warblers to me. And a whole squad of them, when we have only to deal with chiff-chaffs and garden warblers and the willow warbler and a few more.

But what about my ducks? There is nothing in Peterson that exactly corresponds, but the harlequin duck is not a bad fit. The harlequin duck has brown sides, glimpses of blue at the tail and is described as 'smallish slaty duck with chestnut sides and odd white patches and spots'. And – aha! – the range is right and the habitat is described as 'tumbled mountain streams, rocky coastal waters'. Plenty of rocky coast where Betty was driving. So I choose to think that the kettle-holder ducks are the old lady's personal take on the harlequin duck. And she worked them in the fine tradition of American folk art, probably just as her own mother and grandmother had done.

I have a copy of American Peterson because for as long as I can remember I have bird-watched, in the most amateur way possible, just if and when an opportunity arose. I have a *Field Guide to the Birds of Australia* as well, and I sometimes take that up just to browse in wonder among its esoteric offerings: Helmeted Friarbird, Australian King Parrot, Flame Robin. And to remember the morning a kindly couple of ornithologists in Adelaide took me to a salt-marsh bird sanctuary: pelican, egrets, ibis, storks. And the rosellas in suburban gardens, the flocks of sulphur-crested cockatoos in the bush, the tiny sapphire wren I once saw. Australian bird-watching made our own homely collection seem tame indeed.

So the Maine ducks tap into a lifelong fringe interest, for me. I always notice birds. A small triumph when I have spotted egrets in the Exe estuary from the train, going to a literary festival. Keeping an eye out for red kites over the Berkshire Downs, driving to Somerset with Josephine. Looking for the pair of jays that sometimes appear in my London square. And, time was, I kept the Official Duck End Bird List beside my desk in Oxfordshire; species seen as I worked there. The rule being that the bird must have been seen as I sat, without getting up. Around thirty, I think, including treecreeper, nuthatch, all three wood-peckers, flycatcher, all the tits. I can't think how I got any work done.

In Orkney, once, we had the experience of being taken to a sea-bird cliff on Papa Westray by the young woman ornithologist whose summer job was to record the success or failure of the nesting birds – a daily record, with each nest site plotted on transparent paper laid over photographs of the cliff. The populations to be thus assessed, and whether stable or falling. The cliff face was a tenement, its assorted occupants at different levels – fulmars, razorbills, guillemots, kittiwakes . . . And other treats in Orkney, flagship of the Royal Society for the Protection of Birds: an outing with Eric Meek, its area manager there, who would indicate a speck on the far side of a loch – 'and there's a female merganser', pick out a hen harrier amid a distant flock of gulls, stare at something bobbing about invisibly in some reeds – 'A phalarope!' The real ornithologist sees with enhanced vision; they speak another language. But the rest of us can potter about on the nursery slopes, finding out.

What is it about birds? The Royal Society for the Protection of Birds' current membership stands at over one million, topped only by the National Trust. Is it that they are ubiquitous – town or country? That we have been educated by television nature programmes? That we recognize the last gasp of the dinosaurs? Perhaps that bird-watching as an activity costs little – unless you insist on some state-of-the-art telescope – can be done almost anywhere, including out of your own window. Garden bird-feeders are national suburban equipment, and apparently make a significant contribution to the survival of some species. Suffice it that many people respond to birds, more than to any other creature. I once stood watching a pair of pied wagtails on a railway platform – you don't so often find wagtails making a living at a train station. They were largely ignored, and then I noticed a woman intent upon the birds; we exchanged little conspiratorial smiles: 'You too!'

I have never seen a harlequin duck, and I don't expect I ever shall. But somewhere there is one foraging on a rocky coast, tenuously linked to the kettle-holders in my kitchen.

The blue lias ammonites

Fossils. Two little curled shapes, an inch across, that hang in the grey ocean of a sea-smoothed flat pebble of blue lias, itself just larger than an opened hand. I picked it up on the beach at Charmouth, in Dorset, long ago. I have other ammonites – exquisite polished sections, but bought from the fossil shop at Lyme Regis, which is not nearly as satisfying as the one you found yourself. They amaze me, these small creatures that expired together once, in just such proximity, I suppose, so many million years ago, and remain thus, propped on my bookshelf.

Between one hundred and ninety-five and two hundred million years ago, since the blue lias is late Triassic and early Jurassic, the seam of rock that runs down across the country from Yorkshire to the south coast at Dorset, taking in north Somerset and parts of south Wales. Ammonites are marine invertebrates, and, quite apart from their own immense antiquity, their very name races back through time, owed to Pliny, who called these fossils 'horns of Ammon' because their spiral shape resembled tightly coiled rams' horns, associated with the Egyptian god Ammon. It is like the night sky being named for Greek mythology – Andromeda, Cassiopeia, Aquarius, Orion, Pegasus – the physical world demanding a much deeper reference than our own small slice of time.

Ammonites lived in open water, for the most part, cruising in ancient seas, myriads of them, falling on their death to the sea floor where they were gradually buried in the accumulating sediment. The ammonoids show rapid evolution; species evolve and become extinct at faster rates than other groups, making them useful index fossils, used to date the sedimentary rock in which they are found. Our own Jurassic ammonites seldom exceed nine inches in diameter – my two are mere babies at an inch. But there was a German monster over six feet across and others in North America at four feet, while the Portland stone here can offer a two-foot species.

Ammonite taxonomy is vast – there were masses of them, evolving, becoming extinct. Because of where they were and when, my two in their little slab of blue lias must be some kind of asteroceras or promicroceras, but it is impossible to tell which, or what they were within their genus – *Asteroceras confusum* (is that a joke?), *Asteroceras stellare*, *Promicroceras pyritosum* – goodness knows.

Palaeontology is awe-inspiring, sobering. Deep time. It puts you in your place – a mere flicker of life in the scheme of things. I take note of that whenever I walk on one of the north Somerset beaches. The blue lias surfaces here, lifting out of the Bristol Channel – the grey and pink pebbles at Watchet, the cliffs seamed with equally grey and pink alabaster. My aunt Rachel used the alabaster for sculpting, foraging for chunks at the foot of the cliffs after winter storms. It was tiresome material to sculpt – too soft, too liable to crumble under her tools – but we have two of her successes, a long, grey, rather primeval-looking fish, a relative of the coelacanth, I'd say. And a little maquette, a Henry Moore figurine. I've often picked up ammonites at Watchet, both embedded in a stone or as an isolated snail shape. Belemnites, too, those pointed tubular forms. In fact, I think it was on Watchet beach that the deep past first signalled, when I was ammonite-hunting as a teenager.

Ammonites and a palaeontologist have surfaced in fiction, for me – an instance of the way in which the things that alert the mind then insert themselves into what gets written. Shape it, indeed. Watchet beach and its ammonites somehow prompted a novel in which the central figure is a palaeontologist, whose career trajectory begins when as a child he heaves up a lump of blue lias at Watchet, and sees something intriguing upon it. I don't think I would have made much of a palaeontologist myself – I don't have a sufficiently scientific turn of mind; he is a surrogate, perhaps. And, for a novelist, it is the accumulation of all these matters grabbing the attention over the years that will direct the sort of stories that get told, the kind of people who will inhabit them. Every aspect of time, for me, from the deep time of the ammonites through the historian's attempt to analyse the past, to the bewildering operation of memory.

But rocks and fossils never seem like putative material, at the time – they are just something that has made the mind sit up and pay attention. I wish I had paid attention more systematically – done some rock-watching in the way that I have bird-watched, and checked what I was looking at. The blue lias is all that I can recognize, and Devon's red sandstone, and Oxfordshire's oolitic limestone, which built two of the houses in which I have lived. The regrets of old age are polarized: you wish you had not done certain things – behaved thus, responded like that – and you wish you had seized more of the day, been greedier, packed more in. I wish I had packed in more rocks – on foot, legging it, learning what it was I walked over, looked at. Walking was a central pleasure, time was – Offa's Dyke, when the going was good, Wenlock Edge, a bit of the Pennine Way. I looked up, and around – birds, wild flowers – but didn't focus on down, on the deep time over which one was walking.

The naming of things. I have always needed that, where the physical world is concerned; much poring over bird books and my forty-year-old copy of Keble Martin's *The Concise British Flora in Colour*. It annoys me that I can't identify my blue lias ammonites; just 'some kind of asteroceras or promicroceras' won't do. The world and its life are the abiding delight and fascination, and to savour them to the full you want to have things labelled, named, classified; a tree is not just a tree, it is a particular tree, or you are only enjoying it as an agreeable sight. I can understand exactly what drove Linnaeus, despite being myself quite unscientific. Taxonomy is crucial, essential – the majestic discipline that marshals the natural world, so that everyone can know what is what and what it is not. Perhaps this urge for identification began for me in the nursery in Egypt (it never did get known as the schoolroom) when Lucy and I did Natural History on Wednesday mornings out of Arabella Buckley's *Eyes and No Eyes*, that late nineteenth-century guide to the flora and fauna of the English pond and stream: caddis fly larva, water boatman, dragon-fly. And, indeed, out of Bentham and Hooker, the standard wild flower manual; we searched the fringes of the sugar-cane fields for scarlet pimpernel, shepherd's purse, vetch.

The Jerusalem Bible

It is New Testament only, quite small – about nine inches by five – and it is bound with exquisitely inlaid mother-of-pearl, making it feel heavy, chunky. This must be real mother-of-pearl. If it were a tourist offering of today, I would propose plastic imitation, but plastic was not around in 1942, so it must be the real thing, ripped probably from the floor of the Red Sea, and this is therefore an environmentally reprehensible Bible. But environmental concern was not much around either in 1942.

Lucy bought it for me at the Church of the Holy Sepulchre in Jerusalem, and has written in it: Penelope Low from Nanny. It was late summer 1942, when Rommel's army in Libya had advanced to within a hundred miles of the Egyptian border, and British families were advised to leave the country. My mother had opted for Palestine, as opposed to Cape Town, the alternative; my father stayed at his job with an Egyptian bank. This would be only a temporary interruption to the status quo, seems to have been the assumption, we would soon be going home – as was indeed the case, but the bland optimism now seems strange: it looks today as though Egypt could very well have fallen to the German advance, and must have done so at the time to anyone facing the facts.

The title page of the Jerusalem Bible says, at the foot: 'The American Colony Stores, Jerusalem, Palestine'. I am sure that this means simply that it was produced for this outlet, which presumably then supplied some bookstall at the Holy Sepulchre, because I am certain that Lucy's purchase took place there. More on the American colony in a moment; for now, we are in the crowded, incense-reeking interior of the church, and somewhere in a crevice of memory that day lingers, this carefully considered purchase – which would have been quite expensive, and I was grateful, and proud of this new treasure – and Lucy's prickly response to this place: its clamour, its rituals, the smells and bells, the mass of people. She had good reason; Lucy was paid-up Church of England, and the Church of the Holy Sepulchre was everything but that. This was a long way from the measured sobriety of Cairo's Anglican Cathedral. The Church of the Holy Sepulchre is – was – the headquarters of the Greek Orthodox Patriarch, and control of the building is shared between several churches – Roman Catholic, Eastern and Oriental Orthodoxies. Anglican and Protestant Christians have no permanent presence. Lucy was feeling herself to be on alien territory, and was probably bothered about this because she was quite devout, and this after all was the site of Golgotha, where the Crucifixion took place, and where Christ was buried. Perhaps the purchase of the Bible was a small defiant statement: we too are Christians.

And it must have caught the eye. It is handsome – on the front a Greek cross, set in a circle within a diamond of mother-of-pearl inlay, further small inlay slabs all around, forming a nest of rectangles, the whole thing iridescent – a shimmer of blues, pinks, greens, pearly whites. Mother-of-pearl; nacre.

Nacre is the inner shell layer of some molluscs,

long valued as a decorative material – all those bil-
lions of pearl buttons, for starters. I have a butter
knife with a mother-of-pearl handle; many such were
manufactured during the last two and three centuries, no doubt. But nowadays the species supplying
this industry are endangered, and plundering the
oceans in the service of buttons and knives is frowned
on. That shop in Covent Garden that used to have
baskets stacked high with giant shells and nacre molluscs has long since closed down.

So, thus, that morning in 1942, and the Bible that
remembers the Church of the Holy Sepulchre (and,
at one remove, the vibrant life at the bottom of the
Red Sea). We were there as tourists, and must have
seen its sights, but of those I remember nothing. I
was nine.

Hadrian built a temple on the site, originally – the
temple of Aphrodite – which was demolished by the
Emperor Constantine in around 325 when he had
required his mother Helena to build churches on all the
sites associated with the life of Christ. Helena is said to
have discovered the True Cross during her excavations,
though it is not clear whether it was under her auspices
that it eventually got broken up into relics that would
provide churches everywhere with enough fragments
to marshal a whole army of crosses. The medieval
relics marketing industry is fascinating: ideally, a
splinter of the True Cross, or a Holy Thorn, failing

that, hair or toenail of a saint, even a more substantial chunk of bone. Christ is of course the problem, there never having been an available corpse; but never mind, that can be got round, with a bit of ingenuity: a phial containing the breath of Christ. A religious tourist trade that has diminished today to Bibles and postcards.

Constantine's edifice was built as two connected churches, most of which were destroyed in 1009 by the Fatimid caliph, though in a later deal between the Fatimids and the Byzantine Empire some rebuilding was allowed and a mosque reopened in Constantinople. Then came the Crusades; the objective of every Crusader was to pray in the Church of the Holy Sepulchre. Jerusalem was taken, and throughout the Crusader period there was much rebuilding and excavation of the church and its site, until the city fell to Saladin in 1184, though a treaty allowed Christian pilgrims to enter the church. Effectively, the site was a battleground for centuries, the building itself rising and falling, knocked down, restored, revived, neglected, fought over. And, it appears, this tradition survives with occasional brawls between the contemporary occupants; in 2002 the Ethiopian contingent objected to a Coptic monk having moved his chair from an agreed spot – eleven people were hospitalized after the resulting commotion.

Representatives of all these sects would have been there on that morning in 1942 – Greek Orthodox in full fig, monks and priests and a herd of tourists that would have included plenty of those displaced by the war, like ourselves. Soldiers everywhere, and RAF and ATS and WAAF; we were connoisseurs of categories and uniforms – some Aussies over there, and those are New Zealanders, and he's Free French. Jerusalem would have been a favourite leave destination.

Lucy and I were living in some style. We were at Government House, by invitation of the British High Commissioner's wife, because before Lucy took me on she had looked after their children. And thus it was, there, that I saw General de Gaulle in his dressing-gown, but that too is another story. My mother had not been invited to Government House, and was staying more modestly at the American Colony Hotel, which I remember as having a lovely courtyard with orange trees, resident tortoises, and amazing ice-cream. It was the hotel of choice for the discriminating: charming, cheap, more select than the cosmopolitan and pricey King David, and with an interesting background.

The hotel was run by descendants of an American religious group. I gave an inaccurate description of these in *Oleander, Jacaranda*, drawing on remembered hearsay. I am now better informed. They had left Chicago for Jerusalem in 1881, so as to be there well in time for the Second Coming at the millennium. They were joined by others from America and from Swe-

den, and eventually formed a community of a
hundred or so, who engaged in good works, diversi-
fied into farming, and, after the Second Coming failed
to take place, the surviving family of the original
group founded the hotel, sited partly in the historic
'Big House' just east of the Damascus Gate which the
first arrivals had made their home. There my mother
stayed, modestly, and there could I, today, though
rather less modestly.

The American Colony Hotel is five star, now, and
when I Google it I can indeed see a garden courtyard,
and very inviting it looks. 'Privately owned boutique
hotel . . . an oasis of timeless elegance.' Swimming-
pool, complimentary internet access, TV with
in-house video. And there is obliging availability: I
can have a standard double room tomorrow night for
£175, or – if I want to push out the boat – the Deluxe
Pasha King Room for £345. Are there still tortoises, I
wonder? And do they still produce Bibles bound in
mother-of-pearl?

I have four more Bibles, as well as the Jerusalem
Bible. So I am an agnostic who owns five Bibles. One
is the battered old King James Version with which I
grew up, from which Lucy and I read every morning
at the start of the day's lessons: Bible Study. Then
there is something called the Bible Designed to be
Read as Literature, which seems to bestow literary
status on the original text simply by knocking out the

traditional verse numbers. Given to me by my grand-mother. And then there is a dreadful thing called the Good News Bible, which has little cartoony illustrations and has debased the language of the King James Version to such an extent that I shall not even give a quote, to spare those of you who have not come across it. And there is a further offering called the New International Version, which is somewhat less debased but why bother at all, when you have the King James? These last two were acquired by myself, when I noticed them in churches I was visiting – Pevsner in hand, usually – and thought: what on earth is going on?

The language of the King James Version was laid down in my mind, as a child, like some kind of rich sediment: those cadences, the rhythm of the phrases. The fact that we met unfamiliar words and that meaning was occasionally obscure bothered neither Lucy nor me. Lucy was there for reasons of piety and the requirements of the National Parents Educational Union's daily timetable; I rather enjoyed the stories. Intensive exposure to that beautiful text, to the liturgy, to the narrative, has not made me a Christian, evidently, but I am profoundly grateful for it. If you don't know something of the biblical narrative you are going to be bewildered by most early art and by innumerable references in English prose and poetry. And if you have not known the King James Version you will not have experienced the English language at its most elegant, its most eloquent.

I am an agnostic who relishes the equipment of Christianity: its mythologies, its buildings, its ceremonies, its music, the whole edifice without which ours would be a diminished world. I like to attend a service. I am a church-visiting addict, with cathedrals the ultimate indulgence. An ambiguous position; some may say, hypocritical. I want it all to go on, I want it all to be there, but I can't subscribe to the beliefs. I am accredited – baptized, confirmed; but nobody asked me if I wanted to be, at some point scepticism struck, and I stepped aside. But not very far; there remains a confusing, or confused, relationship with this physical and mythological presence, which is in some way sustaining. Perhaps this is because I grew up with the Bible and the rituals of the Church of England; perhaps it is because, however secular-minded, you can recognize the effect, the allure of religion (which is why I call myself an agnostic rather than an atheist). Jack shared my unbelief. A friend and colleague of his, Father Conor Martin, was a Jesuit priest, a fellow political theorist and an academic in Dublin; Conor perfectly accepted Jack's position, but had also his own subversive comment: 'Ah, but Jack, you're a spiritual man.' I think I know what he meant.

The Gayer-Anderson cat

It is seated upright, seventeen inches tall, an improbable cat in that its front legs are unrealistically long, but otherwise entirely cat-like, sinuous, elegant, prick-eared, its back legs invisible beneath its haunches, its tail lying straight alongside. It has a powerful presence – its cavernous eye sockets seem to stare enigmatically. It wears gilt earrings and a nose-ring, a silver necklet, and there is a winged scarab on its chest and another on its forehead.

The original is a familiar presence in the Egyptian hall of the British Museum. Mine is a replica, sold by the Museum's shop and a Christmas present from Jack over twenty years ago. The shop still sells them, online, for £450. Not as much, I trust, back then. The cat is a representation of the cat goddess Bastet, likely to have been a votive statue, and dates from what Egyptologists call the Late Period – about 664–332 BC. For the Museum, it is one of its most iconic objects, much viewed and admired, and, as I write, I learn from the internet that it is on loan this year to the Shetland Museum at Lerwick. You can't get much further than that from ancient Egypt.

The cat was given to the Museum by Major R. G. Gayer-Anderson, who had collected it in Egypt in the 1930s along with much else by way of Egyptian antiquities – 7,500 items of all periods were given to the Fitzwilliam in Cambridge by him and his twin brother. A sizeable haul, back in the days when hoovering up antiquities from Egyptian traders was a favourite activity of foreign visitors. Today, removal of antiquities is strictly forbidden; you can't – or shouldn't – smuggle out so much as a potsherd.

Gayer-Anderson acquired the cat from a dealer and went to work on it to get rid of the accumulated surface incrustations, and to repair some of the damage it had suffered. His repairs seem to have been reasonably skilful but the cleaning process rather too enthusiastic; the original surface is now lost, and its present appearance – that gleaming greenish-black – is not what it would have been when it was created.

Gayer-Anderson was a friend of my London grand-parents, and family legend has it that when he came back to England after his long residence in Egypt he loaned the cat to my grandmother for a while before giving it to the Museum, and it formed the centre-piece of her dining-room table at 76 Harley Street (my grandfather had been a surgeon in the days when such medical people owned an entire Harley Street house, and brought up their families there).

I wonder if this is true. Neal Spencer, in his booklet for the Museum on the cat, gives an account of its movements after it arrived in England which makes the family story somewhat unlikely, on the face of it. The cat seems to have spent the late 1930s and the war period in a sealed wooden box in the vault of Lloyds Bank in Lavenham, Suffolk, while a lady called Mary Stout, a friend of Gayer-Anderson and temporary cus-todian of the cat, argued with the Museum about the terms of the bequest. But . . . it is possible; there may have been some interlude when it fetched up with my grandmother – she was certainly also a close friend, and this legend must have sprung from somewhere.

By the time I came to that house, in 1945, the cat

was gone – if ever it was there – and Gayer-Anderson
had died. But I had met him as a child, in Egypt,
when my mother and I were occasionally invited to
tea at the Bayt al-Kritiliya, the restored seventeenth-
century Mameluke house in old Cairo where he lived
and which he had made a sort of Arabian Nights
incarnate with its fountains, mashrabiya windows,
oriental furnishings. The tea served was conventional English afternoon tea, but the rest was exotic,
magical; I adored it. Alas, of Gayer-Anderson Pasha
(the honorific bestowed on him by King Farouk) I
remember little. Large, jolly – that is the impression.

He had lived in Egypt for many years, having been
seconded to the Egyptian army from the Royal Army
Medical Corps after training as a doctor. There, he
became Egyptian Recruiting Officer, and, later, Oriental Secretary to the High Commission – the British
High Commission in Cairo, that is. This must mean
some kind of adviser, I suppose – the chap who knows
a lot about how things operate around here. Gayer-
Anderson probably did, and described himself as an
Orientalist – that now somewhat discredited term.
He contributed to a memoir of my Harley Street surgeon grandfather, and described their initial meeting
at Gallipoli in 1915, on the Base Depot Ship *Aragon*,
over a dinner with 'many a good yarn capped by a
better'. My grandfather was notoriously genial, and a
raconteur, and they clearly hit it off, all amidst the

carnage of the Gallipoli campaign, with my grandfather honing his surgical skills when not breaking
off for a convivial evening.

They met up again a bit later in Cairo, where Gayer-
Anderson showed my grandfather around and
described him as 'unfailingly courteous and consider-
ate' towards Egyptians of all classes 'as is not always
the case with Europeans'. I'm rather pleased to hear
that, and I note Gayer-Anderson's implied disapproval
of the prevailing attitudes of the day; he was only too
right, and it was much the same twenty years or so
later, when I was growing up there.

So what does the Gayer-Anderson cat mean to me,
staring inscrutable from one corner of my book-
room? Its presence, first and foremost; even this
replica has a force-field – your eye is drawn to it, sitting in that room I feel as though I am not alone.
Despite being unrealistic it is essentially cat-like – not
so much related to the comfortable complacent
domestic cat we all know but to some more ancient,
self-sufficient, prototype cat. I am reminded of the
paper-thin feral cats of Cairo that I saw when last I
went there, flitting the streets like ghost creatures.
Perhaps they are just that, ghosts of all those cats
turned into mummies in Pharaonic times – eviscer-
ated, wrapped, stacked up in their thousands in
animal cemeteries as tributes to the god.

I find myself responding to religions that recognize

animals – that revere animals, indeed. Ancient Egypt above all, with each god having his or her own dedicated species. But it is universal in time and space, animal worship, animal respect. Christians and Muslims seem the only people to have abandoned it. We use animals – eat them, farm them, labour them – but we have lost touch with that elemental instinct to accord them status. We may abuse them less – in some parts of the world – but we can't any longer see them as totemic, as imbued with individual significance: Ibis, Crocodile, Hawk, Bull, Bear, Monkey, Serpent. And Cat. My cat reminds me of that loss.

It is an emblematic cat, then – essence of cat. And it is also, for me, a cat that resonates in time and space, within my own time-span and beyond; it speaks of that tall house in Harley Street, of a Mameluke house in Cairo, of a ship anchored off Gallipoli in 1915.

Elizabeth Barker's sampler

It is dated 1788. I doubt if Elizabeth Barker was a child; children usually give their age, on a sampler. No, a grown-up, I think, and while her sampler is not especially accomplished, it is pleasing, with text surrounded by stylized trees with birds and butterflies, and, below,

two small stags and a pair of even smaller dogs, one brown, one black. It is the black dog that perhaps makes this my favourite sampler, along with the fact that it is the only one I have from the eighteenth century. The feisty little stitched black dog stands out, demanding attention from 1788.

At some point, way back, I thought I would start a sampler collection. I rapidly ran out of steam, partly because this proved a somewhat expensive undertaking, but also, I think, the commitment waned. So I have just eight samplers. I am still interested in, attracted by, samplers, but I feel a certain ambivalence. One of mine claims to be the work of: 'Sarah Nottage. In her 7th year. 1836.' I sincerely hope it wasn't. If six-year-old fingers really toiled over that canvas, made those tiny stitches, then that was child abuse. I hope – and suspect – that an adult hand helped out, at the very least.

Sarah's text is a standard one:

> Food, raiment, dwelling, health and friends
> Thou, Lord, has made our lot
> With Thee our bliss begins and ends
> As we are Thine, or not.

And so forth for two more verses . . . Piety is always the textual note.

Anna Maria Stacey, aged ten, in 1846, has:

> Jesus permit thy gracious name to stand
> As the first effort of an infant hand . . .

Which is straight out of the pattern books from which both texts and designs were taken. Pious sentiments, and formal designs of trees, flowers, animals, which may form a border round the edge, or motifs within. In a child's sampler, there is often an alphabet somewhere.

All of mine are fairly run-of-the-mill samplers. One is a map of England, another popular choice.

All are worked in basic cross-stitch, and none have the elaborate originality of Victoria & Albert Museum quality samplers, as I realized when I looked into the matter once. In fact, the most interesting is perhaps the least immediately appealing – not well laid out, rather crudely worked. But the text is odd:

> Then ill [I'll] be not proud of my youth or my beauty since both of them wither and fade but [be?] in a good name by well doing my duty this will scent like a rose when I am dead.

Entirely secular; no religious sentiment. What is going on here? The next line is the key: 'This was done at New Lanark School by Janet Martin aged 11 years. Finished her sampler 7 April 1813.'

What is going on here is the first breath of utopian socialism. Robert Owen – the industrialist and social reformer. New Lanark cotton mills in southern Scotland came under Owen's management in 1800. Thinker and philanthropist, he believed in the alleviation of poverty through socialism, and had conspicuously rejected formal religion: 'all religions are based on the same ridiculous imagination, that make man a weak, imbecile animal; a furious bigot and fanatic; or a miserable hypocrite'. So, no 'Jesus permit thy gracious name to stand . . .' in his school, and the very existence of a school on that industrial site is a testimony to enlightenment.

I don't know where I acquired this, and I didn't realize its significance until some time later, deciphering that puzzling, awkwardly stitched text, and thinking: oh! New Lanark! Robert Owen! That sampler should be my favourite, for its historical and ideological freight, but I'm afraid Elizabeth Barker's little black dog has always elbowed it aside.

Samplers have had a further, personal relevance. My Somerset grandmother made one of her home and its setting, an exquisite, original design that shows the house, the garden pond with frogs and dragonflies, the white fantail pigeons, the dogs, the horses in the stables and, at the bottom, a row of small embroidered children – the wartime evacuees. She finished it in 1941, and it is my most treasured possession; an heirloom, indeed. Furthermore, set against my routinely worked nineteenth-century samplers, this is in a different league. My grandmother's work is indeed of Victoria & Albert Museum quality.

Her design was creative, elaborate, ingenious. She used not just basic cross-stitch but a wide variety of stitches, thus giving depth and texture to her piece. And she worked with specially dyed wools in a subtle palette of blues, greens, buff and a soft plum colour.

Is this art or craft? And wherein lies the distinction, anyway? My grandmother had done fine needlework all her life: drawn-thread work, Assisi work with silks, Winchester wool work. The essence of this is craft, I suppose, but she had always created her own designs – not a pattern book in the house. And with the sampler it seems to me that craft segues into art, if what is implied is a grander concept, an enhanced vision. Her sampler is an embroidered painting, a fond and sometimes witty image of a place, executed with elegance and imagination. I am always a little awed by it, knowing I could never have aspired to such work myself.

The leaping fish sherd

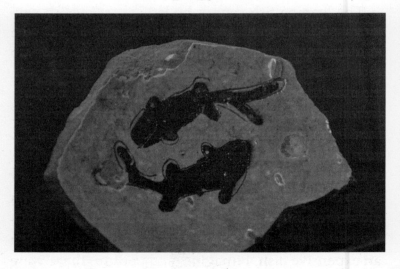

It is about four inches across; it is slightly curved and is clearly the fragmented base of what has once been a wide, shallow dish, with the round foot behind and the glazed surface above. The glaze is a rich honey colour, and on it dance two small black fish. This sherd is twelfth century, possibly earlier, and came from Fustat, the first capital of Egypt, which is today a vast rubbish tip outside Cairo.

A friend gave me the sherd, twenty years or so ago, and it has sat on my mantelpiece ever since, relished for its survival, for its provenance, because it says that a potter a thousand years ago had seen fish leap, because it has travelled through time and space like this, fetching up in twenty-first-century London, a signal from elsewhere.

The leaping fish cannot be later than twelfth century because Fustat was burned to the ground in 1168, an order given by its own Arab vizier so as to keep the wealth of the city from falling into the hands of the invading Crusaders. But they could be earlier, because Fustat had been the thriving capital since the seventh century, with a population of two hundred thousand by the time of its destruction. Artefacts from as far away as China have been excavated at Fustat, so it was trading, but it was itself a centre for the manufacture of Islamic art and ceramics; whoever made the dish was in the business. Quite an expensive dish, I imagine, and perhaps there were more fish, or a further elaboration of the theme – other sea things.

There is something highly evocative about sherds – the detritus of the past. Crucial archaeological evidence, of course, and, if you are not an archaeologist, this vivid, tangible reminder of people who have been here before, making things and using them and discarding them. The past seems to echo with the sound of breaking crockery.

I am an archaeologist manquée, in a sense; that is the path I might have taken, had life run differently. It ran into fiction writing instead, but I do have a large cake-tin full of sherds. Personal archaeology; garden archaeology, from the two old houses in which I have lived, one sixteenth-century, one seventeenth. We didn't acquire them for the sherd potential – I discovered that by degrees, as gardening enthusiasm grew, and my spade began to turn up items that invited close consideration. The sixteenth-century house had been a rectory, and its incumbents had clearly lived well: many oyster shells, and, most eloquent, chunks of the curved thick glass bases of eighteenth-century wine bottles. Both gardens threw up bowls and stem pieces of clay pipes. The clay pipe was tiresomely brittle, it seems; the past must echo also to expletives as yet another damn pipe fell to bits.

The seventeenth-century garden yielded most – perhaps because it was there that the most intense vegetable growing took place, in an area that had been the farmyard. Much deep digging on my part, the fruits of which have filled the cake-tin. Blue and white willow-pattern china in quantities, which probably dates from late eighteenth century to early twentieth. Other china – particularly pretty green and white fluted sherds with a floral design, remains of some treasured best tea or dinner service, I decided. And, reaching further back in time, a couple of sherds of seventeenth-century salt-glaze – the deep yellow glaze with scribbled lines and loops in dark brown. And a fragment of broken handle in the other kind of salt glaze – mottled brown. Much plain earthenware, evidently from large crocks and smaller ones. And there was some glazed earthenware mottled with green that looked like the medieval pots in the Ashmolean and, if so, might have dated from even before the construction of the farmhouse in 1620. An entire sequence of domestic crockery, silent testimony lying there in that richly fertile soil – 'scarce below the roots of some vegetables', as Sir Thomas Browne put it. My vegetables, now.

There were other tantalizing finds. A tiny green glass bottle, just over an inch high. Nineteenth century, by the look of it. But what could it have held? And a little, delicate, cream-coloured horn spoon; another valued item, surely, lost rather than discarded.

This was not archaeology, of course. It was fortuitous discovery. And these homely Oxfordshire finds seem a far cry from the exotic implications of the leaping fish sherd. But, for me, all fed into an insatiable fascination with what has been, what is gone but survives in these glimpses afforded by something you can hold in your hand, these suggestions of other people who also held this, used it, made it.

It is not enough to live here and now. Not enough for me, anyway. I need those imaginative leaps out of my own time-frame and into other places – places where things were done differently. Reading has provided me with that, for the most part, but it is objects, things like these scraps of pottery, that have most keenly conjured up all those elsewheres – inaccessible but eerily available to the imagination. The past is irretrievable, but it lurks. It sends out tantalizing messages, coded signals in the form of a clay pipe stem, a smashed wine bottle. Two leaping fish from twelfth-century Cairo. I can't begin to understand what that time was like, or how the men who made them lived, but I can know that it all happened – that old Cairo existed, and a particular potter. To have the leaping fish sherd on my mantelpiece – and all those other sherds in the cake-tin – expands my concept of time. There is a further dimension to memory; it is not just a private asset, but something vast, collective, resonant. And all because fragments of detritus survive, and I can consider them.